PENGUIN BOOKS

THE PREDATORS' BALL

Connie Bruck is a senior reporter for *The American Lawyer.* Her articles have also appeared in *The Atlantic, Manhattan, inc., The Washington Post, The New York Times,* and *Regardie's.* She received the John Hancock Award for Excellence in Business and Financial Journalism in 1984. Connie Bruck lives in New York City with her son.

D0036597

THE PREDATORS' BALL

*The Inside Story of
Drexel Burnham and the
Rise of the Junk Bond Raiders*

CONNIE BRUCK

PENGUIN BOOKS

PENGUIN BOOKS
Published by the Penguin Group
Viking Penguin, a division of Penguin Books USA Inc.,
40 West 23rd Street, New York, New York 10010, U.S.A.
Penguin Books Ltd, 27 Wrights Lane,
London W8 5TZ, England
Penguin Books Australia Ltd, Ringwood,
Victoria, Australia
Penguin Books Canada Ltd, 2801 John Street,
Markham, Ontario, Canada L3R 1B4
Penguin Books (N.Z.) Ltd, 182–190 Wairau Road,
Auckland 10, New Zealand

Penguin Books Ltd, Registered Offices:
Harmondsworth, Middlesex, England

First published in the United States of America by
The American Lawyer/Simon and Schuster 1988
Published with a new chapter in Penguin Books 1989
Published simultaneously in Canada

10 9 8 7 6 5 4 3 2 1

LIBRARY OF CONGRESS CATALOGING IN PUBLICATION DATA
Bruck, Connie.
The predators' ball: the inside story of Drexel Burnham and the
rise of the junk bond raiders/Connie Bruck.
p.   cm.
Reprint. Originally published: New York: American Lawyer: Simon
and Schuster, 1988.
Includes index.
ISBN 0 14 01.2090 4
1. Consolidation and merger of corporations—United States.
2. Junk bonds—United States.   3. Milken, Michael.   4. Drexel
Burnham Lambert Incorporated.   5. Stockbrokers—United States.
I. Title.
[HD2746.5.B78   1989]
332.63'2'0973—dc19   88–7993

Printed in the United States of America
Set in Aldus

FOR ARI SCHLOSSBERG

CONTENTS

Prologue:
The Ball

In THE third week of March 1985, the faithful, fifteen hundred strong, came to Beverly Hills to pay homage to Michael Milken, the legendary junk-bond guru of Drexel Burnham Lambert whom many of his followers called simply "the King." For the next four days, they would savor the world he had created for them.

By five-thirty each morning, an armada of about one hundred limousines glided into position around Beverly Hills. Dozens of them ferried guests from the lush green-and-pink medley of the Beverly Hills Hotel—then owned by arbitrageur Ivan Boesky, his wife and his in-laws, and completely booked by Drexel for these four nights—through the city's wide, stately, palm-tree-lined streets. Their destination was the Beverly Hilton, where the annual Drexel High Yield Bond Conference—by now known as the Predators' Ball—was being held, just a few blocks from Drexel's West Coast office.

Breakfast was served at 6 A.M., a concession to popular tastes by Milken, who was at his desk each day by 4:30 A.M. Then came the perpetual round of presentations, sometimes three simultaneously in different rooms, given by heads of companies. These were nearly all Drexel clients, typically the small and medium-sized companies—run by entrepreneurs with healthy ownership stakes—with whom Milken had carved out his historic franchise when he started doing financings for them, back in the late seventies and early eighties.

Because of their small size, or their lack of credit history, or their leveraged capital structure, these companies had been rated below investment grade by the rating agencies and thus had not been able to raise money by issuing bonds in the public market. The only way for them to borrow money was in short-term loans from banks or in private placements with insurance companies, which carried covenants so restrictive that they made the money almost not worth having.

Then, one day, Drexel's investment bankers had come knocking at the door. Drexel would underwrite their bonds, low-rated though they were, for the public marketplace. Michael Milken, a most extraordinary junk-bond trader, could raise $50 million, $100 million or more—the kind of long-term, relatively covenant-free capital that was available to these companies nowhere else. All they had to do was pay the price: a high yield to the investors, and an enormous fee to Drexel.

Now hundreds of buyers were in the audience for these presentations. There were the players who had turned nondescript or failing financial companies into dazzling success stories, based on the yield of the bonds that Milken offered them. And there were the money managers—people who ran investment portfolios for thrift institutions, insurance companies, public and private pension funds, mutual funds, offshore banks, college endowments, high-yield funds.

Many of them had been converted into believers by Milken back in the seventies, when he had begun tirelessly preaching an esoteric gospel: that in a diversified portfolio of high-yield bonds, otherwise known as "junk" bonds, the reward outweighs the risk. This was a proven theory, well documented by academician W. Braddock Hickman in his enormous multivolume tome *Corporate Bond Quality and Investor Experience*, published in the fifties. All that remained, for everyone to make money, more money probably than they had ever imagined, was to put theory into practice.

Hand in hand with Milken, these buyers had put theory into practice—and now they were players in a $100 billion market. The intense young man with the ill-fitting toupee, the set jaw, the air of utter confidence and the greatest sales pitch that any of them had ever heard had been right.

Some of these buyers thought nostalgically of the way it had been at the beginning. Just six years earlier, Milken had staged his first West Coast high-yield-bond conference at the Beverly Hills Hilton for about sixty people. The buyers had sat around conference tables with the issuers and engaged in the kind of substantive dialogue, replete with hard data, that allowed them to decide whether they wanted to own a company's debt or not. That immediacy was gone now. The presentations were made to hundreds of buyers in huge conference rooms with floor-to-ceiling screens on which the speaker's immensely magnified image appeared, and they were driven not by hard data but by slick, soft-sell videos. "Instead of a dialogue, it's like watching TV," complained James Caywood of Caywood-Christian Capital Management, who manages about $2.2 billion, mainly for savings-and-loan associations (S&Ls), and is an old-timer in the junk market. "The conference has become—excuse my language—a gangbang."

It had also, this year, become the Predators' Ball. There was a new gospel—or, more, a kind of added liturgy—being preached these days by Milken, who had become more messianic, more fevered, more *wired*, than ever. His message, received with wild excitement by this congregation, was that they should save corporate America from itself.

Milken had long professed contempt for the corporate establishment, portraying many of its members as fat, poorly managed behemoths who squandered their excess capital and whose investment-grade bonds, as he loved to say, could move in only one direction—down. He had made fortunes for himself and his investors by identifying assets undervalued by the market. In the seventies Milken had done this primarily with the debt securities of troubled or bankrupt companies. But by the early eighties the clearly undervalued asset was corporate America, and the biggest play was in the takeover game.

This was a game for which Milken was a natural by temperament and talent. When Wall Street's elite investment banking firms were pocketing huge fees from the mergers-and-acquisitions (M&A) game, Milken and his corporate finance partners at Drexel had been left out in the cold, too déclassé to be hired by the major corporations that had bank lines big enough to play. Unable to attract those clients, they had finally decided to do something beguilingly simple: they would create their own.

Who needed Chase Manhattan or Manufacturers Hanover when Carl Lindner, Sam, William, and Hyman Belzberg, Saul Steinberg, Victor Posner and the entire host of institutional junk-bond buyers were ready—at Milken's behest, and on hours' notice—to sign up to buy the junk bonds that would finance a takeover? Just as Milken had given medium-sized companies access to amounts of capital that had been wholly out of their reach before, so now his chosen takeover artists could set their sights on targets that but for him would have remained the stuff of their dreams.

"Capital is not the scarce resource," Milken had been instructing his followers for several years and, to their delight, proving over and over again.

Now, in March 1985 at the Beverly Hilton, on the eve of an assault that would shake corporate America to its roots, he declared that the combined buying power of his assembled guests was three trillion dollars.

It was a heady message, and made more so by events of the preceding two weeks. The junk-bond-financed takeover had not sprung, fully functioning, from the minds of Milken and his Drexel colleagues; it had needed crafting and fine-tuning. T. Boone Pickens Jr.'s peanut-sized Mesa Petroleum had made a run at mammoth Gulf Oil in early 1984. Pickens had ultimately driven Gulf into the arms of its white knight, Standard Oil of California. Then Steinberg's Reliance had mounted its raid against Disney. Carl Icahn had launched his bid for Phillips Petroleum, after Pickens' Mesa had taken its turn and been bought out. These raids—all financed by Drexel junk bonds, except for Pickens' run at Phillips—had thrown off hundreds of millions of dollars to the raiders and to Drexel. But not one had acquired its target. Corporate America, therefore, had been able to deride these bids as nothing more than stickup artists' bluffs.

They couldn't do that anymore. A week before this Predators' Ball, the first Drexel junk-bond-financed takeover had actually swallowed its target. In a deal that started hostile but turned friendly, the Coastal Corporation was acquiring American Natural Resources Company for $2.46 billion—$1.6 billion of it from bank loans and $600 million from Milken's junk (an amalgam of notes, or debt, with high-yielding interest and preferred stock with high-yielding dividends). Oscar Wyatt, chairman and CEO of Coastal, had become a sudden star.

There were lots of people at this conference who were shaking Wyatt's hand, wishing him luck—and picturing themselves in his shoes. One of them was Nelson Peltz. Just a week earlier, Triangle Industries, a company with a $50 million net worth run by Peltz and Peter May, two unknowns, had made a $456 million bid for National Can, to be wholly financed by Milken's junk bonds.

Coastal was a substantial company, and Wyatt, while he was anathema to the corporate establishment, was an experienced operator. But if Triangle Industries, a vending-machine, wire and cable company with little to its name besides the cash raised from previous junk-bond offerings, could succeed in taking over a major industrial company like National Can, then that meant that no prey was too large and no predator too inconsequential—so long as Milken could tap into his magic pools of capital. Overnight, all the rules of survival in the corporate jungle had been rewritten. The weak could become the strong, and the strong the weak. It must have not only excited but tickled the fancy of Milken, an amateur magician who occasionally does tricks for his friends, to be able to wave this particular wand.

The honored guests of this conference, therefore, were the takeover artists and their biggest backers—men like T. Boone Pickens, Carl Icahn, Irwin Jacobs, Sir James Goldsmith, Oscar Wyatt, Saul Steinberg, Ivan Boesky, Carl Lindner, the Belzbergs—and lesser lights about to shine, such as Nelson Peltz, Ronald Perelman, William Farley. The names tend to meld into a kind of raiders' litany, but they are not all the same. For Milken, they would have separate roles during the coming months, performing discrete functions in a vast, interlocking machine of which he alone would know all the parts.

What all these men did share, of course, were enormous egos and appetites, and they did not think of themselves as Milken's functionaries. Each thought he was using Milken to attain his own goal. This was true. But the larger truth was that they were joined in an effort to satisfy an appetite that dwarfed all of theirs, so enormous that all that their deals would throw off to Drexel and to Milken—billions in fees and in equity stakes—would only whet it.

On the second night of the Predators' Ball, while the lower-ranking troops (money managers and executives of medium-sized companies) were sent in buses to a show at a movie lot, some one hundred of the real players—takeover entrepreneurs, major investors, arbitrageurs, deal lawyers—attended a cocktail party at a bungalow at the Beverly Hills Hotel. From there they were chauffeured to dinner in a private room at the swank Chasen's in Beverly Hills.

In addition to Drexel's female employees, there were a number of extremely attractive young women at this dinner—so good-looking, in fact, that one takeover lawyer, George Katz of New York's

Wachtell, Lipton, Rosen and Katz, renowned for his naiveté, remarked to a companion, "I've got to hand it to these guys—I've never seen so many beautiful wives!"

In fact few if any wives attended this dinner. An assessment closer to the mark was made by arbitrageur Martin Weinstein, who, noting that Irwin Jacobs had been deep in conversation for hours with one of these women at the far end of the room, commented to a friend, "Tell Irwin he doesn't have to work so hard. She's already paid for."

According to Julian Schroeder, a former corporate finance partner at Drexel, the "girls" have been a staple of the conference since the early years. They were seen as necessary bait for clients in the days when Drexel was "laughed at" by those whom he and his colleagues called for business. These women were recruited chiefly by Donald Engel, a close associate of Milken and a longtime managing director of Drexel. In 1984 Engel resigned and became a "consultant" to the firm, but he continued to carry out his traditional function vis-à-vis the "girls."

Fred Sullivan, chairman of Kidde, Inc., who has attended the conferences for years, confirmed that the women were paid by Drexel—"varying amounts, depending on how pretty they are, and what they'll do," said Sullivan, with a chuckle. "Don [Engel] always says to me, 'How could I get all these guys to come, if I didn't have the girls?' "

Following the dinner at Chasen's, many of the guests and the women had repaired to Bungalow 8 at the Beverly Hills Hotel, where the cocktail party had been held earlier that evening. Bungalow 8, the one Engel traditionally occupies for the conference, is situated at a far remove from the hotel and most of the other bungalows, and is therefore quite private. As in past years, Engel was sharing it with a Drexel client, Joel Friedland, a partner of the Pritzkers. As one participant who partied there late into that night puts it, "All these big takeover guys were in that place together, and we've all got tremendous egos, we're all trying to prove ourselves all the time, to show we can get the girl we didn't get in high school, we're basically a bunch of exhibitionists—things just got out of hand."

On the final night of the conference, there was a gala dinner and show for all fifteen hundred guests, held in a huge auditorium at the Century Plaza. During dinner, Milken did a video presentation, courtesy of Lorimar, a Drexel client. There was a takeoff on the E. F. Hutton commercial. "When E. F. Hutton talks . . ." says the buttoned-down gray-suiter, pausing as a woman sashays by him. "Did you see the tits on that broad?" There was an adaptation of the theme from *Ghostbusters*, with the chorus "When you need money, call Drexel!" Milken tried for levity, but his natural demeanor is so unmistakably serious and intense that the strain showed. It didn't matter. The applause was deafening. He was the King.

Then it was time for the performer of the evening. In the early years of these conferences, Stephen Wynn of Golden Nugget—who, as he has said, was "made" by Drexel—was the dinner speaker. Then, in 1984, Wynn recruited Frank Sinatra as a surprise guest. This year too, the identity of the performer was a well-kept secret. It had been a matter of speculation among some of the lesser troops at this conference, who were awestruck at being in such proximity to this tidal wave of money and power that was building. "Everyone was saying," recalls one portfolio manager for a savings and loan, " 'It's going to be either Michael Jackson or God.' "

It was Diana Ross. According to Wynn, Ross entertained gratis, in return for the chance to invest in one of Milken's investment partnerships, Reliance Capital Group, L.P. She was in the same well-heeled company there that she was on this night—with Wynn, Steinberg, the Spiegel family, Ivan Boesky, Victor Posner, the Belzbergs, Mantar Associates (a partnership of Milken and his Drexel colleagues) and others.

After about forty minutes of a dazzling performance, Ross began circulating among the guests. Finally she settled on the lap of straitlaced Baptist Carl Lindner and sang to him.

MILKEN IS SAID by close associates to spend barely a moment in his twenty-hour workday that is not dedicated to business purpose. It is not surprising, therefore, since this extravaganza was his creation, that it was such an intensely purposeful event.

It was an evangelical happening that stirred a mass excitation in its participants, many of whom felt they were part of a large and unstoppable force destined to change the world. It was deal heaven. There seemed to be a deal for everyone. Money, as Ivan Boesky once told a group of prospective investors in his arbitrage partnership, was falling off the trees. It was a glorified road show for the buyers and for the scores of companies that made presentations, many of whom would soon be doing junk-bond offerings. It was a reunion for Milken's high-rollers, whose camaraderie, if not collusion, he encouraged. One Drexel lawyer later recalled having seen Ivan Boesky, Carl Icahn, Carl Lindner and Irwin Jacobs huddled in a corner. "*Anything* could have been happening there," he remarked with a laugh. It was a good time. Bungalow 8 would not soon be forgotten, and client loyalty gets forged in sundry ways.

And it launched Milken's now full-blown tour de force. Within the first two weeks of April 1985, hard on the heels of the Predators' Ball, five more Drexel clients—in addition to Triangle Industries—would make bids for companies, all backed by Milken's junk bonds.

Mesa Petroleum, with a net worth of $500 million, would go for Unocal.

Lorimar, with a net worth of $105 million, would offer $1 billion for Multimedia.

Sir James Goldsmith would make a bid for Crown Zellerbach Corporation for $1.1 billion.

Golden Nugget, with a net worth of $230 million, would go for Hilton Hotels for about $1.8 billion.

And Farley Industries, with earnings of $6 million, would go for Northwest Industries, for about $1.4 billion.

Other bids would take longer to germinate—but they would turn out to be the most fruitful of all.

NELSON PELTZ went through the four days of the Predators' Ball, as he would later say, as a "nervous wreck." Peltz, who had a track record in business that can be described as lackluster, saw National Can as the opportunity of a lifetime. He had run his family's frozen-food business, expanding it through acquisitions and then selling it in the midseventies; it later went bankrupt. Peltz had struggled for years, been close to broke, finally managed in 1982 to acquire with Peter May a controlling block of Triangle Industries, which he intended to leverage up as his vehicle for acquisitions. Until now, nothing had worked. And he was terrified that this deal too would somehow get away from him.

What had probably gotten Peltz to this point, however—to be one of Milken's players, on the verge of acquiring one of the largest can-manufacturing companies in the United States—was his long-time conviction that he would someday make it very, very big. This was a conviction shared by few others, and unsupported by events. But it made him persist, and continue to think in grandiose terms. Now he began to picture the vistas that would open to him if he were to acquire National Can. At Don Engel's cocktail party at Bungalow 8, Peltz was introduced to Gerald Tsai, then the vice-chairman of American Can. "Someday," Peltz said eagerly, "I'd like to talk to you about buying your cans."

RONALD PERELMAN brought more to the party than Peltz did. Perelman, for whom Drexel had been doing junk-bond financings since 1980, had boot-strapped himself into a series of acquisitions—keeping the profitable core, selling off the pieces, paying down the debt and leveraging up for the next acquisition. They were small by Drexel's new standards—who had ever heard of Ronald Perelman in 1985?—but at least they had worked.

With Drexel's assistance, Perelman had just taken private his mini-conglomerate, MacAndrews and Forbes. And he was in the process of acquiring Pantry Pride, a supermarket chain discharged from Chapter 11 bankruptcy reorganization in 1981, which had a huge tax-loss carryforward of over $300 million that could be used to shelter income. It would be his vehicle, he hoped, for the kind of acquisition exponentially bigger than anything he had attempted before, something that would vault him forever out of the minor leagues. For the last month or so, Perelman, a crude Napoleonic type who was drawn to glamour and status, both in companies and on the social scene, had been eyeing Revlon.

At the conference, Milken and Perelman had agreed that when the Pantry Pride deal closed, Milken would raise about $350 million for that company in a "blind pool"—for the purpose of an acquisition, but with no target identified.

CARL ICAHN had been successful for years at threatening companies with a takeover only to have management buy his stock back at a premium not offered to other shareholders—a practice that came to be known as greenmail. He had started doing business with Milken just about six months earlier. Strong-willed, fiercely independent, smarter than most, he could not be controlled by Milken in the way that Peltz and Perelman could. And Milken's was a construct—intricate, highly interdependent, requiring constant fine-tuning—where control mattered. As one former Drexel employee puts it, "Mike feels most comfortable when you owe him your life." And most of the people Milken touched owed him.

Nonetheless, Milken and his colleagues had sought Icahn out, offering to refinance the bank debt he had used for his acquisition of ACF (only the second company he had acquired in six years, during which time he mounted a dozen major campaigns) and to provide him several hundred million dollars in surplus funds for what they called a "war chest." Icahn had just completed his raid on Phillips—where Milken had stunned the corporate world by raising commitments for $1.5 billion in forty-eight hours—and had walked away from that ten-week escapade with a profit of $52.5 million.

Icahn gave a presentation on ACF at the conference and then wandered about, dropping in on others'. One he found especially interesting was given by Robert Peiser, the chief financial officer of TWA (Drexel had raised $100 million for the airline in the past year). He asked Peiser several questions. It made Peiser uneasy. Afterward, a few onlookers warned him that Icahn was up to no good.

THE WORLD that Milken created for his faithful would last much longer than those four days and would extend far beyond the enclave of Beverly Hills. Before his awesome machine was forcibly slowed nearly two years later, it would transform the face of corporate America.

It would introduce terror and mayhem into countless corporate boardrooms. It would cause frightened managements to focus on short-term gains and elaborate takeover defenses rather than the research and development that make for sustained growth. It would cause the loss of jobs, as companies were taken over and broken up.

But it also would help to bring the owner-manager back to American business. And it would dramatically accelerate the trend toward restructuring, as once-placid managements hastened to take measures—such as selling low-earnings assets, pruning work forces, renegotiating labor contracts, closing hundreds of older, outmoded plants—before others did it for them.

In doing all these things, the good and the bad, Milken's machine would stir hatreds and prejudices as bitter as those in any social revolution—not surprisingly, since that in part is what this was. The denizens of corporate America would be challenged, and some would be dispossessed. In their place would come Milken's own—a band of mainly small-time entrepreneurs, raiders, green-mailers, the have-nots of the corporate world, who had had only bit parts to play until Milken made them its stars.

Experts would long debate whether the value that Milken's onslaught had added to American business outweighed the damage it had done. Some of the raiders' cant, of course, had been self-serving, but some of it was true. What was not debatable was that Milken, some of his Drexel colleagues and his anointed players had made more money in a shorter period of time than any other individuals had done in the history of this country. And they may have broken lots of rules and perhaps even a few laws to do it.

PART ONE

Spreading the Gospel

1

The Miner's Headlamp

AT 5:30 A.M. each weekday in the early 1970s, a bus pulled up to a stop in Cherry Hill, New Jersey, and a young man lugging a bag that bulged with papers mounted its steps. He was making the two-hour commute to New York City, where he worked at the investment-banking firm of Drexel Firestone. The train would have provided a more comfortable and faster ride; but, for those very reasons, it also offered more opportunity to meet other Wall Street acquaintances. They would want to engage in the kind of idle small talk that commuters share to pass the time. The thought must have been intolerable. He did not wish to be rude, but he wanted no interruption.

As soon as he had settled into his seat, being sure to take one with an empty one adjacent, he unloaded a mountain of prospectuses and 10ks (annual Securities and Exchange Commission filings) onto the seat next to him. On winter mornings the sky was still pitch black and the light on the bus was too dim for him to be able to read. He wore a leather aviation cap with the earflaps down; he had been bald for years, and although he wore a toupee his head always felt cold on these frosty mornings. Now over his aviation cap he fitted a miner's headlamp—strapped around the back of his head, with a huge light projecting from his forehead.

Michael Milken was as anomalous at the impeccably white-shoe Wall Street firm of Drexel Firestone to which he traveled each day as were the low-rated bonds that he traded there. He came from a middle-class Jewish family. He had no aspirations to climb any social ladder. He was painfully uncomfortable, moreover, in most purely social situations. He was oblivious to appearance—not caring what kind of car he drove, or what kind of clothes he wore, or whether his aviation cap and miner's headlamp made other passengers stare at him. Milken was occupied, at every moment, with his own thoughts, and those thoughts were riveted on the bonds.

Milken had grown up in the well-to-do, largely Jewish enclave of Encino in Los Angeles' San Fernando Valley. His father, Bernard Milken, was an accountant; from the time he was ten Michael watched at his father's side as he prepared tax returns. A boyhood friend, Harry Horowitz, recalled that the kinetic quality so marked in Milken in later years was present when he was young. Even as a teenager he slept only three or four hours a night. He was a high-school cheerleader. And then as in adult life he eschewed all stimulants—no drugs, alcohol, cigarettes, coffee or carbonated beverages.

He graduated from Birmingham High School in neighboring Van Nuys in 1964 and then attended the University of California at Berkeley, graduating Phi Beta Kappa in 1968. While that campus was roiled with the protests of the militant left, Milken majored in business administration, managed a few portfolios for investors and was active in a fraternity, Sigma Alpha Mu.

Milken married his high-school sweetheart, Lori Anne Hackel, and headed east to the Wharton School, the University of Pennsylvania's business school. Horowitz, visiting him during Milken's first week at Wharton, attended an orientation dinner with him. The two were a little taken aback by Milken's fellow students, Ivy League graduates dressed in navy blazers and smoking pipes, and they in turn were struck by the two Californians. "They were making fun of us, though in a sort of nice way," Horowitz recalled. "And I remember Mike told me that evening that he was going to be number one in his class." Milken did have straight A's, but because he was short one paper he did not graduate with his class. He later co-authored a paper with one of his professors and received his M.B.A. degree.

Milken had come to the Philadelphia office of what was then called Drexel Harriman Ripley to apply for a summer job while he was at Wharton, in 1969. Anthony Buford, Jr., then a director of Drexel, recalled that a professor at Wharton, Robert Hagin, recommended Milken for the job. "Bob told me, 'This is the most astounding young man I've ever taught,'" said Buford.

Buford was involved in a corporate-planning effort, analyzing all aspects of the firm. Like many other firms in the late sixties and early seventies, Drexel Harriman Ripley was struggling to weather the crisis of the "paper crunch," in which back-office systems buckled and sometimes collapsed under the burden of trades, and records of stock and money delivered and received were lost. When Milken arrived, Drexel was in the throes of making the transition in its back office from the clerk with the green eyeshade to computers. Milken, who had spent the previous summer at the accounting firm of Touche Ross, was dispatched to the troubled area.

While he quickly believed he had divined the solution to the problems, his plan was not implemented. Most of the people in the back office from whom Milken tried to garner information had no more than a high-school education but many years' worth of experience at their jobs. "Mike was like a bull in a china shop," recalled a former Drexel executive. "He was *terribly* arrogant. And he didn't have the facility to shroud his ability, couldn't keep it from being threatening and abrasive. This army of operations people were so far beneath him in intellectual powers that he couldn't deal with them, he could only beat on them. Soon their attitude was, Go talk to somebody else. So he never was able to unlock the system.

"Mike's difficulty, gigantic, was that he simply didn't have the patience to listen to another point of view," this former executive continued. "He would assume he had conquered the problem and go forward. He was useless in a committee, in any situation that called for a group decision. He only cared about bringing the truth. If Mike hadn't gone into the securities business, he could have led a religious revival movement."

Whatever his interpersonal shortcomings, Milken was recognized as so high-powered intellectually that he was moved on from the back office to do other special projects, as assistant to the firm's president, Bertram Coleman, and then his successor, James Stratton. He worked at Drexel part time throughout his two years at Wharton.

Perhaps his most significant contribution to the firm was his analysis of its securities-delivery system. Drexel, like many Wall Street firms, used to ship securities from city to city and borrow the price of the securities until they were delivered. That delivery often took as long as five days. Milken realized that delivery should be made overnight, thereby cutting the period of interest payment from five days to one. According to its vice-president of operations, Douglas Clark, that idea saved the firm an estimated $500,000 annually.

When he left Wharton in 1970, he was hired full time at Drexel, to work in the Wall Street office as head of research for fixed-income securities; from there he moved into sales and trading. While Milken's academic record was superb, he lacked all the other requisites —Ivy League school, social standing, physical presence—for acceptance at one of the premier firms on the Street, such as Goldman, Sachs. Drexel, while it was in a state of decline, at least had a major-bracket franchise. Besides, Milken tended always to stick with what was familiar. He had already spent two years working at Drexel; he would stay there.

Drexel prided itself on its lineage. It had been founded in 1838 in Philadelphia by an established portrait painter with financial acumen, named Francis Drexel. In 1871 the firm of Drexel, Morgan and Company was opened in New York; these two firms were later consolidated into a single partnership, engaging in both commercial and investment banking, under the name of J. P. Morgan and Company in New York and Drexel and Company in Philadelphia. The two firms epitomized the elite in investment banking, though Drexel was overshadowed—as was every firm and every financier— by the legendary J. P. Morgan, so formidable that he is credited with saving the United States Treasury from collapse in 1895 and averting a Wall Street panic in 1907.

With the passage in 1934 of the Glass-Steagall Act, which mandated the separation of investment-banking activities from commercial banking, J. P. Morgan and Company and Drexel and Company became entirely separate organizations. The Morgan firm opted for commercial banking and is now known as Morgan Guaranty Trust Company. Drexel stayed in investment banking. In 1966, Drexel merged with Harriman Ripley and Company.

The Philadelphia-based Drexel was strong in money management and in research, while the New York–based Harriman Ripley and Company had blue-chip investment-banking clients. It should have been a perfect marriage. But, like so many mergers of investment-banking firms which would occur over the next two decades, this one was fractious. Some key partners of both firms left, taking clients and capital. By 1970, Drexel Harriman Ripley investment banker Stanley Trottman later recalled, "we were afraid to open the paper every day—for fear we'd see yet another deal for one of our clients filed by someone else." That year Drexel Harriman Ripley was able temporarily to stanch the hemorrhaging by obtaining an infusion of capital—$6 million—from the Firestone Tire and Rubber Company. It changed its name to Drexel Firestone.

When Milken arrived as a full-time employee in its bond-trading department, Drexel still had some portion of its once-encyclopedic gilt-edged client list intact. Those triple-A credits, however, held no lure for him.

The universe of corporate bonds that Milken was entering consisted mainly of "straight debt"—bonds whose holders receive fixed-interest payments, typically every six months, until maturity, when the principal is repaid. A much smaller, more arcane part of the market consisted of convertible debt—bonds whose holders have the option to exchange them for other securities, usually stock. Corporate bonds are rated by rating agencies, such as Standard and Poor's and Moody's. Those companies with the strongest balance sheets and credit history, the elite of corporate America, are rated triple A. When they issue bonds in order to raise debt capital, the interest those bonds pay is not much higher than that of risk-free U.S. Treasury bonds. These are known as "investment-grade" companies.

A bond that is issued as investment grade and is subsequently downgraded because of a perceived deterioration in the company's condition trades at a discount from its face, or par, value. Below-investment-grade bonds are rated Ba1 or lower by Moody's, BB+ or lower by Standard and Poor's, or are unrated. In the early seventies, these were known as "deep-discount" bonds or "fallen angels." Also inhabiting this netherworld were those bonds known as "Chinese paper," which were issued in the course of highly leveraged acquisitions by the conglomerateurs of the sixties.

It was these discounted bonds, both straight and convertible, some of them selling as low as ten or twenty or thirty cents on the dollar, that fascinated Milken. He had been under their sway since the sixties, when he began investing in them with money given him to manage by some of his accountant father's clients. To persuade them to entrust him, a college student, with their money, Milken made a deal in which he would take 50 percent of all profits and 100 percent of all losses. Years later he commented (as reported in *The Washington Post*) that this arrangement had given him "a healthy respect for principal."

Milken encountered the Hickman study while he was at Berkeley. W. Braddock Hickman, after studying data on corporate bond performance from 1900 to 1943, had found that a low-grade bond portfolio, if very large, well diversified and held over a long period of time, was a higher-yielding investment than a high-grade portfolio. Although the low-grade portfolio suffered more defaults than the high-grade, the high yields that were realized overall more than compensated for the losses. Hickman's findings were updated by T. R. Atkinson in a study covering 1944–65. It was empirical fact: the reward outweighed the risk.

Milken said in an interview with this reporter that the Hickman study "was consistent with what I had been thinking about for a long time." It also represented the kind of thoroughness that won Milken's respect. "Hickman had studied every bond for forty-three years," Milken remarked. "He had done very thorough, original work, without machine support and the kind of data bases that would be available today."

While Milken had been entranced with these low-rated bonds before he found Hickman, Hickman lent legitimacy to the gospel Milken began to preach at Drexel Firestone. In the summer of 1970, Drexel published listings and commentary on convertible and straight high-yield bonds—something rarely if ever done before on Wall Street, and the result of Milken's labors. Hickman had documented this discontinuity in the market, but it was Milken who had the conviction and the nerve to take a retrospective, academic thesis and to play it prospectively as a trader and salesman at Drexel Firestone—giving much-increased liquidity to these bonds that had heretofore been only lightly traded. Before Milken, most institutions that bought them had socked them away until maturity.

Milken found his métier researching and trading these bonds. First he learned everything he could about the companies whose bonds he would be trading, preparing for his hours on the trading desk as though it were orals. Then he was ready to make his bet.

Explaining their allure, Milken said, "The opportunity to be true to yourself in high-yield bonds is great. It is not like buying a stock. With a stock, its value is generally dependent upon investors' collective perceptions of the future. No matter how much research you have done regarding a particular stock, you don't have a contract as to what the future price will be. But with a high-yield bond there is a date certain in the future when it matures, and if you hold it to maturity and your analysis is correct, you will be correct in your calculation of your yield—and you do have a contract as to future price. One is certain if you're right. The other is not."

"Trading was perfect for Mike," one former Drexel executive remarked. "You have to assess the many complex forces at work on a particular transaction. And then the question is, do you want to do it at this price—and do you have the guts to act on it? For Mike, it's not even a guts question. It was religion. If he didn't act on it, he was being unfaithful to his God."

Most of his colleagues, however, looked askance at Milken and his low-rated bonds. "The high-grade-bond guys considered him a leper," a former executive of the firm recalled. "They said, Drexel can't be presenting itself as banker to these high-grade, Fortune 500 companies and have Mike out peddling this *crap*."

While they ostensibly objected to his merchandise, some of his colleagues apparently had antipathy for the peddler. Stanley Trottman recalls that the two high-grade-bond salesmen most vociferous about Milken and his low-grade wares were virulent anti-Semites and wanted Milken moved to another floor; when they failed in that, he was segregated off in a corner of the bond-trading floor.

But while Milken was proving Hickman's theory by making consistent profits on this much-disdained paper, those who scorned it, and him, were losing their shirts. When one of these high-grade-bond salesmen finally took his case to an executive of the firm, arguing that Milken should be fired, the executive responded, as he would later recall, "Let me ask you something. Milken on a modest capital base is making money, while your high-grade department on a large capital base is losing it. Now, whom should I fire?" Milken stayed, and, not long afterward, his antagonist left.

By the early seventies, Wall Street was littered with dead and dying firms. The recession of those years crippled the securities markets, and spiraling inflation then delivered the death blow to many smaller securities firms, which had limited resources. Between 1968 and 1975 over 150 firms were absorbed or closed. And by 1972, Drexel Firestone was in critical condition.

FOR BURNHAM AND COMPANY the financial crisis meant opportunity. The firm had been founded in 1935 by I. W. ("Tubby") Burnham II, the son of a physician and grandson of the founder of I. W. Harper Gin, a distillery. Tubby Burnham's grandfather wanted his offspring to work for a living and so gave them no money once they were grown; when Tubby Burnham asked him for $100,000 to start a brokerage firm in 1935, his grandfather replied that he would loan him the money—but it was only a loan. Indeed, when he died he left his entire estate to a wildlife refuge and park, the Bernheim Forests, in Kentucky, and he stipulated in his will that the $100,000 with which his grandson had started his brokerage business should be repaid. It was.

By 1971, Burnham and Company was a small brokerage house, with about forty-two partners and capital of $40 million. It had a good research department, and its international equity (stock) arbitrage and retail businesses were decent. While it was undistinguished, the firm had always been profitable. Burnham husbanded its capital strictly.

At that time Wall Street adhered to strict procedural rules designed to perpetuate the establishment, and none was more inviolate than "bracketing," which refers to the order in which underwriters are listed in tombstone ads announcing securities offerings. The top spot was reserved for the special-bracket firms, then came the major bracket, and then the submajor and regional brackets. The higher the bracket, the bigger the underwriter's role in the offering—so it was not merely a matter of status, but of dollars.

In 1971, in the special-bracket elite were Dillon, Read and Company; the First Boston Corporation; Kuhn, Loeb and Company; Merrill Lynch, Pierce, Fenner and Smith; Morgan Stanley and Company; and Salomon Brothers. After that came about seventeen major-bracket firms, and then twenty-three submajors. Burnham and Company, a submajor, decided that the only way for the firm to establish an investment-banking presence was to acquire a major-bracket franchise.

That was what Drexel Firestone had. In addition, it had close to $1 billion under management, some investment-banking clients and cachet, and about $10 million of Firestone money.

Burnham paid visits to Gustave Levy, who had built Goldman, Sachs, and Robert Baldwin, the chairman of Morgan Stanley, which was a cousin to Drexel Firestone. Both men said they would support a merged Burnham and Company and Drexel as a major-bracket participant. The Drexel name, however, had to come first. As one former Drexel director remarked, "It was a classic case of the last gasp of the old guard—insisting on getting first billing."

"If I had called it Burnham, Drexel, we'd still be a submajor,"

Burnham confirmed. "I remember I told my mother about it, and she said, 'How can you? The firm has been Burnham since 1935.' I said, 'Mother, I want this. It will be worth millions to us.' "

It would, of course, be worth not millions but billions, and would raise the little Burnham and Company from the nether regions of Wall Street to its zenith of money and power less than fifteen years later—before it all threatened to come undone. But in 1973 Burnham had no idea that the value of Drexel Firestone resided not in its major-bracket franchise but in one rather odd, intense figure segregated off in a corner of the trading floor. The juxtaposition of the names was the most costly part of the transaction for Burnham. Beyond that, he paid book value (the capital its partners had invested in it), mainly with subordinated debentures.

Now Drexel, home to the kind of white Anglo-Saxon Protestants who took their genealogy seriously, not only had a Jewish trader peddling schlock bonds but had been taken over by a Jewish firm. Although Burnham and most of the top executives of the firm were Jews, Robert Linton, who became the firm's chairman in the early eighties and who changed his name from Lichtenstein, demurred slightly at this characterization of Burnham and Company. "It was not a Jewish firm in the sense of an Ira Haupt or a Newburger [other brokerage firms]," Linton declared. "None of the top people practiced their religion. I mean, we weren't lighting candles. My family came to this country in 1770."

Burnham was curious about whether there were any Jews at venerable Drexel Firestone, and he asked its president, Archibald Albright, who told him that there were three or four (out of 250). "He said, 'They're all bright, and one of them is brilliant. But I think he's fed up with Drexel, and he may go back to Wharton to teach. If you want to keep him, talk to him.' " One of Burnham's advisers recalls that Albright told Burnham he would have to give this young man a substantial piece of the action to keep him.

Burnham called Milken that day and asked him why he wanted to leave. "He said, 'They won't give me capital.' He had a five-hundred-thousand-dollar position overnight."

Burnham gave Milken a position of $2 million, which was a large amount of trading capital in 1973. That year Milken made $2 million for the firm, a return of 100 percent. The next year Burnham doubled the capital. According to one Drexel executive, Milken received 35 percent of his small group's trading profits as a bonus, to be distributed as he saw fit. This fixed percentage had no cap, and it would remain unchanged over the next fourteen years.

Milken told his boss, Edwin Kantor, who was in charge of all fixed-income trading, that he wanted to create an autonomous unit, with its own sales force, its own traders and its own research people: the high-yield- and convertible-bond department. Selling these low-rated bonds, he explained, was more like selling stocks than it was like selling high-grade bonds. If a bond was rated triple A by a rating agency, institutions bought them based on that rating —not on the salesman's pitch about the company. But to convince an investor to buy a bond with a C rating you had to tell the company's story. You had to know the company's management, its product, its balance sheet, its earnings trend and cash flow—just as you would in trying to sell the stock of a little-known company. You had to convince the investor that the rating agency had been too hidebound, or too cursory, or too blind to see that there was ore to be mined in this foundering company's bonds. And, finally, you had to persuade the investor that an analysis of the assets showed that if the worst happened and the company went into default, there was a safety net of value below which the bonds could not fall.

As one competitor of Milken's commented later, "Mike was the first to come up with the idea that he wanted a specialist—a salesman who lives and dies in this one specialty."

At another firm, Milken's desire for such an autonomous, self-contained unit might have incited turf battles and been too disruptive to be allowed. But Drexel Burnham was so embryonic, its territory so unclaimed, that Milken got what he wanted. And while it was true that these bonds were a specialty product that could benefit from a specialist's expertise, it was also true that having his own unit would satisfy Milken's powerful desires for secrecy and for control. These bonds, moreover, which in the main did not trade on any public exchange with electronic trading screens flashing prices, but in private transactions, trader to trader, were his perfect medium.

Milken would in effect create his own firm within the firm of Drexel Burnham, one which its members would refer to simply as "the Department." He laid the groundwork for that autonomy in 1973. From the very beginning, Milken made it mandatory that a certain portion of his people's profits were reinvested in trading accounts which he ran. It was a system of forced savings, in which these salesmen and traders were able to watch—from a distance—their wealth accumulate. With the kind of return Milken got, no one really had much to complain about. On the other hand, if one decided to leave him on less than amicable terms, as one trader would, there might be difficulty in getting one's money out. It was a powerful disincentive to taking any secrets from Milken's operation to a rival firm.

OVER THE NEXT several years, Milken began to cultivate a group of increasingly satisfied customers. There were a handful of institutions, like Massachusetts Mutual, and discount-bond mutual funds, including Keystone B4, Lord Abbott Bond Debenture, and National Bond Fund. These tended to play the market according to Hickman, going for the yield over time in large, diversified portfolios.

There was also David Solomon, of First Investors Fund for Income, known as FIFI. FIFI was converting its high-grade-bond fund (with bonds that had suffered in the recession) to a high-yield fund in 1973, at about the time that Solomon was employed to manage it. According to former members of Milken's group, Milken soon took Solomon in hand, and the returns on Solomon's portfolio showed the effect. In 1973, the return on this fund's portfolio was minus 14.02 percent; by 1975, it was plus 39⅛ percent, according to Lipper Analytical Services. In 1975 and 1976, it was the number-one performing bond fund in the United States. Almost overnight, Solomon was transformed into a seeming portfolio wizard. But, especially in the first few years when Solomon was a neophyte in this field, Drexel employees claimed it was Milken who pulled Solomon's strings.

While portfolio managers played for the yield, Milken always played—for himself, his colleagues, the firm and a growing body of wealthy individuals—for the upside. In the seventies, in near-bankruptcies and also bankrupcies (where only a portion of the bond's value is lost), that upside could be enormous. As Hickman had noted, "Corporate bonds were typically undervalued in the market at or near the date of default. As a result, investors selling at that time suffered large losses, while those purchasing obtained correspondingly large gains."

This was not an original concept. The renowned trader Salim "Cy" Lewis of Bear, Stearns had made a fortune buying the bonds of bankrupt railroads in the forties. Milken would follow in Lewis' footsteps by buying Penn Central bonds, on which he and his clients made killings. Milken, however, bought not just in one industry as Lewis had but across the whole landscape of troubled companies; as default was thought to be near and bondholders panicked, Milken was there to pick up the distress-sale merchandise, often at ten and twenty and thirty cents on the dollar.

Milken was also buying the bonds of the near-bankrupt real-estate investment trusts, known as REITs. Many of these trusts had issued investment-grade public debt which had now sunk as low as ten cents on the dollar. The REITs were much like mutual funds except that instead of stocks their portfolios consisted of real estate or financial instruments associated with realty, such as mortgages or leases. These trusts had grown out of the 1960 legislation that provided effective exemption from the corporate income tax for qualified trusts—the thought of Congress having been that this would provide the small investor with an opportunity to have an ownership interest in real estate. The REITs grew gradually through the sixties, and then they skyrocketed. In 1968 their total assets were $1 billion; in 1969, $2 billion; in 1974, $20.5 billion.

That year, the party ended. When the recession hit, the growth and earnings at many REITs slowed dramatically. However, the debacle was not all-inclusive; some REITs continued to perform well through the midseventies. Some faltered but came back. Milken analyzed them and chose those that he thought would either make it or have a liquidation value of, say, seventy-five cents on the dollar—so they were a bargain at twenty cents. "What we did with the REITs was to create a kind of unit trust for certain customers," Kantor said. "We would say, 'Take ten or fifteen of these—if just two of them make it, you'll do great.' And they did."

Not all of Milken's gambles received Tubby Burnham's blessing. Burnham had survived and prospered by being conservative with his capital, and some of the paper Milken bought made him nervous. When he could, Kantor made himself the buffer between Burnham and Milken. "I insulated Mike," Kantor declares. "I got the calls on Sunday morning—'What are you *doing?*' "

At one point Burnham ordered Milken to get the firm out of the REITs, and Milken formed a syndicate among his colleagues, customers and himself to buy out the firm's position. "Mike and the rest made a fortune on that," Mark Kaplan, who was then the president of the firm, said later. Milken was also doing well in the deal he had struck with Burnham. Kaplan recalled that in 1976, Milken and his principal trader, Charles Causey—with whom he was then in a fifty-fifty partnership—each received $5 million in compensation.

Among Milken's early, delighted customers were Carl Lindner, Saul Steinberg, Meshulam Riklis and Laurence Tisch. Tisch, Steinberg and Lindner bought mainly for their insurance companies' portfolios. Often it was the debt and equity of each other's company that they were buying. Lindner, for example, through American Financial, had been the second-largest shareholder of Steinberg's Reliance Financial through much of the seventies. He also became a major shareholder of Riklis' Rapid-American in the midseventies. And he was in the late seventies the second-largest shareholder in Tisch's Loews Corporation. The four were generally friendly business associates, though they may have been personally rivalrous. In an SEC deposition in 1982, Lindner would remark of Tisch, "You know Larry, he's worth a billion and a half dollars, he and his brother, and you'd think that he was looking for cigarette money most of the time."

Of the four, Tisch would be the only one who would distance himself from Milken in later years, as Milken's machine grew ever more gargantuan and controversial and Tisch began to affect the role of elder statesman. While Tisch would remain personally aloof from Milken and his junk bonds, however, the insurance company Tisch had taken over in a hostile raid in the s......es, CNA, would continue to invest heavily in them. Milken would testify in a deposition taken by the SEC in October 1982 that there were extended periods during the preceding two and a half years when he spoke to CNA's portfolio manager every day. Moreover, Tisch's son, James Tisch, would be an investor, along with the Belzbergs, in a risk arbitrage partnership, Jamie Securities, run by John Mulheren—who took enormous positions in takeover stocks (many of them Drexel-backed deals) and was, of all arbitrageurs, probably closest to Ivan Boesky.

Meanwhile, Lindner, Steinberg and Riklis would become among the most devoted stalwarts of the Milken empire.

Lindner and Steinberg—who is about twenty years younger than Lindner—had followed somewhat similar career paths. Both were outsiders, who had amassed their own fortunes, and who had forever alienated the establishment with their onslaughts on major banks. And both acquired property- and casualty-insurance companies which would assume significant stock positions (in Steinberg's case, sometimes with hostile intent) in other major companies.

Lindner, a secretive, publicity-shy Cincinnati financier who did not finish high school, had built a milk-store business into a major supermarket chain and then had invaded the financial world— where his prize catch in 1966 was Cincinnati's Provident Bank, one of the pillars of the city. He had continued on his financial-service acquisition trail, acquiring a major property- and casualty-insurance company, Great American. By 1974, about the time he began buying bonds from Milken, his mammoth holding company, American Financial Corporation, had equity of $192 million and debt of $692 million: a debt-to-equity ratio of roughly 3.5 to one.

One Drexel employee maintains that officials at Drexel had turned Lindner down as a client about six months before Milken met him and began doing business with him, because they were worried about Lindner's reputation. He was known then to be the target of an SEC investigation, and he would be charged by the SEC with violating anti-fraud and anti-manipulation provisions of the federal securities laws in 1976 and in 1979. But Milken is said to have persuaded others at the firm to overcome their compunction, and by the midseventies Lindner became Drexel Burnham's biggest client, both in trading and in corporate finance. He would also become, of all Milken's clients, the one Milken would respect the most.

Steinberg had started a computer-leasing business, Leasco, when he was just a couple of years out of Wharton, in 1961. That very profitable company's stock had soared in the heady stock market days of the late sixties, making it possible for little Leasco to take over the conservative, 150-year-old Reliance Insurance Company, nearly ten times its size, by tendering to its shareholders a package of the highly valued Leasco paper.

Then, in a far more audacious move—one which rocked the corporate establishment, stirred currents of anti-Semitism, and foreshadowed the kinds of epic struggles that Milken would finance some fifteen years later—Steinberg in 1969 had targeted for conquest the $9 billion Chemical Bank. By the time he surrendered, those who had so effectively combined against him included not only the directors and management of Chemical, but most of the banking business, Governor Nelson A. Rockefeller and the legislature of New York State, and members of the Federal Reserve Board and the Senate Banking and Currency Committee.

Riklis had never set his sights on a major bank, but he was every inch the renegade. Like Steinberg and Lindner, he had created his own fortune, relying on leverage, invention, keen business acumen and a disdain for the unwritten as well as some of the written rules. Like Lindner, Steinberg and Riklis by the midseventies signed consent decrees with the Securities and Exchange Commission—a standard securities-law-enforcement plea bargain—in which they neither admitted nor denied their guilt but agreed to desist from violations of securities laws in the future or face criminal-contempt charges.

An Israeli emigrant, Riklis had started out with a stake of just $25,000, buying and combining small companies in the 1950s. By the time he met Milken in about 1970, Riklis controlled a conglomerate, Rapid-American, which had sales of close to $2 billion. It included such companies as International Playtex, Schenley Industries, Lerner Shops and RKO–Stanley Warner Theatres. What Riklis had done was acquire one company and then use its assets to acquire the next, and that company's to acquire the next, in ever larger circles. He acquired these companies by issuing mainly bonds, or debt, in exchange for the company's stock. As Riklis liked to say, Rapid-American owed its success to "the effective nonuse of cash."

The major difference between Riklis' debt-laden acquisitions and those of Milken's later acquirers was that Milken's chosen would issue the bonds for cash and then give the cash to the shareholders, while Riklis would issue the bonds directly to the shareholders. Both Riklis and his successors a generation later, however, would be using to their advantage the same debt-favoring provision of the U.S. tax laws: interest (on bonds) is deductible, but dividends (on stock) are not. Therefore, assuming roughly a 50 percent corporate-income-tax rate, a company that can pay shareholders a rate of return of 7 percent on dividends can just as easily pay 14 percent interest on subordinated debt, because it can deduct the interest.

"I started this thing," Riklis would claim in an interview in 1986. "When Mike entered the market [in about 1970], I already had over a billion dollars of these bonds outstanding."

Riklis' method of dealing with the day of reckoning on all this debt would also be used in later years by many of Milken's issuers.

Riklis has been the master of the exchange offer. In order to post-pone the date of repayment of principal, he would offer a slightly more attractive bond—with a longer maturity—to his bondholders. And after another few years he would offer another. "You *have* to do the exchange," Riklis declared. "Otherwise the bonds will come due!" On several occasions, he has reportedly commented that his bonds will never be repaid in his lifetime.

After years of encountering resistance from the SEC to his tak-ing his company private, Riklis worked out the guidelines with the SEC's then head of enforcement, Stanley Sporkin, in 1980—and pro-ceeded to take Rapid-American private. He was followed, in short order, by Lindner, who took American Financial private, and Stein-berg, who did the same with Reliance. According to one former employee of Reliance, all three transactions were influenced by Milken. Since these three members of Milken's coterie sometimes owned each others' debt and/or equity, Drexel became the nexus for a lot of trading activity among them at this time. A 1982 SEC investigation explored, among other things, trading that had oc-curred in the securities of these and other companies from January 1980 through May 1982. The investigation was closed without any action being brought by the SEC.

Some of the earliest buyers of the high-yielding Rapid-American bonds Milken was hawking remember frequent meetings with Rik-lis, Milken and about a half-dozen buyers at the Pierre Hotel in the early seventies. At that time, Milken had only about twenty-five different issues to trade. There were fallen angels—including the airlines' busted convertibles (securities whose underlying equity is trading far below the bonds' conversion price) and "Chinese paper" like Riklis', which had been issued in the context of an acquisition.

They also remember when Riklis' companies got into trouble in the midseventies and his bonds went down to twenty and thirty cents on the dollar. Riklis had recently been divorced, his personal life was a nonstop party, and his attention had strayed from busi-ness.

At that time, Milken, Drexel, and Milken's customers are said to have owned about $100 million of Rapid-American's debt. Before Milken, debt holders had traditionally been a passive lot. But Milken made it his habit to accumulate with his fellows such enor-mous positions that he could demand attention from heads of com-panies. Sometimes it worked and sometimes it didn't; when Milken in the midseventies went to lunch with Sanford Sigoloff, then head of Daylin, and announced how much of that company's debt he owned and what he thought Sigoloff ought to be doing with the balance sheet of the company, Sigoloff replied that the last time he had checked he was chief executive officer of the company, and that lunch was over. But Riklis was more desperate and more receptive. Milken gave him a business plan. As Riklis recalled:

"Mike said, 'You're working for me. You own a lot of the equity in your companies, but I own your debt. And your equity is not worth the paper it's printed on unless your bonds are valuable. Riklis is working for Milken.'

"If you say that Mike rescued me, it would be wrong," Riklis continued. "But if you say Mike chaperoned me, it would be right. He oversaw everything that I did. He had to—in order to know whether he should sell these bonds or not, and what was the bargain price. He had to be constantly monitoring what we were doing."

Over the years, Riklis became a friend and a great fan of Milken, whom he considers "a creative genius." "All my dealing with Drexel," Riklis said, "is based on the fact that Mike exists in Drexel."

Riklis claims that the word "junk" to describe these low-rated bonds originated in one of his and Milken's early phone conversations, in about 1970. "He looked at my bonds and he said, 'Rik, these are junk!' And I said, 'You are right! But they pay interest, and they sell at a discount.' Mike called them junk bonds, he created that name, unfortunately as a joke to start with. Today he would like to get rid of that joke, but sometimes it's very difficult.

"Today, Mike would kill to have everybody know it as a high-yield bond, but it's too late, so he might as well accept it," Riklis concluded. "A pogrom is a pogrom."

2

Dr. Feelgood

WHILE MILKEN was forging the client relationships that would one day power his juggernaut, the man who would be his crucial partner and ally, Fred Joseph, arrived at Drexel Burnham. In later years, when the firm's profile became highly visible, Joseph would be Milken's face to the world. While Milken and his cadre would remain secluded from the press, Joseph would be supremely accessible—and so politic, so polished, so affable, so disarming, this silver-haired, soft-spoken Bostonian, that he would lend his mantle of legitimacy to the Milken operation.

And while Milken drove the money machine, Joseph would concentrate on building the institution—recruiting talent from rival firms with piles of money, watching for signs of restiveness within his team, carrying out the managerial responsibilities of the role he had assigned himself as, in his words, the "Dr. Feelgood" of Drexel.

Behind the scenes, Joseph would at times attempt to rein Milken in. When one of Milken's troops threatened a prospective client in order to get his business, Joseph would try to make amends. It was his job to bring the veneer of the civilized world to the brute force of the Milken crew. But however effectively the two men complemented each other, in at least one way they were more alike than different: both had a rapacious hunger for market share.

JOSEPH, ARRIVING at Drexel Burnham in 1974 via E. F. Hutton and Shearson, was a thirty-seven-year-old with a couple of false starts and an itch to do something grand in investment banking.

The son of Orthodox Jews, he had grown up in the blue-collar Roxbury neighborhood in Boston. He attended public school there and then went to Harvard on a partial scholarship. Majoring first in physics and then in English, Joseph decided on business school by default: he considered himself no physics genius and no poet, but he thought he was good enough at numbers and he knew he could sell.

After graduating from Harvard Business School in 1968, he applied for a job at E. F. Hutton, where he was interviewed by John Shad, who would later become the chairman of the SEC. Joseph recalled that after listening to Joseph explain his ambitions, Shad asked him three questions:

What kind of name was Joseph? Jewish.

What did his father do? He was a cabdriver.

What had he been best at, at college? Boxing. (He had won a collegiate championship three out of his four years.)

Joseph thought his answers were sure to lose him the job, but Shad read them to mean that he was highly motivated, and hired him. He made partner in four and a half years, which put him on an exceptionally fast track. But then Shad, who was his mentor, became embroiled in a power struggle to head the firm, and Robert Fomon seized the helm. Joseph had been Shad's campaign manager, and the bad blood between him and Fomon meant that there was no future for him at the firm. He left and went to Shearson, as a first vice-president in corporate finance.

After he had been at Shearson for a couple of years, Joseph became assistant to Alger (Duke) Chapman, the president of the firm, and was given the job of trying to salvage the firm's failing retail business which was losing money. Within a year it had become profitable.

After about eighteen months, Joseph was made Shearson's chief operating officer, its number-two position. By this time the firm was in desperate need of capital, and Joseph was one of the major negotiators of its merger with Hayden Stone. When that was finally completed, in September 1974, Joseph decided that he wanted to get out of his management role and go back to investment banking. But the head of corporate finance at Shearson Hayden Stone was a good friend of his. Rather than displace him, Joseph once again began looking for another job. He wanted a major-bracket firm. It had to be a major in trouble, though, because Joseph's résumé—bouncing from one submajor in turmoil to another—wasn't made for the establishment powerhouses. Drexel Burnham fit the bill. It had just become a major, and Tubby Burnham and the firm's president, Mark Kaplan, were looking for someone to exploit that opportunity.

The merger of the old Burnham and Company with Drexel had taken place more than a year before Joseph joined as co-head of the newly constituted firm's corporate-finance department. Joseph found no trace of assimilation. The two firms, moreover, were such stereotypical opposites, each almost a caricature of its kind—the classy Drexel, genteel to the point of being effete, and the brash, bucket-shop Burnham and Company—that the place lent itself to parody.

One Drexel investment banker would later say, "The Drexel people were sitting at one end of the hall, waiting for Ford Motor Company to realize it had made a mistake and call us up and tell us that they'd really appreciate it if we would take them back. And you had the guys from Burnham and Company running around Seventh Avenue trying to underwrite every schmate factory they could find."

Culture clash was the least of Drexel Burnham's problems. In 1975 the firm did very little investment banking; nearly all of Drexel's venerable old Fortune 500 clients had fled. Only Philadelphia Electric and a handful of smaller companies remained.

The firm's self-image, as it would later be recalled by one Drexel executive who arrived at the firm in the mid-1970s, was terrible. "Physically, Drexel Burnham was a pigsty. It was cheapskate in all its dealings—I once had a t and e form [an expense-account form] returned to me because I had taken a taxi where I might have taken a subway. And there were spotty compensation deals throughout the firm. It had a case of Monty Hall–itis." Moreover, Drexel Burnham was peopled largely by "leftovers, people who hadn't worked out elsewhere, whose will had been broken."

If Joseph was daunted, he did not show it. After six months at Drexel he told Kaplan that given fifteen years he could create something that might be as important as Goldman, Sachs, which was arguably the premier investment-banking firm on Wall Street and had been molded by one man, Gustave Levy.

Joseph's strategy was to develop an "edge." And the first edge to work on, he decided, was service to medium-sized, emerging growth companies. There was nothing so original about this; many firms had such a goal. Joseph, however, believed they gave it only lip service. At most firms, when a young partner brought in a deal for a small company, the firm wouldn't support the research and wouldn't make a market in the stock; while if another young partner obtained for the firm a co-management in an underwriting for IBM, he would be promoted. Drexel, Joseph determined, would say that it wanted to build medium-sized companies, and would mean it.

Joseph's strategy made particular sense because by the midseventies most of these companies had lost their investment bankers. They had been served by the submajors, but in the early seventies the ranks of those firms were decimated. In 1971 there were twenty-three submajors, among them Burnham and Company; by 1978, there were two. A handful had moved up into the majors, and the rest had disappeared.

Joseph fired six of the eighteen professionals in the corporate-finance department and began assembling his team. Although his nominal co-head of corporate finance, John Friday, a patrician, low-keyed holdover from Drexel Firestone, would remain at the firm until 1982—as a vocal, if solitary, critic of the junk-bond business —from the moment Joseph arrived Friday was history. Joseph made a decision not even to try to recruit bankers from Goldman or Lehman, but to take them from submajors like Thomson McKinnon or Dominick and Dominick—on the theory that morale would be better among people who were making a step up (to a major, albeit a ragged and schizophrenic one) than a step down. By mid-1976 he had assembled a group of twenty-eight in his corporate-finance department. Many had worked with him at Shearson (they became known as the "Shearson Mafia") or had bounced around the submajor circuit.

Joseph wanted to make the compensation system as entrepreneurial as possible. Previously, the firm had allocated some portion of corporate-finance profits to the department as a bonus pool, and Friday had divided it up. Those early pools were not more than $50,000.

Joseph instituted a formula for corporate finance's bonus pool that made it more substantial—and would make it exponentially more so in years to come. What went into the bonus pool was a fixed percentage of the operating profits of the department, with extra credit given for certain kinds of deals. As the firm became more successful, salaries remained moderate, and the real money was in the bonus pool. Joseph doled out from this pool according to explicit criteria he developed, rewarding the kinds of traits he prized for the firm's culture, penalizing those he wanted to extirpate.

Joseph's game plan was well suited to the times. And his ambition for the motley Drexel Burnham was enormous. But that game plan, fueled by his own fervor, would in all likelihood have produced one more small dot on the pointillist landscape of investment banking in the seventies and eighties, were it not for his alliance with Milken.

Several months after Joseph arrived at Drexel, he heard there was a "bright guy down on the trading floor doing deep-discount bonds." "I went down and met him and it took me a while to figure out how good he was," Joseph said. "It was clear he was very smart, but it was hard to interpret his fast trader talk, and he didn't know anything about banking and I didn't know anything about high-yield bonds, and it took us a while. We both kept looking at each other, thinking, Gee, I could probably do something with that guy."

The first business on which Milken and the investment bankers coordinated was the REITs. Milken was trading the REIT bonds, and he began sending REIT managements over to the corporate-finance department. In 1976 there were 130 REITs. By 1984, Drexel would have done fee-paid transactions for about 95 of them.

The REITs, however, were only a warm-up. It was in the early spring of 1977 that Milken and Joseph decided to collaborate on an undertaking that would provide an "edge" commensurate with Joseph's ambition and would launch the firm on its trajectory. Lehman Brothers Kuhn Loeb, then one of the most prestigious investment-banking firms on Wall Street, had just underwritten several novel issues of low-grade, high-yielding bonds—$75 million for LTV Corporation, $75 million for Zapata Corporation, $60 million for Fuqua Industries and $53 million for Pan American World Airways. Until now, high-yielding bonds were the Chinese paper from the conglomerate-building exchange issues of the late sixties and from various and sundry fallen angels, high-grades which had been downgraded, including the REIT bonds. But these Lehman-underwritten issues were bonds which started out in life as junk.

Milken, who bought some of these bonds, pointed out to Joseph that he had the buyers for such low-rated paper—the clients he had

done business with since 1970. For by 1977, prior to the public issuance of non-investment-grade debt—as Milken would later note
with some pride—there was already a thriving, vital high-yield
market. "The value of this thesis was tested in 1970, and even more
in 1974," said Milken, adding that the bonds of many companies,
including Loews, Rider, Tandy, Westinghouse, and Woolworth's,
had plummeted in price in 1974; but within the next two or three
years those prices rose dramatically.

"By 1977, what was important was we'd just gone through a
difficult economic period, and people who had invested had had a
very, very successful experience," Milken continued. "Those investors who had confidence in '74 achieved rates of return in excess of
forty percent. And it was their enthusiasm that then fueled this
market in 1977."

The high-yield bond was indeed, as a Drexel publication put
out by Milken's department would say some years later, "a financial
instrument whose time has come." Historically, low-rated companies had borrowed money short term on a senior, secured basis from
banks, and longer term from insurance companies in private placements (although some companies were too low-rated to qualify
for the private placements). But those loans had been laden with
restrictive covenants. The other source of capital, of course, was
equity offerings—but those diluted the value of the stock already
outstanding. Furthermore, the equity markets had been so depressed
through the seventies that for many companies—particularly the
contingent Drexel was attempting to serve—an equity offering was
not even an option.

Milken was offering these low-rated companies a new financial
instrument that blended the best of equity and debt: long-term,
dilutionless, less restrictive capital. The average life of these bonds
was fifteen years, with no principal payments due for ten years.

This was subordinated debt too, which meant it was subordinated to the claims of any senior-debt holders. If they wished, the
companies could continue to acquire senior debt at a lower interest
rate from banks—which would draw comfort from the level of subordinated-debt capital beneath them. Like a mountaintop-real-
estate developer who builds one row of homes with spectacular
views, sells them and then builds another in front, repeating the
process until the latest row has reached the very cliff, the companies
could continue to acquire senior debt, without interference from

the subordinated-debt holders, who would be relegated to increasingly junior positions.

For Milken's investors, there was not only the appeal of the high interest rate, to compensate for the additional risk, but some upside: these companies' ratings might be upgraded. Furthermore, Milken guaranteed the investors liquidity. He told them that he would be there to make a bid on the bonds—it might not be a bid for what they had paid for the bonds, but it would be a bid. In essence, Milken was replacing more covenants (which an insurance company would have exacted in a private placement) with liquidity; so if an investor didn't like what a company was doing—as his mountaintop view was obscured—he could always sell his bonds.

And for Drexel, these bonds offered a walloping commission of 3–4 percent of the principal amount, as contrasted with the standard rate of seven eighths of one percent charged for underwriting high-grade bonds. The firm was embarked on what Joseph would later describe as its "high-value-added" course: as the years went on, Drexel would charge ever more astonishing fees for doing what no one else could do.

Milken had his stable of clients, but if this market was to thrive it would need a much broader base. Milken and Joseph quickly determined, however, that they would not distribute the bonds through Drexel's retail system. Milken followed the old Hickman credo on diversification. The retail customers with their small holdings would not have diversified portfolios, and without diversification Milken was convinced he would ultimately kill his clients.

The way to reach those retail buyers, Milken and Joseph decided, was to invent high-yield-bond funds, where the portfolio *would* be diversified. First Investors Fund for Income (FIFI) had been operating essentially as a high-yield-bond fund since Milken began tutoring David Solomon, in the midseventies. In 1976 FIFI had asked Drexel to raise capital for it. The project had foundered for close to a year, and now, in the spring of 1977—with the new junk bonds starting to be issued—Drexel's G. Christian Andersen and David Solomon set out on a cross-country road show to raise about $17 million.

"We took the story of high-yield bonds to the masses and to Wall Street and started to acquaint people with what the performance record [of FIFI] had been," Andersen noted. "I saw there was a real market out there."

FIFI became the first of the new "high-yield" funds, followed by Drexel-led underwritings for about a half-dozen more before the end of 1977. This was when the nomenclature, at least at Drexel, changed. As one Drexel investment banker remarked, "We knew we couldn't go to the public and ask them to invest in 'junk.' "

For the public, the allure was simple: riskless Treasury bonds were then offering a return of about 7.5 percent, while the funds' target was in the area of 10 percent. And for the fund managers whom Milken was assiduously courting, this new area sounded exciting. Mark Shenkman, who would later become a Milken devotee and was then equity-portfolio manager at Fidelity, had his first meeting with Milken at breakfast in 1977: "Mike said, 'Why just be an equity manager when you could have a specialized niche, which takes into account equity research and trading inefficiencies, and offers good performance?' " Shenkman relayed the Milken pitch to Jack O'Brien, in charge of product development for the Fidelity funds, and soon Fidelity started its first high-yield-bond fund.

While the Lehman issues had been sizable, Drexel started out small. In April 1977 its first deal was $30 million of subordinated debentures at 11.5 percent for a highly leveraged oil-and-gas-exploration and equipment-manufacturing company, Texas International. Though in later years Milken would forsake the notion of a syndicate and loathe the existence of even a single co-manager— why give bonds to other firms to place when he had more demand than he could fill, and why risk their finding out anything about his distribution?—in the beginning he did spread the risk. In the Texas International deal, Drexel Burnham took $7.15 million of the bonds to distribute, and the rest were allotted in tranches of under $1 million to fifty-nine other firms. The underwriting fee on the deal was 3 percent, or $900,000, of which Drexel collected the lion's share. In those days, that was a dramatically large fee.

By the end of 1977, Drexel did six more deals, all in modest amounts—ranging from $7.5 million to $27.5 million—and its total for the year was $124.5 million. While Drexel had done more deals than Lehman, Lehman ranked first for the year in amount, its total twice as large as Drexel's. Moreover, White, Weld and Company, E. F. Hutton and Company, and Blyth Eastman Dillon and Company all gave Drexel a run for its money, weighing in with fewer deals but in dollar amounts that came close to Drexel's.

That was the last time in junk-bond history that Milken's competition would be able to touch him. In 1978 Drexel did fourteen issues for a total of $439.5 million, and its closest competitors for number of issues and amount did six issues and $157.9 million respectively. From then on, the numbers would tell a story of Drexel's dominance that grew more mammoth with each passing year, as the firm seized close to 70 percent of market share.

Lehman Brothers might have competed at the outset, but the business was too dicey for that high-class firm. Lewis Glucksman, the volatile trader who would for a brief, cataclysmic period several years later head Lehman, liked the junk business and believed the firm should make a strong commitment to it. But his partners on the investment-banking side disdained it. Lehman did only one more deal after that first batch and then turned down seventeen. They all went to Drexel.

Mark Shenkman, who left Fidelity in 1979 to set up a junk-trading operation at Lehman Brothers Kuhn Loeb, later recalled that "the big concern at Lehman was, 'What will General Foods say [about its investment banking firm peddling such déclassé merchandise]?' All the establishment firms were slow coming into this business because they wanted to protect their franchise with the blue-chip companies. Drexel had no franchise to protect."

And Drexel's lack of ambivalence showed in its commitment of capital to this new business. In 1976 Drexel Burnham had merged with William D. Witter, a research boutique in which the Belgian Compagnie Bruxelles Lambert, just months earlier, had purchased a controlling interest for about $20 million in cash. Drexel thus became Drexel Burnham Lambert, with a capital base of $67 million, and Bruxelles Lambert—controlled by Baron Léon Lambert—owned a 28.3 percent stake in the newly merged firm. Now, with the junk-bond business under way in the late seventies, Burnham says he went back to his Belgian investors for two separate infusions, of $10 million each, mainly for the Milken-Joseph venture. The Bruxelles Lambert stake in the firm went to 35 percent.

By 1978, Joseph had assembled his core corporate finance group, the half-dozen investment bankers who over the next eight years—to their astonishment—would each amass many millions of dollars. Among them was Stephen Weinroth, who arrived at the firm that year after stints as an investment banker at L. F. Rothschild and Loeb Rhodes and then as the chief operating officer of a private company.

Weinroth was drawn to Drexel because he saw a "happy constellation" in place. The medium-sized companies Drexel was targeting were indeed an underserved market, the high-yield bond was its perfect product, and Milken was already dominant in trading those bonds. Moreover, Weinroth—avuncular, rotund, hardly an investment banker in the white-shoe mold—felt temperamentally suited to these clients and the role he would play. "With medium-sized companies, you can really get to know the managements, and you can really help them. I figured I could make a difference. I wasn't dealing with an Exxon."

After Weinroth had been at Drexel for about six months, he would tell Fred Joseph that when he was at Loeb Rhodes two things had always scared him: when he was pitching a piece of business he was afraid he would lose it to Goldman, Sachs, and then if he got it he was afraid the firm would not be able to perform. At Drexel, these fears vanished. "I said, 'Freddy, it's *too* easy. This isn't even fair, it's so easy.' "

3

Transformation

WITH THE FIRM flexing its muscles so pleasurably in this burgeoning market, Milken in early 1978 announced to his immediate boss,
Kantor, that he wanted to move his entire high-yield group to Los
Angeles. He and his wife were both L.A. natives. The winters in the
East were too hard on her and their young children, who were sick
a great deal, and he and his wife were intent on going home. It was
important to him to make the move soon, as his father was ill with
cancer and he wanted to be near him. Furthermore, it made business sense: he would be able to work a longer day, since California
was three hours behind New York.

There apparently were other factors. As one Drexel executive
would put it, "The nervous Nellies at the firm, especially Tubby
Burnham, were driving him crazy, always worrying about the size
of his positions, and he wanted to put some distance between himself and them."

Others said Milken wanted to escape the bureaucracy that was
a requisite part of life in the firm, even for him, who had managed
to shun much of it. Out in L.A. he would be far freer, while Joseph,
more important to him than ever, would be his proxy back in New
York. In sum, Milken would have his own fully integrated, insular,
autonomous and delightfully faraway shop—the natural extension of what he had begun five years earlier, after the Burnham
merger.

Milken's decision hit the firm like a thunderbolt. It would cost
the firm millions to open up a full-scale trading operation in Los
Angeles. The very engine of the firm would be situated three thou-

sand miles away. Milken, who was fiercely independent and aggressive, would be harder than ever to keep in check.

But the point is that it was Milken's decision, not his request. Kantor said later, "What could we do? Mike was making one hundred percent of the firm's profits."

It was not as though Burnham and Company had been a shell when Milken arrived. The firm had been profitable every year of its forty-odd-year history. It had had the strength to take over Drexel Firestone at a time when many submajors were folding or being absorbed. But Milken's profits were so astronomical that when the profits and losses of all the departments in the firm were calculated, the others canceled one another out and Milken's profit figure was that of the firm, overall.

Almost as stunning as the fact that a thirty-one-year-old trader could dictate to a Wall Street firm that it move its major base of operations to the hinterlands of Los Angeles (where no other firm had even a meaningful outpost) was the fact that Milken convinced his entire East Coast staff of about twenty traders and sales and research people to move with him. The only people he lost were clerical.

The incentive, of course, was not mysterious. Through the investment partnerships that Milken ran, by 1978 his top people had already become millionaires. They were the envy of Drexel. An invitation to join them was a ticket to wealth. Gary Winnick, who had sold furniture before coming to Drexel in 1972 and by 1978 was selling high-grade bonds to institutions, recalled how Milken recruited him for the move West.

For the past two years, Winnick had worked across the trading floor from Milken. They had a passing acquaintance. Winnick said that he came in early and left late, as of course did Milken, and Milken noticed this. Later, Milken would tell him that he admired his work habits. In the spring of 1978, shortly after Winnick heard that Milken was moving his group to L.A., Milken—who had spoken to Winnick infrequently—asked him as they walked out on a Friday afternoon what he was doing that weekend. Winnick replied that he and his wife were going to look for a house to buy in Westchester County. "Don't buy anything," Milken said.

He's got something in mind for me, Winnick thought to himself. He felt as though his heart were going to jump out of his chest. Winnick was then making about $50,000 a year. Milken's people

were widely rumored to be making half a million, a million, more
—and they were no more gifted than anybody else in the business.
He raced home to tell his wife what the wizard had said, to puzzle
over those three words, to dream about what he knew could be—if
the words meant what he hoped—one of life's greatest opportunities. Several weeks later, Milken finally asked him to join.

Winnick was not alone in his assessment of Milken's people as
being notable only for their newfound wealth. "None of Mike's guys
was anything when he took them on—he created them," declared
one former Drexel executive. "What he wanted was bodies—but
loyal bodies. Disciples."

His faithful cavalcade moved west. In later years, Milken—
who, though he would avoid the press, was not loath to cultivate
the legend that grew up about him—would tell friends that he and
his wife made the trip west by car, so as to afford him time away
from the phone. She drove, and he sat in the backseat, mired in
prospectuses.

Another story he told about this trip is more revealing. Not long
before Milken and his wife began their journey, he (in Drexel's
account) had shorted some bonds with warrants (to buy stock at a
given exercise price) attached. When you short a security, you sell
it to another party at a given price, for future delivery. What you
are betting is that by the time of delivery, when you have to buy
the security, its price will have dropped, so you will buy it for less
than your selling price. As the Milkens started out, however, the
company's stock took off on one of the greatest runs of all time—
and escalating with it, of course, were Milken's shorted bonds and
warrants.

"Mike said, the warrants were going up and up, there was nothing he could do—he just kept stopping and making calls from phone
booths all the way to California. It was a very long trip," recounts
one former Drexel employee. "It would have been a very hard hit if
it had been the firm's capital that took the loss. But by the time
Mike got to California, he had managed to lay off the position on
his clients. He told that story laughing—especially the part about
how he'd been able to lay it off."

MILKEN AND HIS ENTOURAGE opened shop in a skyscraper at
1901 Avenue of the Stars, in Century City, on July 3, 1978—the day
before Milken's thirty-second birthday. For months there was no

name on the door behind which they were trading. Some of Milken's associates say he did this in order to show Burnham that the business was his and he didn't need the Drexel name. Others insist that he felt a sign was unnecessary—his was not a walk-in business for the public—and that the anonymity suited him. "All Mike has ever wanted," maintained one longtime associate, "is to be left alone to do business."

Milken was serious about the longer workday. He set the clocks to New York time, so that everyone would remember that they were living by New York market hours. He expected his people to arrive by 7:30 A.M. New York time—4:30 A.M. California time.

He bought a house in Encino in the San Fernando Valley, near where he and his wife had grown up. Encino is a pleasant, well-to-do California suburb, but it has none of the palatial sweep of Beverly Hills or Bel Air. Milken, however, has no taste for such splendors. In Encino he was surrounded by family. When he arrived, his parents (his father has since died) lived nearby in a modest California ranch house, as did his brother, Lowell (in a larger one). His cousin Stanley Zax had just become chairman and president of the Zenith National Insurance Company, and the large Zenith building (with a Drexel retail branch on the first floor) was a half block from Milken's parents' home.

The nucleus of Encino is Gelson's, the superfancy supermarket where Milken would often go on a Saturday morning, accompanied by a flock of his children and their friends from the neighborhood. These were not stolen, unproductive moments. Milken enjoyed doing this because he was interested in the business of Gelson's and liked to see how things were priced and displayed. He likes children, generally feeling more comfortable with them than with adults, but their presence too had purpose: they would pick out their favorite products, and then Milken knew what was hot. "For Michael, there are no chores. Everything is a learning experience," said Harry Horowitz, his friend since boyhood.

As homey a tableau as this makes, the house the Milkens chose was not without a certain cachet. It had been the guest house on the Clark Gable and Carole Lombard estate. When Gable died, in the midseventies, the land had been divided into numerous, relatively small lots, so, while some of the homes that were built there are large and ornate, most of them are close together. The overall impression of the area, now known as the Clark Gable Estates (with street names like Tara and Ashley from *Gone With the Wind*) is of an extremely upscale, nouveau-riche development.

The Milkens' home, however, is different. Secluded, at the top of an uphill driveway, it is only partially visible from the street: a deep-blue multilevel shingle house with enormous stone chimneys. While it does not seem very large from the front, it opens up into large, airy spaces. "Mike paid $750,000 for it in 1978, and I remember we were all agog," says one member of Drexel's corporate-finance department.

Within several months of Milken's move, his brother, Lowell, two years his junior, left the prestigious, hard-driving Los Angeles law firm of Irell and Manella where he was an associate to join Milken at Drexel. Lowell Milken, who graduated summa cum laude from UC Berkeley and then graduated from UCLA Law School, where he was the editor of the law review, had been a highly regarded fourth-year associate at Irell, clearly destined to make partner. But with his brother, at Drexel, he could utilize all he had learned at Irell and Manella and do much more.

Michael Milken had been investing for his brother as well as for himself for years, and by this time the Milken assets were probably between $25 million and $50 million. Lowell Milken came in to manage those assets; as those of Milken's high-yield group grew, he would manage those as well. At Irell he had done tax work for small entrepreneurs; now he set about constructing tax shelters for his, his brother's and the group's incomes. Movies, including those produced by Dino De Laurentiis, became a favorite shelter. According to two former Drexel partners, they believed that these shelters were so effective that Michael Milken paid relatively little in taxes.

During the next several years, Lowell Milken would form a company at Drexel named Cambrent Financial Group, which would function as a service arm for the Milkens and the high-yield group and employ a handful of lawyers. Lowell Milken would draw on his Irell and Manella connections for talent, hiring two of the firm's outstanding lawyers, Edward Victor and Craig Cogut. Richard Sandler, who had been Lowell's close friend when they were growing up and had attended UC Berkeley and UCLA Law School with him, also joined and functioned as Michael Milken's personal attorney. Cambrent would be located at Drexel—adjacent to Milken's trading floor, in fact. But it would have no relationship to Drexel. And its very existence would underline the utter separatism of the Milken operation.

Lowell Milken was the technician with the green eyeshade, the administrator of the empire. But he would also be his brother's closest adviser and probably his sole confidant. His office was shouting distance from Michael Milken's desk in the center of the trading floor. Friends of both say that Michael trusted his brother to do the equity analysis that he did not have time to do himself. While Michael was a creative fount of ideas, in perpetual intellectual motion, Lowell distilled, rejected, organized, and attended to the legalities. He was a fail-safe mechanism for Michael. Michael made no important decision without consulting his brother.

Other functions of Lowell's are less touted. Shorter than Michael, also sporting a toupee, Lowell was so abrasive that he would soon make Michael—notorious for driving his people by insult—look almost beneficent. The two did an effective good-guy/bad-guy routine. Michael would say, in response to a request from a group member, that it was fine with him, just check with Lowell; and then Lowell, his rage triggered at its mention, would summarily reject it. Lowell came to be regarded within the firm as Michael's hatchet man and would be feared and disliked by some in Milken's group. He shared his brother's obsession with control, and it seemed to lapse over into his personal life as well; Lowell's wife was said by employees at Drexel to wear a beeper. But however much animus existed between group members and Lowell, no one could come between the two brothers.

Michael Milken's power did not go to his head in a way that impaired him as a salesman. Not long after he arrived in L.A. he called James Caywood, who had just arrived in Houston to run a high-yield-bond fund named American General Capital Management.

"Mike said, 'I hear you're the new high-yield manager,' " Caywood recalled. " 'I'm Mike Milken. Why don't you get on a plane, come out here, we'll spend some time and talk about the high-yield market?'

"I said, 'Mike, I've been in this business ten years as a salesman. I know it's customary for the salesman to come to see the customer.'

"He said, 'You know, you're right.' And he walked in the door one day later," Caywood added.

Milken arrived carrying under his arms two enormous files, like carousel cases, each weighing about thirty pounds. "He said, 'Every bond you want to talk about is either in here' (pointing to the files) 'or in here' (pointing to his head). There were about 150–175 issues

—however many, he could tell you the name of the chairman's cat. He cut the wheat from the chaff—'This is what's good about these guys, this is what's bad.' "

Caywood thought that Milken had to be the world's best bond salesman. He had an almost unbelievable memory for prices that bonds had traded at years earlier. Caywood also thought Milken was a workaholic, and told him so. "Mike got sort of insulted. He said, 'I don't think I should be criticized for working hard. Some people like to play basketball. Some like to play golf. I like to work hard.' "

That night, after Milken and Caywood had dinner, Milken boarded a plane for Los Angeles at eleven o'clock Houston time. Caywood estimated that Milken would have arrived at his home in the San Fernando Valley about four hours later. "When I got to work the next morning—it was five A.M. California time—Mike had already called. The man is a *machine*."

By late 1978, demand was outpacing supply in the junk market. There were eleven high-yield mutual funds. At American General, Caywood had $150 million to invest and was receiving $1–2 million more a day. Like other high-yield funds, American General promised clients large monthly dividends—"so even if the bonds didn't make sense to buy," Caywood said, "you had to buy them."

Offerings, moreover, tended to be small. "You were lucky to get ten percent of a twenty-five-million-dollar offering," Caywood declared. "So that was two and a half million. Hell, I was getting in two and a half million a day."

Whatever the investment demands of Caywood and other portfolio managers of these funds, which generally had $50–150 million, they were dwarfed by David Solomon's at FIFI. By the end of 1978, Solomon had $400–500 million. Solomon, therefore, could not afford to be choosy, and he opted of necessity for a bottom-fishing approach, buying up the dicey bonds, the junkiest of the junk.

Less than two years after Drexel had issued its first junk-bond offering for Texas International Company, then, a market with well over $2 billion in new issues had been created. Companies were lining up to issue the bonds. Buyers were clamoring for them. And Milken, with his core group holed up in Century City, was the undisputed patriarch of this new universe.

Years later, junk buyers who met him then would recall the fervor of Milken's pitch. "He didn't just say, he *preached*," one buyer recalled. "He was like a messiah, preaching the gospel. He had this total singlemindedness of purpose."

"If my purpose was to try to help people, maybe I was single-minded," Milken responded, in an interview in 1987. "The marketplace was willing to invest in long-term, fixed-income securities of non-investment-grade companies. I felt it was our responsibility, in terms of making a contribution to both parties, the companies and the investors.

"To me," Milken continued, "it was a form of discrimination —to discriminate against the management and employees of a company which offered value-added products and services, all because he didn't get a certain rating. It seemed grossly unfair. So I would not have been true to myself if I didn't use the tools I had, to try and raise capital for these people.

"If you say to me, 'What characterizes Drexel?' " Milken concluded, "it's a commitment to helping people—being there when they need you."

What Milken had formed went far beyond his inspired salesmanship. One buyer who accepted his invitation to come out to see him in Century City in January 1979 was Howard Marks, who had managed money at Citibank for pension clients and was about to start managing a high-yield mutual fund there. Later Marks moved to L.A. to join Trust Company of the West, where by the mideighties he would be investing a portfolio of about $2 billion in junk bonds.

After his visit, Marks thought that Milken's operation would make a great case study for Harvard Business School. He was struck by the completeness, the circularity, what he calls the "yin/yang" of Milken's creation. As Marks recalled, "He had the issuers. He had the buyers. He had the most trading capital of any firm. He had the knowhow. He had the best incentive system for his people. He had the history of data—he knew the companies, he knew their trading prices, probably their daily trading prices going back at least to 1971. He had boxed the compass."

It was, indeed, all in place. A springboard moment. And now Milken was about to add a new dimension to his fabulous farrago. For the past ten years he had been building his following, earning their fealty. With his extraordinary acumen and Tubby Burnham's capital, he had been able to line the coffers of already wealthy men like Lindner, Riklis, Steinberg and Tisch. Others, less successful when Milken found them, owed him more. He had transformed

David Solomon of First Investors into a star portfolio manager. And, through his trading partnerships, he had transformed his key people from nonachievers into millionaires, binding them to him with their newfound, albeit largely untouchable wealth.

As Milken's universe expanded from trading to incorporate the original issuance of junk, however, the bounty that was his to distribute increased exponentially. Now he had a product which would not simply allow some wealthy investors to make a killing (buying for the upside) but could transform a dissolute financial institution into a powerhouse. And he had pools of capital that could be tapped to transform small-time entrepreneurs into major, and ever grateful, corporate players. There were many who would profit from Milken's new, expanded abracadabra powers—and who would jump to do his bidding. As the first of them, Stephen Wynn, would say to *Forbes* magazine years later, about Drexel, "They made me."

SHORTLY AFTER Milken arrived in Century City, Steve Wynn came to see him. Five years earlier, Wynn had taken control of a foundering, third-rate casino in downtown Las Vegas, the Golden Nugget. He had added a hotel to the gambling operation. Golden Nugget's pretax profits had been $1.1 million the year before Wynn assumed control; by the end of 1978 they were $7.7 million. But the Golden Nugget was still a sleazy joint, and Wynn had bigger ambitions.

He had spent Memorial Day weekend in Atlantic City, where he visited the newly opened Resorts International. The crowds, in lines dozens deep for the slot machines and the gaming tables, had stunned him; he had never witnessed such raw, pent-up demand. Wynn had decided that Atlantic City was the future and he was going to get a piece of it. All he had to do was raise $100 million to build a Golden Nugget there.

"One hundred million, for a company which had a ten-million net worth and three million in income! It was ridiculous!" Wynn exclaimed in an interview in 1986.

Wynn's close friend was Stanley Zax, the chairman of the Zenith National Insurance Company. "Zax knew I was dealing with a small broker," Wynn recalls. "He said, 'Get your ass on a plane and meet me at 1901 Avenue of the Stars, the thirteenth floor, and I will introduce you to the only guy who can do this—my cousin.'

"I got there and Stan introduced me to this young kid, thirty-two, wearing jeans, a plaid sports shirt and black loafers. Stan told him he'd known me for ten years and that I was good at my business.

"I told Mike about Atlantic City. He asked me brief, terse questions. He asked for annual reports of Golden Nugget. Asked where I'd gone to school (I'd gone to Wharton).

"He said, 'I'm in the bond department, I don't bring in clients, that's the job of corporate finance. On the other hand, I usually can persuade them to look at things my way.' (I didn't realize how humorous that was).

" 'I'll tell you what I'm going to do. You think you need a hundred million. I think you need a hundred twenty-five million. I don't like people to be underfinanced. I'm going to do your deal. The firm has turned down Harrad's, Bally's and Caesar's—they don't want the gaming industry, don't want the association. I don't think they should have turned down Harrad's.

" 'Get in that plane and go to see Fred Joseph in New York. Be there at eight A.M. Monday. Joseph will go and try to convince Tubby Burnham and Bobby Linton [who had become president of the firm, succeeding Mark Kaplan]. Wear a regular suit. Do you have shoes with laces?' " Wynn shook his head. " 'Well, dress conservatively.' "

Linton was nervous, but Burnham finally overruled him and decided in favor of it. There were good reasons to take the gamble. Wynn had a track record. He had his own money in, something which carried a lot of weight at Drexel; nearly his entire net worth, about $2 million, was in Golden Nugget. Moreover, the gaming industry was essentially without investment-banking services because no other firm wanted the taint and gaming was not considered a growth industry at the time; if Drexel could overcome its queasiness, it could probably have the whole industry. And besides—Milken wanted it.

Over the next two years, Drexel raised not $125 million but $160 million for Wynn's idea. The capital came largely from mortgage debt, with some subordinated debt and small equity offerings—so Wynn's ownership stake, roughly 20 percent, was barely diluted. And six years later Wynn's $2 million stake would be worth about $75 million and he would sell the Atlantic City casino for $440 million. It would turn out to be, as one corporate-finance professional who worked on the deal says, a "grand-slam home run."

"I was the first [investment-banking] client that Mike brought in," said Wynn proudly. "He *saw* it. He saw that Drexel could get control of the whole gaming industry. And they did."

But in the beginning Milken had raised $160 million for something that was little more than a gleam in Steve Wynn's eye. One buyer, James Caywood, recalled that as hungry as he was for junk at that time, investing in the Golden Nugget bonds had required a leap of faith. "It was a dream. The balance sheet was nonexistent. Those of us that bought were doing nothing but betting on, number one, Drexel, and, number two, Steve Wynn," said Caywood.

Wynn concurred. "We symbolized, in terms of timing and our essential posture, the archtruth of Drexel's philosophy. There we were, wanting more money than anyone could argue we had a right to. It was venture capital, masquerading as debt finance," he concluded, capturing the essence of Milken's operation.

Even with the enormous demand in the junk market in 1979, it took almost two years to raise that $160 million. Wynn crisscrossed the country, visiting scores of mutual funds and other institutions. In one fourteen-day period he did road shows in twenty-five cities. "Mike told me at the start that I'd have to sell them hard," Wynn recalled. "He said, 'Tell your story. If your deal works, and it will, inside of five years you'll be able to do five hundred million over the phone.' "

And that, Wynn added, was exactly what had happened. Over the next six years, Drexel raised about $1 billion for him. He had never had to do another road show. He had never had to wait for the authorization of Burnham, or of anyone else at the firm. "If I want two hundred fifty million dollars, I just call Mike. Done. In one issue, Mike took forty million himself. Personally."

Though the intense Milken and the flamboyant Wynn (now known through his television commercials, in which he features himself with Frank Sinatra, Dolly Parton and other stars) would seem to make an odd duo, the friendship had purpose. Wynn would be useful to Milken as an entertainment arm, providing stars as entertainers at the Predators' Ball. He would be a business-getter, bringing to Milken clients such as Circus Circus and Lorimar. And, through Golden Nugget and also his personal portfolio, Wynn would become a major investor in other Drexel deals, including the hostile megadeals. Briefly he would become a principal in the hostile game, making a bid in 1985 for Hilton Hotels for $1.8 billion, which he then dropped.

Interviewed in mid-1986, Wynn indicated that he planned to return to the hostile arena and was only waiting for the right moment with the right target. "Mike and I have never fired both barrels. When we do, it won't be for any little four-hundred-million-dollar acquisition. It will be a tidal wave. It will be a two-, three-, four-billion-dollar deal."

"This," Wynn declared, pausing for effect, "is how real wealth moves. It gallops."

4

Merge with Mike

NOT LONG AFTER Milken and his cadre had moved to the West
Coast, their colleagues back in corporate finance in New York began
to feel that the epicenter of deals, money and power was decidedly
westward. Indeed, with Milken out in L.A., Drexel Burnham in
New York had the quality that Gertrude Stein delineated in Oak-
land: "There is no there, there."

In September 1979, Joseph and a select group from his corporate-
finance department held a session with Cavas Gobhai, a consultant
whom he had used for years and whom Joseph's colleagues teasingly
referred to as his "guru," to address their unease. It was a three-day
meeting, held at the Barbizon Plaza on Central Park South because
Bruxelles Lambert owned an interest in the hotel.

Gobhai's groups are reminiscent of the sixties' encounter or
T-groups; the goal of those earlier human-potential movements, of
course, was spiritual or emotional development, while Gobhai's—
fittingly for the late seventies and the eighties—is the achievement
of business purpose. But the process is similar. About a dozen people
participate in intense, almost unbroken morning-to-night sessions
held in a hotel suite and usually lasting for two or three days. There
is comfortable furniture and a blackboard, on which Gobhai writes
ideas which seem exciting. There are no telephone calls, no intru-
sions from the outside world. And there are rules for the interaction.
Gobhai is enforcer and leader.

Born in Bombay, India, Gobhai graduated from MIT with a
degree in chemical engineering and worked for a number of years
with another creativity-facilitating group before branching out on

his own. One of Gobhai's key premises is that most great ideas are, as he says, "born bad"—by which he means that one is more likely to make one's way to the great idea from the seemingly crazy or outrageous than from the cautious and sensible.

Gobhai believes, however, that most of us—certainly investment bankers, by and large a conservative, literal-minded group—are conditioned to attack these outrageous ideas "with heat-seeking missiles" as soon as they appear on our intellectual screens. The sine qua non of his groups, therefore, is that they provide a climate in which all ideas are allowed expression and respect. For example, one idea that would emerge in his group in later years, shortly after Joseph had become chief executive officer of the firm, was that Joseph quit his new post and become Milken's assistant. (The problem for which this was posed as a solution was that Milken was working too hard, and Joseph was the only one whom Milken would trust to shoulder some of his burden. No solution was found, however.)

"The big bad idea they started with at this session," Gobhai says of the 1979 meeting, "was, what if there were no difference between corporate finance and the high-yield-bond department?"

At another firm, such a thought might have been unthinkable, with or without Gobhai to ward off the "heat-seeking missiles." Traders and bankers had long occupied enemy camps on Wall Street. Ten years earlier, the investment bankers in establishment firms were a pedigreed class who originated underwriting business because of their family, school or social-club connections. The traders, disdained by the bankers as brutish types with microsecond attention spans, existed mainly to offer supplemental services to the bankers' clients.

The seventies, however, had seen a revolution on Wall Street. The end of fixed commissions in 1975 incited free-for-all competition, and traditional, long-standing investment-banking relationships came to an abrupt end. Relationship banking, in which corporations gave their business to investment-banking firms they had known for years, gave way to "transactional banking," in which investment banks competed anew on every deal. At the same time, wildly fluctuating interest rates caused tremendous volatility in the market. As new financial products were introduced, what became crucial was the ability to perform transactions, and to do it instantly before the opportunity passed.

As life was becoming more difficult for the bankers, then, the traders' star was rising. Trading became a strong profit center in most major investment-banking firms, often surpassing the bankers. Notwithstanding the traders' much-amplified contributions to the bottom line, however, the bankers continued to scorn them. And the contempt was mutual: the traders generally regarded their corporate-finance partners as masters of little but the long lunch. The clash of these two cultures was endemic on the Street.

But not at Drexel Burnham. There, there was no war, because there was nothing about which to fight. The firm had had no investment-banking culture, and no trading culture. What had come down the pike was an almost miraculous trader who was single-handedly responsible for the profits of the firm. These Drexel investment bankers weren't proud; they wanted to be part of the Milken trading bonanza.

Gobhai, who encourages the use of metaphor and animal imagery in his groups, recalled that someone in the room put forth the idea that most investment-banking firms functioned as a pride of lions, in which the male lions (the investment bankers) ate their fill first, and then the remains of the kill came down the line (to the traders, the salesmen and the research people). What they ought to do at Drexel, someone else ventured, was function as a wolf pack, with all of them bringing down the kill and all eating together.

Put more directly, Milken and his group should not have the lion's share. There could be no question of these investment bankers having the lion's share in the traditional mode, since Milken was the engine that empowered them. He needed the product they brought him, it was true; but he could replace them in a moment. They could not replace him.

But should they be more like him, should they (to adopt the metaphor) run with his pack? Traders typically had a principal mentality (often using the firm's capital to take positions), whereas investment bankers tended to have an agent mentality (facilitating transactions on behalf of a client, who was in turn the principal). Milken had a principal mentality with a vengeance. He invested not only the firm's capital but his own and his people's profits. At this point, he was buying the bonds of bankrupt or near-bankrupt companies, at enormous discounts, and investing in some venture-capital deals. While his partners in corporate finance did not know just how much money Milken and his associates were making in these trading and investment partnerships, they rightly surmised that it was a king's ransom next to their own incomes (which in 1978 were under $100,000 a year).

The issue on the table, then, was whether they should become more entrepreneurial—like Milken, and like the clients whom they were financing with the junk bonds. Someone drew a bar graph of investment-banking firms from one to ten, with one being the most institutional and ten being the most entrepreneurial (firms which made a practice of putting their own capital at risk in deals). Merrill Lynch was at one. At two were Morgan Stanley, Goldman and Salomon Brothers. E. F. Hutton and Dean Witter were at three. Lehman Brothers was at five, Lazard Frères at six. Kohlberg Kravis Roberts and Company, Oppenheimer, and Allen and Company were all at ten. Milken was beyond ten, off the chart. After a vote, this group decided they wanted to be at about eight.

Then there was the matter of Milken's closest clients. Should they continue to do business with the Lindners, the Riklises and the Steinbergs of the world—and if they did, would they lose the chance of ever being able to do a better grade of business?

They made a number of resolutions, all recorded as part of the notes of the meeting by a young corporate-finance associate who had recently joined Drexel, Leon Black. While this meeting was attended mainly by the more senior investment bankers, Black was exceptional. He was very bright. And, as one Drexel investment banker put it, "He had more contacts than all the rest of us put together." Leon Black was the son of Eli Black, the rabbinically trained corporate chieftain of United Brands Company who in 1975 had jumped from his forty-fourth-floor office in New York's Pan Am Building, shortly before it became known that United Brands had been paying bribes in foreign countries. Eli Black had had many friends in the business community, and his son could have capitalized on his father's contacts to go to one of the prestigious investment-banking firms. But he wanted to make his own way. So he had interviewed with Fred Joseph and, as he would later say, "bought Fred's act."

Now Black wrote that they should find those "robber barons" who would become the owners of the major companies of the future —but they should not do this to such a degree that they would share the stigma of such clients.

Most of the resolutions, though, had to do with strengthening their Milken connection:

Service Milken as a new business source—pick his brain.

Get Milken to share investment opportunities.

Get Milken to manage corporate finance's money.

At one point during this session, investment banker Fred McCarthy said something that Gobhai immediately wrote on the blackboard. Years later some of this group's members would use that phrase as a buzzword for much that happened in the amazing times that followed.

Gobhai wrote: "Merge with Mike."

As DREXEL BURNHAM metamorphosed from a nondescript brokerage to a Wall Street powerhouse over the next five years, it was cast more and more in the image of its principal-minded trader. On the entrepreneurial one-to-ten scale, the firm coalesced with Milken, off the chart. And by the end of that time Drexel's and Milken's power would be so great that the other major investment-banking firms would be forced to imitate them.

Drexel became a pioneer in what Wall Street would by the mideighties loftily call merchant banking (a term borrowed from the British), which simply meant that a firm was using its own capital to finance deals (as a debt and/or equity participant). Harking back to the merchant banks of the robber-baron era, and to J. P. Morgan in particular, Fred Joseph declared to Business Week in mid-1986, "We're going back to our roots." By that time, Drexel had equity stakes in more than 150 companies that it had financed.

Some of these equity stakes were acquired through Drexel's investing directly in deals as equity participants, some through exchange offers (where Drexel owned debt which was then exchanged for stock), and some through warrants, securities exercisable into stock at a given price (which the firm routinely demanded as part of its fee in junk-bond underwritings, starting in the late seventies, and especially in its financing of leveraged buyouts, beginning in the early eighties). Taking warrants as part of a fee was not a novel practice, but was shunned by the more respectable investment-banking firms. At Drexel, however, it fit the firm's principal-mindedness. The deals Drexel was underwriting were high-risk, at least by conventional perception, and the capital it was providing was not widely available; so, the reasoning went, Drexel deserved to share in the upside with these companies. Furthermore, equity stakes provided some discipline. Theoretically at least, they were a deterrent to doing bad deals, and they added extra incentive for Drexel to devise some solution if a company got into trouble.

The owner-manager was a natural corollary of Drexel's own principal-mindedness. Drexel wanted to share risk and reward with companies controlled by managers who were driven by the same incentives of ownership.

Milken points out that he had seen the value of an owner-manager for many years before Drexel began doing original issuance of high-yield debt for its entrepreneurial clients. He had seen it when he called on Riklis, Tisch and Charles Bluhdorn (of Gulf + Western) and bought their bonds. He says he first understood its importance as a child, when he was helping his father prepare tax returns and had the opportunity to meet some of his father's clients. The difference in the attitudes of those who were owners and those who only felt like employees was clear to him.

"If you get a guy with some of his money in a company, he's going to do better than people who are getting a salary and bonus based on the size of the company," declared Joseph, delivering the Drexel exegesis. ". . . We wanted to finance companies of the future by picking guys who were going to be successful entrepreneurs, and our main discipline was getting them to have their money in the company. And we insisted on it."

It may be that the only clients available to Drexel were the aggressive entrepreneurs who seemed to reflect the firm's image— but Joseph claims that those were also the clients that he and Milken wanted. From the early days of the Predators' Ball, introductions of clients giving presentations typically included a reference to the size of those clients' stakes in their companies.

Often it seemed as though they all—this entrepreneurial, underdog firm and its entrepreneurial, underdog clients—were in business together. Not only did Milken and Drexel have a substantial stake in many of these companies, often owning both their debt and their equity, but Drexel's corporate-finance professionals would typically sit on their boards, in order to further solder the relationship.

And the connections did not go only vertically between client and Drexel but also horizontally between clients. For many would be both issuers and buyers; client A would buy client B's paper, and client B would buy client A's. This was not simply fortuitous. While with the inner circle it may have happened more naturally, later issuers—for whom Drexel would typically raise more capital than was needed, in a deliberate overfunding—would be told that investing in other junk was part of being in the game. So the matrixing never stopped.

Milken liked it that way. He thrived on connection. He placed these companies' debt; he knew where virtually every bond was (and had it all entered on his supercomputer system); he owned some of the debt himself; he owned some of the equity. Connection was generative. It helped to insure client loyalty, increased the flow of information, acted as a means of control.

Lines would blur in the investments too. Sometimes Milken invested his own capital, sometimes that of the firm, or of his group, or of a group from corporate finance. For, by 1981, corporate finance had finally prevailed upon Milken to start an investment partnership for them. In order to make it a large enough pool (the investment bankers did not have huge sums to invest), Milken agreed to match the assets invested by corporate finance with those from his people.

Most of the people in corporate finance to whom this partnership was open chose to participate. One who did not was Julian Schroeder, who would leave the firm in 1985 and wage an unsuccessful campaign for Congress. Schroeder said he passed on the investment because he "never felt comfortable about it, and didn't like the liability." It was structured as a general rather than a limited partnership, which meant that all who participated would have been individually liable.

Another former partner who refused the opportunity said he was disturbed by both the liability and the nondisclosure provision, which stipulated that the only individual to whom Milken would disclose his investments was Fred Joseph. "Here we would have this individual liability, which extended to the shirts on our backs, and Mike would not disclose to any of us what he was buying. It was weird.

"But most of those characters thought he was the Messiah," this investment banker added. "The theory was that he could turn lead into gold."

Investment banker Stanley Trottman put $100,000 into the partnership in 1981, and by the end of 1985 it had grown to $1 million. The partnership's return was rarely if ever less than 50 percent a year, and in 1985 it was close to 100 percent.

Given Milken's passion for secrecy, the firm that was being molded in his image could never become a public company. But in 1981 Tubby Burnham, who was at that time still the chairman of Drexel, brought the issue to debate. Milken, of course, was adamant. In a public firm he would never be able to run his trading partnerships for whomever he favored, never be able to build his own, autonomous shop based on them, never be able to keep secret what he was buying, what he was making, what he was sheltering. And some executives at the firm were also loath for the world to know what the profits of Milken's department were, compared to the rest of the firm's—since it would become clear, as one partner said, "that you could just take him out of the firm and have all its value." Milken had his way, Burnham was, as he said, overruled, and the firm remained private.

IT WAS AGGRAVATING to some at Drexel—among them Robert Linton, who became president in 1977—that while Milken held magisterial sway over the firm, he chose to own none of its stock. Drexel was a firm that prided itself on its equity being broadly spread among its employees (unlike, for example, a firm such as Goldman, Sachs, which kept the ownership in the partnership very narrow). Indeed, given Milken's explicit conviction about the importance of feeling like an owner rather than an employee of one's business, and given his practice of accumulating equity stakes in scores of the companies he financed, it was utterly incongruous that he should refuse to own stock in Drexel. Linton is said by others at Drexel to have concluded that Milken's continuing refusal was evidence that the autocratic salesman-trader had no interest in the future of Drexel and was merely using it as his vehicle while it suited him.

Now Joseph persuaded Milken to make a show of good faith by taking some stock. Milken agreed, on the condition that the firm offer him a special issue—a bond with a warrant, a kind of hybrid convertible. Since this issue and a second issue several years later were made available only to Milken and some of his designated people in L.A., it became known within the firm as the "Western convertible."

"Was a special deal created for Mike, different than for anybody else? Yes," said Edwin Kantor. "Did he deserve it? Yes, again."

Milken, of course, had not done this solely as a peacemaking gesture. As one former member of his group explained, "Before that [Milken's taking stock], he just thought of it as a place where he had a nice deal. But by this time he saw that what he was creating was going to be unbelievable, and the profits were spilling over to the firm, in corporate finance and so forth. So why shouldn't he get his money both ways [in his percentage-of-profits deal and as an equity holder in the firm]?" He added that many members of Milken's group—who heretofore had not owned a significant stake in the firm—now followed Milken's lead. By 1986, Milken would be the firm's largest individual shareholder, owning about 6 percent of the firm's stock, according to an estimate in *Forbes*.

BY 1980 THE recession had hit, and Milken's business was especially vulnerable—for as interest rates skyrocketed, bond prices plummeted. But Milken was in his element. His friend Stephen Wynn asserted, "Mike does better in hard times than good. He goes hundreds of millions long. I remember I called him one day [in the early 1980s] and said, 'How are you doing?' 'Wonderful,' he said. 'Down eleven million today, after sixteen million yesterday. I'm stuck for a hundred eighty million in all.' He was *cheerful*.

"Mike knows the market is crazy, but it will come back," Wynn continued. "But the people who run money panic, they want to get out, so they start selling everything—and Mike will make a bid. Then he sits there. And when it does come back, he makes out."

Milken does not run with the herd. He is, said Joseph, "one of the greatest natural contra-thinkers I've ever seen. If you say, 'It's a nice day,' he thinks about the fact that people think it's a nice day, maybe it's not nice somewhere else, maybe it's not gonna be nice, compared to what, what do you mean, nice day? He really thinks that way. That is perfect for an investor, or a trader, to be a contra-thinker. It turns out it is perfect for a finance business, trying to figure out what's going to happen in the future."

In the early eighties, Milken took Drexel's junk-bond business characteristically against the current. While other investment-banking firms, some of which had been only gingerly testing the waters in junk, pulled back in the recession, Drexel kept pushing ahead, taking ever greater chunks of market share. In 1979 there were sixteen firms in addition to Drexel in the junk market; in 1980 that number dropped to twelve, and in 1981 to five. The total amount of junk issued in these years did not vary that much, hovering between $1 billion and $1.5 billion—but Drexel came to be responsible for nearly all of it.

In 1979 the total issued was $1.22 billion, and Drexel had issued $408 million of it. By 1981, the total issued was $1.47 billion, and Drexel had issued $1.08 billion of that total. Drexel did twenty deals that year, and its closest competitor did three.

That competitor was Merrill Lynch—a firm that would try over the next two years to stay in the market and challenge Drexel's hegemony. By this time, Milken was already known for the ferocity with which he responded to challenges on what he viewed as *his* domain. And he and his crew responded to Merrill with the kinds of tactics that would ultimately make them hated by all their rivals on the Street.

Drexel and Merrill were co-managing a junk issue for Volt Information Services in 1981. Drexel arranged the road show that introduced the company's managers to prospective bond buyers. On the plane to Chicago the Merrill bankers found themselves in coach, while Drexel went first class with the Volt executives; and when they all arrived in Chicago, Drexel and Volt were in one hotel, Merrill in another. But the coup de grace came when the Merrill bankers arrived at the site of the road show and discovered—too late to notify their customers—that the location had been changed.

According to one Merrill Lynch banker, this was no anomaly but almost routine in the early eighties. "It got so that when we were co-managing a deal with Drexel and going to a road show, we always checked with their customers, to be sure that Drexel hadn't changed the location, at the last minute." Drexel stopped this practice by 1984–85, he added.

Drexel's dominance was not founded on dirty tricks, only accompanied and perhaps protected by them. Fred Joseph emphasized that it was his and Milken's creativity that allowed them to keep doing so much junk business in the recession. By 1980, soaring interest rates were already causing bondholders to suffer. So, in order to keep luring bond buyers into the market, Milken and Joseph came up with newfangled pieces of paper over the next several years. High-coupon, high-premium convertible bonds (if the related common stock declined, the high yield would offer significant downside protection). Bonds with warrants. Commodity-related bonds: four were exchangeable into silver, one into gold, two had returns related to the price of oil, and one had a coupon which would increase based on the volume of trading on the New York Stock Exchange.

"I used to sit with a company and say, 'What do you want?' " Joseph recalled. "I've got to give the investor the potential to earn the return that he thinks is fair for this package. But I can give him the return any way I want. I can give it to him by giving the money back sooner, or by giving him a higher interest rate, or by giving him more stock, or the stock cheaper.

" 'Tell me the one thing that's the least important to you, and if you give me control of one variable, there's nothing we can't do.'

"All the other firms didn't have the confidence of having a Mike Milken who could sell this paper," Joseph added. "So they had to look at spread sheets, figure out what had been done, and do one just like it. But we could just sit there with our minds wide open, smoke pot"—he laughs—"daydream, and say, 'What do you want?' "

Even with its inventiveness, Drexel was having trouble finding companies willing to pay what it took to raise money in 1981–82. And in its push to keep doing junk deals, Drexel did a couple that were notably outrageous. One was a $30 million offer in 1982 for Flight Transportation, a company which billed itself as offering jets for private charter to the Caribbean. There were, however, no jets, only a scam, and the FBI closed in shortly after the offering, while most of the money was still in escrow. Many of the bondholders sued, and they eventually achieved nearly full recovery in a settlement with Drexel.

"It was deliberate fraud on the part of Flight Transportation, but if we had been more careful we should have been able to spot it," conceded Stanley Trottman, the investment banker whose deal it was. After the Flight Transportation debacle, Drexel instituted some controls on the freewheeling junk-bond enterprise. A private investigator, Jules Kroll, was hired to do background checks on Drexel clients. And the Underwriting Assistance Committee (UAC) was formed (in response to Flight Transportation and a couple of other bad deals that occurred just prior to it). A group of about eight to ten senior corporate-finance people and executives, the UAC was to review and authorize every deal the firm underwrote.

Trottman, who described the aftermath of Flight Transportation as "the worst period of my life," suffered financially as well as emotionally. For by this time Fred Joseph had added the accountability factor to his entrepreneurial system of compensation in corporate finance. "More than most other firms, we understand that we're a middleman in the marketplace," Joseph claimed. "We have clients on both sides. And because Mike is so powerful, we have really been serious about that ongoing responsibility to buyers. It is a long-term approach to your business, instead of just do the deal, get the fee and get out of there.

"If you do a deal here that goes bad, we're the only firm that keeps you accountable down the road. You've gotta fix it. If you don't try to fix it, I'll kill you. If you try to fix it and do fix it, you'll almost recover the ding. If you try to fix it real hard and don't, you'll recover some."

There was nothing Trottman could do to fix Flight Transportation. He received $50,000 as his bonus for 1982, while others in corporate finance received bonuses as high as $250,000–$300,000.

At least in Flight Transportation, Drexel was able to plead ignorance in the face of outright fraud. But in Drexel's deal for American Communications Industries (ACI), the situation was different. There, the risks were apparent.

In February 1981, Drexel issued $20 million of bonds for ACI, a movie production and distribution company which had been formed in 1978. The prospectus admitted that the company might not have sufficient earnings to cover the interest on the debentures. This was a foreshadowing of the statements that would later become boilerplate in Drexel's junk-bond prospectuses in its megadeals—but in those deals, like the $1.9 billion issue done in 1984 for Metromedia Broadcasting Corporation, for example, there would be assets that could and would be sold. Here there were none.

There was considerable compensation to the investors for their risk. The investors got bonds with a 12¾ percent coupon (the coupon indicates how much interest is to be paid, usually semi-annually) which were issued at a 70 percent discount. Warrants, included as sweeteners, were issued with the debentures in a unit.

These "unit" deals, which Milken had started issuing in 1980, had a special advantage for him. Typically, bond buyers and equity buyers are different groups, and many of Drexel's bond buyers therefore would not be interested in a company's warrants (exercisable into equity). Indeed, some high-yield mutual funds—which by the early eighties were still a giant part of this market—were not allowed to own equity. And these warrants were detachable from the bonds. So Milken would strip off many of the warrants, sell the bonds separately and—according to sources both inside and outside of Drexel—sell them to favored clients at very favorable prices.

How risky a deal ACI was viewed as at Drexel may be deduced by noting not only what the investors got but also what Drexel got. Drexel claimed its lion's share of the 3 percent underwriting discount, which was $600,000. It also received stock in ACI, which the company had the right to repurchase up to a certain date at a maximum price of $700,000. Furthermore, ACI entered into a "consulting agreement" with Drexel, for which the firm would be paid $4,000 a month until April 1983 (for a sum total of $100,000). Such side deals were generally not a part of underwriting agreements at any major investment-banking firm.

The ACI offering took place in February 1981, and the first interest payment came due the following August. ACI became the first company in junk-bond history to default without making even one interest payment. One buyer said, "They didn't do what they said in the prospectus they were going to do. They were supposed to make only low-budget films. They got the money, and five months later it was all gone—along with everything else."

By late 1981, other companies for which Drexel had raised money began to falter and have trouble meeting their interest payments. This was not unique to Drexel clients. Corporate profits nationwide plummeted in 1981–82, and bankruptcies reached record post-Depression levels. But Drexel had carved out its niche with companies that were by definition high-risk, that few others would finance. One such marginal client in the midseventies had had to pay Drexel its fee in merchandise—thirty-three pinball machines—in lieu of cash.

"There were a bunch of these companies in trouble. We started a Special Planning Committee, which was the workout committee, except that Freddy [Joseph] didn't want to call it Workout," Weinroth recalled. "We met on Friday afternoons. We'd walk out late on Fridays, and I'd say, 'Freddy, I want to kill myself,' and he'd say, 'Can I go first?' We'd never dealt with issues going bad before."

Joseph remembered a meeting of the corporate-finance group at the Manhattan apartment of David Kay, who was one of Joseph's "Shearson Mafia" hires and was the head of the fledgling mergers-and-acquisitions group. Milken, in from L.A., came to the meeting.

"Mike was upset that all the deals hadn't turned out the way we'd expected," Joseph said. "We educated him that having access to a company's numbers doesn't make you a prophet. He allowed that, but said it was no reason for having him sell his clients paper that turned bad. So fix it."

What evolved from this dialogue was Drexel's creation and virtual monopoly of a new business: the unregistered exchange offer. In a registered exchange offer, a company goes through the months-long process of registering a security with the SEC before offering it to bondholders in place of a formerly issued security. These had been done for many years. Riklis' exchange offers, for example, in which he extended the date of maturity again and again in each issue of his "Chinese paper," were registered.

But whereas Riklis' exchange offers were motivated by his desire to postpone into the far-distant future the day when he would have to repay the principal, these Drexel-created exchange offers were designed to loosen the noose of interest-payment obligations on strangling companies. Milken's theory was that many companies don't go broke on the operating-profit line; rather, it is often financial charges that kill them. If there were a way of reducing or removing those charges, these companies might survive and ultimately return to health.

Drexel investment banker Paul Levy, who would come to specialize in this area, stated that its key is the concept of the "flexible balance sheet," or adapting to a company's changing needs. If a company is being choked by its interest-payment obligations, why not make those payments in common stock? Or why not just exchange the old debt paper for common stock, and eliminate the charges entirely? In this new-age finance, nothing is written in stone. "People used to issue bonds, and after twenty years they would repay them," Levy said. "That's hogwash!"

The bondholders would tend to accept these offers, no matter how displeasing, because they would find themselves between the proverbial rock and a hard place. As Levy explained, these exchange offers are essentially an arbitrage. If a buyer purchased at par a bond which then came to trade at sixty cents on the dollar, he would probably be willing to exchange it for a piece of paper trading at sixty-five cents—especially if he thought his alternative was to be stuck holding the bonds of a bankrupt company.

For these remedies to spell salvation for companies in such dire straits, however, they would have to be completed quickly; there was no time for the months-long process of registering with the SEC. Drexel investment banker James Schneider, in the firm's San Francisco office, had had workouts on his mind through most of 1981, since ACI was his deal and he had had the responsibility for trying to salvage it. In early 1982, Schneider, who had obtained a law degree before turning to investment banking, claims he realized that the way to achieve these exchange offers with the requisite speed was through the window of Section 3(a)9 of the Securities Act of 1933. That provision allows companies to offer new paper in exchange for old, without having to go through registration. It stipulates, however, that investment bankers are prohibited from accepting fees for selling or promoting unregistered securities, and they may not solicit for the exchange. All the investment banker is allowed to do, then, is advise the company on what kind of exchange is most valuable to the company and most likely to find favor with the bondholders; after that, the solicitation is supposed to be left to the company.

Over the next four years, most other investment-banking firms would shy away from these transactions on the advice of their lawyers. Their attorneys took the position that it would be hard to define what was "promoting" or "soliciting" in these highly complex exchange offers, in which bondholders typically need a lot of explaining and persuading, and that their clients, the investment bankers, would be thrusting themselves into what was at best a gray area. Other investment-banking firms differentiate between the carrot-and-stick exchange offers for troubled companies—in which the bondholder has to be persuaded it is better to accept a less attractive piece of paper than risk default—and exchange offers done often in a defensive buyback, where the offer is so patently attractive that no solicitation would be required.

Commenting on this problem, Drexel's corporate-finance partner Mary Lou Malanowski said, "The buyers can talk to *us*—we just can't solicit them. And since we're in the aftermarket so much, talking to buyers all the time, we know what they want, they can talk to us, we can tell the company." Malanowski added that the 3(a)9 for the troubled company has another advantage from Drexel's point of view, which is that it carries no underwriting liability. ⟨Sinc⟩e the securities are unregistered, Drexel's name does not appear ⟨in th⟩e prospectus.

⟨D⟩rexel completed its first 3(a)9 in 1981. Over the course of the next five years, it would do about 175 of these exchange offers, the majority for troubled companies, involving a total of $7 billion of junk debt. According to an article by Randall Smith in *The Wall Street Journal* in September 1986, while other investment-banking firms that aggressively entered the junk-bond market through the eighties tended to experience high rates of default on their under-writings—9, 10, even 17 percent—Drexel with its lion's share of the market would have a default rate of just under 2 percent.

Drexel's low default rate was certainly not wholly attributable to its use of the 3(a)9. It had been in this business longer than nearly all its competitors, and its knowledge—reflected in its credit anal-ysis and fashioning of the proper covenants for a given issue—was unrivaled. Still, those 3(a)9s did play a role in keeping Drexel's record—and, indeed, the record of the whole junk market, since Drexel did not limit its 3(a)9s to issues that it had underwritten—more default-free than it would otherwise have been. According to the *Journal* article, $2,927,000—or 3.4 percent—of all the public new-issue junk debt underwritten by the top fifteen underwriters from 1980 to September 1986 (totaling $86,043,000) went into de-fault. Drexel's 3(a)9s were not exclusively for new-issue junk debt, so the comparison is imprecise. Nonetheless, if one assumes most conservatively that without that $7 billion of 3(a)9s another $2–3 billion of new-issue debt would have gone into default, then the dollar amount of defaulted debt noted in the *Journal* would have roughly doubled.

It seems plausible that a higher default percentage, or a sudden slew of defaults of Drexel-underwritten issues, might have dulled the growing institutional appetite for junk in this country in the early eighties. But if there ever was the possibility of an externally generated braking to Milken's machine, the 3(a)9 removed it. And with the 1981–82 recession weathered and the problem deals at least temporarily fixed, Milken was ready to move to a new plateau.

5

The Cloister
at Wilshire and Rodeo

IN 1983 THE WORLD of junk exploded in size. By the end of 1983, 40 percent of all original-issue debt outstanding had been issued within the year—$7,310.2 billion. Twenty-three offerings of $100 million or larger were issued, compared to only eight in 1982. Drexel did $4,690 billion of junk offerings—three times the amount it had done the previous year.

In one ten-day period in February 1983, Drexel underwrote seven new issues totaling $500 million. In April, Drexel did the largest junk-bond offering ever, raising $400 million for MGM/UA Entertainment Company. And then, in July, $1 billion for MCI Communications.

Drexel's leap to these megadeals was not as smooth and effortless as it may have appeared to outsiders. One former Drexel employee recalls that Milken and his team were extremely nervous about the MGM/UA deal, since it was about four times bigger than anything they had ever done. "One of Mike's guys called me, wanting me to take ten million," said this former Drexel retail salesman. "Now, whenever they had a good deal they didn't want to give it to me, because Mike hates retail, he has no use for it, he doesn't want to have to take calls from somebody asking for a million dollars of bonds when he wants to be dealing with a hundred million. And here they were asking me to take it. They said, you know, be a team player. So I did.

"Then it got oversubscribed. I got a call: 'We want it back.' I'd already placed it with my clients. I said, 'Forget it.' Then Mike's hit man [another of Mike's salesmen] called me. 'You rotten . . .'— every obscenity in the book. Finally we compromised—I would cut back five million, they would cut back five million. Even after that [he] started to call again, shouting that they had to have the rest.

"Mike plays very tough," he said. "He doesn't get in there and do it himself—I've never heard him raise his voice. But he has people who do."

The MCI deal started out at $500 million. Milken's sales force, however, kept coming back to him with reports of bigger and bigger demand; Milken moved to $600 million, then $800 million, then finally $1 billion. After all, the MGM/UA deal had been oversubscribed. But then, as the deal grew, the Street cooled; some buyers began to say that $1 billion was too much debt for the company, and that there would be too much dilution of the equity (warrants were being issued with the bonds).

At most investment-banking firms, if they had filed to do a junk underwriting for $100 million but found they could sell only $50 million, they typically would cut the deal back to whatever they could sell. But Milken had for years now made it a point of honor that he would not cut back a deal. As he would testify with apparent pride in a deposition in mid-1986, "I would say also that in my entire career on Wall Street I have never backed out of a transaction once I've agreed to stand up to it, no matter how onerous it turned out to be."

This policy presumably sprang not only from Milken's sense of probity, but from his knowing it was good for business. It was meant to—and generally did—incur a sense of deep indebtedness in the client. Marshall Cogen of General Felt Industries, for example, recalls that in the hard times of 1980 Drexel filed to raise $60 million for General Felt but found they could sell less than half of that; the firm took the rest. As Cogen said in an interview in 1986, "I have never seen that done by another investment banking firm—*never*. Today everyone wants to bank us—Goldman, Lazard. But no one else would have raised that money back in 1980. And without it I never could have developed the base I have."

In the $1 billion MCI offering, according to this former employee, Milken was able to place only about $750 million. The firm took the other $250 million. But not for long.

A couple of months after the MCI offering, HITS was born. HITS is Drexel's own high-yield mutual fund, sold by Drexel's retail staff to the public. And in its portfolio was a healthy slug of MCI paper.

HITS was not a dumping ground for bad paper, but an outlet

for deals where Drexel had trouble selling the paper and so had to buy a lot of it. HITS became one more cog in the increasingly well-integrated, high-powered Milken machine.

As the number and the size of deals increased in 1983, so did Drexel grow and prosper. The firm employed about fifty-five hundred people that year, up from three thousand in 1979. Milken's group had grown from the twenty or so with whom he had arrived in Century City to 130. In 1978 Drexel had placed eleventh among corporate-bond underwriters; now it was sixth. And the firm that had earned $6 million in profits in 1979 earned an estimated $150 million in 1983.

In 1983 Milken and his brother Lowell, in partnership with several other investors, bought a four-story building at what is probably the most exclusive commercial address in Beverly Hills, at the intersection of Wilshire Boulevard and Rodeo Drive. They then leased the building to Drexel, and it became the new Milken headquarters.

It was also a statement, a graphic précis of things to come. Milken had chosen to live in relatively unpretentious Encino, but that was for his tiny sliver of private, family life. For his business, which consumed virtually all his waking hours, he was now setting a very different stage. Milken's new office was smack in the middle of one of the most ostentatious displays of wealth that exist in this country, in a town that spawns every excess that money can buy. Milken chose this as his made-for-the-movies mecca. Over the next several years the stretch limousines would begin lining up at 4:30 A.M. on the cobblestone driveway just behind Wilshire, their passengers—not only raiders but corporate chieftains as well—come for an audience with the King.

By 1983, too, Milken's investment partnerships—the repositories of much of his and his people's wealth—were multiplying. Other privately held firms on the Street had investment partnerships that were firmwide, as well as some in which certain partners participated and others did not. But only at Drexel was there a system so Byzantine, and so custom-made for patronage, manipulation and control by a single individual.

One of Milken's earliest investment partnerships, formed for him and his group even before he moved out to California, was Otter Creek. Then, according to the registration statements in Los Angeles County (where some but by no means all were filed),

Milken and his brother, Lowell, started one partnership, GLJ, in August 1978, immediately after he had moved to L.A. According to Milken's testimony in an SEC deposition in 1982, both Otter Creek and GLJ had accounts not only with Drexel but with Bear, Stearns. A National Association of Securities Dealers (NASD) rule stipulates that any employee of a broker-dealer who has a brokerage account at another firm must disclose its existence, and make its records available, to officers of his firm. There was no indication that Milken had not done this. In later years, Drexel would institute a policy forbidding employees from maintaining such outside accounts.

According to the L.A. County records, in 1982 Michael and Lowell Milken started three more, WB Associates, WRC Associates and Lobon Associates, and Lowell started a fourth, Carlyle Associates. The Milkens were the first-named partners, followed by various combinations of people in Michael Milken's group. By the end of 1983, there were two general partnerships, for Michael and his wife, Lori (RA Partnership), and Lowell and his wife, Sandra (EJ Associates), started on the same day; and then there were Chanticleer Investors Ltd., Dunmore Partners Ltd., Moredon Partners Ltd., and Canterbury Group, again with various combinations of the members of Milken's group, and also two lawyers working for Lowell in Cambrent. One of them was Richard Sandler, Lowell's boyhood friend, with whom he had gone through college and law school. Sandler was often the filing individual for these partnerships, some of which he participated in, and he was also trustee for Milken's children in some trusts. Given Sandler's relationship with Lowell, he was closer to being family than any other lawyer the Milkens might have found.

Probably one of the more lucrative of these investment partnerships was one formed to create a Chicago brokerage firm named Belvedere Securities, in early 1981. Belvedere was somewhat unusual among Milken's investment partnerships in that it had people participating in it who were not members of Drexel. At the outset, Belvedere Securities had among its general partners two money managers whom Milken had done business with since the early seventies, James Regan and Edward Thorp. Regan and Thorp controlled a number of entities, including an arbitrage fund, Princeton-Newport Partners, and Oakley-Sutton Management. Three other general partners of Belvedere had all been previously associated with a Regan-Thorp group. The sixth general partner, which contributed 75–100 percent of the firm's capital, was Milow Corporation (seemingly standing for Michael-Lowell). Lowell Milken was president, director and shareholder of Milow, and Richard Sandler was vice-president, director and shareholder. Within the next couple of years, Milow was deleted from membership and the capital contribution of Michael Milken (who was a limited partner from the beginning) rose to the category of from 50 percent to less than 75 percent.

Among its other limited partners, some of whom were added on through the early eighties, were Lowell Milken, GLJ, two corporate profit-sharing trusts at Irell and Manella (Lowell's old firm), Saul Steinberg's Reliance Group Holdings, and a large number of the more senior members of the Milken group.

Belvedere's main purpose was to engage in the stripping of Treasuries, trading the corpus, or body of the bond, and its coupons separately. These transactions enjoyed an extraordinary tax benefit, in large measure because the stripped Treasuries were newly created instruments for which the law was unclear. It therefore gave Milken a chance to operate in a gray area, his favorite terrain. Milken (through the Milow Corporation) and the Regan group had first started doing this in the late seventies at Belvedere's predecessor organization, Dorchester Government Securities. The Dorchester entity was located at the same address in Chicago as Belvedere later would be—One First National Plaza, Suite 2785—and all the general partners of Belvedere were also general partners of Dorchester Government Securities.

By the early eighties, zero-coupon Treasury bonds (which were the corpus) and the coupons or strips (known popularly as Tigers, Cats, Cougars and other names) were a multibillion-dollar business on Wall Street. In 1982, with the Tax Equity and Fiscal Responsibility Act (TEFRA), the tax laws changed. Until then, one did not have to allocate one's basis (assign costs) to the various pieces of paper, so it was possible to create an artificial tax loss. TEFRA closed that loophole. But until its passage, the tax benefits of these instruments, as used by Milken, made them perhaps the most powerful of all the financial tools he had at his disposal. According to two former members of Milken's group who were limited partners of Belvedere, they believed the Treasury-stripping idea had been brought to Milken by James Regan in the late seventies—which would explain the presence of the Regan-Thorp group in these partnerships.

It was noteworthy, too, that Milken carried out this gold-mine business through a separate brokerage firm created for this purpose, its majority interest owned by him, participated in by his favored—but not by Drexel. That is not to suggest, however, that the business activities of Drexel and Belvedere were not interrelated. In the course of taking a deposition from Milken in 1982, as part of a wide-ranging SEC investigation which focused on trading in the securities of companies including Reliance, Golden Nugget, American Financial, Rapid-American, CNA and First Executive, the SEC lawyer stated (in an exchange with Milken's counsel) that Belvedere had been selling the securities of Reliance and Leasco (another Steinberg-controlled company). The SEC lawyer also stated, "It is our understanding that there are orders placed with this firm by individuals who are members of the high-yield department for clients of the Drexel Burnham firm. Are you at all familiar with that?"

"No," Milken replied.

Asked whether Edwin Kantor, the head of all fixed-income trading at Drexel and the person who theoretically had to approve all of Milken's transactions, knew of the existence of Belvedere and the fact that members of Milken's group were its limited partners, Milken replied that he did. Asked furthermore whether Kantor was aware that this brokerage firm sold securities that the Drexel Burnham firm also sold, Milken replied, "It's quite possible. I'm not aware that Mr. Kantor gets a copy of all trades this firm does."

Milken gave some indication of the level of wealth in these partnerships when he talked to Robert Wallace, a Drexel employee in its Palo Alto office, about joining his cadre, in mid-1983. Wallace, who would later leave Drexel to form his own San Jose, California, investment company called Gateway Advisers, liked and admired Milken but decided not to join him because, he says, he didn't want to "jam bonds down clients' throats."

He was, however, tempted. "Mike told me," Wallace recalled, " 'No one who has been with me for five years is worth less than twenty million.' "

Wallace says that Milken was referring to his core group of a dozen or so—including Gary Winnick, Peter Ackerman, Dort Cameron, Charles Causey (Causey retired in 1981) and others. These were the "loyal bodies" Milken had gathered in the mid- and late seventies, most of whom had been either adrift or relatively low-achieving when he found them. He had collected a heavy toll from them. Julian Schroeder, a former Drexel investment banker, said, "Mike sits in the middle of that X of the other desks so that he can see everyone, and then he screams and yells. He cracks the whip. It's a slave ship out there—high-priced slavery."

There were other compensations, in addition to the material. Many of Milken's people felt that he extracted their very best from them—because he would tolerate nothing less. "Mike challenged you constantly in terms of your level of knowledge, and he helped you operate at the best level you possibly could," said one former member of the group. "If it weren't for Mike, I'd be a good high-grade-bond salesman, making a hundred thousand a year."

Many, too, were mesmerized by Milken's brilliance and awed by his sense of mission. The group was not unlike a cult: intensely secretive, insular, led by a charismatic and messianic leader whom many of his followers came to see as larger than life. "We owe it all to one man," declared one member of the group, "and we are all extraneous. Michael has denuded us of ego." One of the original cadre, Dort Cameron, added, "Michael is the most important individual who has lived in this century." Another former member will take it a step further: "Someone like Mike comes along once every five hundred years."

While his followers deified him, Milken resisted all outward signs of his station. He displayed an utter indifference to title, with a kind of reverse snobbism (what Drexel-given title could possibly matter, when in reality he was the King?). When questioned about his title in an SEC deposition in 1980, Milken replied, "I'm some kind of a vice-president. I'm not sure exactly whether I'm senior or executive or first. It keeps changing."

In what long seemed almost a fetish, he refused, year after year, to have his name or picture in Drexel's annual report. Even Drexel's fiftieth-anniversary retrospective, in 1984, made no mention of Milken. Milken finally explained, in an interview with this reporter in late 1987, "I feel it is not fair for my picture to be there and not everyone else's. It detracts from the community feeling. Everything we do is reflected in that. I sit with all my people as an equal. Our Christmas card lists everyone, whether it's the person who's parking the cars or the head trader.

"People are much more productive," Milken continued, "when they feel they're part of a team. It should be a collective force. No one should stand on top of someone else. I have always felt it is a human weakness to feel you're better than someone else.

"Watch the movie *Gandhi*," he added. "It is harder to motivate people if you are in a limousine and others are walking barefoot."

Milken's preoccupation with collectivism and antihierarchical form—more suggestive of a leftist leader of the sixties than of a financier of the eighties—was further reflected in that 1980 SEC deposition. Asked how many subordinates he had in the high-yield- and convertible-bond department, Milken objected, "I don't necessarily view them as subordinates."

"Well, how many people are subordinate to you in the hierarchical structure of the firm?" asked the government lawyer.

"We don't really have a pecking order."

"How many people are assigned to the high-yield- and convertible-bond department in addition to yourself?"

"I would estimate—I don't know exactly, but I would say between thirty-five and forty-five."

"Now, do each of these people report to you?"

"Since I'm the manager, you could say that [but] I may not speak to them for eight months."

"But you don't report to them?"

"No."

"You're not subordinate to any of these thirty-five or forty-five people in your department?"

"By subordinate, you mean accountable?"

"Yes."

"I'm not—I'm accountable in I'm trying to do a good job. Again, we don't have people that check in with one another."

"Well, do these people report to you? Are you denominated the boss?"

"Yes."

As though to underline this desire for structural egalitarianism, Milken had no office. On the infrequent occasions when he was away from his desk in the center of the trading floor, he urged others to use it. Meetings were generally open to all who were interested. People were encouraged to perform numerous functions. In a later SEC deposition, given in 1982, Milken described some people in his group as "quasi-trader salesmen," explaining that "on a given day he could be primarily selling, and another day he could be trading. Another day he could be doing something else."

In this group in which no one was to be placed above anyone

else, Milken had no second in command. One former member of his group says that even when Milken had to be absent from the trading floor for a day, he would not deputize anyone—and he would not, in this disciple's view, because it would mean ceding control. In an SEC deposition in 1985, when he was asked who was second in command in his department, Milken expounded on this point, saying, "I would say there is no second in command. You could say on some days there's one hundred seventy people that are second in command, and other days, you know, there's ten. It depends on what's happening, what the situation is. People have responsibilities, rather than a formal organization chart."

Indeed, someone once tried to draw an organization chart of Milken's group and it became a joke, a maze of crisscrossing lines, which was then screened onto T-shirts. Thenceforth, Milken's group was dubbed the "T-shirt organization."

If the absence of clearly defined responsibilities caused some pushing and shoving among a highly aggressive and incentivized group of people, Milken probably did not mind. According to one former member of this group, Milken preferred that there be a certain amount of friction among his people, so that they would not develop alliances—and he could better maintain control.

Milken kept his group cloistered. He demanded that his people shun publicity, as he did. He was convinced there was no upside— "Mike would always say, 'You can't make a dime off publicity,' " Steve Wynn recalled—and there was considerable downside. If his people started seeing themselves in print, he once commented to this reporter, they would get their heads turned, they would think they were famous. "They won't work as well. I want them there at four or four-thirty, ready to work, until eight o'clock at night. That's what we do, that's our responsibility. I don't want them to think of what's outside."

As though hearing the ring of the despot in his words, Milken quickly added, "I don't expect anyone to do any more than I do. I sit among them, my desk is the same as theirs."

Milken doubtless did inspire by his example. In an SEC deposition in 1982 he described what generally happened in his workday —which started a little later then than it would in later years and was not as frenetic as it would become. "I come in in the morning sometime between four-thirty and five," Milken began. "I generally read *The Wall Street Journal*. I generally write notes for the people in the department, put them on an administrative person's chair. By five-fifteen she's put them on everyone's chair in the department, so if they're not in they can't sit down without picking up their note.

"I then direct administrative people to make phone calls for me and get people on the phone, and that generally runs till around two o'clock in the afternoon.

"Sometime around ten forty-five to eleven-fifteen they put some food on my desk which I eat in anywhere from one to five minutes. Sometime in the afternoon it's possible corporations would come in for meetings and there would be meetings in the department with representatives from various corporations.

"Sometime between four and six a position sheet is put out as to what the position is for the department at the end of the [day], which I start to review. And if I'm not too tired, I then start writing out notes for the people in the department, asking them why they bought or sold a security, if I have an opinion, or I don't think that's a good idea, or that it might be a good idea.

"When I'm exhausted, I go home and I get ready for the next day."

Milken also made it clear that whatever happened on that trading floor was under his control. "I have good hearing, and over the years it developed that I can hear most conversations in the department. It's a small area they're going on. I might overhear someone doing a trade that I don't think's a good idea and might scream at them before they've completed that trade, or try to provide direction."

For Milken, weekends were an extension of his weekday treadmill. Maurits Edersheim, who had been at Burnham and Company since the forties and was deputy chairman of the board, recalled that he had a friend who was so eager to meet Milken that he agreed to the only time Milken had available: 5:30 A.M. on a Sunday. "Then Mike called me," Edersheim said, "and said that he hadn't realized that the clocks would be moved that Sunday for Daylight Saving Time, and could my friend come at four-thirty instead?"

Sometimes it seemed that the very notion of his taking time off was so at odds with his self-image that it offended him. In the above SEC deposition, the government attorney was questioning Milken about having been in Sun Valley, where Milken had seen Steve

Wynn. ". . . I'm not quite sure what the circumstances are here. Were you on a holiday?" asked the lawyer.

"I took off Friday and was there Friday, Saturday and Sunday," Milken replied.

"Okay, and at some point you saw Mr. Wynn at this holiday?"

". . . I had my briefcases with me, so I was reading at the time. I don't know if you want to call it a holiday—one has their own interpretation."

The example Milken set must have done much to bind his people to him—an example of sublimation of all things personal, and utter consecration to his mission, which was framed not just as money-making but challenging the prevailing misconceptions of the financial world with respect to low-rated debt and moving capital into the hands of a new order of manager-owners. But when all is said and done, the real glue was probably the money. Milken had made his key people fortunes that made the incomes of the investment bankers at Drexel—or at any firm on Wall Street—seem penurious. And this was true despite the fact that incomes for Wall Street's investment bankers were skyrocketing. In 1983 the top earners in Drexel's corporate-finance department were making over a half-million dollars—and that was roughly double what they had made the year before.

By this time, the discrepancy in income between the bankers in New York and the Milken group had spawned internecine rivalries. Many of the bankers envied the gold mine in Beverly Hills, while Milken's group—at their desks at 5:15 A.M., under their master's lash—disdained the bankers as lazy. Indeed, it became customary for bankers arriving at their New York offices at 7:30 or 8 A.M. to find that Milken had already called; they would return his call, and start the day with a Milken harangue. As one former member of the Milken group remarked, voicing the common West Coast bias, "The corporate-finance guys in New York are yentas—they have nothing to do but sit and talk all day."

And much of that talk, he believed, consisted of speculation about just how much lucre was being amassed in Beverly Hills. "They didn't know how much we were making, but they suspected. Even within our group, no one knew what anybody else was making."

6

The Air Fund

IT WAS NOT only within the Drexel enclave that lives were being transformed by Milken's Midas touch. By 1983, Fred Carr, of First Executive, a life insurance company, and Thomas Spiegel, of Columbia Savings and Loan, were building powerful, fast-growing institutions—each a maverick within its industry, each based upon and thriving with Milken's product.

In the late sixties Fred Carr racked up stellar returns as head of a go-go mutual fund called the Enterprise Fund and then departed in 1969—just months before the fund's collapse. His timing may have saved money and pride, but not his reputation; the Enterprise Fund failure would dog him for years. Then, in 1974, he was hired to run First Executive, a company with about thirty employees, teetering on the verge of bankruptcy. Friends wondered what the lure in a moribund insurance business could be for this shrewd equities analyst.

But "the fact that it had the name 'insurance business' had nothing to do with Fred's going to First Executive," declared Naftali Teitelbaum, who worked with Carr for years at that company. "He went there because he would have the opportunity to exercise his concepts in investments unfettered."

Carr quickly allied himself with an actuarial consultant, Alan Jacobs, who provided Carr with the insurance business expertise that he lacked himself. Over the next twelve years Jacobs would quietly, very much behind-the-scenes, design many of First Executive's innovative insurance products.

In 1975 the company began marketing the single-premium deferred annuity, or SPDA, in which the buyer made one payment and then collected the payout, tax exempt, a given number of years later. The SPDA and the other annuity products that followed it over the next decade—including structured settlements and guaranteed investment contracts, or gics—were custom-made for Carr's desires, since they brought in large sums of money up front for him to invest. And if Carr could promise a higher return than the next annuity-marketer, he would dominate this burgeoning business. All he needed, then, was a crackerjack investment strategy.

By 1977–78, he had it. He would eschew real estate, common stocks, mortgages, all the traditional investment instruments of the stodgy old insurance giants (many of which would have shown enormous losses, if they had had to mark their portfolios to market, showing their current market value), and he would go into bonds in a big way. Junk bonds. Indeed, according to an associate of Milken, Milken was convinced that one of the many benefits of his moving to L.A. would be his ability to cultivate a relationship with Carr and First Executive.

In 1978, the year that Milken moved to the West Coast, First Executive bought some portion of 66.7 percent of all the public junk issues Drexel offered. In 1979 it bought in 73.3 percent of the issues; in 1980, 86.7 percent; in 1981, 100 percent; in 1982, 92 percent; and in 1983, 100 percent.

In little more than a decade, Carr's investment strategy would turn First Executive from a nearly insolvent company to a pioneer in new-wave insurance products, with assets of $12 billion and a net worth of about $1.3 billion. Not surprisingly, Carr's investment portfolio would be yielding nearly 13 percent, compared to an industry average of 9.9 percent. And by the time First Executive's assets reached that $12 billion mark in late 1986, the amount invested in junk would fluctuate from about $5 billion to $7 billion.

Thomas Spiegel would seem to owe Milken even more than Carr did. Carr at least had a track record replete with highs as well as lows, before his and Milken's needs converged so perfectly. Spiegel, on the other hand, had not distinguished himself before Milken took him in hand.

In the early seventies Spiegel was a salesman in Drexel Burnham's retail department in New York. One Drexel executive recalled that Spiegel excelled as a playboy. "He would be out till four A.M., never got in to work until ten-thirty or eleven—then he was hung over." Spiegel then tried his hand at real estate, marketing condominiums in Iran for Starrett Corporation. In 1974, Spiegel's father, Abraham Spiegel, bought an ailing thrift in Beverly Hills, Columbia Savings and Loan Association, and in 1977 brought his son Thomas in as its president and chief executive officer. Its net worth was then $3 million. Under Thomas Spiegel's aegis, it continued to flounder.

Of course, Columbia was not the only thrift in trouble. By 1980–81 a large majority of the nation's three thousand S&Ls were caught with the same devastating mismatches that Columbia was: it had made long-term, fixed-rate mortgage loans, with funds provided by passbook and other short-term savings accounts. Those mortgage loans had been made at rates like 4 and 5 percent. And when interest rates in 1980–81 spiraled to 15 percent, thrifts had to compete with the new money-market mutual funds and thus were forced to shift from passbook accounts to certificates of deposit with adjustable rates.

Deregulation, in an effort to aid the failing thrifts, came with the Garn–St. Germain Depository Institutions Act in 1982. Congress authorized federally chartered thrifts to make commercial loans and invest in corporate-debt securities as well as other assets. Some state legislatures then passed similar bills, affecting state-chartered thrifts.

Thus, Congress provided Milken with a brand-new pool of capital to tap: the nearly $1 trillion in portfolios of savings and loans. While federally chartered thrifts would have ceilings (not more than 10 percent of their assets) on their junk investments, some state-chartered thrifts—including California's—would have virtual investment autonomy. And thrifts, moreover, make great investment vehicles because they have enormous built-in leverage: they can take in $100 of deposits for every $3 of equity or subordinated debt.

Spiegel's new strategy was to achieve a high yield from his investments (moving from a mortgage-loan portfolio to junk bonds) and to cure the mismatch of the maturities of his assets and his liabilities. To this end, over the next several years Columbia floated several billion dollars' worth of intermediate and long-term, non-withdrawable certificates of deposit, sold through a retail distribution network by stockbrokers nationwide. The average maturity of Columbia's liabilities increased from 3.6 months at December 1982 to 2.9 years at March 1986. So now Spiegel had capital he could rely on, that couldn't be withdrawn overnight. He then invested a substantial portion of those deposits in junk bonds, locking in an enormous spread.

In December 1981, Columbia had $373 million in assets; by year-end 1986, it would have roughly $10 billion—with at least 26 percent of its total assets invested in junk.

One former Columbia employee recalled that Spiegel bought his first junk bond for Columbia in 1982 and quickly began investing hundreds of millions in them. "But Tom was a newcomer to this market. It was all Mike—there was no research staff at Columbia, no documentation, everything was in two file cabinets."

By 1986, Columbia would have a full research staff working on its junk investments. Spiegel, now a hard-working executive, would point to that staff and claim that Columbia made its own investment decisions, independent of Milken. He would, however, tell *Business Week*, "Mike has really been the major influence in expanding my business perspective." He would have expanded, too, from junk to include major investments in mortgage-backed securities, and also equities in a risk arbitrage operation.

Spiegel's high-risk investment practices would earn him the displeasure of the Federal Home Loan Bank Board. Thrifts theoretically exist to finance the housing industry. And Spiegel was playing the junk game with federally insured funds. The Bank Board would conduct a review of thrifts' investments in junk, considering setting a ceiling on those investments for Spiegel and all other state-chartered institutions, but by the end of 1987 it had taken no action. At the insistence of that agency, Spiegel's 1985 compensation would be reduced from nearly $9 million to $5.1 million—which still made him the thrift industry's highest-paid executive.

Spiegel was no favorite of the government, but he had—with Milken's product and guidance—created one of the most profitable and best-capitalized thrifts in the country. By the end of 1986, while Columbia's profits continued to grow, nearly one of every four federally insured savings and loans had lost money for the year, and their losses had more than doubled from 1985.

In speeches Milken gave in 1986, he took pleasure in alluding to these successful upstarts, First Executive and Columbia, which had flouted conventional industry practices. Milken was the proud progenitor of both institutions. And his relationships with them continued to be incestuously close as they came of age. He sold them the junk bonds that were the engine of their phenomenal growth. He raised capital for them. And he was their substantial shareholder. According to one former member of Milken's group, Milken and some group members provided Carr with much-needed capital by buying his stock and warrants when he was starting to build First Executive. By the end of 1981, Milken and a Drexel group owned 50 percent of First Executive's reinsurance subsidiary, later renamed First Stratford. By December 1984, Milken—through his children's trusts, in a purchase of securities for which the only named individual was his lawyer Richard Sandler, as trustee for those trusts—would own 9.9 percent of Columbia's stock. Also in December 1984, the Drexel Burnham Lambert Group would control 10.3 percent of Columbia. In effect, then, Milken and Drexel would control over 20 percent of the institution.

What set First Executive and Columbia apart from other institutions and companies with which Milken was playing his multiplicitous roles by 1983 was the degree of their metamorphosis. Others had benefited from Milken's performance, but they had not been so utterly transformed from flounderers to titans—and titans whose sustenance, in large part, continued to come directly from Milken. The bigger their appetites for junk became, the more useful First Executive and Columbia would be—ultimately functioning as enormous appendages of Milken.

For the moment, in 1983, Carr and Spiegel performed their functions in Milken's machine by joining the other members of Milken's extended business family—including Carl Lindner through American Financial, Saul Steinberg through Reliance Insurance, Meshulam Riklis through Rapid-American, Victor Posner through several of his companies, the Belzbergs through a number of their companies, and others—who issued their own paper and bought one another's and traded, with Milken the nexus for it all.

But as important as these players were, by year-end 1983 the junk market was far broader and deeper than Milken's coterie of high-rollers. From 1977 to 1983, 225 industrial and finance companies issued approximately $19.5 billion of junk debt. According to Milken's estimate, by the end of 1983 the junk market totaled over $40 billion par value (including those issues which had been downgraded into the junk category, as well as originally issued junk). And since the entire straight corporate-bond market was about $375 billion, the junk sector was roughly 13 percent of the total.

Even as this market won more and more buyers—or, in Milken's lexicon, "disciples"—it still was not a mainstream kind of investment, so the yield spreads remained impressive. At the end of 1983, Milken estimated that for several years the typical high-yield bond had outyielded long-term U.S. Treasury bonds by 300–500 basis points (paying 13–15 percent, compared to a 10 percent yield from a Treasury bond).

Among those who had profited from these yields, First Executive and Columbia were by far the most aggressive for their respective industries, but other insurance companies and thrifts were entering the market. The original handful of high-yield mutual funds that had been created at the inception of junk had grown to twenty-six, with assets of $5.5 billion. Pension funds had come into the market; the World Bank's was one of the first, with a $20 million investment in junk in 1980, and it was followed over the next several years by those of such blue-chip corporations as IBM, Xerox, Atlantic Richfield, Standard Oil, General Motors and others.

There were many tributaries, but virtually all flowed through Milken. Many of the pension-fund managers, for example, asked Milken to refer them to someone with expertise in junk bonds, and Milken steered some to the mutual-fund managers. Says one mutual-fund manager who claims to have turned down such an offer, "It happened to every mutual-fund guy at some point—Mike would say, 'Want to run some private accounts?' And if you said yes, then you'd owe him."

One who did not turn down the favor was David Solomon, who ran First Investors' high-yield mutual fund. Solomon ran some of the pension-fund money of the World Bank (he had been recommended along with several others by Milken) and other corporations, as private accounts under a separate group, First Investors Asset Management. This business became so lucrative that in early 1983 Solomon walked out of First Investors, taking the entire junk-bond staff and five of the company's seven private-account clients (which had an aggregate portfolio of nearly $300 million). He set up his own company, Solomon Asset Management. Among the clients Solomon took were the World Bank pension fund and First Executive (which pulled out $80 million from its $120 million First Investors portfolio and invested $90 million with Solomon).

Every business and profession has its network, through which referrals and favors are exchanged. What set this one apart was its utter dominance by a single individual. Milken, and Milken alone, was in a position continuously to demand and to dispense favors. He had the product. He had the trading capital. He knew, with his phenomenal memory augmented by his computer system in Beverly Hills, where nearly every bond was. He dominated not only the primary market (of original issuance) but the secondary market (trading). As one junk aficionado put it in a frequently uttered refrain, "Michael *is* the market."

No buyer of junk who might suddenly need to get out of a position could afford to be on Milken's bad side—for having refused to buy some bonds Milken needed to unload, for example. "Mike's favorite expression," said one mutual-fund manager, "is, 'I'll make it up to you.' "

And the controls which Milken manned so zealously, in his twenty-hour days, operated a financial machine of increasingly awesome power. For the 1983 junk-bond conference, Milken performed what would become his annual ritual: he calculated, roughly, the total of his guests' buying power. "Our access in this room," he declared, as recalled by one guest, "is one hundred billion dollars."

These yearly announcements always bore the embellishment of Milken the showman, since—even with his legendary persuasiveness—his guests' portfolios were not wholly consecrated to junk. But, Milken's hyperbole notwithstanding, it was clear by this time that he had tapped a demand so massive that it could outstrip the supply that was available from Drexel's "traditional" financings. If his machine were to achieve its fullest potential—and if he and Drexel were to continue to dramatically beat their profits from the previous year—he would have to find a new source of product.

Increasingly, he and Joseph were both convinced that the wellspring had to lie in mergers and acquisitions, or M&A—where investment-banking firms were reaping multimillion-dollar fees for their firms on a single transaction. As the profitability of Wall Street's traditional businesses had declined with the slashing of commission rates through deregulation, and long-standing ties between corporations and their investment bankers had been replaced with a free-for-all competition for underwritings, M&A had emerged as the Street's hottest growth business. Before 1976, most investment-banking firms had not even had separate M&A groups, but by 1983 at the premier firms—Goldman, Sachs; Morgan Stanley; First Boston; Kidder, Peabody—these were major profit centers.

This latest merger wave was the fourth that this country had seen. The first occurred in the late 1890s, when monopolies like U.S. Steel and Standard Oil were formed. The next lasted from 1919 to 1929, the year of the crash, when companies like General Motors and Pullman expanded. The third occurred from 1960 to 1969, when the bull market fueled what were essentially paper deals, and conglomerateurs were able to acquire much larger companies with their companies' overpriced stock.

The current wave began in 1974, when one pillar of the business establishment, International Nickel Company, raided another, ESB. International Nickel, moreover, was aided in its depredations by the ineffably white-shoe Morgan Stanley. With that, the class barrier was broken, and hostile takeovers became acceptable for elite companies and their investment bankers and lawyers. The International Nickel raid was followed by other hostile cash takeover attempts by blue-chip companies, all looking for quality, well-managed target companies.

While the volume of these deals was much diminished from the late sixties, the size of the transactions began to grow. In 1975 there were fourteen mergers with a value in excess of $100 million; in 1977 there were forty-one; in 1978, eighty. By 1979 the deals could be tallied according to those with a value of $1 billion or more: there were three that year, one in 1980, nine in 1981, five in 1982, and nine in 1983.

This wave had been triggered in part by the market crash of 1974, which created abundant bargains. Then inflation swelled the value of corporate assets, but the stock prices did not rise to reflect those values. So it became much cheaper to buy a company than to build one.

The country's tax and accounting system, moreover, encourages the assumption of debt—as occurs in these leveraged takeovers —at the expense of equity. Corporate income is taxed to corporations, and dividends are taxed to shareholders, creating a double tax. It is easier for a corporation to pay interest (on debt), which is tax deductible, than to pay dividends (on stock), which are not. A company in the 50 percent tax bracket can afford to pay a rate of 16 percent interest as easily as a rate of 8 percent in dividends. And the individual investor, who has to pay taxes on either the interest or the dividend, will generally prefer the higher interest payment.

By the early eighties, additional factors had come into play.

With the Reagan administration, antitrust restrictions became obsolete. Giant oil-company mergers that would never have been allowed in the Carter years became boilerplate. And companies of many parts that had been assembled in the conglomerate era began selling off odd pieces and acquiring other companies in their main line of business.

Banks—the crucial participants—had joined the M&A fray with a vengeance. Although in 1975, when Crane made a tender offer for 25 percent of the Anaconda Copper Company, no big New York bank would even act as an exchange or escrow agent for the bonds, such inhibitions had now been overcome. With deregulation, banks lost most of their low-cost deposits and were forced to offer money-market and other high-interest-bearing accounts. Furthermore, profit margins on short-term loans to corporations became thin because the banks had to compete with commercial paper. So the highly lucrative loans for takeovers became much-sought-after business.

With the 1981 Economic Recovery Tax Act, the tax system slanted the board still further toward the assumption of debt in these leveraged deals. This legislation was intended to spur economic growth by allowing companies to take extra-rapid depreciation. When they did that, cash flow grew faster than reported earnings. Stock prices, therefore, did not get the boost that they would have gotten from higher earnings, but the added cash flow increased companies' ability to service debt—and enhanced their appeal as targets.

In addition to all these factors which gave rise to acquisition fever, there was Wall Street, fanning the flames. By 1983, investment bankers had abandoned their traditional roles as passive advisers and were now shopping deals frenziedly and becoming expert at handling multibillion-dollar transactions. But Drexel could not win the blue-chip clients that were the real players in this arena, and so it was relegated to the periphery, with small-time deals.

By the end of 1983, Drexel's M&A group had produced $10 million in fees, up from $6 million the year before. The group was run by David Kay, one of Joseph's "Shearson Mafia" hires from the seventies, a dapper type who seemed more Seventh Avenue than Wall Street ("We'll take a gross of zippers, David," one of his colleagues would kid him). Joseph recalled telling Kay that in the major firms' corporate-finance departments M&A was accounting for 40 percent or even 50 percent of revenues. Drexel's corporate-finance department that year had had revenues of $115 million (including M&A's $10 million). So, Joseph argued, Kay was not even close to pulling in his competitive share. "I told him that it was time for us to make a quantum leap in M&A, and that I thought we had to do it by tying in our financing.

"We had some other ideas," Joseph said, "like underwriting dispositions for companies—using our financial muscle to go to a company and say, You want to sell that division? We'll guarantee you a price of forty million dollars. And then if we couldn't get the forty million we'd make up the shortfall, but at least it would give us the merchandise."

Drexel could not shop deals the way other firms did, because it had no merchandise. A firm like Goldman, Sachs, with its roster of Fortune 500 clients, often served as a marriage broker between those clients and made princely fees. But Drexel had no sizable M&A product, and no entree to the world that had it.

Six years after Drexel began underwriting original junk, it had created a $40 billion market, increased its profits geometrically, made fortunes for Milken and his chosen, provided what was essentially venture capital to scores of midsized companies, and brought bountiful returns to thrifts, insurance companies, pension funds, high-yield funds and others. But it was still an outcast in the major corporate world.

Drexel had found the "edge" for which Joseph had been casting about back in the seventies, and it was lined with gold. But money had never been the touchstone for Joseph. His aim, from the start, had been to create a world-class institution. And he was convinced now that Drexel—like the firms that laid claim to such status—needed to become a big player in the M&A field.

What would become Joseph's "quantum leap" was actually only a small conceptual step forward from what the firm was already doing. Starting in 1982, Drexel had begun raising the "mezzanine" financing—by selling junk bonds—in leveraged buyouts. In a leveraged buyout, as it came to be known in the eighties, a small group of investors, usually including management, buys out the public shareholders by borrowing against the assets being purchased and then repays the debt with cash from the acquired company or, more often, by selling some of its assets. LBOs are structured like an inverted pyramid, with senior, secured debt at the top (typically about 60 percent, provided by banks); mezzanine, unsecured debt in the middle (about 30 percent, which Drexel provides with junk bonds); and a smidgen of equity, the prime filet of the deal, at the bottom.

A number of firms—among them Kohlberg Kravis Roberts and Company, Forstmann Little and Company, Clayton & Dubilier and others—had been specializing in LBOs for many years, some starting in the early sixties. The LBO is, after all, simply an investment technique, in which you hock the assets of the company in order to buy it—similar to the way many real-estate deals are done, with second and third mortgages. The LBO firms would buy companies in partnership with their management. By being made equity partners, those managers were given incentive to trim costs and augment efficiencies. And by the use of leverage, the value of the equity holders' investment often grew phenomenally.

In the sixties and seventies, the LBO market consisted mainly of buying private companies or divisions of public companies. LBOs that involved taking sizable public companies private did not start until about 1980.

And it was not until William E. Simon, former U.S. Treasury Secretary, pulled off the Gibson Greetings deal that the LBO became the craze of Wall Street. Wesray, the private investment group that Simon headed, acquired Gibson Greetings from RCA in 1982. In 1983, when Gibson Greetings went public again, Simon's group emerged with a remaining holding of about 50 percent in Gibson— and a profit of $70 million. By 1984, the dollar amount of completed LBOs would increase fourfold within the year, to reach $18.6 billion.

Though Drexel had not pioneered the LBO, it was a match made in heaven. It was a philosophical fit: the LBO represented a shift of control from a bureaucratic organization into entrepreneurial hands. And it was an extension of what Milken had been doing since 1977, when he started to help his clients to leverage their balance sheets with high levels of debt, through the issuance of junk bonds. Indeed, that realignment of the balance sheet—in which debt, with its tax-deductible interest payments, was so favored— had been explored by Milken in the paper he wrote in 1973 (after leaving Wharton) with one of his professors, James Walter. Entitled "Managing the Corporate Financial Structure," the paper examined ways of optimizing investor returns by modifying a company's capital structure, and compared that to the management of an investment portfolio.

"Notwithstanding the focus of most corporate executives upon the operating side of the business, opportunities for profit enhancement also exist in the financial end of the business," Walter and Milken wrote. "The liability and net worth segments of the balance sheet represent portfolio positions that are subject to modification as conditions warrant. Neglect of such matters is patently inconsistent with rational behavior."

In raising the financing for LBOs, Drexel would be doing what it did best—for the mezzanine level of unsecured debt in these highly leveraged deals was by definition junk. Before Drexel, that financing had generally been raised from private placements with a handful of insurance companies. But Milken had his legions of ready buyers, raised on a diet of just such high-yielding debt from companies with highly leveraged balance sheets. In 1982 Drexel placed the mezzanine financing for two deals, and in 1983 it did two more. Investment banker Leon Black, the only one in corporate finance besides Fred Joseph who seemed to have Milken's respect, headed the LBO group.

From there, it was a natural progression. If Milken could place the most difficult portion of debt in an LBO, which is a friendly, negotiated takeover, why couldn't he do the same thing in an "unfriendly LBO"—which is a hostile takeover using debt?

In November 1983, Joseph, Milken and members of their respective teams met with Cavas Gobhai in a suite at the Beverly Wilshire Hotel, next door to Drexel's new Beverly Hills office, to engineer the quantum leap. As Joseph recalled that meeting, "We started by asking, 'Where does our financing muscle really come into play?' One thing that's hard to finance is unfriendly acquisitions. You can't finance them, because you can't tell people you're going to do the deal, and you don't know if you're going to need the money, and you don't know how much money you're going to need, because you may have to raise the price, and you don't have access to the inside information, and a lot of people don't like to get involved in unfriendly deals."

Those were the problems. By the end of that two-day session, Milken, Joseph and the rest had decided to find a candidate so that they could start experimenting with solutions to them in the real world. Within a few weeks, T. Boone Pickens, targeting the Gulf Oil Company with his pygmy-sized Mesa, became their first test case.

But the germ of this new wildly egalitarian system—in which, before long, *anyone* (with Milken behind him) could take over any company, no matter how large—had begun to grow about a year earlier, at yet another Gobhai session.

"We wanted to position ourselves so that Drexel had an awesome M&A capability," Joseph recalled, "because we had the access to the money and the power." They wanted to become so strong that companies doing deals would clamor to hire them—even if only to neutralize them. At the time, it was the stuff of fantasy, the daydream of omnipotence of every have-not.

At that 1982 session, Joseph and the others drew up a list of the people who were the stars of the M&A world. It included Martin Siegel of Kidder, Peabody; Eric Gleacher of Lehman Brothers; Bruce Wasserstein of First Boston; Felix Rohatyn of Lazard Frères; Ira Harris of Salomon Brothers—and lawyers too, like Martin Lipton of Wachtell, Lipton, Rosen and Katz, and Joe Flom of Skadden, Arps, Meagher, Slate and Flom.

At a Gobhai session, of course, all ideas are entertained, no matter how outrageous. This list, therefore, was not a literal recruitment list; Flom, for example, was not seen as a potential candidate, although his ties to the firm would grow as Drexel became one of his firm's five biggest clients over the next few years. But Joseph would later say that there were four on that list whom they did want—and Martin Siegel was at the top. "I took Marty on then, as my assignment to recruit," Joseph would say four years later, in an interview in mid-1986 shortly after Siegel had left Kidder to join Drexel.

When that list was drawn up, the idea of persuading any of those individuals to join Drexel was, as David Kay put it, "chasing rainbows." Before it could have even the faintest hope of luring one of those stars, Drexel had to bust its way into the M&A preserve, through sheer financial force. And one way to do that—which would be implemented not literally but in spirit—emerged at this session.

Drexel's problem was that it had no Fortune 500 client with a billion-dollar bank line to wage a takeover. But what if *Drexel* had the billion dollars, at the ready? Or what if they said they did (and got it later)? And what if, by their staking the word of the firm on this claim, the world believed it and acted accordingly? In the new lexicon—and universe—that Drexel would soon create, this concept would become known as the "highly confident" letter. But for now it was christened (for its emptiness) the Air Fund.

"We would announce to the world that we had raised one billion dollars for hostile takeovers," one Drexel executive recalled. "There would be no money in this fund—it was just a threat. The Air Fund stood for our not having a client with deep pockets who could be in a takeover. It was a substitute for that client we didn't have.

"That concept led to our making Carl Icahn real instead of nettlesome. Carl ended up being our Air Fund. Boone ended up being our Air Fund. We manufactured out of thin air—almost thin air—a credible takeover guy."

PART TWO

Pawns Capture Kings

7

Triangle-National Can: Kingmaker

On April 2, 1985, the conference room on the eighth floor of the no-frills National Can headquarters in southwest Chicago was packed with the usual armies of deal advisers—M&A lawyers from Skadden, Arps, Slate, Meagher and Flom as well as from Paul, Weiss, Rifkind, Wharton and Garrison, and investment bankers from Salomon Brothers. There were some new investment-banking faces too, troops who were still a little green but who had launched a juggernaut that was now commanding the attention, and fear, of corporate chieftains across the country, as well as the one in this room.

Drexel—in the spirit of the GI Joe poster hanging behind the desk of one of Drexel's senior executives, a poster which had been designed as a mock ad for the firm and featured the hero leading his platoon, their guns spitting fire—had arrived.

Two weeks earlier, Triangle Industries, controlled by Nelson Peltz and Peter May, had made a Drexel-financed, unsolicited $41 all-cash tender offer for all outstanding shares of National Can. Now, with other options for the company having failed to materialize, it looked as though a friendly deal might be struck. Frank Considine, the silver-haired, patrician CEO of National Can, threaded his way through the crowd and asked Peltz to come into his office. May was Peltz's one-third partner, but Peltz was the lead player and deal-maker. Alone with Peltz, Considine told him that he might be willing to do the deal, but the shareholders would have to get a better price. The two men talked for about ten minutes, and then Peltz raised his offer to $42 a share.

"Nelson did that dollar totally on his own," said Fred McCarthy of Drexel, who was advising Peltz. The additional dollar raised the price of the deal by $9 million. "Leon [Black] and I thought it was outrageous, but once he'd done it, what were we going to do? At that point we could have said, 'We won't play anymore.' Instead we said, 'Don't do it again.' "

The negotiations continued. James Freund of Skadden, who was representing National Can, continued to pound away at Peltz, trying to get him to go up another dollar—which would have raised the price of the deal by another $9 million—but Peltz, now chastened, resisted. "I *wanted* to give another dollar," Peltz said. "A dollar in this deal meant nothing. What was a dollar? But I had to get the OK from Mike Milken, and he was in Hawaii."

According to one long-standing acquaintance of Milken, his wife, Lori, had made him promise that on his vacation he would not work from 9 A.M. on; so Milken took his family to Hawaii, where he slept for a few hours in the late evening, rose at 1 or 2 A.M. and worked until 9 A.M.—by which time it was 2 P.M. in New York and most of the business day was over.

"Mike was unreachable," Peltz said. "They [his Drexel advisers] were blocking my calls. They thought I was being too gracious."

Freund said, "I knew he wanted to go up a buck—assuming he could get the money. But I finally realized I was working over the wrong guy. All the discipline was being imposed by Milken and company."

Peltz was indeed—as his Drexel advisers, McCarthy and Black, had so heavily reminded him—not the true principal here, only Milken's chosen agent. He had come into the breach when Victor Posner, one of Milken's longest-standing clients and a member of the high-rollers' coterie, had been cornered. Posner had owned 38 percent of National Can. In February 1985, National Can, along with an employee stock-ownership plan, had launched an offer for 51 percent of the company's shares which would have left Posner— who was in desperate need of cash to make interest payments on debt for at least two of his companies—with a sharply devalued minority position. If Posner was to be rescued from this worst-of-all-worlds situation, a competing bidder would have to be brought in.

By this time, in early 1985, Milken was moving his players across the M&A field as though it were a chessboard. The Air Fund had matured into the "highly confident" letter, in which Drexel would announce that it was "highly confident" it could raise a given sum, necessary for its client to take over his desired company. It then would obtain from its buyers "commitment letters," in which each promised to buy a certain amount of junk bonds. These bonds would be issued by the shell corporation formed to acquire the target, and secured by the assets of the target.

It was an evolving strategy, changing slightly each time it was implemented. Thus far Milken had launched the junk-bond-financed hostile takeover on behalf of T. Boone Pickens, in Mesa's run at Gulf; Saul Steinberg, in Reliance's bid for Disney; Carl Icahn, in his bid for Phillips Petroleum; and Oscar Wyatt, in Coastal Corporation's bid for American Natural Resources (ANR). Only one of these targets, ANR, had actually been acquired—less than a month before Triangle made its offer for National Can.

Even for Drexel—home of the underdog and the proverbial outsider—Peltz and May were small-time. All they had to their names was a controlling interest in a tired old vending-machine, wire and cable company, Triangle Industries—its 1984 revenues were $291 million, compared to National Can's $1.9 billion—plus about $130 million of cash that first L. F. Rothschild and then Drexel had raised for Triangle from the sale of junk bonds. But none of the bigger players to whom Drexel had shopped the National Can deal had been interested. None considered the deal a bargain. And as one longtime associate of Peltz said, "The others all had more at risk—only Nelson had so little to lose."

So Peltz and May were brought to the fore. And on April 4, 1985, they reached an agreement with National Can to acquire the company at $42—not needing to go up the extra dollar after all.

For a while, Peltz recalled, everyone held his breath, waiting to see whether this paper miracle would collapse. The only other Drexel-backed takeover to achieve consummation, ANR by Coastal, was a sturdier construct. "There is no comparison between Coastal and this," Peltz asserted, visibly offended at the suggestion that Triangle was not the first of Milken's minnows to actually swallow a whale. "Coastal was a big company, with significant assets. It wasn't so leveraged. Triangle was a company with a fifty-million-dollar net worth. This was the first of the superleveraged buyouts to go through."

The acquisition of National Can cost $465 million. Triangle contributed $70 million as equity, to which another $30 million was added through its sale (underwritten by Drexel) of preferred stock;

the debt portion layered above that consisted of $365 million raised with junk bonds by Drexel. And after the deal closed, Drexel raised another $200 million from junk bonds, in order to pay down National Can's preexisting bank debt. So the total debt of National Can, once the $200 million was added to the preceding $365 million, was $565 million.

Five hundred sixty-five million dollars was a towering debt load for $100 million of equity to carry. And Peltz pointed out that even the $70 million from Triangle, at the equity base, came from its earlier offering of junk. "We put the hundred million in the sub [the subsidiary, Triangle Acquisition Corporation, formed for the buyout]. But it was all debt! We called it equity here [at Triangle Acquisition Corporation], but it was debt over here [at Triangle]. Do you understand the leverage in this deal? It was eleven to one!

"And for the next two months, every Friday after the market closed, Peter Ackerman [Milken's key aide for buyouts] would call me and say, 'You're going bankrupt! You're going bankrupt! You miscalculated the debt!' And I'd say, 'You guys did the calculations. What are you talking about? What kind of smoke is blowing through the air-conditioners out there on Wilshire Boulevard?' "

Leon Black acknowledged, "We *were* nervous. The first year or two of these buyouts is very risky. We have a franchise to protect. It's not unusual in the early stages for us to make sure that the runners of these companies are keeping their eye on the ball. We hadn't seen Nelson manage much of this size before."

Peltz appeared to share little of his bankers' anxiety. In mid-1985 he purchased through Triangle a $2 million apartment in Paris. "Mike made him put it on the market," commented one Drexel investment banker, "which was the right thing to do. We have a responsibility to our bondholders. What's he going out and spending the company's money like that for, when he's got this mountain of debt?"

By the beginning of 1986, however, the first good news was in (and Peltz took the apartment, still unsold, off the market). National Can had had a record year in 1985; its earnings (for April 17 through December) were $162 million, up from $68,775 the year before; Triangle's stock had quadrupled, making it the third-best performer on the New York Stock Exchange. With interest rates down, Peltz and May were refinancing the company's acquisition debt, meaning they were paying down that debt and replacing it with newer debt at lower interest rates. And their combined personal stakes in the company had gone from a market value of roughly $8–9 million when they purchased the controlling block of Triangle stock, in 1983, to about $34 million. Adding in a premium for control, which would have been present if they were to sell their block, it was now worth more than $40 million.

Alan Brumberger, another Drexel banker who worked on the National Can deal, noted in mid-1986, "All my clients were pleading with me, 'Make me Nelson.' "

NOWHERE WAS Milken the magician's prowess—creating out of (almost) thin air a takeover entrepreneur—more stunningly displayed than in the case of Nelson Peltz and Peter May. Others he backed before and after—T. Boone Pickens, Saul Steinberg, Oscar Wyatt, Carl Icahn, Ronald Perelman, Sanford Sigoloff, William Farley—were all given access to pools of capital that they could only have fantasized about were there no Michael Milken. But each of them had been successful in his sphere, however much smaller—and in some instances disreputable—it may have been before they joined the Drexel party. (For Icahn, for example, it was greenmailing.) Only Peltz and May were virtually empty-handed when they arrived at the threshold. And when it was all over, they would reign over an empire with $4 billion in revenues.

Peltz's love of luxury did not stem from early deprivation. Asked where he thinks his younger brother Nelson acquired his opulent tastes, Robert Peltz says, "He had them from the first moment he opened his eyes." The Peltzes were a comfortable upper-middle-class family. When Nelson was small they lived in the Cypress Hills section of Brooklyn, later moving to Park Avenue in Manhattan. Nelson attended a private school, Horace Mann. In 1960 he entered the Wharton School at the University of Pennsylvania, in 1961 he took a leave of absence, he returned in 1962 and he left later that year.

He went to work for what was intended as a brief stint in the family food business, Abe Peltz and Sons (started by Nelson and Robert's grandfather). It was then a $2.5 million business with about a dozen employees, which sold frozen foods to institutions. Peltz says he intended to stay there for two weeks, just long enough to earn his fare out to Oregon, where he had a job teaching ski-racing to youngsters. But he got hooked.

While his brother managed the day-to-day operations of the business, Nelson set out on an acquisition course, buying up small food businesses along the East Coast—among them a company called Flagstaff, whose name he adopted in 1969. In 1972 he took Flagstaff public; through his acquisitions, the company now had sales of $50 million. Robert Peltz was chairman of the board of this newly public company, and Nelson was its president.

In the process of taking the company public, Peltz met Peter May, who was then one of his auditors at Peat, Marwick, Mitchell and Company. Like Peltz, May came from an upper-middle-class family in New York. He had received an M.B.A. from the University of Chicago, and, like Peltz, he was hoping for far greater vistas in business, seeing his stint at Peat, Marwick as a stepping-stone. He went to work for Peltz at Flagstaff.

Nelson Peltz's grand plan was to use Flagstaff as a vehicle for acquisitions by doing stock swaps. "But the stock never really performed, so we couldn't use it for acquisitions," said May. "Instead, we did acquisitions for debt. This was, of course, before Milken. So we were limited to bank debt, which was keyed to standard ratios. If we had a twenty-million net worth, we couldn't borrow a hundred million." In 1975, Flagstaff bought 51 percent of Coffee-Mat, a maker of vending machines for beverages and snacks, and the following year it acquired the rest of the company.

By the late seventies, Peltz was leading a fast-track social life. He had a press agent. He often showed up in the "Suzy Knickerbocker" column. His lifestyle, one friend who knew him then commented, was like an Oriental potentate's. He and Saul Steinberg (chairman of Reliance, Inc.) were notorious for throwing wild parties at their respective summer houses in Quogue, Long Island. The story that floated around the Drexel corridors, one which may be apocryphal but which was told and retold so many times that it became legend, featured Peltz and Steinberg as hosts to a women's tennis match—four topless women on the courts, and Peltz and Steinberg the spectators.

But Peltz's business life was considerably less fast-track, and he was frustrated. He couldn't even expand the food business the way he wanted to, and his real aspirations were for something far more glamorous.

"Nelson didn't want to be in the food business," a friend declared. "He wanted to be a big shot! He wanted to buy Columbia

Pictures! He was assiduously cultivating Herbert Siegel [CEO of Chris-Craft Industries], Charlie Bluhdorn [chairman of Gulf + Western], Saul Steinberg. He was like the kid who wants to hang out with the varsity football team."

Peltz did make overtures to Herbert Allen of Allen and Company, which held only a relatively small block of Columbia Pictures at that time but was nonetheless viewed as being in control of the company. According to one insider, Peltz called Herbert Allen and said he would be interested in buying a controlling block, but Allen never took him seriously because he did not believe that Peltz had the means to buy any sizable block. "It was just that Peltz wanted to go Hollywood," the insider said. "He wanted to socialize with Herb Allen."

Even the limited expansion of the food business had not worked. In 1978, the food businesses of Flagstaff were sold to a group headed by Philip Sassower, Lawrence Schneider and Ben Jacobson for approximately $31 million (most of which went to pay off the bank debt accumulated in the acquisitions). Robert Peltz stayed with the food business and its new owners, while Nelson and Peter May set out to make Coffee-Mat, all that was left of the public company that had been Flagstaff, their new vehicle. They renamed the company Trafalgar. Robert Peltz remarked about the grand expansion engineered by Nelson that ended with selling out, "It could have made sense. It could have become a Staley or a Kraft, if things were done differently. But they weren't."

"The company was not performing," one insider said. "Too many luxuries were taken. A food company doesn't need offices on Madison Avenue [where Nelson Peltz moved the offices], they should be over a warehouse. And it doesn't need layers and layers of nonproductive management."

What happened to Flagstaff after the buyout is a lesson in the perils of leverage when interest rates climb. The Sassower-Schneider-Jacobson group had acquired Flagstaff in a leveraged buyout, with variable-rate financing, in 1978. In the next two years, interest rates skyrocketed, the interest on the Flagstaff notes went from 8 percent to 20 percent—and in 1981 Flagstaff went into Chapter 11.

Meanwhile, Coffee-Mat had deteriorated severely since Peltz took it over. Its earnings went from $1,111,000 for 1976 to a loss of $2,291,000 by 1978. Over the next several years the losses continued. But throughout these losing years, Peltz drew an annual salary of at least $230,000. Says an insider, "Coffee-Mat had been dominant in its industry for many years. But by the early 1980s it was damn near bankrupt."

In 1979, Trafalgar had a $1 million capital-loss carryforward, and Peltz was looking for an investment to take advantage of it. Saul Steinberg introduced him to Michael Milken. "Mike and I were remembering the other day that he had come to call on me at Coffee-Mat," said Peltz, "and we were laughing, saying he must have really been desperate." Milken persuaded him that Trafalgar should buy Penn Central bonds, then selling for thirty cents on the dollar; in the end, Trafalgar got the full dollar.

Peltz commented, "Milken has always been very private. He has a lot of information, and he channels it very carefully."

Peltz recalled an incident at his office, where his son had dropped off a parrot he had just bought. "Mike calls, and immediately the parrot started to squawk—no words, just squawking. Mike said, 'Are we alone?' I said, 'Yes.' 'What's that noise?' 'A parrot,' I said. 'Call me back when the parrot's gone,' Mike said, and hung up."

While the investments Milken recommended were successful, nothing else was. Peltz and May had planned, initially, to use Trafalgar as a vehicle for acquisitions, but by the early eighties it was clear that that had been a pipe dream; they'd be lucky to keep it out of bankruptcy. They started a consulting company called NPM, to do workouts for troubled companies; the first client was their own former company, Flagstaff, which went into bankruptcy despite their efforts. In 1980 they acquired a 9.5 percent position in Sterling Bancorp, a New York bank holding company, but management repulsed their advances. Peltz went on the board, briefly. But in 1981 they sold their position for roughly the purchase price.

Friends of Peltz recall his hard times in the early eighties, but say that Peltz somehow managed to maintain the trappings of wealth. "He always had a big, fancy home and an expensive car," recalls one old friend, "even when he was all but broke."

Then, in late 1982, Peltz seized upon the idea of acquiring a controlling block of Triangle Industries, the vending-machine, wire and cable company, from New Jersey businessman Arthur Goldberg. What Triangle had that was most interesting to Peltz was cash flow —not a great deal, but some. Cash flow is a company's earnings plus bookkeeping charges that don't involve current cash outlays—for example, charges for depreciation, amortization and depletion, which reduce net income without taking cash out of the till. "I learned that from the grocery business," Peltz declared. "What matters is what is in the cash register at the end of the day."

This is a homely-sounding precept, but one that would effectively function as the first commandment for the raiders of the eighties. Earnings might be unimpressive (and therefore the stock price low) but if there is a great deal of depreciation, for example, then cash flow can be high. And it is cash flow, in its ability to service debt by making interest payments, that makes a highly leveraged acquisition viable. In his original issuance of junk bonds, Milken had recognized the importance of cash flow, more than earnings, in assessing whether the leveraged companies he was underwriting would be able to meet their debt payments. Now that he had moved from $25 million offerings to multibillion-dollar deals, the calculation was not so different—just bigger.

Peltz understood that if he was to have a vehicle for acquisitions, that vehicle would have to have cash flow sufficient to make the interest payments on its debt. Trafalgar had almost no cash flow. And no one—including the hungry Milken—would raise any junk-bond financing for him until he had a company with some kind of cash flow.

Goldberg, however, believed that Peltz did not have the wherewithal to be a buyer. Peltz appealed for assistance to Jeffrey Steiner, whom he had met about five years earlier through Schneider, Sassower and James Goren. Steiner had easy entree to Goldberg because he was partners in a scrap business with Goldberg's brother-in-law. He also had the financial muscle that Peltz lacked.

Born in Turkey and raised in Austria, Steiner had made a great deal of money as an oil trader in Europe and the Middle East, and then, in 1981, he decided to get out of oil trading and into "the takeover business." He set up an arbitrage operation in New York and kept homes in Paris and London as well. Through his European connections, Steiner was able to raise huge sums of money overnight. When Peltz appealed to him for his help with Goldberg, Steiner had just raised $20 million in twenty-four hours for Carl Icahn in Icahn's bid for Marshall Field.

Steiner and Goldberg met for breakfast at the Plaza one Sunday morning in early 1983, to discuss Triangle. While they had breakfast Peltz waited outside. Steiner said that he might be interested in investing in the deal himself, and he could in any case raise financing for Peltz in Europe. Although Steiner then dropped out (he was in the midst of a divorce and was distracted from the deal), he had opened the door for Peltz.

In April 1983, Peltz and May (in a two-thirds/one-third partnership) purchased Goldberg's block, 29 percent of Triangle's shares, for about $14 million. Two million was lent to Trafalgar; twelve million was lent to Peltz and May, from Manufacturers Hanover and Bankers Trust. Bankers Trust took the stock as collateral; Manufacturers Hanover took Peltz's and May's signatures and a lien on Peltz's house in Quogue.

Peltz recalled that it took all his powers of persuasion at the bank, and that when he finally walked out of Bill Rykman's office at Manufacturers Hanover with the certified check in hand and met Goldberg, Goldberg told him that he couldn't do the deal after all, because the Triangle board would not approve the change of control. "I literally ran the check under his nose, the spittle started to come out of his mouth, he was dying to put his arms around the money," Peltz declared. "I said, 'Let me try, let me talk to the board, let me show them I don't have horns.' "

But one Triangle insider remembered, "It was a conservative board, and Peltz and May made them *very* nervous. Their image was of some guys who were real operators, trying to do something on a house of cards." Finally, the board compromised by requiring Goldberg to remain as chairman and chief executive officer for six months.

With Triangle, Peltz and May finally had acquired their long-sought vehicle. They decided to raise $75 million from the sale of junk bonds, underwritten by L. F. Rothschild. According to May, Milken wanted to do only a $35–50 million offering of senior subordinated debt, whereas Rothschild—then pushing hard to compete with Drexel in the junk business—was willing to do the larger amount, as subordinated debt (not senior, and therefore less secured); so they chose Rothschild over Drexel.

In September 1983, Rothschild did a "unit offering"—bonds coupled with warrants, which are securities that are exercisable into common stock and can be stripped off and traded separately. Unlike Milken, who liked this unit form because he could dispense the warrants to his favored, Rothschild apparently did not know what to do with them. "There were about one million one hundred thousand warrants, and no one wanted them," recalled Peltz. "So [through Triangle, in 1984] I bought back nine hundred thousand for about five million dollars. Two years later, they were worth ninety million."

Triangle's banks had been pressuring Peltz to sell off the wire and cable business, in order to raise the cash to pay down the banks' loans. Peltz and May decided instead to fund the business, which has since done well, and they paid off the banks' $30 million loans with the money from the junk offering. The rest, May said, they began investing, mainly with Milken and mainly in junk. Once you're carrying money at 15 percent, nothing but junk will do. Then they went shopping for targets.

In early 1984, Peltz and May became interested in Beverly Hills Savings, and they promptly enlisted Drexel's help in financing its acquisition. A thrift, of course, with its wondrous leverage potential, would have suited Peltz's proclivities. Though it was state-chartered (and therefore much freer to invest in junk bonds than federally chartered thrifts), Beverly Hills Savings at this point had not yet invested in junk. But Thomas Spiegel, just a few blocks down Wilshire Boulevard, was already blazing the junk trail with Columbia Savings and Loan.

Beverly Hills Savings was caught in a struggle for control between its then chief executive, Dennis Fitzpatrick, and Paul Amir (a cousin of Thomas Spiegel), who was waging a proxy fight. Peltz, a potential white knight (that bidder to whom a target turns in order to escape the clutches of another, unfriendly bidder), negotiated a deal with Fitzpatrick in which his expenses for conducting a "due diligence" (inspection of the books) investigation—which came to about $675,000—would be paid by the bank.

But the thrift already had a terrible reputation among many in the financial community. One director of Triangle is said to have told Peltz, when he heard that Peltz was intent on making the acquisition, that he would resign if that occurred. And, according to Peltz and May, it did not take them more than several weeks to see signs of what would become public just one year later, when the Federal Home Loan Bank Board closed Beverly Hills Savings and reopened it as a federally chartered S&L. The Federal Savings and Loan Insurance Corporation then filed a $300 million suit against several of the thrift's former officers and directors, alleging that they had wasted its assets by making questionable loans and real-estate investments, and by investing in junk bonds.

Interestingly, the thrift's portfolio of junk originated—and spurted to about $300 million, or more than 10 percent of its assets —in 1984, after Peltz and May withdrew from the scene and Paul Amir took over. Peltz and May had been examining the thrift's books with advisers from Drexel, investment bankers Fred McCarthy and David Kay. Donald Engel, the host of the annual Bungalow 8 party at the Predators' Ball, who had known both Peltz and May for many years, went on the thrift's board with Peltz while they considered the acquisition. So Drexel was well aware of the dying S&L's flawed loans, which Peltz describes as "one horror story after another."

According to the FSLIC suit, the $300 million of junk bonds with which Beverly Hills Savings gorged itself between March 1984 and December 31, 1984 were primarily bought from Drexel. The losses to the thrift from this investment are claimed by FSLIC to exceed $10 million (an amount which was dwarfed, however, by the losses from real-estate investments). One former executive of this thrift claimed, "Milken used Beverly Hills Savings as a dumping ground. And when they got to the end, and really needed to sell for liquidity, all of a sudden he wasn't there."

The "dumping ground" contention would seem to be supported by allegations made in a suit filed in July 1986 against Drexel and a senior vice-president, James Dahl, by Beverly Hills Savings. Dahl was one of Milken's most favored trader-salesmen, someone who, as a former member of Milken's group put it, "could sell you a third eye." Dahl would be a defendant along with Drexel in another, more important suit, too, which would be filed in early 1987. Here, the Beverly Hills Savings complaint alleged that Dahl called the thrift in April 1984 and recommended that it buy a half interest (Drexel owned the other half) in a bond from a company called Cell Products. He allegedly said that the bond would be secured by a first-trust deed on the company's manufacturing plant, and moreover that the company was a vital, growing concern, whose stock had quadrupled in the past year. Beverly Hills bought a 50 percent interest in the security for $3.69 million.

Absent from Dahl's pitch, according to the complaint, was the information that Cell Products had lost $6.7 million in the previous two quarters and had missed the April 1 interest payment on the bond. The suit also claimed that, contrary to Dahl's alleged assertion, the bond was not backed by a first-trust deed, but by a claim that was subordinate to an $8 million first-trust deed. And, the suit claimed, that made the Beverly Hills claim worthless, since the Cell

Products site was appraised at a maximum value of $6.4 million. All this became more than academic when Cell Products went into bankruptcy, some months after Beverly Hills Savings bought the bond. Now Beverly Hills Savings was suing Drexel for more than $6 million in damages.

So while Peltz passed on Beverly Hills Savings as too moribund, it appears that Milken found in that very morbidity the thrift's usefulness. Peltz, meanwhile, was continuing to scour the landscape for a more desirable target. And though he had yet to find one, he decided to raise more cash. According to one source, he explored the possibility of another underwriting with L. F. Rothschild, which had raised the $75 million for him in September '83, but he was told that it wasn't feasible. The junk salesman there had already called in all his chips on the first deal, and less than a year had passed.

So, in July 1984, Milken underwrote $100 million of junk bonds for Triangle "for possible future acquisitions and other general corporate purposes." The fee was steep: Drexel demanded warrants to purchase 240,000 shares of common stock, about 12 percent of the company. The firm also was guaranteed the placement of its designee on Triangle's board. Donald Engel, who in 1984 resigned from Drexel but continued as a consultant to the firm, joined the board for Drexel.

This $100 million was one of the early "blind pools" that Milken would raise in order to build "war chests" for his players. Just one year later, in the summer of 1985, Ronald Perelman would be launched into the hostile arena with a $750 million blind pool—although there would be some question as to how "blind" that pool really was (or whether investors were told that the target, already chosen, was Revlon). And in the summer of 1986 Milken would raise for Wickes, run by Sanford Sigoloff, a blind pool of $1.2 billion—the biggest ever.

But in July 1984 raising $100 million for nothing more than an acquisitive urge was still novel. Asked whether he had hesitated to raise $100 million for who-knows-what, Peltz eyed his questioner incredulously. "If I could have raised four hundred million, I would have raised four hundred million! I did what I could. Now I had about a hundred thirty-five million in cash, and I had to be taken seriously. In those days," he said with a chuckle, "that was a lot of money."

Over the next six months, Peltz and May made a number of

overtures, but nothing worked. After arbitrageur Ivan Boesky made his run at Scott and Fetzer (maker of Kirby vacuum cleaners, *World Book* encyclopedias, and other consumer products) and was rebuffed, Peltz made his approach—and was also rebuffed. (The company was ultimately acquired in a friendly deal by Berkshire Hathaway, whose controlling shareholder and chairman is Warren Buffett.)

Triangle then accumulated a position slightly over 5 percent in Great Lakes International, a dredging company, but its CEO was also not interested in doing a friendly deal with Peltz and May. And given Drexel's fees, Peltz says, the downside in a hostile offer would have been too steep. Peltz was irritated. It did not help to receive a note from Arthur Goldberg, who had greenmailed Great Lakes some months earlier, saying, "I'm glad to see you're following in my footsteps." (Less than a year later, Great Lakes would be acquired in a friendly deal by Sam Zell, the Chicago real estate magnate who is another Drexel player.)

While Peltz was priming himself for a leap, he also was severing a relationship with Gerald Guterman, a New York developer. The loans for $12 million to NPM (Peltz and May) from Manufacturers Hanover and Bankers Trust had been conditioned on their being reduced by $3 million ($1.5 million to each bank) in a short period of time. Peltz and May, therefore, had to sell some of the Triangle stock to another investor and pay down that portion of the bank loan. That investor was Guterman, who had been a friend of Peltz and had been involved in other deals with him.

In June 1983, Guterman purchased roughly $3 million of Triangle stock from NPM and acquired a position that was roughly one third of NPM's. About six months later, after accumulating more stock in open-market purchases, Guterman said he wanted to go on the Triangle board. Peltz demurred. Guterman became convinced that Peltz wanted to freeze him out.

Two bankers at Drexel say they advised Peltz that Guterman would be a liability if Peltz were to attempt a hostile deal. Guterman had a Selective Service conviction dating back to the early sixties: he had spent some time in jail, then served and received an honorable discharge.

In the fall of 1984, Guterman began to accumulate more Triangle stock. By mid-November, he stated in his 13D, a filing which must be made with the SEC within ten days of one's acquiring 5

percent or more of a public company's stock, that he was considering waging a contest for control. He also stated that he intended to
communicate with other stockholders about his concern that Triangle management was "engaging in self-dealing transactions and
other acts of corporate mismanagement." Then, suddenly, the matter was settled, and Guterman sold his stock back to the company
at the market price.

Guterman remains fiercely bitter, convinced that Peltz knew he
was about to be launched by Milken and didn't want to share the
bonanza. He told friends that he had helped Peltz when he was
down and out, put up money for him when Peltz wanted to invest
in Guterman's real-estate deals, paid off interest on notes Peltz had
at banks when Peltz had no cash. Then Peltz found in Milken the
ultimate deep pocket and had no more use for him, Guterman complained.

Peltz and May insist that had Guterman not insisted upon joining the board and begun his aggressive stock accumulation, they
would have let him remain a shareholder. Instead, they say, he
became the victim of his own poor judgment. "Gerry left thirty-five
million dollars on the table," May declared, calculating the profit
Guterman would have made on his Triangle stock had he held it
through 1986.

"I settled the deal with Guterman the day before Thanksgiving
[1984]," Peltz recalled, "and then I went out to L.A. for a meeting
with Michael, six A.M. that Sunday morning, Thanksgiving weekend. It was costing nine million dollars to buy Guterman out, and
Michael wanted to be sure about the balance sheet. We issued some
preferred. And that's when Michael said that he didn't think Victor
[Posner] was going to do the National Can deal, he was thinking
about a backstop for him—and I should take a look at it."

VICTOR POSNER had long been a much-valued Drexel client. In
the midseventies he had joined Milken's early group of satisfied
customers who bought the bonds of fallen angels that Milken recommended when they were at twenty or thirty cents on the dollar,
and then made killings when they rose. By the early eighties he was
on the short list of people—including Fred Carr, Tom Spiegel, Carl
Lindner, Meshulam Riklis and Saul Steinberg—whose companies
were busily buying one another's Drexel-issued paper. And he
would also participate, along with Steinberg, Spiegel, Steve Wynn,

Ivan Boesky, Ronald Perelman, the Belzbergs and others, in one of Milken's lucrative investment partnerships, Reliance L.P.

Posner made a fortune in real estate in the 1930s and 1940s, led a life of retirement in Miami Beach for about ten years and then, in 1966, began to acquire controlling chunks of small industrial companies. In 1969, through NVF Company, which had sales of only $30 million, he made a bid for Sharon Steel, which had sales of $220 million. This had not been accomplished with cash raised through Milken's junk bonds, of course, but with that era's version—the Chinese paper that Riklis too had used to advantage. Posner offered Sharon stockholders a package of bonds and warrants, and won nearly 90 percent of the stock in what was then one of the fiercest merger battles ever.

For a number of years, Posner's empire did quite well. In 1969, after the major group of eight companies had been acquired, they earned about $10 million on sales of $400 million. By 1975, they earned about $22 million on sales of $600 million. By 1976, moreover, the package of subordinated debentures and warrants that NVF swapped for Sharon shares—in 1969 selling for $25—was worth about $140. By contrast, the packages handed out by Gulf + Western and Litton Industries—other great acquirers via stock swaps at that time—were worth less than the shares for which they had been exchanged. While other conglomerateurs were attracted to companies for their glamorous earnings growth (much of which had evaporated by 1970), Posner, the shrewd old real-estate shopper, bought companies that were asset-rich.

By the midseventies, however, the quintessential Posner traits were already in evidence. He paid himself so well that he was one of the three or four highest-paid executives in the country, though the combined sales of his companies did not exceed $1 billion. His family members were well represented on his company payrolls and boards. And he had signed a consent decree with the SEC for having allegedly misused pension funds from Sharon Steel. All this made his declaration to *Business Week* in 1976 the stuff of satire. "I'm not in this for the money," Posner protested. "I want to create a good product."

At Drexel, stories about the eccentric Posner are legion. One investment banker described Posner's Miami Beach offices, located in a somewhat run-down building that used to be a hotel, as "out of a comic opera—overly ornate, with all this weird, schticky stuff." The office featured an array of couches, a pool table, a pinball machine, enormous plastic hampers in which the mail was placed, and Posner's desk, which was raised, on a platform—to compensate for Posner's being so short, some associates speculate. Two, sometimes four, guards were present at all times, their guns bulging under their jackets. Posner is reclusive, rarely traveling, seeing few people, carrying out most of his business contacts by phone.

He married his first wife when she was seventeen and he was in his midthirties, and in his late sixties he preferred girls in their teens. His most recent girlfriend was the daughter of a former mistress; several years ago Posner stopped having an affair with the mother (who had become an officer of his various companies) and began an affair with her daughter, then in her teens. According to one banker at Drexel, their affair ended when she turned twenty. "He couldn't talk to her anymore," quipped this investment banker.

Drexel's David Kay recalled one meeting, more unusual than some others, at the Posner headquarters. Donald Engel was the Drexel investment banker in charge of the Posner account until he resigned from the firm to become a consultant. He has continued to serve as a director on the boards of Posner companies. For years, Posner was Engel's biggest client, and Engel was always shuttling back and forth to Miami. On this morning, he arrived in Posner's office and mentioned that he had just had breakfast with Posner's son Steven. " 'You did *what?*' Victor yelled, leaning over his elevated desk. 'Didn't you know that Steven's children have—' " Kay broke off, then continued, "some contagious disease, like hepatitis or something, I can't remember exactly. So Victor had his office fumigated. Later that day we had a meeting there. We all had to wear hospital masks, and Donnie wasn't allowed on the floor. He had to sit downstairs and participate through the speaker phone.

"Victor is a living legend," said Kay, smiling. Kay had had dinner with Posner at Côte Basque in the late sixties, when Kay was at Shearson. With Kay was a stockbroker from Shearson. The stockbroker asked Posner how he had become so successful, and Posner responded by describing his first business venture: As a child he had lived in Baltimore with his parents and seven brothers and sisters, and his father had a newspaper stand. When he was thirteen he demanded that his father give him 50 percent of the interest in the newsstand. His father, pointing out that he couldn't put one son ahead of his wife and all his other sons and daughters, refused. So the boy opened a stand selling candy and newspapers, across the street from his father's—and in six months, Posner declared, he had the whole family working for him.

"The amazing thing," Kay concluded, "is that he told that story with pride."

Posner began acquiring his 38 percent block of National Can in 1979. After he called the company's chief executive officer, Frank Considine, to tell him that he had bought more than 5 percent of the company's shares, Considine met with Ira Harris of Salomon Brothers and Joe Flom of Skadden, Arps. "Joe said, 'Sue—but I can't guarantee you'll win,' " Considine recalled. "Well, I didn't like the idea of suing if I wasn't going to win."

Posner told Considine that he wanted his position only for investment, and that he thought Considine was doing a good job. And for several years—as Posner was accumulating his stock in the open market at bargain prices—he didn't interfere in the running of the company, and he and Considine got along.

Posner did not ask to go on the board. "He felt comfortable that I wouldn't deceive him—and I never did, until the very end," said Considine, looking strained. In the end, Considine with his advisers came up with the idea of National Can's management in conjunction with its ESOP (employee stock option plan) doing a leveraged buyout of the company. Had that buyout occurred, it would have left Posner with a sharply devalued minority position. Considine did not tell Posner about this plan in advance, but allowed it to be sprung on him as a surprise.

No two men could be more disparate than this Midwesterner and the Miami wheeler-dealer, and no notion more incongruous than of these two "visiting," as Considine put it, in Posner's baroque enclave. But, as Considine's erstwhile adviser and close friend Ira Harris says, "Frank Considine takes people at face value, and he took Posner that way. Whatever Posner's track record with others had been, his with Frank was good—and until he did different, Frank wasn't going to cross him.

"Considine is the kind of person," Harris added, "that if he walked into the room and there was a dollar bill on the floor, he would spend ten minutes trying to find out who had dropped it."

In late 1983, Posner's passivity ended. The relative prosperity of his companies in the midseventies was gone; once-profitable conglomerates like NVF, DWG and Pennsylvania Engineering were showing some heavy losses. But while profits plummeted, Posner's salaries escalated. In 1984 he collected $7.6 million from NVF, which lost $146.5 million for the year. National Can, with its steady cash flow, must have become too tempting to resist.

National Can had asked Salomon Brothers, which had traditionally been its investment banker, to underwrite $100 million of senior debt, accompanied by a small amount of warrants. The warrants, exercisable into common stock, were intended as an equity kicker to make the bonds more attractive; they would also have diluted Posner's position slightly. Posner objected, arguing that subordinated debentures would be better. (Senior debt is more secure, since its claims on the assets of the company come before those of the subordinated debt. Also, senior debt generally carries covenants restricting the company's leveraging itself further. Since it carries less risk than subordinated debt, it pays a lower interest rate.)

Posner sent Don Engel out to see Considine. According to Walter Stelzel, National Can's chief financial officer, Engel offered a subordinated-debt package that would have carried a one percent higher interest cost than the senior debt underwritten by Salomon, but would have fewer covenants. "Because of the covenants on the senior debt, we couldn't have leveraged up. But that was OK with us, because we didn't *want* to leverage up," Stelzel said. "In those days, we didn't know what leverage was.

"We said to Posner, 'OK, if you're going to start interfering, let's do something different.' And he said [we could] buy him out at fifty-two (the stock was then in the thirties) or do a buyout with [him and] management participation."

The board decided that the company should pursue the buyout with Posner. Stelzel added that the management at National Can did worry about being in a Posner-controlled company, but that they drew up an agreement with strict operating rules, which would have prohibited too much leverage as well as interference from other Posner companies. By April 1984, the proposed merger agreement between National Can and Posner's NVF was ready: Posner would buy out the shareholders at $40 a share, and NVF would own 80 percent of the newly constituted company, while National Can's management would own 20 percent.

The cash buyout would cost $410 million. Drexel was to raise the mezzanine financing through the sale of about $155 million of junk bonds, which would come beneath the $255 million of senior debt lent by Manufacturers Hanover. According to Drexel's Leon Black, he and others at the firm held meetings to structure the deal, in the summer and early fall of 1984.

"We would have done it then, but Posner kept procrastinating," Black said. "And by the late fall he started having real difficulties, with Evans [Products] and Sharon [Steel], and the banks were getting more and more nervous about the interlocking pyramid of his empire. By November or December, we'd decided that we didn't want another big slug of his private paper out, leveraging him further, making him more illiquid."

Drexel's concern was not disinterested. Drexel had not issued any paper in the two Posner companies that were in the most trouble—Evans and Sharon Steel. But Drexel was already working on one of Sharon Steel's famous 3(a)9 swaps (unregistered exchange offers), in an effort to avert Chapter 11.

Moreover, since 1982 the firm *had* floated nearly a half-billion dollars for various companies of Posner's, in three private placements (of securities that are not publicly registered and therefore can be issued more quickly and require less disclosure) and two public deals. One of them, issued for DWG back in 1982—$50 million of zero-coupon bonds (which are sold at a discount and pay no interest until the annual accreted interest is paid at maturity)—had a short maturity, due in 1986.

Among the heaviest buyers of Posner's paper, furthermore, were members of Milken's select coterie, those he most protected. In one $25 million issue for a Posner company in 1982, for example, according to a November 1984 article in *Forbes* magazine, Fred Carr (First Executive) and Carl Lindner (American Financial) bought the entire issue. Defaults by Posner could cause a strain on some of Milken's most important client relationships.

Drexel's most recent financing for Posner had been a $206 million private placement for his acquisition of Royal Crown, in June 1984. Stephen Weinroth noted, agreeing with Leon Black, "We had a growing conviction, in the fall of 1984, that we shouldn't be financing anything Victor did. We'd done Royal Crown, and already we were having misgivings. It has worked out OK, but only OK. It probably would have been better if someone else had done it."

According to National Can's tender-offer document, however, Posner continued to tell Considine, through December, that both Drexel and Manufacturers Hanover had committed to do their respective financings—though as the offer states, when Considine contacted both Milken and the bank, neither confirmed that their commitments were in place. Finally, at the end of January—after having enjoyed what had amounted to a one-year option on the company—Posner told Considine that he had decided that the transaction as proposed was too leveraged and he preferred to either (a) remain a 38 percent stockholder and obtain control of the board, (b) acquire 51 percent and obtain control of the board or (c) be bought out at $60 per share. Furthermore, he told Considine, after obtaining control he planned to cause National Can to acquire for cash the retail building-materials group of Evans Products, which was on the verge of bankruptcy.

Considine said later, "Victor is too proud—he would never say that he couldn't do the transaction. He always, to the end, said he could. He needed the money—but you'd never know that. One of Victor's sayings was, 'I don't care, whatever happens, it's not going to change my style of living.' He would always say that, in a friendly way—kidding but also serious."

On his buyout price of $60 a share, Considine added, Posner was "absolutely rigid." "The stock was selling at thirty-four dollars. We couldn't possibly have done it—there would have been shareholder suits. I told Victor that. He would say, 'Never mind. Some strike lawyer out there will always sue. Never mind the lawsuits.' "

So Considine and his advisers came up with their leveraged-buyout plan, in which the company and an ESOP comprised of two thousand salaried workers would purchase 51 percent of the company's shares for $40 a share, using mainly borrowed cash. And at the time of the offer, in late February 1985, National Can's board issued preferred stock with four million votes to the ESOP, virtually eliminating any chance NVF would have had of mounting a successful proxy fight. At the buyout's completion, the ESOP would have had 50.1 percent of the company's voting rights.

Once National Can made its LBO offer, Milken's troops moved into high gear. Leon Black recalled that he and others at the firm made "probably twenty calls" to find someone to top that offer. Black brought it to Carl Icahn and to Henry Kravis, of the leveraged-buyout firm of Kohlberg Kravis Roberts. The Belzbergs and Ronald Perelman gave it a fairly cursory look. Milken sent materials on the company to Sam Zell. Don Engel urged repeatedly that it be given to Peltz, and Peltz began lobbying Milken for it in February.

But, said one of the people involved in this marketing process, "Nelson was Mike's last choice."

Peltz knew there was competition for the deal ("I was seeing boogeymen in all the closets") and says he was "dying for it." May uses the same language. "We were dying for a deal. We'd been sitting on the money for a year and a half [starting with the Roth-schild offering]. We knew National Can had developed a strong market position, that it was a strong cash generator. Considine had a great reputation. It was not sexy, but a sound business."

On March 6, 1983, Peltz flew out to see Milken and "camped out at Drexel for a couple of days." "I said to Mike, I want this deal, I don't want you to finance it for anyone else, I'm not leaving until you agree." By the time he left L.A., on March 8, Peltz was convinced that if any Drexel client was going to get the deal, he would be the one.

According to Leon Black, he and others at Drexel had been finding that National Can was a hard sell for three reasons: it was perceived as being in a declining industry; it had had problems in the bottling part of its business; and the management buyout which had to be topped appeared fully priced. Of all the prospective buyers to whom Drexel was shopping the deal, only Icahn showed interest.

On March 7, Icahn crossed the 5 percent line, and through the next week he continued to accumulate National Can stock, at prices ranging from about $37 to $39 a share. On March 15, on his way out to vacation in Colorado, he stopped off to see Frank Considine. "I liked Carl, he struck me as straightforward and honest," Considine declared later. But Considine was intent on achieving the management-ESOP transaction, and Icahn was talking about an offer that would not be all cash, but cash and paper—which would make it less desirable.

Jeffrey Steiner, who has invested in every deal of Icahn's start-ing with his raid on Marshall Field in 1982, said that Icahn's interest in National Can was only passing. "Carl looked at it, but he didn't see a white knight coming in, and he didn't want to run the com-pany. Carl wants to buy assets at a discount," Steiner said. "Nelson, on the other hand, didn't care if he was buying assets at a premium. He just wanted a company, and wanted it to work."

About Peltz's having said that he believed Drexel was commit-ted to his doing the deal from March 8 on, Black asserted, "Our feeling was, we had to get a deal done, given the pressure of the deadline on National Can's offer [which would expire at midnight, March 21]. So we were working on a few horses."

Icahn's intentions were, as always, opaque. "Of all the players out there, Carl is the master of confusing the other side as to whether he really wants to do it or not. He straddles that line better than anyone," Black said. "Here, I talked to both him and Nelson at the end of that week [before the weekend-long negotiations], and Nelson was the one who really wanted to do the deal. I felt more comfortable that with Nelson it would happen."

Peltz was chosen by default. As Milken had resisted giving National Can to Peltz, he must have wanted to find *some* deal for him. Milken had raised $100 million for Peltz eight months earlier, and the interest payments (variable rate, starting out at 14.25 percent) had to be met.

Moreover, Peltz had already shown himself as pliant, someone who understood what it took to play the Drexel game. A dues-paying member of the club, he had put up his Drexel-raised cash for each of the new junk-bond-financed takeovers as it came down the pike: $20 million for Phillips, $25 million for Coastal. Indeed, in the next month, even after his own deal had closed and he no longer had over $100 million burning a hole in his pocket, he would still find $35 million to commit to Unocal. And he knew he had to give up equity, both to Milken and Drexel and to those buyers who took the riskiest pieces of his paper. Drexel already owned 12 percent of Triangle from the warrants it had received as part of its earlier financing, and it would cut another 4 percent piece of the pie for itself here.

All that remained, then, was to negotiate with Posner for his 38 percent block, obtain commitments for the financing, and make the tender offer; by this time, the expiration date of the National Can offer was just four days away. For the past two weeks, however, Posner had been elusive. Peltz tried daily to reach him, unsuccessfully.

Victor Posner had been pursuing another option. The various investment bankers at Drexel who have worked with Posner over the years all agree that Posner traditionally had not been a seller. And he was thought to be especially loath to sell his position in National Can, where he had bided his time in good behavior for so long, and where he—perhaps more than anyone else—saw great value. But Drexel was refusing to finance the transaction, which must in itself have come as a shock to Posner, a member of Milken's coterie for so long. According to one investment banker who visited Posner in Miami, his phone had a series of buttons for direct lines; the first was to Jefferies, the Los Angeles stock-brokerage firm, and the second was to Milken.

By February 1985, Posner must not have felt that Drexel was his special friend. He is said by one source to have gone to Bear, Stearns for financing and been turned down. First vice-president Paul Yang of E. F. Hutton, who was already working on some matters for Posner, said later that an associate of Posner called him in mid-February, to talk about Hutton's raising money for Posner to do the acquisition of National Can. Yang then spoke with Posner, who said that he felt "Hutton deserved a try." Yang and Daniel Good, then head of Hutton's M&A division, had visited Posner in Florida in the fall, and they were eager to break into the lucrative junk-bond-financed takeover business.

National Can would have been Good's and Yang's first major junk-bond deal. On February 24, two days after National Can had launched their offer, Yang met with Donald Glaser, Posner's in-house lawyer, in the apartment in the Waldorf Towers that Posner keeps as his New York residence, to discuss his fee structure. "Then we began soliciting from various sources commitments to acquire high-yield paper," Yang recalled.

On March 11, however, Posner's Evans Products—flagging under a debt load of $540 million—filed for bankruptcy. "With that, we stopped the effort," said Yang. "The whole thing had taken about two weeks. And shortly after that, Mr. Posner sold his block of National Can [into the Triangle offer]."

That was not done without a great deal of angst on all sides. Peltz and May, their lawyers and a cadre of investment bankers from Drexel spent the weekend of March 16–17 in negotiations with Posner's lawyers from Paul, Weiss and with Donald Glaser. According to several of those present, the structure they arrived at by Sunday night allowed Posner's stake to be bought out, except for about $30 million, for which he would be given preferred stock in the new company and roughly 20 percent of voting control. Peltz and May, through Triangle, would be putting in roughly $65 million, for which they would receive 80 percent of voting control. That $95 million or so from Posner and Triangle would form the equity base, upon which the remaining $365 million of debt would be layered.

But when Glaser called Posner Sunday night, to finalize the deal, Posner vetoed it and suggested to Peltz that they be fifty-fifty partners. "I said, 'Victor, I love you, but I'm not doing that,' " Peltz remembered.

May put it more bluntly: "The twenty percent [which Posner would hold] was bad enough, but fifty percent was out of the question. I did not want to be associated with Victor Posner."

Peltz and May went home, convinced that they had lost the deal. But at about two o'clock the next morning Leon Black called Peltz and asked him to come back, saying that Drexel would raise the $30 million of preferred that would have been Posner's. By mid-morning on that Monday, March 18, Posner had committed all his stock to the transaction at the $41-a-share price, and Milken and his team of salesmen were at work raising the $395 million of commitments from their buyers.

The "commitment letter" was a crucial part of a new structure Drexel had devised. Much as banks give commitment letters for their part in these financings, so Drexel's buyers made their commitments. And whether the deal went through or not, they would receive a "commitment fee" for their trouble. Here it was three quarters of one percent of the amount for which they subscribed.

For its services in raising this money, Drexel was to receive one half of one percent of the $395 million in financing commitments, or about $2 million. In addition, Drexel received an advisory fee of $500,000. Upon consummation of the deal, Drexel received fees ranging from 3.25 percent to 5 percent of the varying pieces of paper totaling $395 million that it placed, less the $2 million it had received for securing the commitments. Also upon consummation, Drexel received a further fee of $2.5 million, plus warrants which if exercised would give the firm 95,000 shares of Triangle stock. All told, its fees came to roughly $25 million. Combined with the warrants Drexel had obtained from its earlier financing, the firm now had warrants for about 16 percent of Triangle stock.

This financing was done as a private placement (with rights to register as public securities later), rather than in the public debt markets. In the last year or so, Drexel had turned increasingly to private placements, especially in the leveraged buyouts. And for the hostile deals, especially, they would now become the weapon of choice. Registering public securities with the SEC at the outset would have made the process too slow and cumbersome.

There were, however, some disadvantages to doing these as

private placements. It narrowed the market of buyers; most mutual funds, for example, buy only public securities. And it was generally more expensive for the issuer, because the buyers demanded a higher yield to compensate them for a lack of liquidity, since privately placed bonds are not supposed to be freely traded. Moreover, since these placements *are* private, buyers can demand individualized rewards—such as a given number of warrants to accompany a certain amount of securities. While this kind of demand and free-form allotment was not advantageous from the issuer's standpoint, it was perfect for Milken's system of repayment of favors, and rewards.

This was the third time in two months that Milken's troops in Beverly Hills had been thus mobilized—having just raised $1.5 billion in commitments for Phillips and $600 million for Coastal. "The way it works," explained Drexel's John Sorte, who worked on Phillips and would soon work on Unocal, "is that the salesmen call up and ask people if they're interested, and in which kind of paper— the senior notes, or what. And if they are, the book is delivered to them the same day. Then they call back, and if they're interested the allocations are made and the commitment letters sent out by Telecopier.

"In Unocal, for example [in mid-April 1985, three weeks after National Can], we raised $3 billion in commitments from a Monday to a Friday. There were six Telecopier machines, and commitments from 140 institutions. The machines got all backed up, papers were lost in space. The mechanics of these things are a nightmare. It's like running an army.

"We use our own people, not messenger services, because we really can't rely on anyone else," Sorte continues. "So we put the secretaries in limousines, and send them off to get these things signed."

Compared to the challenges of Phillips and Unocal, National Can's $365 million seems like child's play. But according to Drexel's Mary Lou Malanowski it was not an easy sell. "This was one of the first hostile deals, and it required a lot of marketing to get people interested in playing," Malanowski said. "We had no real numbers on the company, because we weren't inside. And usually when we raise money the buyers care a lot about the management, they want to meet them. Here there was no time. And Nelson and Peter had no track record, just this little company, which was peanuts."

Still, it was all done in just under thirty-six hours. The riskiest piece that Drexel had to raise was the $30 million of preferred that was to have been Posner's. In these buyouts, the riskier pieces of paper are generally accompanied by equity kickers, so that the investors have the chance of sharing in the upside in return for their risk-taking. Coastal's takeover of ANR had been an exception, since Oscar Wyatt had been unwilling to give any equity; Milken and his colleagues at Drexel had been so eager to bring one of these takeover bids to consummation that they had acceded to his terms.

For Peltz, however, there were no such allowances. The $30 million of preferred was accompanied by warrants to purchase 19.9 percent of National Can. And the lenders who committed to buy it, $15 million apiece, were Carl Lindner's American Financial and Charles Knapp's Trafalgar Holdings Ltd.

After Knapp was fired from the Financial Corporation of America, the once-high-flying California thrift which under his control nearly became insolvent, Milken had attempted to raise $1 billion for Knapp in his new private partnership, Trafalgar Holdings. Why anyone should have wanted to invest with Knapp, given his track record, is not clear, and apparently Milken's would-be lenders felt that way, too, because the $1 billion did not get raised. (Knapp denies that Milken attempted to raise the money.) What Knapp ultimately did, according to one friend, was create a fund in which investors placed, say, $140,000 to reserve the right to come into the first six deals he offered them, with the proviso that if they came into none they would suffer a 50 percent penalty, of $70,000. "It was nothing—just window dressing," said this friend. According to one investor, however, Knapp told him that he had the $1 billion on hand. In other words, it was the Air Fund come to life in its original, unadulterated form.

Here, Knapp presumably had the $15 million he committed to invest—but he nevertheless backed out of the deal at the last minute, when it was time to fund the deal. "We couldn't find anyone to replace him on such short notice," Malanowski said, "and we couldn't let the deal crater. So Drexel came in for the preferred, just to save the deal. It was done so fast that there wasn't even time for it to go through the UAC [Underwriting Assistance Committee, which is supposed to approve all financings the firm does]." Drexel bought $10 million of the preferred, and the other $5 million of Knapp's portion was bought by Atalanta/Sosnoff Capital Corporation, a money-management firm which has over $5 billion under management and is run by veteran investor Martin Sosnoff.

According to documents filed with the SEC, Carl Lindner (through American Financial) not only bought the biggest piece of the preferred but also assumed the lead in the debt portion of the deal, committing to buy $50 million of senior notes. The next-largest commitment was made by Sallis Securities Company—which was Fred Carr, of First Executive, using a "Street name," or pseudonym—coming in for $33 million. After that came more heavy chunks, of $20-25 million, by more disguised buyers: 338 Rodeo Corporation, which is Thomas Spiegel's Columbia Savings and Loan; and Worldwide Trading Services, which is Atlantic Capital. By early 1985, Atlantic Capital—a private investment company just across the street from Milken's Beverly Hills headquarters, its investment portfolio run by a former Drexel employee named Guy Dove III—had amassed about $3-4 billion of mainly municipal funds to invest. Over the next year or so, this secretive organization would probably be Milken's single largest source in the hostile megadeals—his private pool in the woods.

After these classic high-rollers came an assortment of corporations, insurance companies, thrifts, mutual funds, a couple of individual investors, a bank trust account. One of these buyers, experienced in the junk market, said that he bought because of what he had heard about Posner's actions. "Victor was in no condition, half dead, but he was still bidding," says this buyer. "He let it [National Can] go with his last gasp. He obviously thought it was a gem—and the guy's not stupid."

There was Ronald Perelman (MacAndrews and Forbes), paying his dues before his mega-blind-pool offering three months hence, committing $7.5 million. And faithful Meshulam Riklis (Schenley Industries), coming in for $10 million. Riklis said, "I didn't know anything about Peltz, anything about the company. I bought the ten million dollars of bonds because Mike was offering them."

Knapp was apparently not the only buyer to appear on the commitment list submitted by Drexel to the SEC who was replaced by different buyers by the time the offer was funded, several weeks later, according to a source at National Can. Investment banker Alan Brumberger of Drexel says substitution happens fairly often in the hostile deals, when speed is of the essence. "Someone will say, 'I'll come in for fifty [million], but I'd like to get down to twenty-five [million].' And then they're replaced." They still make the commitment fee, for having signed on.

According to one SEC attorney, it is lawful for substitution to occur as long as amendments to the original 14D document (which lists the buyers, the type of securities and the amount) are filed so as to keep disclosure current. At least in this deal, no such amendments were filed.

Probably more serious, in terms of noncompliance with SEC rules, is the way these bonds changed hands after they were bought. Though the debt in the big hostiles was raised through private placements, the bonds were issued with registration rights and were supposed to be registered with the SEC within a timely period, generally three to six months. Then they would become public securities and could be traded freely. Until that time, the underwriter could sell the bonds only to sophisticated investors who stated that they were buying the bonds for investment purposes, not with an eye to reselling them. The purpose of this regulation is to prevent a widespread distribution of the bonds, which would effectively circumvent the registration requirement.

Here, the securities were not registered for about fourteen months. "There was so much else going on, we just didn't get around to it," May said. This delay did not seem to impose any undue hardship on his bondholders who may have wanted to trade out of the bonds, however, since they did that anyway.

By the time the securities were registered, only one of those who had originally committed to buy the senior notes was among the fifteen holders of those notes (although three of the fifteen holders were Lindner-affiliated insurance companies, holding about $38 million, which might have been part of his original $50 million). Of the seventeen senior subordinated note holders at registration time, only four were members of the original group. And of the nineteen subordinated bondholders, only three belonged to the original group.

In sum, at least four fifths of the bonds in Triangle–National Can had changed hands at least once by the time they were registered. According to one former Drexel employee, this was no anomaly but paradigmatic, and fundamental to the smooth functioning of Milken's machine. "The way the game works, the first people to get the deal are the friendly, docile, captive accounts," this man says. "Then they'd move into a second tier, obviously at a higher price. So the first group got the premium, for being less shy. The docile ones served as warehouses [until Drexel was ready to move them to the next tier]. Everybody knew that Carr's account, for example, did. They [Milken's salesmen] would call Fred up and say, 'We're buying [whatever] today,' and he'd say, 'OK, what are you paying?' "

In this deal, many of the bonds had moved out from the first-tier buyers into the portfolios of insurance companies big and small (from Prudential Insurance Company of America, with assets of about $134 billion, to Guarantee Security Life, a company with assets of about $370 million), bank trust accounts, thrifts and even a few blue-chip companies like Conoco and Atlantic Richfield.

Seen in the larger context of Milken's machine, this mass movement of privately placed bonds was sublimely purposeful. It meant that the first-tier high-rollers, the most crucial players, were kept happy not only with the commitment fees but with the profits upon trading. It meant that they were also quickly freed, to go on to the next megadeal. It meant that the more risk-averse, who didn't want to go through the exposure and aggravation of being publicly identified as financing junk-bond takeovers and subpoenaed for depositions by the target's lawyers, were still enabled to play the game—although they paid a price for their reticence. It meant that there really was liquidity, for anyone who wanted to get out before the bonds were registered. And it meant that Drexel had a virtual monopoly on the secondary trading, since no rival had enough information about the bonds or their whereabouts to compete effectively.

Those were the advantages. The only disadvantage was that it may have been illegal—or at least pushed the outer limits of the regulations. While four fifths of the bonds changing hands as they did in Triangle–National Can is suggestive of the kind of widespread distribution the rules were designed to prohibit, as long as those investors were sophisticated and would testify that they had not bought the bonds with an eye to reselling them, but had later changed their minds, no illegality would be established. To prove illegality, the government would at least have to show by a pattern of repeated instances of such movement—as appeared to have been institutionalized at Drexel, from the first-tier to second-tier buyers—that it was deliberate and predetermined, and that the investors were indeed buying with an eye to reselling.

This mass movement of privately placed bonds was not unlike Drexel's 3(a)9 deals. Both were brilliant adaptations that made Milken's machine, an engineering marvel of synchronous and complementary forces, function more efficiently, more powerfully. Both were the kind of innovation that in Drexel's heyday its boosters might have pointed to as an example of the firm's creativity. And both showed Drexel's apparent willingness to treat the law as if it were a stultifying system of rules and regulations meant for the world's less able.

As SPEEDY AS Milken was in raising the commitments from his obliging first-tier buyers, the Triangle offer was just under the wire. "I came in with twenty-four hours to go [before the deadline for tendering shares into National Can's own offer]. It would have been *his* company," Peltz declares, referring to Considine. With the offer about to be announced, Peltz, hopeful that a friendly deal could be negotiated, went to Chicago to see Considine. The CEO was non-committal. The board would consider the proposal, he said. In fact, as Peltz feared, Considine was attempting to obtain financing to top Triangle's bid.

Just a week later, on March 27, Peltz and May arrived at the 1985 Predators' Ball. Peltz, too inconsequential, had not been asked to give a presentation. He wandered around, buttonholing anybody who he thought might know something. He asked Donald Drapkin, a Skadden, Arps lawyer, who had come to the conference with his friend and key client Ronald Perelman, and whose partners, led by James Freund, were representing the management of National Can. "What have you heard?" Peltz demanded. "What are they doing? Can you call someone?"

"I was a nervous wreck," Peltz recalled. "Everybody kept coming up and congratulating me, but I was a total basket case."

At Don Engel's celebrated party in Bungalow 8, Engel introduced Peltz to Gerry Tsai, then vice-chairman of American Can; and Peltz, the wistful can magnate, made his first overtures. Also at that party was William Farley, who had recently joined the growing group of Drexel takeover entrepreneurs. (In May he would launch a successful raid on Northwest Industries, in Chicago.) "Farley told me that he knew Considine, and that Considine felt more rapport with me than Nelson because at least I'd gone to the University of Chicago," May remembered. Later, in the Polo Lounge of the Beverly Hills Hotel, Drapkin taunted Peltz, saying, "Considine doesn't like you, Nelson. He likes Peter."

"I'm sure the truth was that he didn't like either one of us," May said. "Frank is a real gentleman, and he plays everything very close to the vest, so he's never said. But I'm sure that he thought of us as two Jewish guys from New York he'd never heard of, and we were the last thing he wanted."

LESS THAN TWO weeks later, on the night of April 4, the merger agreement was ready. Peltz had gone to $42 on his own and outraged his Drexel bankers. Then—unable because of Milken to go up another dollar—he had come up with the idea of a $4 million bonus pool for the employees ("I said to Considine, 'I don't need my bankers' approval for this, because it will come out of earnings . . .' " he recalled). And after some further negotiations, in which Peltz agreed to stipulate that National Can would stay in Chicago and he would not strip off assets, all that remained was the signing.

Peltz was nervous and exhilarated that night. "I was sitting in the National Can offices with May and Lovado [chief financial officer of Triangle], and I said, 'You guys excited?' Lovado said, 'Don't ask me. I'm just a bean-counter.' "

For Considine, the experience was also intense. He had had a heart attack a couple of years earlier, and that night, as the documents were being finalized, he recognized recurrent symptoms. He went home, leaving his chief financial officer, Walter Stelzel, to sign the agreement.

Considine, who had hoped to do the management buyout, topping Triangle's offer, said that Citicorp had indicated that they had the financing all but ready. But at the last moment, with Triangle's offer only a couple of days from expiration, Citicorp had backed out. "We wasted four or five days that might have made the difference with someone else," he said ruefully.

Then, referring to the ease with which Drexel had raised the money, virtually overnight, he added, "We weren't in the network. If we had been, we could have done the deal ourselves."

BY THE FALL of 1986, it was clear that the paper miracle of Triangle–National Can had assumed proportions that exceeded any of its architects' expectations. All the elements that make for success in this kind of superleveraged transaction converged. In the general economic environment, interest rates dropped dramatically and the stock market went up; at National Can, earnings rose, its stock price quadrupled—and management, which was excellent, stayed.

In the familiar catch-22 of Wall Street, however, the feat, once so demonstrably successful, could not be replicated, though it was much imitated. In October 1986 Drexel's David Kay commented, "Today you couldn't do a National Can. Then hardly anyone had beaten out a management LBO, no one knew how it would work. Now there's a feeding frenzy the minute one of these deals is announced, like Warnaco [where in the spring of 1986 management announced it was taking the company private, and a bidding war ensued that drove the price up to a point where Drexel's bidder finally stopped].

"There's too much money chasing too few deals," Kay lamented.

In the spring of 1985 Drexel had raised a total of $595 million for the acquisition of National Can—$395 million for the acquisition itself, and another $200 million for the payment of its bank debt. By September 1986, thanks to falling interest rates, the rising stock market, and the company's performance, only about $80 million of that original debt remained outstanding. The rest had been retired with money from a new bank line, and from an offering of convertible debentures and convertible preferred, which were later converted into common equity. Some of the original debt, then, had been turned into common equity, and the bulk of what remained had been refinanced at 8–9 percent instead of 14–16 percent. These refinancings brought Triangle's annual interest charges down from about $85 million to about $35 million.

"We've really taken the leverage out of the leveraged buyout," crowed Drexel investment banker Fred McCarthy. "In the beginning, a company that had $65 million of equity borrowed $700 million—your basic ten-to-one ratio," he said with a laugh. "Now it's $500 million of long-term debt, and equity of about $350 million—one and a half to one."

Business at National Can has been helped by a number of factors—none of which was foreseen by the corporate-finance people at Drexel who structured this deal and gave it their blessing. Consumer-sector growth was one. Another was the decline in the prices of energy and aluminum, both used in the production of cans. And pricing in the glass business, which National Can entered several years earlier, became stronger.

Earnings have also been boosted by the introduction of an investment portfolio, which ranged from $200 million to $500 million in 1986. Here Peltz—who oversees the portfolio—played an interest arbitrage. Triangle pays an after-tax cost of roughly 5 percent on its debt (because interest payments are tax-deductible), while earning roughly 8 percent after tax on junk preferred (for a corporate holder of preferred stock, only 15 percent of the dividends earned are subject to federal income taxation—so 85 percent of those dividends are tax-free to corporations). According to Peltz, 20 percent of Triangle's income comes from its investment portfolio.

Peter May, when asked to explain the upturn at National Can, cited several of the fortuitous changes in the business environment. Then he added, "The business was on the brink of turning around significantly—we can't take credit for that. But the great intangible is the change in atmosphere. They were unable to make any long-term business decisions because of Victor Posner, and now they know we are committed to the company's long-term growth. And there is also the intangible of showing the new owners how good you are."

Peltz is more apt to claim credit, but in one frank moment he did not. In an interview in mid-1986 he remarked that National Can's earnings were the same as they had been two years earlier, before all the debt of the acquisition was laden on the balance sheet. Asked what he would attribute this to, Peltz replied, "Not my management expertise!"

Considine was interviewed by this reporter in September 1986, the week after *Business Week* canonized Peltz and May, featuring them on its cover as "The New Aces of Low Tech," and publishing a separate editorial which stated, "Peltz and May are . . . what the U.S. needs more of: entrepreneurs with long-term vision." Asked what made the business suddenly so great in 1985, Considine answered sharply, "It didn't just suddenly become great. It's been going on for ten years. We got ourselves in shape, positioned ourselves to be the low-cost operator in the right markets. We expanded the glass business when everybody—including articles in *The Wall Street Journal*—said I was nuts. We bought when everyone else was selling. So we positioned the company. And last year, putting aside any expenses associated with the rhubarb, *was* a record year. This year's going to be another very good year."

Posner shared this long view of the company, believing in its strength, and missed out on the bonanza. Ever since he was forced to sell his National Can holdings, things have gone from bad to worse for the reclusive financier:

In early 1986, Posner's DWG defaulted on the principal payment of its Drexel-underwritten notes. Lindner lent Posner $55 million so that the notes could be paid off.

Evans Products went into bankruptcy (advised in its reorganization by Drexel), and Posner—for the first time—was forced out of a company he controlled.

Sharon Steel, advised by Drexel, continued throughout 1986 to extend its debenture-swap offer—making it the most extended swap in history—until April 1987, when Sharon Steel followed Evans Products into Chapter 11.

In May 1986, Posner was featured on the cover of *Business Week* as America's highest-paid chief executive—who also returned the least to shareholders for the money. He took total compensation of $12.7 million in 1985 from DWG, a holding company that earned $5.6 million on $989 million in revenues in '85 and that in the first nine months of fiscal 1986 lost $5.9 million.

In July 1986, Posner was convicted of having evaded more than $1.2 million in federal income taxes by inflating the value of land he donated to a Bible college in Miami. He was subsequently granted a new trial because of juror misconduct, but he later pleaded guilty and avoided a jail sentence by agreeing to pay back taxes and fines totaling at least $4 million, and to spend $3 million on the homeless and devote twenty hours a week for five years to working with them. His legal fees to Edward Bennett Williams were paid by the ailing Sharon Steel, in an arrangement made by that company's board in 1982 but not disclosed until 1985.

Had Posner succeeded in his buyout of National Can—and had he been able to maneuver it into the interlocking pyramid of his troubled empire—it would have been manna. But Posner, in a rare interview, asserted that he has no regrets about having let National Can go, and that he wants to clear up some prevailing "misconceptions."

He claimed that the reason he did not proceed with the buyout of National Can was that he believed the transaction was too leveraged, and the cash flow would not be adequate to cover the debt service. "We *had* the money," he insists, in response to a query about Drexel's having been unwilling to finance the transaction.

"Drexel told us they would arrange it. There was no problem with the money.

"I told Considine I wanted to go to fifty-one percent, and the company could have stayed with the same small amount of debt it always had, and he could have continued to run it the same way he always had. But he didn't want that. I think that that twenty percent [which management would have gotten in the management buyout] did something to turn his head," Posner declared.

Asked about Dan Good and Paul Yang of E. F. Hutton attempting to raise the financing for him, Posner said, "They said, 'Please give us a shot.' I said I wasn't convinced that they could do it—and we didn't need them, because we had the money [committed from Drexel] and I wasn't going to do the deal anyway.

"From the moment Considine wouldn't do the fifty-one percent deal, I only wanted to sell. And then Milken came to me [with the Triangle offer] and he says, 'Vic, this is a helluva deal.' "

Posner added that he cleared $80–90 million profit from the sale of his stock into the Triangle offer. "I would do the same thing again today," he declared. "I thought the debt load was too high—interest rates have come down, so it's worked so far, but I still think there is too much leverage."

Drexel's David Kay, who has known Posner for many years, said, "There can never be too much leverage for Victor. The sad part is that when Victor tells you that, he believes it's true. How could it be otherwise? Everything is as Victor mandates."

Posner became a dinosaur at Drexel, a relic of the not-distant but prehistoric past when the firm was more than happy to underwrite securities for just about anyone. In the eighties, however, while the firm's fortunes skyrocketed, Posner's went into a free-fall. By 1986, Posner was an embarrassment to many at the firm, an unlikely candidate for future Drexel financings, a reminder of a past that the members of this aspiring world-class institution preferred to forget.

If Posner symbolized the old Drexel, however, Peltz—to his astonishment and the astonishment of many at Drexel—became for a brief, halcyon time the sign-bearer of the new. After one interview in early 1986, Peltz remarked to this reporter, somewhat wistfully, "Will you write something good about me? Nobody's ever written anything good about me." Then came the Business Week article in September 1986—in the issue that featured Peltz and May on the cover—breathlessly lauding them as revitalizers of smokestack America, who had not stripped off assets for a quick profit but were strengthening the business for long-term growth. Their key investment banker at Drexel, Fred McCarthy, chortled, "The question now is, will success spoil Drexel Burnham? Will we become hoity-toity?"

Peltz no longer had to camp out on Milken's doorstep, begging for a deal. When Milken traveled to Boston to address a group of security analysts in February 1986, Peltz met him in Boston and then—over a six-hour strategy session—flew him back to L.A. "Nelson was so excited, so thrilled, to have had Mike to himself for all that time," exclaimed one friend of Peltz. "He came home bursting with ideas."

Indeed. Within the next five months, National Can reached an agreement to acquire American Can Company's packaging operations, capping Peltz's courtship of Gerry Tsai that had begun in Engel's Bungalow 8 the year before. The purchase price of $560 million would be raised by Drexel.

And Avery, a tiny holding company that was a leftover from the Trafalgar days and is controlled by Triangle, agreed to buy Uniroyal Chemical Company for $710 million.

Finally, it was decided that the third segment of the Peltz-May empire—a target then unknown—would be acquired by Central Jersey Industries (CJI), the shell of an old railroad company with a tax-loss carryforward, which is 38 percent owned by Triangle. In August 1986, Drexel raised $381 million as a blind acquisition pool for CJI. "Play money," Drexel's Fred McCarthy said. "It's all in hundred-dollar bills, and we're filling a pool with it so Nelson can dive in."

Said in jest, it captures the spirit of what Milken has done with Peltz and May. With the American Can and Uniroyal acquisitions, Milken placed them atop an empire with $4 billion in revenues. Peltz and May reached that stratosphere of American industry not by years of work in building companies and creating products, but by putting what little they had on the line, rolling the dice—and issuing mountains of debt. Thanks to Milken the magician, these mountains can simply be moved from one place to another. Not surprisingly, some critical observers, such as Felix Rohatyn, investment banker at Lazard Frères, decried the creation of such empires as being achieved "with mirrors."

Even some at Drexel find Peltz's coronation hard to take, not for ideological reasons but because they feel he was merely their pawn, who never deserved to be king. "Nelson is floating. Nelson the industrialist," commented one adviser drily, shortly after the American Can and Uniroyal acquisitions were announced. "In your [this] book, call him 'Nelson the industrialist' and make us all vomit."

In the truest sense, of course, Peltz was as much a pawn as ever. For what he was really doing as he undertook this dramatic expansion of his empire was satisfying Milken's needs—and, only incidentally, his own. As Meshulam Riklis, who portrays himself as a conservative elder statesman to this new generation of high-rollers, put it in an interview in mid-1986, "What Mike and Drexel must now do is create the guys that will maintain the pressure in the market for the buying and selling of these publicly held corporations. . . . They [Milken and Drexel] will work with me for whatever I need, but I am not interested in buying a company for three billion dollars, I don't want the responsibility. . . . Someone else may do it, who has got nothing much to lose.

"They have to find the one, two, three, four guys who are ambitious, and they're gonna give them the money, and they make bids for companies, and they use those companies to make bids for other companies. They have to create these guys, otherwise their business stops. That's what they're doing, and they're gonna have to do it more and more. They have to create—I call these guys the monsters."

AVERY'S ACQUISITION of Uniroyal Chemical is a good example of one of Milken's created "monsters," Peltz, performing his function perfectly. In April 1985, Carl Icahn made an offer for the outstanding shares of Uniroyal. In response, Uniroyal's management took the company private, with the leveraged-buyout firm of Clayton & Dubilier and Drexel as money-raisers. The debt was designed to be paid down quickly, and it soon became apparent that in order to pay down that debt the company would have to not just sell off pieces but be liquidated.

The chemical business was the core, healthy business of Uniroyal. Salomon Brothers—Uniroyal's longtime banker, which had attempted to fend off Icahn and then brought in Clayton & Dubilier —had the first shot at trying to sell that business, had put an overly rich price tag of $1 billion on it in an auction, and had failed. Then Drexel tried, and after some difficulty with the natural buyers, which were other big chemical companies, Leon Black settled on Peltz. "Avery was a shell, so the leverage was great," Black says. "Avery stock was selling at about two dollars, so if it all worked, and the stock went to fifteen, it would be terrific."

Drexel, of course, would raise the money—$1 billion—for this shell to make its $760 million acquisition. The Milken machine would thus be kept in high gear. The holders of Uniroyal paper would be paid off, in the amount of time allotted in the deal's structuring. And there would be $1 billion of new, 15 percent interest–yielding paper, to feed all the hungry buyers. So the mountain of debt would simply be moved from one place to another (probably with many of the same buyers, since if they liked Uniroyal once, chances were they would like it again) and Drexel would make its fees, again. This story, however, would have a less than happy ending when, a little more than a year after Avery's buying Uniroyal Chemical, it announced plans to sell the company. Peltz would attribute his decision to an inability to build the company into a big concern through acquisition, given the rich stock prices of companies in the chemical industry.

"We are increasingly on all sides of transactions," Black commented in mid-1986. In the negotiations between Avery and Uniroyal, Drexel (mainly Black) was representing both seller and buyer. Moreover, Drexel had an equity interest in both parties, since it had gotten warrants which gave it 10 percent of Uniroyal, and it would be collecting warrants as part of its fee in the $1 billion Avery offering, giving it 12 percent.

Black remembered a time, not long ago, when Drexel was anything but so ubiquitous. It was effectively shut out of the divestiture business—which is the selling of pieces of companies and comprises about 40 percent of M&A—because the big, established companies who were the sellers would never use Drexel. But those companies, one after another, were felled by Drexel's avenging bidders. These companies, all in their past lives the clients of Salomon Brothers, had all now come forcibly, via acquisition, into the Drexel fold: Northwest Industries, Uniroyal, National Can, TWA, Beatrice, Pacific Lumber. "We didn't have the list. We've been *buying* the list," Black concluded. "And all this has given us the M&A product to work with that we never had."

After the Avery-Uniroyal negotiations were completed, Drexel set out to raise Avery its $1 billion. When the prospectus, showing the company's proposed recapitalization, was sent out to potential buyers in early September 1986, there was a lot more dilution than the market had expected. Peltz and May, and Drexel, were buying in at very low prices, prompting mutterings of self-dealing from angry shareholders. The stock dropped fast from $6, where it had been selling ever since the Uniroyal deal had been announced several months earlier, to $2.

Jeffrey Steiner, however, was not among those unhappy shareholders. In the last year, Steiner had left the investors' sidelines and taken his leap as a Drexel player, following in the footsteps of his friends Icahn and Peltz. In late 1985, with Drexel financing, Steiner had taken over Banner Industries, a manufacturer of aircraft replacement parts; he now had a $300 million blind pool, also raised by Milken, which he would use in early 1987 to acquire another company, Rexnord, a manufacturer of mechanical parts, chemicals and plastics. Steiner, still close to Peltz, was the second-largest shareholder of the Triangle-controlled entity CJI, was involved in deals in Europe with National Can, and used the same team of investment bankers from Drexel, led by Fred McCarthy, as Peltz did. He said he bought 160,000 shares of Avery at about sixty cents and sold out at $6—for a profit of close to $900,000—the day before the stock dropped. "I didn't think the six-dollar price could be justified," he said when asked why he sold at that fortuitous moment, "so I sold it."

In the course of being an exquisitely useful functionary to Milken—who has raised close to $3 billion for him—Peltz has arrived at the heights he always dreamed of. His and Peter May's stake in National Can was valued at about $90 million by the fall of 1986, if one includes an estimated control premium, which is the amount one would pay over and above the price of the stock in order to acquire a controlling block. He bought a 106-acre Bedford, New York, estate, High Winds, with a twenty-two-room house, for about $6 million and did extensive renovations. Less than a year later he bought another estate, in Palm Beach, reportedly for $18 million— which was said to be the second-highest amount ever spent for a residence in this country, exceeded only by that of oilman Marvin Davis in Beverly Hills.

Peltz is not the model of the new, lean corporate manager-owner Milken likes to trumpet. While he falls easily into the

Milken/raiders' harangue about the evils of flaccid corporate life in America ("Uniroyal had a corporate staff of two thousand [Uniroyal says two hundred fifty], headquarters in Connecticut that cost a hundred sixteen million to build—I am telling you, old-fashioned American industry is more like Communism than Communism," he rails), Peltz has always been profligate. When he acquired control of Triangle, he caused that humdrum company to lease a limousine, a helicopter to carry him from his home in Manhattan to the company's offices in New Brunswick, New Jersey, and a Lear jet. And, of course, he had spent $2 million of company funds on that apartment in Paris.

One way Peltz has rewarded himself is in the long-standing, and common, use of corporate perks. Another, seemingly more straightforward, is in his and May's stellar compensation, as Triangle's chairman and chief executive officer, and president and chief operating officer, respectively. But they have drawn this income in a way that escaped much attention until 1987. It has all come to them not as individuals but through NPM (which Peltz and May own). This is a system of compensation which Peltz and May instituted for themselves when they bought control of Triangle. (In 1983, NPM received $461,396.) Peltz and May, technically not employees of Triangle, do not appear on the proxy statement list of the company's five highest-paid executives. That list, for 1986, was headed by Frank Considine, at $1.6 million.

For 1986, however, NPM received $7,644,228 (including a $5 million bonus), which was split two thirds/one third between Peltz and May. Those compensations, of $5.1 million and $2.5 million respectively, would have placed both men among the thirty highest-paid U.S. executives, as ranked by Business Week. Only Capital Cities/ABC and Salomon Inc. had two executives who made that list. Furthermore, as of January 1, 1987, the Triangle board raised NPM's annual base fee to $7.4 million.

When asked by Wall Street Journal reporter Randall Smith about his and May's compensation, which was creating a stir among analysts and some shareholders in the spring of 1987 and apparently had hurt the price of Triangle stock, Peltz replied, "The industrialists of the nineteenth century were highly paid and highly criticized, and I guess we'll have to bear that burden, too. But those were the guys that did things. It was under Carnegie that the U.S. steel industry outperformed England."

In reaping the rewards of National Can, Peltz could not be

accused of thinking only of himself. Within months of the National Can acquisition, some of its pension-fund assets were placed under the management of Mount Vernon Associates, Inc., of which William Heffner, a Triangle director, is chairman and president. Heffner is Peltz's father-in-law.

The new Triangle offices, in New Brunswick no longer but in Manhattan, are spectacular. Both Peltz's and May's offices are on the top floor of the Lexington Avenue building, and these rooms have ceilings about thirty feet high, with sloping walls that are all glass and exposed steel beams. They are a far cry from the back room Peltz leased from Sassower, Goren and Schneider (who bought Flagstaff) in the early eighties.

Interviewed in his new digs in the fall of 1986, Peltz offered his visitor coffee in a Triangle mug inscribed with the words "Cash is King." He took a phone call, said heatedly, "You're *wrong!* I'll talk to you about it later, I've got someone here," and hung up on Milken. When his visitor expressed surprise at his tone, Peltz said, "What do you think I do, stand up and face east? That guy gets up and puts on his pants in the morning, just like I do."

PELTZ MAY PROTEST, but he surely knows that Milken has been the true principal here, the shadow behind Peltz's ornate carved-wood chair. It was Milken who determined that Posner would not do the National Can buyout. He canvassed his troops for someone to rescue Posner. He chose Peltz only when no one else was willing. He decided how much would be paid. He put Drexel in for $10 million when Knapp dropped out. He placed the debt as no one else could have, some with lenders who did not know who Nelson Peltz was. He told Peltz to put the Paris apartment on the market. And he has engineered the breathtaking expansion of the Triangle empire.

But Peltz is now enthroned. And publicly, at least, he does not play the role of Milken's subject. He makes fewer obeisances to Drexel than he did in interviews six months earlier, and is less self-deprecating. "We never could have done it without Drexel—but we were the only Drexel client who was in love with National Can. And we were the only ones willing to pay all cash."

Many who have dealt with May and Peltz see May, with his Peat, Marwick background, as the more substantial partner. One longtime associate noted, "Nelson will not make a move without checking with Peter. And if he shows Peter the figures and Peter says no, then Nelson doesn't do it."

One man who has dealt with the two in negotiations for Uniroyal remarked, "Nelson is like a guy in the back of a covered wagon, selling medicine—and Peter May is the guy inside, making the stuff, packaging it, making sure it all works."

Peltz's analysis of the partnership varies from this. "Peter's very good at administration, at neatening things up. I conceptualize, I strategize. In American Can, for example, Gerry [Tsai] and I met privately until we agreed on the price. Then, after that, Peter took over the deal. And on financings I structure the broad outline, he does the details."

As for Considine, Peltz commented, "He has a tremendous amount of independence. I corral my ego. It's done in a way that makes him feel he's leading the band."

In his unimposing conference room at National Can headquarters in Chicago, Considine gave a short laugh upon being told that Peltz said he corrals his ego. "Nelson is chairman and CEO of Triangle and I am chairman and CEO of National Can," Considine said. "That means I run National Can. It's OK with me that he owns the stock—as long as it's clear that I'm running the company." (In January 1988, William Sick would be brought in as chief executive of what was by then called American National Can, and Considine would remain its chairman.)

Considine arrived at National Can as a sales manager in 1961, when he was forty, and worked his way up through the ranks, becoming president of the company in 1969 and chairman and chief executive officer in 1973. He admitted that the transition to life under Peltz has not been easy. "You feel very possessive about the company," he said slowly, "you feel you've built it—but you have to remind yourself that it is a public company. And you have to cross that bridge, it has to be something you accept intellectually. But it's difficult—that's why a lot of CEOs walk out when this happens."

When the deal was negotiated with National Can, Considine received stock options for about one percent of the company—management's stock options, taken all together, were for 2.7 percent. He confessed to sometimes thinking about "what this has cost me personally"—in not having been able to do a management leveraged buyout, or in not having negotiated for a heftier stake of stock options. "I don't really mind. Money's never been what drives me. I have enough to always get by—as Victor would say, I'm not going to change my standard of living," he said, smiling.

"And I don't believe in being greedy," Considine added. "It's just when you look around you and see everyone making so much, and you know that you and your people are the ones who built this company, and instead here is Drexel making all this money. And with the warrants and more warrants, they own sixteen percent of the company. But," he concluded, seeming to chide himself, "you can't spend time looking back."

Considine, of course, is not delivering a polemic against leverage or against takeovers, but is uttering the personal plaint of someone who built a company, tried to take it private, was beaten out—and now watches strangers reaping its rewards. He was beaten because the banks—which until then had happily serviced every request by National Can—would not or could not do for the management of National Can what Drexel did for the unknown, previously feckless Peltz and May. And, while Considine would not say this, he now works for two individuals whom he probably never would have hired, and who could not have gotten in the doors of those banks to discuss this transaction.

About this strange new world—which seems to be borne by one figure, Atlas-like—Considine commented, "It's a different game today. I don't pretend to know how it's going to turn out. You have nonoperating people running businesses. They're financial people—*financial* operators, that's for sure, but they're not operators."

8

Icahn-TWA:
From Greenmailer to Manager-Owner

CARL ICAHN was the living embodiment of a Drexel dilemma as the firm moved into financing the hostile megatakeover. The goal of Milken and his fellows was precisely what Leon Black had recorded at the Cavas Gobhai session back in 1979: to finance the "robber barons who would become the owners of the major companies of the future." But these "robber barons," as Black admiringly called them, or takeover entrepreneurs—men like Icahn, Sam Heyman, Sir James Goldsmith—tended to be a strong-willed, tough and egocentric breed, disinclined to be anyone's pawn, even Milken's. And Milken's construct, of course, placed an enormous premium on control. Still, what choice did Milken have, other than to play only rookies like Peltz? And besides, with legions of captive clients, Milken could tolerate a handful of freer spirits.

No one on the very short list of independent major Drexel players was more autonomous, and more obsessed with his autonomy, than Icahn. Icahn seeks to control every situation that he touches, whether small or global. He talks to reporters only on the condition that any quote be read back to him in context, and he goes over and over the quotes, listening for each nuance, demanding a word change here, a phrase deleted there. He allowed his employees to speak to this reporter on the condition that their quotes too be checked—not with them but with him.

In the early days of Icahn and Company, he had three partners who worked in the business with him and two others who were passive investors; over time, he managed to unburden himself of all of them, with the exception of one who owns one percent. He had partners in his raids, too, in the early eighties, but eventually accepted only limited partners who would have no say. Fiercely self-reliant, for years using no investment banker, sharing none of the decision-making, Icahn has allowed himself to lean for support on only one individual, his financial analyst Alfred Kingsley. Kingsley is described by close associates of the two men as Icahn's "alter ego." Except for one brief hiatus, he has been with Icahn for twenty years. Icahn has refused to make Kingsley a partner.

An only child, Icahn grew up in a small two-family house in the middle-class neighborhood of Bayswater, Queens; his grandfather lived upstairs. His mother was a schoolteacher. His father had a law degree but hated being a lawyer, taught chemistry but hated teaching. He had wanted to be an opera singer and had studied with Enrico Caruso. Unable to break into opera but desperate to have some opportunity to sing, he took a job as a cantor—nonreligious though he was—in a synagogue in nearby Cedarhurst, Long Island. That too proved unsatisfying. Having developed what the family calls "a heart condition" in his early forties, he stopped working and stayed home until his death in 1978. "He read Schopenhauer and listened to records, day and night," one friend remembered.

Icahn's mother had two sisters, also schoolteachers, and a brother who was only about sixteen years older than Carl and was the family's success story. In the thirties, during the Depression, Melvin E. Schnall had attended Yale University, where he was painfully aware of being part of the Jewish quota. He married into a wealthy family, went into his father-in-law's business, became wealthy himself, lived in a lavish home in Scarsdale with a pool and four in help (where Carl was first "exposed," as Schnall says, to the finer things). But the driving obsession of Schnall's life, which informed his decisions about year-round residences, summer homes, private clubs, and schools for his children, was his effort either to pass as a non-Jew or to be the accepted token. In the course of this decades-long struggle, he joined the Unitarian Church and changed his name from Melvin E. Schnall to M. Elliot Schnall.

Carl Icahn, after graduating from Far Rockaway High School, went to Princeton, where he became recognized as an expert chess player, studied philosophy, and wrote an award-winning senior thesis entitled "The Problem of Formulating an Adequate Explication of the Empiricist Criterion of Meaning." At his mother's insistence, he attended medical school at New York University, but he hated it and he has said, as reported in an article about him in the Princeton alumni magazine, that it aggravated a "slight hypochondria." He dropped out after two years and did a stint in the Army (where, he says, he won several thousand dollars playing poker).

In 1961, Schnall got his nephew a job as a trainee stockbroker at Dreyfus and Company. Icahn invested his poker winnings, made $50,000 in a bull market, and then lost it all when the market fell in 1962. "I was so upset that I've really worked like crazy since then," Icahn told *Business Week*.

He decided that he needed a niche. Options—the trading of puts and calls, which are respectively the rights to sell and buy stock at a certain price at a given future time—were then, as Icahn says, "a wide-open field." He became an options broker at Tessel Paturick and Company, where he worked with Joseph Freilich and Daniel Kaminer, and then the three of them moved in 1964 to Gruntal and built its options department. Trading information on options was not then publicly listed; Icahn started publishing a newsletter, called *The Mid-Week Option Report*, and built a strong client base of options sellers. By 1968, Icahn says, his options department was earning gross commissions of about $1.5 million, which made it one of the most profitable at Gruntal.

It was clear that the intense, abstracted Icahn had found his home on Wall Street. The niches he had carved and would continue to carve for himself satisfied his analytical bent. And the money was a perfect reward. At work he gambled, and for relaxation he gambled. One friend recalls Icahn playing not only the usual card games but Monopoly, for real money. "I walked into Carl's apartment, and there he was," recalls this friend, "with this enormous pile of cash, buying Boardwalk for five hundred dollars."

Icahn decided he wanted to open up his own discount brokerage firm, and he asked Schnall whether he could borrow $400,000 to buy a seat on the New York Stock Exchange. Over the last several years, he and Schnall had become close. Schnall was divorced, living on Sutton Place in Manhattan, running a looseleaf-binder company he had bought, and the two would meet at "21" at the close of most business days. Icahn had traded options for Schnall's account and made about a 30–40 percent return for him. In 1967, moreover, Schnall had sold for roughly $3 million a company he had bought two years earlier for about $400,000, so he had plenty of cash on hand.

Schnall received 20 percent of the stock in Icahn and Company.

With the rest of the $3 million he bought tax-free bonds, with an 8 percent coupon, which he subordinated to Icahn and Company to strengthen its capital base. In return, Icahn paid him $100,000 a year. Carl opened an office at 42 Broadway with Kaminer, Freilich and Jerry Goldsmith, another man who had been at Gruntal, as his partners.

Alfred Kingsley also came from Gruntal to the new Icahn and Company, as an associate. Kingsley, seven years younger than Icahn, had started as an undergraduate at Wharton at sixteen, had graduated from New York University Law School at twenty-three and then had gotten his master's in tax law. In 1965, still in law school, he had begun working full time for Icahn at Gruntal.

At Icahn and Company both Icahn and Kingsley began mixing arbitrage with options. What they were practicing then was not risk arbitrage—where one buys the securities of a target company after a deal is announced, betting on the transaction's going through— but classic arbitrage. Icahn would buy a convertible bond at 100, convertible to ten shares of stock at 10, and then he would simultaneously sell ten shares short at ten and one eighth—thus locking in the eighth-of-a-point profit on each share. Then he introduced options into the mix, in elaborate hedging formulas that left him protected on the downside with the potential for an enormous upside.

"There were great opportunities to make money," Icahn said, recalling a particularly gratifying transaction in Polaroid where a combination of buying stock, puts and calls brought him $1.5 million for what he insists was "no risk." "The arbs didn't know options, and the options brokers certainly didn't understand arbitrage. The arbs kept arbitrage very quiet in those days, there were only a few doing it, like Gus Levy at Goldman, Sachs. So when I put together arbitrage with options it was really great.

"Always, I looked for a spot that was not too popular. You want to be in something other people don't see—and which makes eminent sense."

In 1973 the Chicago Board Options Exchange opened, and the field soon became too crowded for Icahn's taste. Kingsley, meanwhile, had been hedging capitalizations of various companies, which he described as "constantly molding a position. It was like a washing machine, going round and round. I'd look at the whole ITT mess [of varying securities], and I'd say, I could buy this preferred, short that [security], and I'll be hedged. And then the next day I'd buy some other issue, sell against that. Round and round. It was driving me crazy, and I started getting really bored."

Kingsley said it was boredom that drove him from Icahn and Company in 1973 and led him to a small firm named F. L. Salomon, to specialize in new issues. One longtime associate of Kingsley disputed that explanation, saying Kingsley left because Icahn was "paying him spit." Icahn is notoriously tight-fisted. It seems to pain him to give another dollar. Even in later years, after he had made over $100 million, he groused when his team of investment bankers, working until 2 A.M., ordered steaks from Smith and Wollensky's restaurant. Law firms that did work for him would often wait months to be paid.

Another of Kingsley's associates said he was disappointed at not having been made a partner in Icahn and Company. But by this time Icahn was shedding partners, not making them. He was already notorious for his sudden rages, and for the abuse he heaped upon employees, minority partners, outside lawyers. No one was exempt. Kaminer left, then Goldsmith left (although he said Icahn offered to increase his equity share if he remained). Freilich was later reduced to his one percent. Even Schnall was relieved of his stake.

Schnall had not been admitted to an exclusive beach club in Southampton, Long Island, and he decided to leave New York, changing his whole social circle (which summered in Southampton), and move to New Canaan, Connecticut. Icahn suggested that it might be a good time for him to take his money out, since Wall Street was in the doldrums and Schnall was nervous; but he asked Schnall to leave his bonds there. Schnall agreed, and continues to receive what Icahn calls his "allowance" of $100,000 a year. To this day Schnall chafes at having agreed to give back his 20 percent.

Kingsley, meanwhile, was finding the world outside Icahn and Company inhospitable. F. L. Salomon went out of business; Kingsley joined another firm, and it soon merged with yet another. "Every three weeks," he says, "there was another name on the door."

If acumen were the only determinant, Kingsley certainly should have thrived on Wall Street. Jeffrey Steiner, who assisted Nelson Peltz and would become one of Icahn's principal investors in the eighties, called Kingsley "the most clever business analyst I have ever met in thirty years in business." But Kingsley, a short, rotund Buddy Hackett look-alike, an Orthodox Jew who leaves work early on Friday so as to be home for the Sabbath before sundown, did not fit—nor did he aspire to—in the white-shoe investment-banking world. And life in the bottom-tier firms that were struggling for survival in Wall Street in 1974 had little to recommend it. In 1975, Kingsley returned to Icahn and Company after less than two years away.

Even while he was away, Kingsley had continued to talk to Icahn. In one of their conversations he had mentioned that he thought there were great investments to be made in "undervalued situations." The one he recommended was a closed-end mutual fund named Highland. Kingsley bought some of its shares for his customers, Icahn bought some, and after Kingsley rejoined Icahn they accumulated a block of about 30 percent—which management (distinct from the company) then bought back in 1976. "It was a two-year play, it took us a lot of time to accumulate," Kingsley recalled. "But we bought at two and we sold at six."

That was the beginning. After that, they accumulated positions of 4.9 percent (at 5 percent a shareholder must file a 13D disclosure document with the SEC) in several more closed-end funds at discounts to their real value, the stock prices then went up, and they made a profit. Because these were mutual funds, all one had to do to determine whether they were undervalued was to compute the value of their portfolio and compare that to its stock price. "That was the chicken way of playing," said Kingsley, comparing it to the task of targeting a company, whose value is harder to quantify. "And after we'd done those, Carl said, 'This is an interesting way to invest—let's do some more.' "

In 1978 Icahn waged a proxy fight to gain control of a real-estate investment trust named Baird and Warner. Like Milken, who had been investing in REIT paper through the midseventies, Icahn recognized that there was a lot of hidden value in the depressed REIT industry. And Baird and Warner was not a troubled REIT, just one whose stock price had suffered because of the REITs' general disrepute.

While Baird and Warner's assets were mainly illiquid at that time, they were worth about $30 million—a nice pool of capital for Icahn to control. Icahn renamed this REIT Bayswater, after his childhood neighborhood, and eventually caused it to revoke its status as a REIT, in order to invest in new types of real-estate-related activities and also in the securities of public companies. Bayswater thus became a vehicle for raids.

The proxy fight—a campaign for the shareholder vote held at a public company's annual meeting—now became Icahn's weapon of choice. In the 1950s, proxy fights had been waged by outsiders, such as Robert Young at New York Central Railroad, to persuade stockholders to throw out incumbent managements and install them instead. At that time, however, the advantage lay with the incumbents; as long as management was paying a dividend and was not tinged with scandal, stockholders would rarely vote for a raider.

By 1979, the odds had changed. *Forbes* magazine reported that a check of twenty-five proxy actions taken that year showed management the victor in twelve and dissidents in thirteen. Icahn and others had started a new-wave proxy fight, in which the aim was not so much to replace management (although Icahn had done this at Baird and Warner) as to attract the attention of third parties to an undervalued company. And the issues in the proxy fight were framed in terms of shareholder profits. Icahn would point out that the stock was trading at some paltry fraction of book value, and that there was real potential for better earnings.

In 1979 Icahn won a proxy fight to gain board seats and then forced the sale of Tappan, the stove-maker—whose stock was trading at around 8 and had a book value of over $20 a share—to AB Electrolux, a Swedish-owned home-appliance manufacturer, at a price that gave Icahn a profit of close to $3 million. "Tappan worked like a charm for Carl," said his lawyer for that deal, Morris Orens of Olshan Grundman and Frome. "It clearly demonstrated that if you are right about the company's assets being undervalued, and the company wishes to put itself up for sale, there will be buyers out there."

Icahn was ebullient. Discussing proxy fights aimed at forcing a sellout, he told *Forbes*, "I think the risk–reward ratios there are a very exciting thing. Much better than arbitrage. It's the wave of the future."

Icahn moved on to Saxon Industries, the copier company, where after threatening a proxy fight he sold back his 9.5 percent stake to the company at a premium over the market, making a $2 million profit. It was his first public greenmailing—selling back to a company at a higher price than was available to other shareholders. But the word "greenmail" had not yet been coined. The activity —which had been carried out by others such as Victor Posner and Saul Steinberg—was known as a "buyback at a premium" or a "bon voyage bonus."

Now that Icahn was launched into this new game, it was time for him to divest himself of his last meaningful partner, Fred Sullivan. From now on he would accept investors in his deals, but would share equity with no one (except Freilich, with his one percent). Fred Sullivan, the CEO of Walter Kidde, a small fire-extinguisher company that he had built into a major conglomerate, had met Icahn when Carl was a trainee at Dreyfus, and Icahn had become Sullivan's broker. In the early seventies, Kidde had invested in Icahn and Company and owned approximately 19 percent. "We sold back about one year after Tappan, at a profit for Kidde shareholders," recalled Sullivan. "Carl wanted to buy it back."

Asked whether he felt he had any choice, Sullivan replied, "Well, he could have just put it [the profits] all in another entity if we had refused. Carl is very clever. And we decided not to test him."

On Icahn's modus operandi in those early raids, Sullivan remarked, "Carl didn't have the money to finish the deal. He genuinely thought that the price of the stock was undervalued, and he genuinely thought that the values could be realized. He bought on that basis. It was only later, when greenmail started to be excoriated, that he defended it on the grounds that these companies were poorly managed."

And when Icahn descended upon his adversaries, the chief executive officers of his target companies, he must have seemed like a nightmare come suddenly to life. After Saxon, Icahn's next target was the Hammermill Paper Company. "Here's this poor guy from Hammermill [Albert Duval, its CEO], a real Ivy League guy," said Sullivan, "and he's sitting there thinking that the world works the way it always has, with his golf club and his graduating class, and he never raises his voice—and all of a sudden, he's got Carl, who is such a fighter. It's terrible. Carl was a scourge in those days.

"Carl is a dedicated capitalist. He is *dedicated* to amassing capital. He decided that he wanted to make money. Now, a lot of us made that decision, but few are as dedicated to it as Carl."

Seven years after Icahn appeared on his threshold owning approximately 9 percent of the company's stock, Duval spoke of him with a bitterness which made it seem like yesterday. "I formed the opinion that this was not for us, in the first few minutes of my meeting with Carl," Duval declared.

Asked what it was that was so quickly decisive, Duval replied, "He said he wanted to piece off the company. He said, 'I'm only in this for the money. I don't know anything about the paper business. I don't care anything about the paper business. All I care about is the money, and I want it quick.' " Duval added, however, that Icahn did not ask explicitly to be bought out. Had he done so, that could have hurt him later in a proxy contest, as the company could have used it against him to discredit all his claims of wanting to increase the company's value—and expose him instead as someone who had asked for greenmail. ("Everyone knew who Carl Icahn was in those days," explained one securities lawyer. "When you're a greenmailer, you don't have to *ask* for greenmail.")

"He said he wanted to get on the board," Duval continued. "He wanted to force it [the company] to a merger. He said repeatedly that he had no interest in the paper business. Well, everybody that worked there did. As far as we were concerned, the company had a future as well as a past and a present—but Carl just wanted to parcel it out as fast as he could.

"I'm sure if I had said, 'Here's your money, at a price over market,' he'd have taken it right then," Duval added. Instead, Duval—with the help of takeover lawyer Joe Flom from Skadden, Arps—instituted anti-takeover measures, mounted his own proxy campaign, and sued Icahn, charging him with disclosure violations and fraud. Icahn filed a counterclaim, alleging violations in Hammermill's solicitation of proxies.

One of Duval's lawyers said, "Duval called Icahn's bluff. He said, 'I'm not putting you on the board, I'm not buying you out, I'm not selling the company right now.' Icahn was a known quantity at that point. He was someone who had about ten to twenty million at his disposal. You didn't have to worry that he'd make a tender offer for the company—he didn't have the money. At ten or eleven percent of the company's stock, he was tapped out."

One of Icahn's lawyers confirmed that Icahn was stretched to his limit in each of these early deals. "He was really a gambler—everything he had was in each of these deals. Each one got bigger, because he would plow the profits from the one before back in. And the leverage was enormous—so a loss would have been devastating."

Icahn narrowly lost the Hammermill proxy contest. To make matters worse, it was discovered that he had voted about seventy thousand shares that he had borrowed, and then returned, after voting day. Icahn's defense was that he had been buying stock through the days just preceding the election and was afraid that not all of it would clear in time for him to vote it, so he had borrowed some in order to be sure he had the full voting benefit of what he owned.

Duval met Icahn in a hotel room in Erie, Pennsylvania, where Hammermill is located, not long after the voting of the borrowed shares had been discovered. Icahn had lost the contest, the company was not offering to buy him out at a premium, but he was sitting there with close to 10 percent of the company's stock—and settlement talks were at an impasse. "I used a lot of vulgar language," Duval recalled. "I said, 'You're the damnedest liar and cheat I know. We're going to take out a full-page ad in *The Wall Street Journal* and *The New York Times* that says, "Icahn Cheats." '

"I walked to the elevator, and he followed me and said, 'Please, come back, we'll talk.' " Duval is convinced that it was that meeting—and that threat—that broke the impasse, since not long after that, at the end of July 1980, they were finally able to reach settlement terms. For the next year, Icahn was prohibited from engaging in a proxy contest with Hammermill, and he granted Hammermill a right of first refusal on the shares owned by the Icahn group; Hammermill paid Icahn $750,000 for his expenses.

Through the next year, Icahn mounted no raids. According to one former insider, he was "stymied," because most of his capital was tied up. He and his investors had invested about $10.6 million in Hammermill stock. Then, when the standstill expired after a year, Hammermill bought him out at a premium. The price of the stock had risen considerably in the past year. Icahn made a profit of about $9 million over his initial investment.

Someone else might have been tempted to sell back without a premium after the debacle of the proxy contest, in order to free up all his funds. But, as one lawyer who has been opposite Icahn on a number of his forays pointed out, "Icahn's style in 1980 was a whole lot of bluff and bluster. His game was, 'I will not be bluffed out.' For him to have sold out at market, after losing the proxy contest, he viewed—I believe—as a signal to the next ten CEOs: Fight the proxy fight, beat him, and he'll go away.

"In those days he never made any pretense to doing something socially beneficial. The Carl Icahn of 1980 was still trying to figure out how this game was played, and what he could get away with."

For Icahn, the lawyer added, the game never became personalized. Icahn would make whatever attacks on management seemed to be required to win a proxy fight, and he understood that his opponents would unleash their armaments on him—but he seemed surprised when he saw how personal was his targets' animus for him. "If Carl had his druthers, these fights would have been like two gentlemen dueling—you take your best pokes, but when it's over why not go out and have a beer together?"

His targets, however, tended not to see Icahn's game as sporting. "People don't like to be challenged," this lawyer commented. "Particularly kings in their own castles."

IN EARLY 1982, Icahn led a raid on the huge retailer Marshall Field that established him as a serious predator. He surfaced, as was his habit, with a little over 10 percent of the company's stock. But one day later Icahn and his group reported that they owned 14.3 percent. One week after that, they filed at 19.4 percent.

What had happened was that additional investors—including British financier Alan Clore, and Marvin Warner, then chairman of the Cincinnati-based Home State Savings Bank—had jumped on the Icahn bandwagon. After his group had acquired nearly 20 percent of the stock, Icahn executed a loan agreement for $20 million with Jeffrey Steiner on behalf of a small bank Steiner controlled in Paris, Banque Commerciale Privée. Under the margin rules (which allow one to borrow up to 50 percent of the purchase price of the stock), this would have enabled Icahn to buy $40 million of stock.

Marshall Field fought back with a lawsuit as Hammermill had, making the usual battery of allegations about violations of federal securities laws, but added something novel as well: a RICO (Racketeer Influenced and Corrupt Organizations Act) count, usually reserved for dealing with organized crime. It charged Icahn with having invested income derived from a "pattern of racketeering" to acquire his interest in Marshall Field, whose activities affected interstate and foreign commerce.

The complaint charged that this pattern (which was defined to include violations of securities laws) could be found in Icahn's history of infractions over the past decade. These were laid out in detail. There was a consent order from the New Jersey Bureau of Securities, a censure from the New York Stock Exchange, a consent agreement with the New York Stock Exchange, an assurance of discontinuance from the New York State Attorney General's Office, and four decisions levying fines against Icahn and Company by the Chicago Board Options Exchange. And, finally, there was a consent decree Icahn had entered into with the SEC in 1981, alleging various securities law violations in Bayswater, Saxon, and Hammermill (involving the borrowed shares).

Marshall Field's legal battle was unavailing, however, and, within days of Icahn's securing the loan commitment from Banque Commerciale Privée, Marshall Field entered into a merger with Batus, Inc., the British retailer. Batus made a tender offer for all outstanding shares at $30 (Icahn's average cost per share was about $17). The aggregate cost of all shares purchased by the Icahn group was nearly $70 million, and Icahn had still not been tapped out. The bank loan of $20 million had never been taken down.

With over $100 million of buying power now at his disposal, Icahn was a more fearsome predator than he had been before. The business establishment took note. One close associate of Icahn recalled that Laurence Tisch, chairman of Loews and now of CBS Inc., said to him, "Tell Carl to cut this out. It's not good for the Jews."

For Icahn, the deal had many satisfactions, and one was the settling of an old score. Back in 1978, when Icahn was just an arbitrageur, betting from the sidelines, Marshall Field had made such a successful anti-takeover maneuver that Carter Hawley Hale dropped its hostile bid for the retailer—causing the price of Marshall Field stock to plummet. Icahn had lost $100,000 in one day.

As much of a triumph as the Marshall Field raid was for Icahn, it soured him once and for all on having anything but passive limited partners. Before, he had formed limited partnerships of investors—college friends; his uncle, Schnall; his landlord at 42 Broadway, real-estate magnate Zev Wolfson. Some entered these partnerships for as little as $50,000, and Icahn charged a management fee of 20 percent; the partners had no say in the decisions Icahn made. But in Marshall Field, for the first time, he had formed a group with individuals who were more than passive: a Netherlands Antilles corporation called Picara Valley, controlled by Alexander Goren, Philip Sassower and Lawrence Schneider—two of whom had been part of the group that had bought Flagstaff from Nelson Peltz in the late seventies. They had introduced Icahn to Steiner, shortly

before this raid. When it was over, Icahn decided that in the future he would always insist upon having complete control and would never accept a partner who would not cede it to him. Neither Sassower, Goren nor Schneider has invested with him again.

Steiner, however, became Icahn's most constant and largest investor. He says he has no problem with Icahn's autonomy. "In this type of business, you can't be in a position where you have to get approval," Steiner declared. "There has to be a captain. Carl is the captain. The key to these operations is being in control."

After Marshall Field, the tempo of Icahn's raids quickened. Marshall Field had given him not only profits of about $17.6 million but a great boost in confidence. He moved from Anchor Hocking to American Can to Owens-Illinois in rapid-fire succession, bought out by each company at a premium over market within a week or two after his stock purchases. By the fall of 1982, Icahn had begun his battle with Dan River—a protracted, acrimonious fight, during which townspeople of Danville, Virginia, who had never owned stock in the company rose up to repel him, buying stock with money saved for vacations and retirement funds. The struggle finally ended in 1983 when management escaped Icahn by taking the company private in a leveraged buyout. Icahn's profit was $8.5 million. In the summer of 1983, Icahn pocketed a quick $19 million—his largest profit to that date—when he sold his Gulf + Western stock at the market price to an institutional buyer, in a sale arranged through Gulf + Western's investment-banking firm, Kidder, Peabody. To reap this profit, he had invested more than $35.5 million, more than twice his commitment to the largest investment he had hitherto made—$14.3 million in Dan River.

In June 1984, Icahn confounded many Icahn-watchers by doing what he had insisted, in the Marshall Field depositions and the Dan River litigation, he had wanted to do all along: he acquired his target. He could have sold his stock in a railcar-leasing company, ACF, to the company in a management-led buyout and made a handsome profit—but chose to top the bid and take the company, for $410 million. National Westminster Bank USA, which had extended a $20 million loan commitment to an Icahn raid in late 1981, now was the lead bank in loans that totaled $225 million. The rest of the purchase price came from the sale of a major division of ACF just before the acquisition (in what was a highly unusual maneuver) and the post-acquisition sale of another division.

Was the greenmail game dead? Had Icahn decided that no

amount of fast-earned dollars was worth being called a racketeer? Was the scourge of corporate America going respectable?

What now seems clear is that Icahn had decided it was time to move to the next plateau. He had been saying for a couple of years that what he really wanted to do was gain control of these companies and sell off some pieces. He no doubt meant this. In a stock market where companies were as undervalued as many were in the early eighties, it was feasible—if one chose the right companies— to gain control, sell off parts in order to pay for the cost of the acquisition, and be left with the best part of the company almost for free. Over the long term, it would be far more profitable than grabbing a quick greenmail.

It would also be less aggravation. Icahn had accumulated a fortune of over $100 million. Even with his rare hunger for dollars, he could now afford to be a little more choosy. Greenmail had become the *bête noire* of corporate America. From now on, taking greenmail openly was going to mean incessant suits from enraged shareholders and incessant beatings in the press.

Moreover, Congress was up in arms about greenmail and it seemed as though legislators might figure out a way to outlaw it. In March 1984 Icahn had testified before a congressional subcommittee and had said—somewhat surprisingly—that he agreed that they should "end buybacks." But if they were going to end buybacks, he had argued, they should also make illegal all the defensive maneuvers open to managements—"Do not let them print up stock, do not let them issue themselves golden parachutes, do not let them sell the crown jewels."

Whether or not Congress outlawed greenmail was almost not the point. The point was, once an activity was so popularized that it was front-page news, what was Carl Icahn doing in it? He had made his fortune by entering a relatively undeveloped field, taking it farther than anyone else, and then—when it got too crowded and visible—moving a small step forward, in a natural progression. He had first gone into puts and calls. As that became more popular, he had mixed it with classic arbitrage. When options exploded, he had gone into risk arbitrage. Then he had decided to better control the arbitrage, by becoming the principal himself. Now it was time to become—at least often enough to give him the credibility he would need to continue his progression—the acquirer.

And this, interestingly enough, was when Leon Black came to

call to offer Icahn a Drexel war chest. For in the summer of '84, at a Gobhai seminar, Black, Fred Joseph and others had been discussing their need to find those players whom no one else could or would finance, who therefore would be desperate enough to pay the price (in interest rates to the junk-bond investors, and fees and equity stakes to Drexel) of Drexel's dollars. Icahn was one obvious candidate. While David Kay, head of Drexel's fledgling M&A group, objected to their representing the notorious greenmailer, that objection was overruled. Icahn was, after all, a singularly able greenmailer; he had amassed over $100 million in about five years, and his annualized return for that period was over 80 percent. It would hardly be like Drexel to place a higher value on respectability than on performance.

Moreover, Icahn fit nicely into a plan that Black, then head of Drexel's LBO group, was advancing—to get cash into players' hands by refinancing LBOs they had already done, replacing bank debt with junk bonds, and adding in a surplus for a war chest. How much surplus was right would vary in each case, depending upon the appetite of the player. For example, Drexel did a refinancing for William Farley, a small-time Chicago entrepreneur, who had acquired a company which he renamed Farley Metals. Drexel raised $80 million for the refinancing and $60 million for a war chest; about one year later, in the spring of 1985, Farley put that war chest (and more) to use when he made a $1 billion acquisition of Northwest Industries.

Icahn's appetite dwarfed Farley's, but he was far less compliant. Farley gave Drexel 5 percent of equity in Farley Metals and accepted a Drexel-designated director, Leon Black, on the board; Icahn refused to give any equity, and he took no Drexel-designated director. In late 1984, Drexel raised $225 million for the refinancing of ACF, and the bulk of the remainder, roughly $155 million, went into a war chest. According to Black, however, Milken would have raised another $200–300 million for Icahn had he been willing to give up equity. Said Icahn, "I don't like giving up equity. I've learned over the years, a dollar bill is a better partner than a partner."

When Icahn found his next target, in any event, he was not hampered by a lack of cash. Drexel was there, ready and willing to back him—in his $8.1 billion tender offer for Phillips Petroleum.

In late December 1984, just weeks after the ACF junk bonds

were sold, T. Boone Pickens, the most sanctimonious of the raiders, who had vowed often that he would never accept greenmail, was greenmailed out of his Phillips stock. Drexel had backed two hostile bids, both unconsummated—Pickens' Mesa Petroleum bid for Gulf Oil, and Saul Steinberg's Reliance bid for Walt Disney. It was eager now for one of its players to pick up the Phillips ball that Pickens had dropped.

Phillips had announced a recapitalization plan in which all shareholders could participate, except that Pickens got cash in exchange for his stock while the rest of the shareholders were offered a package of cash and securities. The buzz on the Street was that the Phillips recapitalization plan was much too low, and that the situation was therefore ripe for another bidder.

"We decided that since a lot of our clients—Ivan Boesky, Irwin Jacobs, Carl Icahn—were rumored to be holding big positions in Phillips stock, we should try to interest someone in doing the transaction," Drexel investment banker John Sorte recalled. "But it had to be someone not wanting greenmail. We'd now used the high-yield weapon twice—in Gulf and then in Disney, where Steinberg took greenmail. And we decided we shouldn't be using this weapon for greenmail. Too much criticism."

Drexel tried to interest companies they thought might be bona fide acquirers of Phillips. Pennzoil (which had recently lost Getty Oil to Texaco) was one. "David Kay thought Pennzoil was a natural," said Sorte, "but I'm not sure they ever returned his phone call. David Kay and others in M&A did lots of cold calls."

In the end, the only interest that Drexel was able to stir was Icahn's. Flush with his ACF war chest, Icahn had begun buying Phillips stock in late December, two days after the company's announcement of its recapitalization plan and its buyout of Pickens. In February 1985 he decided to wage a proxy fight to defeat Phillips' recapitalization plan, which was to be voted on at an annual shareholders' meeting on February 22. He hired another Wall Street firm, Donaldson, Lufkin and Jenrette, Inc., for the proxy solicitation.

The open question was whether Icahn would accompany his proxy fight with a tender offer. In the past he had preferred to combine the two, because used in concert they put far more pressure on the target. But a tender for Phillips would be exponentially greater than any that he—or, for that matter, Drexel—had done before. The junk-bond-financed hostile takeover was so nascent that there was no blueprint.

In Mesa's run at Gulf, before there was any public announcement of an offer, Milken and his troops had obtained commitments for about $2.2 billion from their network of bond buyers. Drexel had circulated not the commitment letters that later became boilerplate, but thick securities-purchase agreements, which were haggled over endlessly by Drexel and the prospective purchasers' lawyers.

Those who were thus solicited became insiders and were prohibited from either trading in Gulf stock or divulging the information. But word did leak out (or some of those solicited bought stock) and the stock price traded up so rapidly that the deal became too expensive for Pickens to make the tender offer. Instead, Drexel had negotiated a $300 million private placement for Mesa with Penn Central, controlled by Carl Lindner, and Pickens had used that to make a far smaller offer—which ultimately sent Gulf into the arms of a white knight, Standard Oil of California.

Now it was clear that, with Phillips, Drexel could not attempt to obtain oral commitments before an announcement and take the risk of a run-up in stock price. Icahn came up with an alternative: to borrow methodology from the establishment. When major corporations launched their hostile takeovers, they did so on the basis of commitment letters for the financing from commercial banks. Drexel, Icahn suggested, should act like those banks and give him a commitment letter.

Sorte and Black thought that Icahn's demand was outrageous. Drexel, they argued, was acting merely as agent for the lenders to Icahn, and if it gave him a commitment letter, the amount would be charged against the firm's capital. In two years, however, this strange notion would be known as "bridge financing" and would be the rage on Wall Street. Investment banks would commit their own capital to a deal, in a "bridge" between the time of the offer and the time it actually had to be funded. By funding time, the investment bank would have placed much if not all of the debt with bond buyers.

Trying to respond to Icahn's demand for a letter of commitment, Black finally ventured, "Why don't we say we're 'highly confident' that we can raise it? It's really different. It hasn't been done before."

"Carl looked at me," Black recalled. "He turned to his lawyer and said, 'What do you think?' His lawyer said, 'Leon's full of shit. It's not legally binding, what good is it?' " Sometime in the early hours of the morning the meeting broke up, with Icahn saying he was no longer interested in doing the tender offer. But the next morning he called Black and said, "You know that 'highly confident' letter you were talking about? . . ."

That was the beginning of Drexel's famed "highly confident"— the pronouncement that would seem, for a time, almost talismanic in its power. One after another, multibillion-dollar tender offers were launched on the power of those two words, uttered by Drexel. It became an article of faith for Milken that once he had said he was "highly confident" that he could raise a given amount of financing for a bid, he would never renege or cut back on the terms, because then, of course, the words would be just words.

(It took some time before Black and his colleagues recognized fully the magic of the "highly confident" letter. In Phillips, they charged Icahn $1 million for it. By the time they launched the Mesa-Unocal raid for Pickens, two months later, they were charging $3.5 million for it—although they changed the words to "firmly believe" because "highly confident" had become too charged a phrase in Congress.)

ICAHN'S BID for Phillips was the first tender offer ever launched without its financing in place, and the first in which no banks were to participate. Icahn was proposing that he acquire Phillips in an $8.1 billion deal that was part cash and part securities. The cash portion, which Drexel had said it was "highly confident" it could raise, was $4.05 billion. And this $4 billion was to be raised from an amalgam of senior notes, senior subordinated notes, and preferred stock—*all placed with Milken's army of buyers*. Thus, Phillips was to be, essentially, a hostile leveraged buyout. Icahn would pay the debt with Phillips' own cash flow.

Icahn formed a dummy partnership, for which Milken would sell junk bonds, ultimately secured by the assets of Phillips. If the transaction went through, Icahn would pay down his mountain of debt—$11 billion, set atop an equity sliver of $800 million—by selling off some assets and utilizing the company's cash flow.

Unlike the friendly leveraged buyouts that Black had structured, in which commercial banks, typically, were the lenders for the senior level of debt and Drexel placed the subordinated debt, with Phillips even the senior level was to be lent by Milken's network. For some time, Milken had been asking his fellows, "Why do we need the commercial banks?" With Phillips, Drexel announced to the world that they did not.

The world, however, was disbelieving. Phillips and its advisers charged in the ensuing litigation that Milken's "highly confident" assertion was nothing but sleight-of-hand. The company ran full-page newspaper ads demanding, "Is Icahn For Real?"

Icahn, meanwhile, had been holding Drexel back from the next step, which was obtaining written commitments from the bond buyers. It was going to cost him, which is why he had been postponing it, but after the taunting ads he gave Drexel the go-ahead. He would have to pay a commitment fee to the subscribers of three eighths of one percent, or $37,500 for each $10 million pledged. In the abortive Mesa-Gulf deal, those who had committed orally to buy the bonds received nothing for their trouble—while Mesa walked away with a net gain of $214 million after taxes. Milken had realized then that his customers would have to be paid to play, in the future.

If Drexel raised these commitments and the deal did not go through, Icahn would have to pay Drexel one eighth of one percent of all the commitments obtained. Drexel had fought hard with Icahn to be paid one percent of the commitments raised, as they had been in Disney. But Disney, Icahn had argued, was a $700 million deal, and this was $4 billion. Instead, he got the one eighth of one percent in return for agreeing to pay Drexel 20 percent of his profits if he sold his stock. This profit-sharing would become boiler-plate in future Drexel-backed raids.

With all these hefty surcharges, therefore, Icahn did not want to raise the entire $4 billion—and with the vote on management's recapitalization plan just a week away, it was unlikely, anyhow, that Milken could raise the $4 billion in time. According to Black, Milken was pressing Icahn to let him raise $2 billion, but Icahn drew the line at $1.5 billion. In forty-eight hours, it was done.

Sorte commented, "Lots of the buyers now were the same ones that we'd lined up one year before in Mesa-Gulf [when they obtained $2.2 billion in oral commitments]. And we kept a lot of our powder dry. For example, we didn't put in the S&Ls, even though we had lots of them. We realized that if we started having lots of S&Ls in hostile deals, we would jeopardize their ability to be in any [because of the growing concern in Congress about junk bonds and thrifts' investments in them]. And a lot of our big buyers weren't there. Executive Life wasn't there. Columbia S&L wasn't there. Carl

Lindner wasn't there. We wanted people to think we were not stretched."

Some of the faithful, of course, were there. Meshulam Riklis (Schenley Industries) came in for $25 million; Nelson Peltz (Triangle Industries), $20 million; David Solomon (Solomon Asset Management), $50 million; and Steve Wynn (Golden Nugget), $40 million. The biggest pieces were taken by the Belzbergs, Charles Knapp and Atlantic Capital.

The Belzbergs, through three of the entities they controlled—First City Properties, First City Financial and Far West Financial Services—weighed in for $287.5 million.

Knapp, through Trafalgar Holdings, signed up for $100 million. Since Milken had not raised that mythical $1 billion for Trafalgar, it seems highly unlikely that Knapp had $100 million to contribute to anything at this point. More likely, this was a way for his Air Fund to earn a commitment fee of $375,000. Two months later, Knapp would commit $15 million to the Peltz and May Triangle–National Can deal—and then back out.

And, finally, Atlantic Capital, which appeared on the list submitted to the SEC under a disguised name, Worldwide Trading Services, came in for $100 million—taking $50 million in preferred stock, which was the biggest chunk of preferred by far.

It seems unlikely that Icahn intended to take the company. One of his advisers recalled the night when Icahn was told that the proxy solicitation was going well and that he might well win the company. "His attitude was, Holy shit! And we sat him down and started to tell him about an oil company. You know, holes in the ground that are called wells. Carl is a very smart man—but he didn't know a helluva lot about the oil business."

In the end, Icahn won his proxy contest. Phillips had instituted a poison pill—the defense mechanism created by takeover lawyer Martin Lipton, which is triggered by a would-be acquirer's buying a certain percentage of the target's stock and gives shareholders such extravagant rights that the company is rendered far less desirable—designed to protect the company from being taken over by Icahn or any other bidder, so the recapitalization plan would seem to have been the shareholders' most attractive option. But in a dramatic display of new shareholder activism, shareholders voted down the recap plan. Then the company sweetened the plan—and Icahn decided to sell his stock and move on. He had invested about $175 million in Phillips stock, mainly with his war-chest money from Drexel's refinancing of ACF. And now his trading profits on the ten-week deal were $52.5 million—more than twice what he had ever made in a deal before.

Icahn did not retreat from the field of battle without a long night of haggling, however. He had declared publicly that he would not take greenmail. But "expenses" were something else. Phillips was prepared to pay him $25 million. Icahn insisted that his expenses were $27 million. One adviser in this deal insisted that even the $25 million was a profit-making, not break-even, deal for Icahn. Hours went by. The other side did not budge.

"In the end he gave in because the Phillips people dug in their heels," said Anthony James, of Donaldson, Lufkin and Jenrette. "The Phillips board had authorized a maximum of $25 million, and they weren't going to meet again. So it was take it or leave it. That's the only way to deal with Carl. You have to cut off your avenues of retreat. Otherwise, he'll just keep nibbling away at you. Carl will fight endlessly for the last million, the last half million. He will fight for the last penny."

While Icahn prides himself, as he so often says, on being "a man of my word," James—who has also been opposite Icahn in deals—counters that Icahn is a man of his word "in a sense. With Carl, the deal's never over till it's over, till you have negotiated every possible last detail. We have corporate clients who, once you've agreed with them on the major piece of a deal, will bend over backwards to be fair, to drive the other ten unnegotiated pieces together so that the deal happens. Carl would take every one of those ten things and use them to negotiate every last advantage."

Icahn, said James, is different from most people who "care about how they appear, and therefore feel certain restrictions on their conduct. Carl is not impeded that way. He is guided only by what is in his economic interest—and so he's been a lot more successful than most."

PHILLIPS WAS Drexel's gala coming-out, the $1.5 billion bash that proclaimed to corporate America and its investment bankers that Drexel had come of age. For Icahn, the feted raider, who heretofore had made his idiosyncratic ascent in measured, self-propelled steps, it was a giant—almost magical—step up.

After Phillips, however, Icahn went his own way. Unlike Peltz, who, once Milken had enthroned him at National Can, made no meaningful move in the M&A world that was not orchestrated by his benefactor, Icahn continued to do what he had always done—choose his targets with Kingsley, move against them on his own. But by mid-1985 Drexel had become so ubiquitous in the M&A world that wherever Icahn turned, Drexel showed up, too.

Sometimes Icahn and Drexel, although independent, seemed to complement each other. For example, in April 1985, Icahn, who had accumulated a 10 percent position in Uniroyal, threatened a takeover; the company's management then took it private in a leveraged buyout—financed by Drexel. And Peltz, with Milken's help, would later acquire the core chemical business of Uniroyal.

But in TWA, Icahn and Drexel found themselves at odds. TWA was a Drexel client, albeit a far more prosaic and less important one than Icahn; Drexel had raised $100 million in financing for the airline in 1984. When TWA executives learned in mid-April that Icahn was accumulating the company's stock, therefore, the first thing they did was seek Drexel's protection, exhorting Fred Joseph to persuade Icahn to retreat. It was in fact Drexel's policy—known as the "Joseph doctrine"—never to assist an aggressor client in depredations against another client, but to go to the defense of the victim.

The necessity for that policy is self-evident, according to Leon Black. Drexel's client list is a roster of raiders. "How could any corporate client open up to us if they thought we would help one of our clients take them over?" Another Drexel executive added that the policy was sometimes phrased more bluntly to prospective clients: "Pay us, become our clients, and we'll protect you."

Adding to the TWA executives' indignation was the fact that their chief financial officer, Robert Peiser, had made a presentation on the airline at the Predators' Ball two weeks earlier. After Peiser's talk, Icahn had introduced himself and engaged him in conversation for about fifteen minutes. "They were casual questions, kind of bantering, but Carl's got a way of asking probing casual questions," Peiser recalled. "And afterwards, a number of people who had been standing around, listening to us, came up to warn me that he was really interested in the cash flow of the company." Now Peiser and others at TWA felt badly used, as though they had been offered on a menu to Drexel's party-goers.

"I *really* tried to dissuade Carl," said Joseph. "I told him that we couldn't support him. Most important, though, I said I didn't think it was a good business for him." Joseph raised a number of disadvantages: "It's capital intensive. It's in the midst of deregulation, so it's a free-for-all, but still regulated enough that you can't do lots of things. There's a history of adversarial labor relations. It's dependent on a volatile commodity—jet fuel. Pricing is a complicated chess game—so if somebody else in the industry makes a mistake, you can get hurt.

"I kept going through this litany," Joseph said, "and Carl kept saying, 'Stop, stop, I'm going to throw up, *stop*.' "

Moreover, from a political standpoint, Joseph thought Icahn's timing could not have been worse. "I told him I'd just been down in Washington, getting screamed at by Senator [Thomas F.] Eagleton." Joseph had recently testified before the Senate Subcommittee on Securities headed by Senator Alfonse D'Amato. The raids on Phillips Petroleum (first by T. Boone Pickens and then by Icahn) and Unocal (by Pickens) had created a backlash, and a lot of anti-takeover legislation was being introduced. A raid which might result in the dismemberment of an airline as symbolic as TWA would add fury to the storm.

Icahn was aware of the trouble in Washington. Just two months earlier—in the midst of his Drexel-backed raid on Phillips Petroleum—he had testified before a House subcommittee. He had lectured the Congressmen on the ineptitude of American corporate management, regaling them with a couple of his usual routines—slightly tempered for this crowd—on his misadventures in a corporate world where, to hear him tell it, he alone had the gumption to declare that the emperor wore no clothes.

Leon Black thought Drexel's warnings just whetted Icahn's appetite. And Drexel was caught in the middle: they had sworn they would not represent the aggressor but were rejected by the victim because they were so close to the aggressor. At the start, the firm acted as intermediary, hosting several meetings between Icahn's and TWA's representatives. Meanwhile, Icahn continued to buy stock. On April 29 he crossed the 5 percent threshold, and when he filed his first 13D with the Securities and Exchange Commission, ten days later, he owned not 8 or 9 percent of TWA's stock, as its management had feared, but 20 percent.

IN THE BEGINNING, the directors, managers and rank-and-file employees of TWA viewed Icahn much as his other targets had—as a pariah. TWA filed the usual battery of lawsuits, seeking an injunction against Icahn's buying any more TWA stock or commencing a tender offer or a proxy fight. The airline petitioned the U.S. Department of Transportation to investigate whether Icahn was fit to run an air carrier. It encouraged the unions to mobilize against Icahn; employees lobbied legislators and wore "Stop Carl Icahn" buttons. TWA solicited help from Congress. And in a congressional hearing in early June, one month after Icahn had surfaced with 20 percent of the company, the president of TWA, C. E. Meyer, Jr., called him "one of the greediest men on earth."

Icahn also testified at that hearing, and he revealed a fine appreciation of his own abilities, a confidence perhaps born of the fact that to this time he had suffered no major loss. Asked by one member of the congressional panel why he had chosen TWA as a target, Icahn responded, "Do you ask Willie Mays why he jumped a certain way for a ball? Or do you ask McEnroe why he holds the racket a certain way?"

In fact Icahn and Kingsley had been lured to the airline in large measure by what they read as its ample cash flow—the raider's lodestone. TWA was basically breaking even, but it had—according to Icahn's calculations—about $200 million in depreciation.

In the Drexel-hosted meetings with Meyer, CFO Robert Peiser and other TWA executives, Icahn had talked a great deal about the airline's cash flow. Meyer had argued that it was unpredictable, because in the crisis-ridden airline business, vulnerable to strikes and to terrorist attacks which halted tourism, it could disappear overnight. Icahn was unimpressed.

But on another point he was persuaded. He had had a tentative plan to partially liquidate the airline (discontinuing domestic routes and selling planes), but in the course of these meetings the TWA officials convinced him that that liquidation plan was not viable.

In an evidentiary hearing before U.S. District Judge John Cannella, Icahn testified to having been so persuaded. "I go by instinct," he said, explaining this sudden sea change in the middle of a deal in which he had reportedly already invested over $100 million. He emphasized that, in fact, he preferred a course that did not require selling off major assets. "I was never in love with liquidating a lot of planes," he testified. ". . . I don't want to get the image of a liquidator."

So the plan changed, but the newly image-conscious Icahn was seemingly undeterred. Judge Cannella found him credible and de-

PAWNS CAPTURE KINGS   173

nied TWA's request for a temporary restraining order against Icahn, which would have stymied him. He continued to accumulate stock. After Cannella's decision, the directors of TWA decided that the company had to be put up for sale. Though Resorts International showed some interest, in the end the only clearly committed white knight was Frank Lorenzo of Texas Air.

FRANK LORENZO, who had started his career as a financial analyst at TWA, had boot-strapped himself into the aviation business by taking over the ailing Texas International Airlines in 1972. He had long harbored an ambition to own TWA. If he added TWA to Continental and New York Air (both owned by Texas Air), the market share of those three carriers would be second only to United Airlines.

Lorenzo was represented by Drexel. TWA had hired Salomon Brothers, not Drexel, because the TWA directors did not trust Drexel. And while Kidder, Peabody had been Texas Air's traditional investment banker, in this transaction—which would be essentially a leveraged buyout, with the financing of about $750 million raised largely from the sale of junk bonds—only Drexel could place the debt.

The Drexel investment banker working for Lorenzo was Leon Black. Black and Icahn had become such good friends during the course of their ACF refinancing negotiations and then the Phillips campaign that, from the start of this transaction, Lorenzo and some TWA advisers were uneasy about the relationship.

One night in mid-June, Icahn, Black and other Lorenzo advisers, and a host of lawyers and investment bankers for TWA held an all-night meeting to structure a three-way peace. Icahn would sell his stock into the Texas Air–TWA merger, making a profit of roughly $79 million, and would also receive an additional package of about $16 million. This was not to be greenmail. Icahn did not want greenmail anymore, but he did want money, so this was a package of "expenses" and other benefits.

Had Lorenzo paid Icahn his price, TWA would have gone down in the annals of corporate raids as a vintage Icahn deal, in which he was a buyer at one price but a seller at another and his advances forced the company to sell to a third bidder. All that would have differentiated this deal from its predecessors would be his profit—at $95 million, his biggest yet.

But because Lorenzo was unwilling to pay Icahn his $16 million greenmail alternative, what should have been the close of the deal became its opening curtain. Lorenzo was not present at that night-long session, and when Black—who had been negotiating with what he and everyone else in that conference room believed was authority from Lorenzo—called him at dawn to say that the deal had been struck, Lorenzo rejected it. Instead of the $16 million, he made a counteroffer to Icahn of $8–9 million, which Icahn refused.

According to former employees of Lorenzo, this is his modus operandi: always to be absent from the negotiating session, so that he is free to say the negotiator had no authority, and then to scrap the deal. For Lorenzo, these former employees say, the moment he sees that a deal in which he is the buyer can be struck at x, that says to him that it could have been done at x minus 3 or x minus 2.

"I argued with Lorenzo. I lost," said Black. "And then *he* lost."

Icahn kept his 35 percent of TWA as the company and Lorenzo proceeded with the deal to have Lorenzo buy the airline—or so they all thought.

"In a vacuum, Lorenzo was right," Black said. "Once he had a merger agreement with TWA, he felt, why should he buy out Carl? Carl didn't know the airline industry. You had to conceive of Carl galvanizing the unions and taking it away. And at that moment no one could have. On the other hand, my feeling was that we weren't talking about a lot of money [the $16 million package]. When you have a 35 percent holder who has proven in the past to be a dangerous adversary, why not take out an insurance policy?"

Of Lorenzo's actions in this deal, Black declared, "If ever defeat was snatched out of the jaws of victory, this was it."

What unfolded over the course of the next two and a half months, at the end of which TWA's board finally voted to accept Icahn's bid and reject Lorenzo's slightly higher one, was a humiliation for Lorenzo and a triumph for Icahn. Lorenzo's poor business judgment was there for all the world to see as he continued to offer higher and higher (though never quite high enough) amounts to buy Icahn out, and as Icahn maneuvered himself into ever more favorable positions. Having refused to spend an extra $16 million to secure the airline, Lorenzo ultimately offered $100 million—to no avail.

And while Lorenzo reneged on a handshake deal and breached

an unwritten agreement, Icahn conducted himself so that he was able to proclaim later that he had been a "man of my word," and everyone in this particular deal, at least, concurred.

Icahn's transformation from hated pariah to a kind of secondary white knight (offering the unions an escape from Lorenzo, after Lorenzo had given TWA an escape from him) was made possible by virtue of one fact. To the unions, Lorenzo was evil incarnate. In 1983 he had sought protection under Chapter 11 for Continental Airlines, abrogated its union contracts and cut wages in half. Then he had proceeded to turn the airline into a money-maker.

Next to Frank Lorenzo, Carl Icahn suddenly looked good. After TWA struck its deal with Lorenzo, and Lorenzo left Icahn free with his 35 percent holding, the unions approached Icahn. TWA's labor costs were dramatically higher than competing airlines', and the TWA management had been readying itself for a strike as its labor contracts came due for negotiation. Now, as they were about to fall into the clutches of Lorenzo, the unions signaled that they would be less intransigent than TWA had feared.

Labor negotiators are known for their stamina in the typically marathon sessions that sometimes seem to exhaust their management adversaries. But, for Icahn—a veteran of hundreds of night-long negotiations who, some have suspected, deliberately prolongs these sessions because he is having such a good time—this situation with the unions was tailor-made. Unlike most managements, which use labor experts to deal with the unions, Icahn dealt with them directly.

Negotiating is probably the thing Icahn does best in life. He brings to it his considerable talents as a poker player, bluffing masterfully, so his opponents never know whether he is going to play or fold. He sketches so many options, and so many variations—or hedgings—on those options, that his adversaries often feel they are lost in a maze. The positions he takes are in such flux that for his adversary to try to challenge or attack them is, as one recalls, like "wrestling with a ghost." And he keeps constant vigil over his own vulnerability. As one individual who has dealt with Icahn says, he is "so paranoid, always looking over his shoulder and behind every door, constantly thinking everyone is screwing him. As a result, Carl gets few surprises."

By early August, Icahn had exploited his talents as a negotiator and the unions' distrust of Lorenzo to reach an agreement with not

only the pilots' union but also the union representing the machinists—a tough, headstrong and volatile group, who were lower paid
than the pilots and thus had less to give away. It amazed TWA
management and their advisers that Icahn had been able to extract
his desired concessions out of the machinists. But there it was: in
return for profit-sharing and stock ownership, Icahn had wrung
concessions from the two unions (though not from the flight attendants)—concessions that would eventually turn the airline from
breaking even to $300 million in profits.

Having made his deal with the unions, Icahn could now top
Lorenzo's bid. Lorenzo, aware that the airline was slipping from his
grasp, raised his bid, and also brought in Martin Siegel of Kidder,
Peabody to advise him. Kidder had been his traditional investment
banking firm, and he had worked with Siegel before. In the last five
years, moreover, the bright, flashily good-looking Siegel had become
one of the stars of the takeover field.

According to two Lorenzo advisers, Lorenzo turned to Siegel as
his distrust of Drexel, particularly of Black, became overwhelming.
He would keep Drexel in the picture as his money-raiser (he had no
choice), but in the ninth inning he was desperate for Drexel-free
advice.

By this time, in the late summer of 1985, it was not easy to
escape the Drexel presence. Unbeknownst to Lorenzo, Siegel had,
since June, been deep in discussions with Fred Joseph about moving
to Drexel. Siegel, of course, was the recruitment "assignment" Joseph had taken after the Cavas Gobhai session three years earlier. It
was only in the last six months, since Drexel entered and transformed the M&A world, that that long-ago goal had become something more than a pipe dream.

Siegel had been in another deal with Drexel recently. In the
Storer Communications buyout, he had represented Kohlberg Kravis
Roberts (KKR), the premier LBO firm. And now he was in TWA. As
Siegel said later, he had watched as his peers at Drexel made five
times what he was making in these deals, and he was not used to
being the margarine spread.

Moreover, in Storer, KKR had beaten out a rival bidder because
Milken could raise $1.466 billion in two days. Black was the Drexel
investment banker on that deal, and he had courted Siegel assiduously. It made Siegel think more seriously about what it would
mean to work for a firm with that kind of muscle.

He was tempted. He knew he could multiply his income if he went to Drexel. His father had gone bankrupt at forty-five, and Siegel believed that this had planted in him a powerful longing for utter financial independence—what he thought of as "fuck you" money. But he was still not sure that the Drexel lucre was worth the taint. Henry Kravis, of Kohlberg Kravis, one of his best friends, had advised him against doing it, for that reason. But he was thinking about it.

In TWA, Siegel was able to do no better for Lorenzo than Black had done. Even though Lorenzo had made a bid higher than Icahn's, once Icahn reached his agreements with the unions he held all the tickets. With those agreements in hand, Icahn could offer TWA labor peace and a financially viable airline. Had the board sided with Lorenzo, on the other hand, they would have had to utilize an anti-takeover maneuver to block Icahn which he would certainly have challenged in court. And if the deal with Lorenzo did survive court challenge, it guaranteed labor havoc. The pilots were promising wildcat strikes, and the machinists let it be known that they might vent their frustration by destroying planes.

So Icahn emerged the unlikely hero. "We got ourselves an airline!" *The New York Times* reported he shouted, donning a pilot's jacket and dancing around his office, when he heard that the TWA board had decided in his favor. The union representatives and their advisers were jubilant, too. Despite the fact that their deal with Icahn prohibited him from giving Lorenzo a standstill (promising to buy no more stock), they had always been fearful that the wily investor was merely toying with them, intent on using their concessions to get a higher price from Lorenzo.

There was certainly an economic rationale for what Icahn had done. Initially, before all the union drama, he had been a willing buyer of the airline at $18 a share, or about $600 million. When Lorenzo offered $23, Icahn had been a seller (except that Lorenzo had balked at the extra $16 million, which had killed the deal). With the $300 million of union concessions in hand, Icahn became a buyer at $24. And he stuck at $24, even though Lorenzo came in at $26, and even though the unions and the TWA advisers begged him to go to $25 in order to make the directors' decision to side with him a little easier. In Icahn's judgment, he didn't have to give that extra dollar, and, true to form, he cut the price to the hair's breadth.

But there was more than economics at work here. By mid-1985,

Icahn was carving out for himself a public image far grander than the one he had had for years as a hard-nosed greenmailer. Some who know him well agree that Icahn's decision to buy TWA was influenced by more than the numbers, which heretofore had been his only touchstone. "Carl got as much of a kick out of being a savior to the unions, a champion of labor, as he did out of owning an airline—maybe more," Black said. "Because it was a nice counterpunch to all the things he'd been being accused of in Washington. He did care about his image. And don't forget, it would have potential, too, for whatever he would want to do in the future."

IN EARLY SEPTEMBER '85, Icahn chose Paine Webber to raise $750 million for his buyout of TWA. Lorenzo, typically, had made a deal for Icahn's purchase of his stock, then unmade it, and then rampaged around for another week or so before finally settling. The explanation offered by both Drexel and Icahn for Icahn's choice of Paine Webber is that in early September Drexel could not obtain a release from Lorenzo, whom they were still representing.

However, one adviser in the deal said that he told Icahn that he thought he could obtain a release from Lorenzo for Drexel, and that Icahn said not to bother. Steiner's opinion was that "Carl chose Paine Webber because they offered to do the deal for a quarter or a half point less than Drexel would have charged." It no doubt suited Icahn too, because it enabled him to be independent of Drexel in a junk-bond financing and have a good excuse for it, so that it would not jeopardize his dealings with Milken.

Joseph Stewart, the Paine Webber investment banker who approached Icahn, thinks he got the deal because he offered to do it for less than Drexel. Robert Peiser, then TWA's chief financial officer, said, "Carl doesn't want to say that he went to Paine Webber because they were cheaper. But he is a great believer in getting service the cheapest he can, and forget the quality."

This was an unusually large junk deal for Paine Webber. But the head of its junk-bond department was David Brown, who had been one of Milken's early hires back in the seventies. In 1984 Brown became the first of Milken's followers who was said to have challenged Milken for a greater share of profits and then to have left with acrimony. At least in theory, Brown knew the Milken network and could distribute to it.

Icahn, of course, is no one's fool. In an apparently unprecedented arrangement—and the terms were to be kept secret—Paine Webber placed $1 million in escrow, to be forfeited if they were unable to do the deal on the agreed-upon terms. The way the deal was structured, the $750 million would enable Icahn to buy out all the shareholders and also take out his investment of about $300 million in TWA stock. In addition to getting all his money out, he planned to take out TWA's computerized reservation system, PARS. It would be given to the Icahn Group as a dividend, and Icahn planned to lease PARS back to TWA for ten years for an amount that would have given Icahn an annual profit of $25 million.

Under this plan, Icahn would have had little more than his pride at risk. He would have recouped his $300 million, he would own the lucrative PARS. And in the worst of all worlds, if the airline went bust, it would be the bondholders, not Icahn, who would lose.

The investment bankers and bond salesmen at Paine Webber wanted to feature Icahn at their road shows. But since Icahn wanted to travel as little as possible, they staged an enormous road show at the Waldorf. In a rare move for an underwriter, Paine Webber paid for prospective buyers to fly in from as far away as California and Japan. According to Joseph Adams, who would later work on the Icahn offering at Drexel, "It was a mistake to feature Icahn—you use the operating guy, that's whom the debtholders want to hear from. And you keep it to relatively small groups. Otherwise, if one person has a valid concern and stands up and voices it, all of a sudden two hundred fifty people who never would have thought of it are worried.

"That wasn't a road show, it was a media event," Adams scoffed. "Icahn at the Waldorf."

Worse, it did not sell. Icahn, apparently carried away by his enthusiasm for PARS, went on at such length about its value that the prospective bond buyers began to wonder why PARS (as well as all Icahn's money) had to come out of the company. In October, Stewart told Icahn that he had placed about $660 million of the $750 million of debt, but in order to place the rest PARS would have to be left in TWA.

Steiner says that Paine Webber asked him to place some of the junk bonds in Europe, and he asked Icahn whether he should. "Carl said, 'They are not going to get the deal done. It is a waste of time. Forget it,' " Steiner recalled.

Now Black returned to the scene, telling Icahn that Milken not only would raise the $750 million with PARS out of the company, but would raise another $500 million war chest, or "blind pool," in the company in which PARS would be placed. Bond buyers who liked the airline could buy its debt; those who were enamored of PARS could buy that company's debt; others could mix the two. The company that would be formed to receive PARS—and the $500 million—would be called Mandrake (as in the magician).

About Paine Webber's failure, Mark Shenkman of Shenkman Capital Management, Inc., one of Milken's early converts to the junk fold, said, "They just didn't have the placement power to do it. David Brown could know the right names and know those people, but you've got to really have their confidence to come in for such a super-high-risk deal. He doesn't have the relationships Mike does. He can't call the Belzbergs, Perelman and the rest and basically call in a chit."

Many in the junk market suggested that Paine Webber's difficulty was exacerbated by Milken's and his crew's bad-mouthing and sabotaging. It was, they say, Milken's public humiliation of his former acolyte, Brown, for having dared to compete. Others had left Milken, but they had generally gone with his assistance to spots where they were, if anything, more useful to him than when they worked for him.

The humiliation was not Paine Webber's only loss. Icahn took the $1 million that the firm had placed in escrow. "They [bankers at Paine Webber] never believed Carl would take the million," said Adams. "When he did, they were just shocked. But Carl said, 'Hey, that was the deal.' " Paine Webber did win its fight to stay in the deal and be listed as a co-manager. But—as was nearly always the case when another firm tried to co-manage a deal with Milken's crew—it was co-manager in name only, and it received a pittance compared to Drexel.

During November and December the numbers at TWA deteriorated rapidly. In November, TWA revised the forecast of its losses for the year from $70 million to $110 million. In early December— the night before Milken was to unleash his sales force to sell this deal—TWA got a reading on its November results, which indicated that losses for the year were going to be $150 million. Milken called off his troops.

Icahn's agreement with TWA gave him two outs: if the airline suffered a "material adverse change" or if he could not arrange financing. Both were available to him. Either he was going to change the terms of his deal, paying less cash and more paper, or he would terminate it and sell his position.

But who would take him out? The only buyer whose interest in TWA appeared undying was Lorenzo. The unions were violently opposed to Icahn's selling out to Lorenzo. One adviser in the deal said Icahn told him that he was dying to sell out to Lorenzo, except that he was afraid the machinists would kidnap his children. Publicly, however, Icahn declared that he felt he had a "moral commitment" to the unions not to sell to Lorenzo.

Then, on December 20, came the terrorist bombings in the airports in Rome and Vienna, which killed several people at TWA ticket counters. Peiser, the TWA chief financial officer, said the bombings "really shook Carl. We had a long conversation about how we could stop the terrorism. We concluded, of course, that we couldn't. It really shook him, that there were these events outside of even *his* control that affected the company. He realized he was not in control of terrorists in Rome.

"He wanted out," Peiser said. "We talked about management's buying him out, and he was interested in that. But we couldn't keep the labor concessions, and we didn't have a lot of time to raise the money. If we could have come up with a proposal to take him out whole, I'm sure he would have taken it then."

Icahn was trapped. His investors too were losing money—he had bought TWA stock at an average price of about $19, and the stock was trading at about $16. He decided to pass up the leveraged buyout. He already had control of the company. He negotiated a new deal with TWA, whereby minority shareholders would have an option to exchange part of their shares for preferred stock. And Drexel said that it would raise $750 million for the deal (with the magical $500 million for Mandrake a thing of the past), but that Icahn could not get more than $100 million of his money out. He decided to leave in the company the $750 million that Drexel was raising. And PARS as well.

An indication of the extent to which Icahn may have felt beholden to Drexel at this point is that he committed $200 million to GAF's bid for Union Carbide, for which Milken was raising $5 billion. Since GAF later dropped its bid, Icahn walked away with a healthy commitment fee. According to Icahn, this is the only Drexel megadeal for which he signed up.

The TWA deal changed one last time when Drexel raised the money, not $750 million but $660 million. The reason Drexel gave for coming up short (in the face of a "highly confident" letter it had given) was that conditions at TWA were so disastrous by early February that many expected the company to go bankrupt.

The list of bondholders submitted to the SEC months later, when the time came for these privately placed bonds to be registered, is not a typical Drexel megadeal list. The most substantial pieces were taken by Fred Carr (adding all his companies together, $72,500,000) and Tom Spiegel (through Liberty Service Corporation, a subsidiary of Columbia S&L, $64,825,000). Ron Perelman, through Revlon, Inc., bought $38,175,000. There were a few other tranches of $30 million and $20 million, but the rest was composed of relatively small purchases. Some buyers came in for as little as $75,000 and quite a few between $100,000 and $500,000. There were executives from Columbia Savings and Loan, a teachers' retirement association, an investment from Middlebury College (one of Milken's protégés, Dort Cameron, is a Middlebury graduate and invests money for the college).

The list *looks* as though it was something of a struggle to create. And that, indeed, was what Icahn told TWA when he announced that Drexel was having so much trouble that they could raise only $660 million, not $750 million, and that therefore he wanted to exercise his option to change the terms one more time. He now wanted to lessen the dividend on the preferred that he was offering to minority shareholders.

Freund, TWA's adviser, called Fred Joseph to ask whether the company was being "jerked around" or whether there really was trouble. "Fred called me back and said we weren't being jerked around," Freund recalled.

A source at Drexel maintained, however, that while raising the $750 million was indeed difficult, it was by no means impossible ("Michael would just have had to make a couple of calls"). But, according to this source, Icahn asked that Drexel claim it was impossible to raise the $750 million, so that he could then have an excuse to change the terms of his deal with TWA. Icahn denies this allegation.

By the time Drexel held its annual Predators' Ball in the first week of April 1986, the TWA financing was completed and the terms of Icahn's acquisition of the airline were, finally, fluid no longer. But events had continued their downward spiral.

Just three weeks earlier, the flight attendants had started a long-threatened strike. While Icahn had prepared for it, training fifteen hundred new hires, the strike had caused enormous disruption and loss of revenue in its first few weeks. The flight attendants were at the Drexel conference, parading with their picket signs around the Beverly Hills Hotel, where so many of the most favored guests, including Icahn, were staying.

On the evening of the first day they took up their post outside Don Engel's famous Bungalow 8, where a cocktail party for the big-hitters was being held, and then followed these guests to Chasen's, the swank Beverly Hills restaurant which hosts a gala dinner at the Predators' Ball each year. By midnight, however, a few of the flight attendants had put aside their signs and joined the Drexel merry-makers at Engel's table in the Polo Lounge. Fred McCarthy, Nelson Peltz's main investment banker at Drexel, remembered, "I said, when we were at Chasen's, 'What a waste of good-looking women, why don't we bring them in here?' "

Icahn was not in the Polo Lounge. He had arrived at the conference earlier in the day, and then came a news broadcast that a terrorist bomb had exploded aboard a TWA flight from Rome to Athens. Icahn turned and headed back to New York. He may well have been remembering his visit to the Predators' Ball one year before. Then, he had had no major company to run. Then, he had had his money in no situation that he could not control. Then, he had been fresh from his Phillips grand slam, where he had played his game and made $52.5 million in ten weeks. And then, he had stopped in at Peiser's presentation.

BY OCTOBER 1986, six months after Icahn had departed hastily from the Predators' Ball, he had subdued—at least for the short term—his demons at TWA. The staggering losses of the first half of the year—$275.6 million—had been stanched. TWA reported third-quarter earnings of $65.2 million, which looked remarkable not only in comparison to the first two quarters, but to the same period one year earlier, when the airline suffered a loss of $13.5 million. (And TWA's operating earnings for 1987, $240 million, would be the best in the airline's history; the second best was $95 million, in 1965.)

There were several factors in the turnaround, and a couple of them—as had been true from the start—were beyond Icahn's control. But now they were going with him instead of against him. Terrorism had subsided; therefore, by the late summer of '86 transatlantic travel was just beginning to return to normal levels. And the price of oil went down, enabling TWA to cut its annual fuel bill by $100 million.

Other factors, however, were Icahn-wrought:

He had taken on the flight attendants, replacing them with newly trained hires, so that while the strike was disruptive the airline was not brought to a halt. The new hires who replaced the veteran workers started at $12,000 a year and abided by tough new work rules. If the flight attendants' union succeeds in its ongoing court battle with Icahn, the airline could be liable for over $400 million in back pay, and it could also be forced to reinstate the former flight attendants. But, for the moment, Icahn was the victor in that contest—and he claimed savings of $120 million a year.

He had negotiated the sale of a half interest in TWA's PARS reservation system to Northwest Airlines, giving the airline an infusion of about $200 million.

And he had negotiated the $242 million acquisition by TWA of Ozark Airlines—an acquisition that the previous management of TWA had been trying, unsuccessfully, to effect for some time. Ozark had been TWA's principal domestic competitor in vying for traffic to and from St. Louis. Now TWA would control over 80 percent of that traffic, giving a large boost to its domestic profitability.

The acquisition of Ozark was an important move to expand and strengthen TWA, but by far the most dramatic results Icahn achieved sprang from his cost-cutting. He had won the early concessions from the pilots and the machinists. He had eliminated layers of bureaucracy at TWA. He had taken on the flight attendants' strike. He had decided not to renew leases for some planes. Thanks to the drop in oil prices and Icahn's talent for chiseling, TWA would see a savings of $600 million for the year.

The praise on Wall Street was not universal. In the view of some analysts, Icahn was running TWA like a classic short-term play—making moves that would translate into quick profits with no long-range perspective. He was not investing in new aircraft, and TWA's fleet was aged. Morale at the company was terrible, with some employees leaving because they were convinced Icahn was only waiting for the opportunity to sell it. Still, TWA was now profitable, making in operating profits about $250,000 a day. It was hard to argue with success.

And with the corner turned at TWA, Icahn emerged in early

October with his most audacious bid since the one he had made for Phillips Petroleum: an $8 billion tender offer for all shares of the mammoth USX, the nation's largest steel producer and a force in the energy business, with about $21 billion in assets. With about $650 million from his usual investor partnerships and TWA (which contributed about one third), Icahn had begun buying USX stock in June and now owned 11.4 percent of the company. And Drexel said it was "highly confident" that it could raise $7 billion.

Icahn's absorption in TWA had not been complete. He had found time and energy in the spring of 1986 to amass a large stake in Viacom International, the broadcasting, cable television and entertainment concern, and to negotiate with that company's management a thinly disguised greenmail package which afforded him and his major investor, Jeffrey Steiner, a profit of about $100 million. But that had been the old greenmailer Icahn, just keeping his hand in, turning a profit.

As a major Drexel player, one of those few with appetites and ambition gigantic enough to be, as Meshulam Riklis had put it, Milken's "monsters," Icahn had been sidelined ever since he took over TWA. For a time, it had seemed that he might be the first of Drexel's kingpins to topple. But he had prevailed, and now he was back with an appetite as insatiable as ever.

Icahn's triumph, of course, was also Drexel's. It meant that they had chosen wisely when they decided to give him a war chest, back in 1984. Nothing Icahn had done, up until that point, proved that Icahn would be able to run a large company. He was running ACF successfully, but that was different.

As Black pointed out, "Carl saw the value in ACF. There were a few things that obfuscated its value to the rest of the public. It had a few nonperforming dogs, which it turned out you could sell for real money. And then there was the railcar-leasing company, which was a gem, a cash cow. So Carl sold off the dogs, and was left with a stable cash cow." Indeed, the takeover of ACF cost Icahn $410 million, but he then raised $400 million by selling off pieces.

"But ACF is not a complicated business," Black said. "Frankly, it was not until TWA that we saw Carl's managerial talents."

With TWA, Icahn became living proof of the raider's catechism that he—and Milken too—had been reciting for years. The fall of '86 was the season of Drexel's triumph, when the business press crowned Milken as the financier of the age, and his raiders as industrialists. Icahn was one of the new celebrities. In October, *Business Week* published his ("I Told You So") essay entitled "What Ails America—And What Should Be Done."

There Icahn delivered a homily. America has lost its edge to foreign competition, in some large measure, because of bad management, he wrote. When America established its economic leadership in the world, its industrial powerhouses had been owned by the Carnegies, the Mellons and the Morgans, to whom managements answered. With the passing of these owners and the dispersion of stock ownership among the public, management answered to no one. It became autocratic and mediocre. It encouraged bureaucracy. But now, declared Icahn—pointing with a flourish to what he had done at ACF and TWA—the manager-owner was back.

In press interviews in which Icahn recently had been challenged about whether he really wanted USX or whether the savvy fast-buck artist was just up to his old tricks, he had pointed to TWA. Skeptics had said the same thing then, he countered, but he did buy TWA, he *had* spent time running it, and the company now was profitable. Now, he told *Business Week*, "I really want USX. Putting it together with TWA—now that is really going to be something. . . . Now if we can turn around a couple of these companies and make them more productive, that will make a statement about what I've been saying. Economic historians will see that I was proven correct."

Among the Drexel-made titans in the fall of 1986, Icahn was the one who most craved stature, the only one who made statements about public policy. Nelson Peltz was interested in expanding his empire and enjoying a life of rarefied luxury. Ronald Perelman was interested in expanding *his* empire and climbing the social ladder. Icahn, clearly, was bent on empire expansion—but he also seemed to be ruminating about posterity. He spoke of writing his autobiography.

He did in fact have more intellectual depth, and a greater range of business talents, than his Drexel-crowned peers. That was why he did not have to genuflect before Milken. The more respect he earned, and the more he publicly articulated the Drexel credo (which was also his own), the more valuable an adjunct (free though he was) he became. Jeffrey Steiner said, "Carl and Mike have a very good relationship. Mike feels, I think, that Carl is different from most Drexel clients—and he is. I don't think that Carl has ever felt as dependent upon Drexel as . . . so many others have."

IN THE OFFICES of Icahn and Company in midtown Manhattan, M. Elliot Schnall was marveling at the fact that after the marathon of TWA his nephew had not even paused for a breather before plunging headlong into USX. Schnall says that he had counseled Icahn, during the TWA takeover battle, to sell out to Lorenzo and take his profits. Sometime during Icahn's travails of the past eight months, he had told Schnall that he wished he had taken that advice. So he had weathered that crisis, only to go into the steel industry! Schnall has invested in nearly every one of Icahn's deals, but when Icahn asked him whether he wanted to join the investment partnership for USX, he declined.

Schnall has done well with Icahn. In 1985, he made over $1 million. But he laments still that he accepted Icahn's suggestion that Icahn buy out his 20 percent interest in the company, back in 1974. He calculates and then recalculates what would have been his. In October 1986, Schnall figured Icahn's net profits at about $300 million and so concluded that $60 million, pretax, would have been his. He and Icahn are close; when Schnall is in Manhattan, mainly in the spring and fall, he comes to Icahn and Company nearly every day. He and Icahn banter about Schnall's fateful error. Schnall laughs, but he has never stopped wondering whether Icahn back in '74 had some sense of the bonanza that was coming—and wanted it all.

Kingsley, whose small warren of an office is shouting distance from Icahn's, has no such lost partnership interests to regret. He has remained an employee all these years, which sometimes bothers him and sometimes does not. He says he has moderate needs, which his salary and occasional bonuses satisfy—like college tuition for his children, a car for his son. He still lives in Forest Hills, Queens, as he did when he first started working for Icahn—though he has moved from an apartment to a comfortable home—and that suits him ("What do I want, to join the jet-setters?" asks Kingsley), although he wouldn't mind having a summer house.

Kingsley's office is a reminder that while he might have made more of a name for himself and more money on Wall Street if he had left Icahn's shadow, at Icahn and Company he has been free to be—himself. Stacks of the *Financial Times*, waiting to be clipped, climb halfway to the ceiling on one side of the room; the window behind Kingsley's desk is nearly obscured by mountains of 10Ks, annual reports, prospectuses; and Kingsley himself is barely discernible behind the cascading piles of papers that rise from his desk. "Mount Everest," remarked a secretary as she tossed a letter onto the top. From beneath his desk, on his visitor's side, papers spill. And there, too, rest unpacked cartons from the peregrinations of Icahn and Company over the past two decades—one from 42 Broadway, one from 25 Broadway.

Out of this strange, unsightly chaos has come what Kingsley says with some pride is the "overwhelming majority" of Icahn's targets. He selects, then he proposes, debates, sometimes is rejected by Icahn. But they have been together for twenty years, and he has a good sense of what will persuade. When Kingsley was arguing for USX, where chairman David Roderick and the steelworkers' union had been at each others' throats, he said, "You know, Carl, you could do again with the unions what you did in TWA." And he is more than Icahn's analyst. Once Icahn is in the midst of a deal, Kingsley is his constant sounding board, really his co-strategist, and they often attend negotiating sessions together.

They are an odd couple, segueing into well-worn routines on cue the way people who have been together for a long time often do. Icahn, who refers to himself as "the Lone Ranger," calls Kingsley "Tonto," and Kingsley obligingly plays the role. A cough from someone in an elevator sends them into a routine of eye-rolling, hypochondriac panic. One longtime friend of the two said, "Carl and Al operate in a kind of mutual hysteria."

Kingsley fans—and there are quite a few in the circle of Icahn investors—suggested that Kingsley is the "phantom" of the operation, the moving finger that picks the right targets, while Icahn is the "front man," with the force of personality and presence to play the game. "Al has always been the perfect foil for Carl," said one. "Carl gets all the money and all the publicity—and Al gets to work at what he loves."

Whatever are the dynamics of the relationship, it has endured. Among those employees who have aspired over the years to play significant roles at Icahn and Company, Kingsley is the sole survivor. One former employee asserts that Icahn has been as ruthless with employees as with the companies he targeted, guided by nothing but his economic benefit. Some employees, therefore, were useful for a time—until they demanded promotions or raises and thus outlived their usefulness. "He is a keen valuer of assets, and that's how he judges people too—how profitable you are to him," said this former staffer. "It's somewhat cold.

"He gets the maximum use out of people, and gives the minimum in return."

Interviewed at his seigneurial estate (purchased from the actress Jennifer O'Neill and named Foxfield, after the Marshall Field raid) in Bedford, New York, Icahn seemed finally to have made the adjustment to wealth. For years after he made millions, he had continued to live as he always had—taking the subway on occasion, eating lunch with Kingsley at a dive called the Dungeon, keeping a spare one-bedroom apartment in Manhattan. But he has finally forsaken the subway and abandoned the dives, and he has purchased a penthouse apartment in the posh Museum Tower, next to the Museum of Modern Art. He has also become philanthropic. He has donated $500,000 to the renovation of Carnegie Hall and funded a center for abused children and the construction of housing for homeless families. In at least one instance, however, an Icahn gift came with strings attached. In 1986 or so, Icahn was discussing making a large donation to his alma mater, Princeton University, but he wanted to become a member of its board of trustees. When his request was rejected, the gift failed to materialize. (By 1988, however, Icahn discussions with Princeton about a possible donation were said by one close to Icahn to be in progress, again.)

Icahn's indulgence in luxury and his forays into philanthropy suggest that his longtime tight-fistedness may be loosening. Certain habits, however, never die. When Icahn, carrying a briefcase, and his uncle, Schnall, carrying an umbrella, go to a restaurant together, Schnall takes Icahn's briefcase so that they don't have to leave more than one tip for the checkroom attendant.

Now he shows a visitor the gardens he has been designing, explaining that it has recently become a hobby. He owns horses with Peter Brant, the polo impresario, in nearby Greenwich, and he has attended the polo matches there. He tells a funny story about having seen Nelson Peltz, his Bedford neighbor, at a polo match. What with Icahn, Peltz and Ivan Boesky, whose mansion is down the road from Icahn's, Bedford (a longtime WASP enclave) is not what it used to be. "I told Nelson," Icahn says of Peltz, "he's Bedford Hills' answer to Beverly Hills."

While Icahn now seems to be enjoying the pleasures and pastimes of the extraordinarily rich, he has no pretensions. He allows, with some self-amusement, that designing elegant gardens is a recent, not a longtime, hobby; and having found himself at those polo matches seems to amuse him, too. His closest friend is Stanley Nortman, who used to have a metals business in Great Neck, Long Island, and now is exploring some way for Icahn and him to get into the movie business. Nortman is a singularly down-to-earth, unaffected individual, who seems closer in style to Bayswater than to Foxfield. And when Icahn's wife, Liba, decided to give a black-tie party at Foxfield for his fiftieth birthday, with a guest list that read like the *Forbes* "Rich List," Icahn insisted that all the employees from Icahn and Company be invited, too—and changed it to optional black tie.

Icahn sets off on his canned diatribe about incompetent management in America. It is for him an oft-repeated spiel about how most of the people running corporate America are former fraternity presidents who got where they are because everybody liked them; about how mediocrity rises naturally to the top because the number-one guy, none too swift, wants someone unthreatening as number two; about how most of these CEOs are aristocrats who live for nothing but the perks of the office.

One of Icahn's favorite lines, now years old, is that whenever he tried to get one of these chief executive officers on the phone, the CEO's secretary would say he was "out of pocket." He always wondered, where do they go when they're "out of pocket"? The only way he could get these guys off the golf course, Icahn would conclude, was by filing a 13D.

Another story, also well worn, concerns his taking over ACF, which had operations in the Midwest and a headquarters staff of 173 in New York. He couldn't figure out what they were doing in New York, so he went to the guys in the Midwest and asked them, How many of these guys in New York do you need to support you? And they said, None—we'd do better without them. But, not to be too hasty, Icahn called in a consultant to analyze the New York operation. Six weeks later the consultant returned with a big black book filled with charts. Icahn said, Don't give me that, just tell me, what do these guys do? And the guy looked at him and he looked at the guy. And then Icahn took out a check and said, Here—I'm paying you no matter what you tell me. Now tell me, what the hell do they do? At which point the consultant said, Mr. Icahn, you've been straight with me, so I'm going to be straight with you. We can't figure out what they do, either. So Icahn closed the New York office.

And Icahn asserts that ACF was well run compared to TWA. At TWA he eventually replaced most of top management. Now he is full of steam. "What I've been saying all these years," declares Icahn, referring to his polemics on the ills of American corporate management, "I never knew how true it was." He listens to his words for a moment, as though hearing them played back, and then laughs at the admission.

These days, Icahn can afford such moments of candor. His most strident critics—who for years derided him as the critic of management who had never managed much of anything—have been stilled by the TWA turnaround. And TWA is news, while the effects of some of the previous forays of this self-proclaimed savior of American business are not. Phillips Petroleum, for example, borrowed $4.5 billion in 1985 to repel Icahn, swelling its debt load to $8.6 billion. The company had to cut $400 million from capital expenses, slash exploration budgets, sell $2 billion in assets and cut its dividends. Its work force fell from 27,000 to 22,000 by the fall of 1986.

Icahn is well aware that he can hold TWA up before his critics like the cross before the vampire, and he does so. He continually trumpets himself as the savior of TWA, insisting that but for his intercession the company would have gone bankrupt.

But the triumph, sweet as it is, is somewhat tinny. "Yeah," he says, "I know, this has stopped the critics. But this was almost easy. I mean, you need entrepreneurial spirit, and you need strength of personality, OK. But after that, it's sort of self-evident what has to be done. I mean, it's almost just common sense. The arbitrage with the options, I think, needed more brainpower."

The measure of success that for Icahn has always been the most compelling is dollars. Friends say that while he has clearly begun to think about his place in history (one said that Icahn sees himself as heir to the merchant-banking tradition of the Rothschilds and Samuel Montagu), his drive for dollars appears unabated. And the two preoccupations are hardly in conflict; the more successful he is as the manager-owner of once-floundering companies, the more money he will make. As one longtime associate said, "For Carl, it's his report card. Every week, every month, every year."

Another friend recounted that he had recently remarked to Icahn, "You know, Carl, before too long you're going to be worth a billion dollars. What will you do, if you're not happy then?"

"And Carl said, 'I will know I made a big mistake,' " his friend recalls. " 'It will mean I picked too low a number.' "

9

Pantry Pride-Revlon:
The Crucial Campaign

IN THE EARLY evening of June 14, 1985, Ronald Perelman appeared at the lavish penthouse apartment of Michel Bergerac. Perelman had just acquired control of Pantry Pride, Inc., a supermarket chain discharged from Chapter 11 bankruptcy reorganization in 1981, which had assets of $407 million and a net worth of about $145 million. Bergerac was the chairman and chief executive officer of Revlon Inc., the cosmetics and health-care giant, which as of December 1984 had over $2.3 billion in assets and net worth in excess of $1 billion. Implausible as it would have been in any era other than this one so dominated by Milken the magician, the small-time, unimpressive Perelman, transfigured by a wave of Milken's wand, had come courting.

The chemistry, however, was all wrong. According to Bergerac, Perelman told him about MacAndrews and Forbes Holdings, the mini-conglomerate he had amassed in the preceding eight years with interests including cigars, chocolates, licorice extract and film-processing. "I'd never heard of it," Bergerac said. Perelman talked enthusiastically about Pantry Pride and its most alluring asset: a huge tax-loss carryforward of over $300 million that could be used to shelter income. The company, which Perelman was in the process of stripping into a corporate shell, was his planned vehicle for acquiring Revlon. He was about to go on a Drexel road show, traveling to cities around the country, making his pitch to junk-bond buyers, in order to raise about $350 million.

"He told me that the dream of his life was to buy Revlon," recalled Bergerac. "I said that that was wonderful, but it was not for sale. He said that he would bid in the low forties. He said that he would do wonderful things for me. I said that I didn't have much taste for being bribed, and goodbye." Perelman had offered "wonderful things"—personal inducements—in addition to assuring Bergerac that all his severance agreements, including his $15 million golden parachute, would be honored, and that he, Perelman, would want Bergerac to stay on as chief executive.

One associate of Bergerac recalls Bergerac remarking angrily, shortly after the Perelman encounter, "Can you imagine this guy, saying he's going to make me a rich man?"

Lawyer Arthur Liman, whose firm, Paul, Weiss, Rifkind, Wharton and Garrison, had been counsel to Revlon for decades, had also worked for Perelman in recent years, and he had arranged this encounter. "Ronald was sensitive to Bergerac's position as the CEO, and he really wanted to please—but he went about it in the worst possible way," Liman said.

Perelman said that he and Bergerac had a "very cordial" meeting, lasting about an hour and a half, and that Bergerac suggested that they make a dinner date to discuss the transaction further. Then, Perelman said, Bergerac canceled the dinner, saying it would be pointless to meet because he was not going to do the deal. Perelman denied that he offered Bergerac extra inducements. "I never even mentioned or hinted or winked about his getting anything."

Associates of both men agree that their personal styles must have blended like oil and water. Bergerac is a courtly, somewhat imperious, urbane, witty Frenchman. Perelman is crude, brusque, humorless, speaks in a staccato manner and perpetually puffs an enormous cigar. "They didn't hit it off," declared Perelman's lawyer and constant cohort, Donald Drapkin, who was at Skadden, Arps, Slate, Meagher and Flom. "Bergerac with his Château Lafite, and Ronnie with his diet Coke.

"And I think that after that meeting Bergerac checked with his friends, and most of them had never heard of Ron Perelman. Or if they had, they said he was young, really aggressive, and Jewish. I think it was just beneath him."

Bergerac had long inhabited the corporate stratosphere. In the 1960s, when Harold Geneen was building International Telephone and Telegraph (ITT) into the world's biggest conglomerate, Bergerac helped negotiate about one hundred acquisitions of companies for ITT in Europe; and in 1971, at the age of thirty-nine,

Bergerac was promoted to the job of running all ITT European operations. During the next three years, he doubled European sales to $5 billion. But in 1974 Bergerac, considered the most likely candidate to follow Geneen as head of ITT, was wooed away by Charles Revson, the legendary founder of Revlon. Revson had courted Bergerac for several years, and when he finally won him Bergerac received what was then an unprecedented bonus: $1.5 million. For a time, the financial press referred to Bergerac as "Catfish," after the Yankees' pitcher Catfish Hunter, who also won a seven-figure contract at that time.

In 1978 Bergerac was the subject of an admiring cover story in *Time* magazine, which noted that the company had survived "triumphantly" the death of its founder, Revson, and that in four years, since Bergerac had taken over, sales and profits had multiplied about two and a half times, twice as fast as the industry average.

In the last several years, however, Bergerac had lost some of his star quality. The company's earnings reached a peak of $192 million in 1980, dropped to $111 million in 1982, and essentially stayed at that level through 1984, though in the first half of 1985—just as Perelman was approaching—they began to rise by about 10 percent. The weakness was in the cosmetics business; when demand slackened in the early 1980s and competition intensified, Revlon lost market share and profits. Meanwhile, however, Bergerac had vastly expanded Revlon's health-care business, making eleven acquisitions and increasing revenues tenfold in the past decade.

With its stock in 1984 trading in the midthirties, considerably below its breakup value, Revlon had attracted the attention of some investors known as the Frates group (after their leader, Joseph Frates, a wealthy Oklahoma investor), who went to Milken to explore financing. According to one member of that group, secret talks were held with Bergerac, who was not opposed to the idea of a buyout in which he would continue to run the company and would own 10–15 percent. Bergerac asked repeatedly whether the financing was in place, and was assured that it was.

But when the group was ready to go public with their proposal and made their formal approach in a meeting at Arthur Liman's office in the spring of 1984, Liman determined—in a call to Milken —that their financing negotiations were in the most preliminary stage. Bergerac, furious, sent them packing with a cursory public denunciation, referring to them as the "gin-rummy gang," saying their only money came from the kitty for their card games in Southampton.

But in the acquisition-happy marketplace of 1984, once the Frates group had made their approach the company was in play. That summer, Alan Clore, the English investor who had climbed on the Icahn bandwagon in Marshall Field, acquired stock. Realizing his vulnerability, Bergerac explored with his investment banker, Peter Jaquith of Lazard Frères, the viability of his leading a management leveraged buyout; but they concluded that the price that would make the deal workable, in the low forties, would not pass muster with the board. And then, for about six months, the rumors quieted, and Bergerac did nothing to pursue his own buyout.

In the spring of 1985, however, Perelman had extended his feelers. Drapkin enlisted the help of Joseph Flom, senior partner of Skadden, Arps. Flom talked to Felix Rohatyn, senior partner of Lazard Frères, about Perelman's interest in Revlon. Rohatyn said later that Flom was talking about a leveraged buyout with management, and that he responded that for Lazard to render a fairness opinion the price would have to be in the midfifties.

Simon Rifkind, founder of Paul, Weiss, and, at eighty-four, a luminary in the bar, dipped his oar into these waters. Rifkind had been on the Revlon board since the late fifties and was executor of the Revson estate; he had also been counsel to the family of Perelman's first wife, Faith Golding Perelman, for generations, and had become a director on the board of MacAndrews and Forbes. Now, just before the June meeting, he spoke to Bergerac on behalf of Perelman, describing him as "a kind of young Larry Tisch."

Arthur Liman, Rifkind's protégé and heir apparent in the Paul, Weiss firm, said Perelman came to have lunch with him and "talked about how Revlon was bound to be sold in any case, and he would do well by the shareholders and well by Bergerac. He said he really needed Michel because he was a wonderful operator and he, Perelman, was not an operating person." Liman also recalled that Flom told him that Perelman had never done a hostile deal—"with the clear implication to me," Liman added, "that he would not."

Perelman felt like a welcome suitor. "The signals we were getting in May and June were all positive," he asserted. "We were hearing back from Felix and Arthur things like 'It [the price] has to start with a five, but it could end with a zero,' and 'We like the music we're hearing.'"

But all this high-powered matchmaking backfired when Bergerac met Perelman in mid-June and the reality of Ronald Perelman and Pantry Pride and Perelman's banker, Drexel, making it all possible via the sale of junk bonds hit home with Bergerac. Bergerac didn't know much about Drexel before Perelman's visit, but he quickly learned. "Michael Milken is very clever," Bergerac declared. "He has done the same thing that Delfim Netto, who was finance minister of Brazil, did there. No one would lend Brazil money, so Delfim Netto said to the bankers, 'What does it cost? I will pay whatever it takes.' Well, Milken realized people would do the same thing—all these people whom the banks would never lend to in a million years, and Milken says, 'Here's a hundred million!' And they say, 'Wonderful!'

"In the old days, people to whom the banks would not lend went to pawnbrokers, who charged an arm and a leg. Now Drexel has inserted itself between the pawnbrokers and the banks."

As Bergerac's comments suggest, Revlon was indeed a class war, between the corporate America and Wall Street elite, and the Drexel arrivistes. It was not simply a turf battle, to be sure; most of the defenders of Revlon in this fight genuinely deplored the junk-bond depredations as financial free-for-alls hurtling toward disaster, and they believed, moreover, that these high-risk players were violating the law to achieve their goals. But beneath these complaints of principle lay something more visceral: the age-old hatred for the outsider, always exacerbated when that undesirable other dares to venture beyond his confines and encroach upon the elite's preserve.

Certainly those in Perelman's camp perceived the violent opposition they encountered as generated by class bias. Howard Gittis, a well-connected Philadelphia lawyer who left his law firm to join Perelman shortly before the Revlon battle, recalled Perelman's early overtures. "At the beginning, we really believed that we would be able to do it friendly. There was a lot of suggestion that, especially with his huge parachute in place, this was a chief executive who would not kick and scream. But I'm convinced that Bergerac's was a noneconomic, emotional reaction. He didn't want Revlon to be sold to Panty Pride, as he called it, and then Marty [Lipton, of the law firm of Wachtell, Lipton, Rosen and Katz] and Felix [Rohatyn] fanned that feeling of Bergerac's. Their attitude was, Who are these people, coming in to buy a company like Revlon—they're upstarts that nobody ever heard of, and they're financed by Drexel, an upstart itself."

• •

"PERELMAN IS one of the great stories of coming from nowhere in the last decade," commented one of his associates admiringly in early 1986. "Seven or eight years ago, when I met him, he didn't even have a business. Today he's worth maybe five hundred million."

Indeed, Perelman's life story reads like a parable of these leveraged times. He grew up in comfortable circumstances in Philadelphia, where his father, Raymond Perelman, owned a small metal-fabricating firm, Belmont Industries. Ronald Perelman graduated from the University of Pennsylvania and then from the Wharton School, receiving an M.B.A. in 1966.

His marriage to Faith Golding—whose grandfather had founded the Sterling National Bank and the Essex House hotel in New York and had amassed a fortune—obviously pleased Perelman's parents. (In an interview in 1986, several years after Ronald Perelman had divorced Golding and married gossip columnist Claudia Cohen, Raymond Perelman ticked off the real-estate holdings of the Golding family and pointed out on the baby-grand piano the numerous photographs of Faith—including her bridal photo—noting rather acidly, "*He's* divorced, we're not.")

For the next twelve years, Perelman worked in his father's business and managed his wife's money. Then, in 1978, at age thirty-five, he decided to venture out. He borrowed $1.9 million to buy 34 percent of Cohen-Hatfield Industries, a jewelry distributor and retailer with $49 million in revenues that year. In 1980, Cohen-Hatfield spent about $45 million to buy MacAndrews and Forbes, a maker of chocolates and licorice extracts, and the Cohen-Hatfield name was dropped in favor of MacAndrews. In the fall of 1980, MacAndrews issued its first batch of junk bonds, a modest $33 million, underwritten by Drexel with Bear, Stearns.

Over the next four and a half years, Perelman set out on a wholly leveraged, though relatively small-time, acquisition trail. He tried and failed to acquire the Richardson Company and the Milton Bradley toy and game company, but he made money in both transactions. He succeeded in buying, for a total of about $360 million, Technicolor, Inc., the film processor; Video Corporation of America, a major manufacturer of home videocassettes; the film-processing assets of Movie Labs; Consolidated Cigar; and a controlling interest in Pantry Pride.

Roughly $140 million of this money came from Drexel junk-bond offerings, the rest from banks—and all built on that original (borrowed) $1.9 million, back in 1978. Perelman chose companies that were strong cash-flow generators and that had problem assets that could be sold off—quickly paying down much of the high-interest debt—leaving the pared-down, profitable core business.

BEFORE REVLON, Perelman's greatest acquisition success story was Technicolor, the film-processing company which he bought in early 1983 for about $105 million (and an additional $20 million of assumed debt). Technicolor was a dominant force in the film-processing industry, but it had made an unsuccessful diversification effort into a chain of one-hour photo-processing stores. Its stock had plummeted from $28 per share in the second quarter of 1981 to $8–10 per share in the second quarter of 1982. Perelman's price, $23 per share, looked rich. He sold off the processing stores and four other divisions for about $30 million (plus notes, receivables and warrants with a value of more than $20 million), as well as some of its California real estate for about $6.4 million, reducing his debt substantially.

In 1983, Technicolor's earnings skyrocketed, and within two years the company had paid for itself. Declares Drapkin, Perelman's close friend and adviser, "Technicolor was the classic Perelman transaction. He paid full price for the company, seeing values no one else saw, sold off pieces and put money back into the core business, and earnings have gone up dramatically."

But if allegations in a suit filed in the Delaware Chancery Court against Perelman, Technicolor, its previous directors and Mac-Andrews and Forbes are found to have merit, Perelman may yet have to pay substantial damages and his greatest success story pre-Revlon will have a rather smarmy postscript. The complaint, filed by Cinerama, which was a stockholder of Technicolor, started out as an appraisal action (claiming that Perelman had not paid a fair price for Technicolor) and then—because of facts learned in discovery—was amended in January 1986 to include claims of fraud and breach of fiduciary duty.

According to the complaint, in September 1982 a banker from Bear, Stearns asked Fred Sullivan, the early Icahn investor and a Technicolor director, to meet with Perelman to discuss Technicolor. Sullivan agreed; a meeting was scheduled in one week's time; and before the meeting Sullivan purchased one thousand shares of Technicolor stock at about $9.50 a share. (As a result of a subsequent insider-trading investigation by the SEC, Sullivan agreed to disgorge all profits made by that stock purchase.)

Sullivan then met with Perelman and became his ombudsman. He arranged for Perelman to meet the Technicolor chairman, Morton Kamerman, and, it is alleged, was the only Technicolor director from whom Kamerman sought advice. The complaint also alleges that Sullivan was retained by Perelman to lobby for the transaction, in return for a fee of $150,000. None of the other directors, it is alleged, knew that Sullivan, who was voting for the transaction, was retained to do so.

The complaint alleges that Perelman sweetened the deal for Technicolor's chairman, Kamerman, by granting an enhancement of his employment contract and a structure for the transaction which would allow Kamerman to receive the best tax treatment for the sale of certain option shares of Technicolor he owned. It further alleges that these sweeteners were negotiated, and the price of $22–23 per share was agreed on, before Kamerman consulted with any disinterested member of the board or with Goldman, Sachs, which later rendered the fairness opinion. Kamerman, however, testified that he did not solicit Perelman's approval of the amendment which was passed by the board.

Furthermore, the complaint charges that a director named Arthur Ryan, who was then president and chief operating officer and has since become chairman of Technicolor, was induced to vote for the transaction by the private promise—told to no other director— that if he did so he would be granted the opportunity to run the company. Ryan, a former Paramount Pictures Corporation executive who had a bitter running feud with Kamerman, it is alleged, was being kept apprised of the deal's progress by Martin Davis, then a senior executive of Gulf + Western who would later become its chairman. Davis is a friend of Perelman and had been Ryan's boss at Paramount, a division of Gulf + Western. Davis allegedly told Perelman that Ryan would be crucial to the company's success, and then relayed the message to Ryan that, under Perelman's aegis, he would manage the company. Within little more than a month after the transaction, Perelman terminated Kamerman and—as he had allegedly promised—made Ryan chairman. Both Perelman and Ryan have denied in depositions that any promises were made.

Taken as a whole, the complaint paints a picture in which

Perelman allegedly used deceit and secret deals—money here, position there, whatever it took—to buy off the necessary people and get the company.

In early 1983, with Technicolor under his belt, Perelman began to move to take MacAndrews and Forbes private. According to close associates, he was influenced by two factors.

The first was that his marriage to Faith Golding was ending in what he knew would be a very messy, publicized divorce, and he did not want the added glare of a public company's spotlight upon him. Perelman had had an affair, as his wife's detectives had been able to document. Moreover, his wife would allege, as part of her divorce action, that he had misused money that came from her family, and she would claim in a filing with the SEC that she owned part of her husband's claimed one-third interest in MacAndrews.

In his divorce, Perelman was represented by his longtime friend Roy Cohn. Cohn told *The Wall Street Journal* that the Perelman divorce-settlement talks almost broke down at the last minute because Perelman disputed one eighth of a percentage point of interest that he was to pay his ex-wife. But the action was settled in 1983, with terms that included Perelman's paying Golding $3.8 million in cash.

The other reason Perelman wanted to take MacAndrews and Forbes private, one associate said, was that he wanted "to do some things which might be criticized in a public company—have his own plane, have his artwork in his office. He wanted to have [MacAndrews and Forbes] as his nest egg—and then he wanted to acquire some other public company, for presenting his face to the financial world."

In March 1984 Perelman took the company private, with Drexel raising the $95 million that the deal required. Then, the next fall, he became enamored of the huge tax-loss carryforward, or net operating loss, in Pantry Pride. He reasoned that this NOL not only could be put to good use in sheltering the income of any company he might acquire, but would give him a substantial advantage in a bidding war. Postbankrupt situations, moreover, were a specialty of Milken, who had made much of his fortune analyzing the securities of bankrupt companies. And by this time, in the fall of 1984, Perelman was being positioned as one of the Drexel players, along with Icahn and Peltz and William Farley, all of them being provided their war chests.

Drexel investment banker Paul Abecassis, who started working on Perelman financings in the early eighties, said Perelman was a logical choice. "Ronnie in his own little way was already doing it. He was acquisition-oriented, using leverage to go after companies and then using the cash flow to pay down the debt. Also, his personality was right—he was extremely ambitious, willing to take risks. It was a natural."

There were obstacles, however, between Perelman and Pantry Pride. The idea had been brought to Perelman in late '84 by Patrick Rooney, a co-founder of the brokerage house of Rooney, Pace Group Inc. (since closed down), which specialized in initial public offerings of small, risky companies—and which had one of the worst reputations on Wall Street. It also had a close relationship with Drexel.

In the summer of 1984 Rooney, Pace had done a $25 million junk-bond offering, at an interest rate of nearly 18 percent, which according to the prospectus was underwritten by Rooney, Pace but which in fact was placed by Milken. One associate of Patrick Rooney said that Milken thus extended himself because "the plan was to have Rooney, Pace pick up the smaller or riskier junk business." A buyer of the Rooney, Pace paper also confirmed that it was sold by Milken.

In late '84, Rooney was about to wage a proxy fight for Pantry Pride. According to one insider, Perelman did not want to join Rooney in that fight for fear that he would be tarred by the Rooney, Pace brush. According to another associate, Perelman also felt that —given the allegations made by his former wife during their divorce —he would suffer in the mudslinging of a proxy contest. And his final problem with joining Rooney was that Drexel was representing Pantry Pride.

"We made Ronnie sit on the sidelines, because we didn't want one client going after another," said investment banker Stephen Weinroth of Drexel (describing the policy that would be invoked less than six months later when Icahn went after TWA).

In Perelman's stead, Philadelphia lawyer Howard Gittis joined the Rooney team (though Gittis claims he was acting independently). Perelman continued to hold a large block of stock. Then, when Gittis and Rooney lost the proxy vote in early 1985, Perelman stepped in. And with the advent of Perelman, Grant Gentry, the chairman of Pantry Pride, who had fought bitterly during the proxy fight, became malleable.

With Drexel representing both sides in the negotiations, MacAndrews and Forbes acquired control of 37.6 percent of Pantry Pride, for $60 million. And Gentry received a payment—some of which was structured to be paid out over his lifetime—of about $3 million with additional payments of $150,000 for the rest of his life, in lieu of a pension.

Now, having had his way with Technicolor and with Pantry Pride, Perelman moved on to Revlon.

IN THE junk-bond-takeover war, which began in earnest in early 1985 with Icahn's raid on Phillips, Revlon was the crucial campaign. That was where the most impassioned corporate defenders were united against Milken's onslaught; where they unloaded everything in the takeover defense arsenal; and where they fought down to the wire, committed to evading Perelman at all costs to the very last moment. What they lost sight of—particularly as Perelman, by the good grace of Milken, kept upping his all-cash bid—was that Perelman's money was as good for the shareholders as anyone else's. In the end, they sought so desperately to escape his clutches that they undid themselves.

To Bergerac and his advisers, and to the rest of the corporate establishment that watched with fear and trembling, the fight for Revlon was a rude introduction to a new world. All the brainpower, clout and class connections that Revlon summoned were no match for the raw financial might of Drexel. Michael Milken had become the great equalizer.

At the outset, it seemed to Revlon's advisers, and to much of Wall Street, preposterous that Pantry Pride would prevail. For all the furor in Congress over Drexel and its junk-bond-financed take-overs, the facts were that by mid-1985 few had succeeded. In the most highly visible and emotion-charged bids—Icahn's for Phillips and Pickens' for Unocal—the companies had fended off the raiders. Triangle's bid for National Can had succeeded, but that had not exactly started out hostile (National Can was in the midst of trying to do its own LBO, and its directors had said they would consider any higher price by another bidder).

Before Perelman made his bid for Revlon in August 1985, the single instance of a Drexel-backed deal that had started hostile and gone to completion was Coastal Corporation's takeover of American Natural Resources Company (ANR), which had turned friendly after two weeks' bitter struggle in April 1985. And ANR, an Oklahoma pipeline-manufacturing company, was not Revlon. As one Pantry Pride strategist recalled, "The attitude on the Street was, How could a major institution like Revlon be taken over by someone like this, a complete unknown—someone who'd made his wealth in cigars and licorice, not to mention with his wife's money?"

Dennis Levine, the Drexel investment banker who represented Pantry Pride in the Revlon battle, recalled Martin Lipton's attitude when the fight was just about to begin, in mid-August. Levine was in Lipton's office at Wachtell, Lipton on another matter. Lipton had just been retained to represent Revlon, and Levine had mentioned that he would be advising Pantry Pride. " 'Don't waste your time,' Marty said. 'Pantry Pride will *never* get Revlon.' "

Lipton brought more than the usual defense lawyer's fervor to this deal. Over the course of the preceding year, Lipton—who had built his firm and his wealth on a takeover practice—had emerged as one of the most outspoken and vehement enemies of what he called the "two-tiered, bust-up junk-bond takeover." "Two-tiered" referred to the fact that bids had featured a front end which paid cash to tendering shareholders and a back end which paid debt securities, thus pressuring shareholders to tender speedily so as not to be left in the second group. But now that Milken appeared able to raise almost any sum of money through the sale of junk bonds, Drexel had moved to the all-cash bid—which would be much harder to defeat in court. "Bust-up" referred to the plan, in most of these deals, to pay down the debt by selling off pieces—if not the entirety—of the company.

During the course of the Revlon battle, Lipton would be moved to new heights, firing off to his corporate clients a memo entitled "Rape and Pillage in the Corporate Takeover Jungle": "This year has witnessed the demise of the few remaining restraints on corporate raiders. They have been let loose to take over and bust up American corporations at will. . . ."

Lipton was drawing a line between the kinds of hostile takeovers he had helped to engineer in the seventies and the Drexel-type wave launched by what he called "takeover entrepreneurs." He drew this distinction in testimony before Congress in the spring of 1985, when about thirty bills to curb hostile takeovers or junk bonds or both were being debated.

Soundly financed acquisitions by successful operating companies seeking to diversify or expand have been an integral part of this country's economic development, and they should not be restricted, Lipton testified. But the bust-up takeovers by takeover entrepreneurs move assets into hands that profit by reducing expenditures for research and development and capital improvements—while a very high percentage of the revenues produced by the acquired assets are diverted to paying the debt incurred by their acquisition. The result is enormous profits for the takeover entrepreneur in the short term—and badly weakened companies, both financially and operationally, in the longer term.

"What we face today," Lipton warned, "is not different in substance from what happened in 1928 and 1929." Privately, Lipton expressed another concern, one shared by many of the businessmen and lawyers who were part of the Jewish establishment in New York, and by some of the Drexel contingent as well. They feared that the common strain among these nouveau entrepreneurs and their nouveau bankers at Drexel—an overwhelming majority were Jews—would unleash a backlash of virulent anti-Semitism. Lipton and other corporate defenders had already felt its undercurrent in the executive suites of the Fortune 500 corporations that had come under Milken's gun. Should the kind of economic disaster that Lipton and others were prophesying take place, they feared that Jews would be scapegoated.

As one Drexel client who shared Lipton's concern put it, "It used to be that the Jews would go into Manny Hanny, or Morgan Guaranty, and they'd beg for money, and they'd be rejected, while the Gentiles would come in and they'd all go to lunch and smoke cigars. Now it's a shift of power to the Jews. Drexel is making these huge sums of money, and the banks comparatively little. The problem is, all the entrepreneurs are Jews with the exception of Pickens and Lindner—and Lindner, a longtime supporter of Israel, is the most Jewish non-Jew I've ever known."

Lipton had been practicing what he was preaching on the public podium. He had refused business from takeover raiders, including former client Sir James Goldsmith. More significantly, he had turned down Fred Joseph's repeated offers to split Drexel's legal work three ways: among its longtime firm, Cahill, Gordon and Reindel; Skadden, Arps; and Wachtell, Lipton.

In fact Lipton had represented Drexel in one vital matter in the spring of 1984, but that was before Milken's takeover machine had really gotten into gear (Milken's only effort, at that point, had been

Mesa-Gulf). Lipton had been invited to speak on a panel at the 1984 Drexel High Yield Bond Conference. While he was there, Drexel executives learned of a planned coup d'état by their 35 percent shareholder, Groupe Bruxelles Lambert S.A. GBL was unhappy, among other things, about the fact that Drexel was reaping so many millions but paying no dividends on its stock.

Lipton organized a defensive maneuver whereby the rest of Drexel shareholders voted to change the firm's charter in such a way as to hamstring their Belgian partners. In the end, a compromise was reached. GBL got its desired dividend in return for lowering its holdings from 35 percent to 28.5 percent. They exchanged common shares for preferred. Since they did that, the value of the common had skyrocketed.

That was the only time Lipton had agreed to represent Drexel. How Lipton had gone from hired gun, who with his friend and rival Joe Flom virtually had created the takeover business in the seventies, to crusader—even turning down business in the name of his cause—bemused many who knew him. Some questioned whether the impassioned polemics sprang at least in part from a shrewd business judgment, to curry greater favor with his beleaguered corporate defense clients and thereby enlarge his franchise—something which Goldman, Sachs had done in the early seventies, when it announced it would not represent aggressors in a hostile deal. Or it may be that Lipton, like certain regents of the takeover world, felt proprietary about it, responsible for it—and abhorred the ways in which the newcomers, Drexel's parvenus, were changing it.

Another outspoken and high-powered foe of the junk-bond takeover by the spring of 1985 was Lazard's Felix Rohatyn, who was now brought in to represent Revlon. Like Lipton, Rohatyn had testified before Congress, and, like Lipton, he had sought to differentiate between those hostile takeovers which were "fair" and "soundly financed" (in which he as adviser, like Lipton, had made much of his money) and the current junk-bond variety.

The risk in financing these megadeals with junk paper is twofold, Rohatyn had testified. First, the paper is not secure; in order to service the high rate of interest, companies have to either improve operating performance significantly or—what is much more often the case—make asset divestitures, which may not be desirable. Rohatyn remarked, "It is an approach that also completely fails to take into account the fact that a large corporation is an

entity with responsibilities to employees, customers and communi-
ties, which cannot always be torn apart like an Erector set." The
second risk, he had continued, lies in the illiquidity of the paper,
since in most cases it is issued not as registered public securities but
as a private placement, ultimately making its way through private
transactions into financial institutions such as savings banks, insurance companies and pension funds. These institutions—many of
them under considerable financial pressure—end up holding securities for which no large-scale liquid, public market exists.

On the issue of fairness, Rohatyn had pointed to the market
speculation that seemed to go hand in hand with these raids, as
arbitrageurs often bid up the price of a stock before any public
announcement of a bid, making it appear an insiders' game. Public
confidence in the capital markets, he had averred, is thus destroyed.
He had pointed out that arbitrageurs manage enormous pools of
money, some of them financed by junk bonds. Raiders also have
huge pools, similarly financed. This creates a "symbiotic set of relationships . . . with the appearance, if not the reality, of professional traders with inside information, in collaboration with
raiders, deliberately driving companies to merge or liquidate."

Also on the Revlon team—though not publicly committed to
repelling the junk-bond invaders—was Arthur Liman, one of the
best-known securities litigators in the country. His firm, Paul,
Weiss, had a conflict of interest, as it had been counsel to both
Perelman and Revlon. Liman decided that it would nonetheless be
appropriate for him to work on the corporate defense for Revlon
(one of the firm's largest clients for over twenty years), but not on
its litigation. Liman brought in Wachtell, Lipton to head the litigation.

Capping the Revlon lineup was Simon Rifkind, a former federal
judge and Liman's senior partner. He was a crucial player. He was
a very influential director on the Revlon board, and the Revlon
lawyers were able to wave his mantle before the court. When Perelman made his hostile tender offer, Rifkind, distressed at having
vouched for Perelman to Bergerac and encouraged their initial
meeting, resigned from the MacAndrews board and remained on
Revlon's.

A day or two before Perelman made his offer, he had asked to
meet with Rifkind. "The judge tried hard to dissuade him," said
Liman, who attended the meeting. "He told him there were greener

pastures elsewhere; he said that Ronald would never be perceived the same again after mounting a hostile raid. He said he wouldn't be following the path of Larry Tisch. But he didn't ask Ronald, for his sake, not to do it.

"As for Ronald," Liman continues, "he obviously cared a lot about what the judge thought of him. He wanted the benediction of Abraham."

The only *éminence gris* that Perelman had in his corner was Joe Flom, a senior partner of Skadden, Arps, who had expanded it from its core takeover business to become a full-service firm and a national powerhouse. Flom is a consummate strategist. Here he played his most significant role at the beginning and at the end. The day-to-day handling of the deal he turned over to Donald Drapkin, the then thirty-seven-year-old Skadden partner who had vaulted over many of his more senior colleagues to become Flom's protégé. He had become Perelman's close friend and lawyer three years earlier during Perelman's failed attempt to acquire Richardson.

In line with the Drexel tenet that people work best when they have an ownership stake, Perelman had made Drapkin a principal in this deal. In June '85, the board of Pantry Pride had loaned Drapkin money to buy Pantry Pride convertible debentures. For a lawyer to become a principal in a deal with a client was a first at Skadden and a practice not followed at any other major New York law firm. It enraged some of Drapkin's partners, but it was a measure of his new clout.

From Drexel, Perelman's senior investment banker was Dennis Levine, a rising star in the firm's corporate-finance department, recently arrived from Shearson Lehman Brothers. Since coming to Drexel, Levine had worked on Phillips, Coastal and Crown Zellerbach Corporation deals.

Perelman also had his longtime sidekick, Donald Engel, who had first brought Perelman to Drexel. Engel had been a Drexel managing director until he resigned in 1984 to become a consultant—but he continued to be involved in Drexel deals and continued to be Milken's trusted aide for entertainment at the Predators' Ball. After his resignation, Engel moved his office into the top floor of the opulent town house owned by MacAndrews and Forbes in which Perelman lived and worked, on East Sixty-third Street in Manhattan.

Finally, and surprisingly, Perelman had on his team Eric

Gleacher, head of mergers and acquisitions at Morgan Stanley, most white-shoe of all Wall Street investment-banking firms. Gleacher had moved to Morgan from Lehman Brothers about a year earlier. He was familiar with Revlon from his days at Lehman, where Revlon was a client; and, according to Perelman, the idea of acquiring Revlon was brought to him by Gleacher, in February 1985. Gleacher, moreover, is said to have mounted a vigorous campaign, against heated opposition from partners in his firm, for their representing Pantry Pride. He is said to have won only on the conditions that Morgan Stanley not be listed as "dealer manager" on the tender offer (which Drexel badly wanted them to do, so as to lend their credibility and also share the heat) and assume a distinctly secondary role to Drexel's—something Rohatyn refers to as "Morgan's back-street arrangement."

Gleacher's partners may have looked askance at representing Perelman's Pantry Pride against a company as august as Revlon, but they had been increasingly tantalized, of late, by the fees in the junk market. In fact, since the fall of 1984 the venerable Morgan Stanley—along with many other investment banking firms on the Street—had been struggling to break Drexel's stranglehold on the junk market. By mid-1985, however, Morgan's record was an embarrassment. One of its inaugural junk underwritings, a $25 million issue for a Houston oil and natural-gas company, Oxoco—a deal which Drexel had declined to underwrite—went into default after about six months. According to *Forbes*, the biggest loser on that deal was Morgan Stanley, which, when it couldn't sell the $25 million offering, took $18.2 million itself (and, after default, with the bonds worth about 35 percent of face value, suffered a loss of over $10 million). Drexel came to the rescue with one of its famed 3(a)9s.

It was one thing to try to break into a market, however déclassé that market was. But it was quite another to join Drexel in one of its most daring assaults on the corporate establishment, and to assume a subordinate role. That Morgan Stanley would play handmaiden to this renegade firm was shocking to the rest of Wall Street and a measure of just how much of a force Drexel had become. William Loomis, a general partner at Lazard Frères, who worked on this deal with Rohatyn, said, "Three things made this deal a departure for Morgan Stanley: that they acted jointly with Drexel; that they acted secondarily to any other investment bank, let alone

Drexel; and that they would go out and attempt to sell things [that their client] didn't own—that is *really* un–Morgan Stanley."

Morgan Stanley was in charge of divestitures in this deal. And the divestitures, of course, were what made it all possible. Perelman's plan, at least at the start, was to do here what he had done on a much smaller scale in his earlier acquisitions, with Technicolor perhaps the best example: acquire the company with virtually all debt and then sell off the pieces he didn't want, using the proceeds from their sales to pay down the debt and getting the remaining business virtually for free.

Perelman made this plan explicit in his tender-offer document, stating that Pantry Pride believed it might be able to realize up to $1.9 billion—the total of his offer, at the starting $47.50 per-share price—from the sale of substantially all the assets of Revlon, excepting the beauty business. And it was, obviously, necessary to firm up these divestiture prices as much as possible, for Perelman— and, more to the point, Drexel—to know just how much they could afford to bid.

One of Revlon's first defensive moves was to try to shame Morgan Stanley out of the deal. "Marty Lipton called them up and said, 'How can you guys be getting in bed with Drexel?' " claimed Dennis Levine.

Bergerac called Robert Greenhill, a managing director of Morgan Stanley, with whom he had gone hunting on big-game safaris. "I said, 'Bob, what are you doing with these clowns?' There was silence. And then I said, 'I understand you are out getting prices for pieces of Revlon, selling a company you don't even own. You know, horse thieves used to be hanged.' " None of these calls to honor met with any success.

The other defector from the corporate establishment, which Revlon executives and advisers also lobbied unavailingly, was Chemical Bank. It had made a commitment to provide approximately $500 million of what was then (at $47.50 a share) a $1.95 billion offer, on a well-secured, "last-in, first-out" basis. Unlike Citibank and Bankers Trust, which were known for their willingness to lend to hostile deals, Chemical had rarely done so, and never for a junk-bond, bust-up raid. Also, its policy was to refuse to lend to a hostile acquirer of a client. Chemical had loaned to some Revlon companies in Europe.

Rohatyn, who says he was "amazed" at Chemical's participation, called Michael Blumenthal, then chairman of the Burroughs Corporation and a director of Chemical; Bergerac called Walter Shipley, Chemical's chairman. Rohatyn recalled, "A number of Chemical directors—Andy Sigler of Business Roundtable probably the most vociferous—were very unhappy about the policy issue. But once the chief executive officer had made a decision, it was difficult to override—and there would have been legal liabilities. But there was lots of turmoil."

"Revlon made some headway in persuading them to back out," added Andrew Brownstein, a partner at Wachtell, Lipton who worked closely with Lipton on this deal, "but the odds were long. Had the bank backed out, we believed it would have been a serious blow to them [Pantry Pride]—first, because Drexel charges more for the money they lend than the bank would, and, second, because it lent credibility for Drexel's investors, to be able to say that a bank was getting up one quarter of the money."

After threatening suit (and even sending to bank officials a draft of the complaint), Revlon finally did sue Chemical, along with Pantry Pride and MacAndrews and Forbes, in federal district court in Delaware, about one week after Perelman had announced his intention to launch a hostile tender at $47.50 per share, on August 19. Not named in the Revlon suit was Drexel—a decision Lipton made because of his prior representation of Drexel in its internecine battle with its Belgian shareholders in 1984.

The Revlon suit marked one of the rare instances in a hostile deal in which a bank was joined as a defendant. Revlon charged, first, that Chemical was a "bidder" for Revlon and had failed to make the disclosures required of one, and, second, that the bank was in violation of the margin rules—rules set by the Federal Reserve which govern loans made on stock purchases.

The claims of margin violation, made against both Chemical Bank and Pantry Pride, were "potential show-stoppers," said Michael Mitchell, a Skadden, Arps partner who was one of the litigators on the Pantry Pride team. Essentially, Revlon was arguing that the loans made to Pantry Pride should be subject to the margin rules set by the Federal Reserve, because Pantry Pride's junk-bond offerings and its Chemical loan were all "indirectly secured" by Revlon stock. The "maximum loan value" of any margin stock is 50 percent of the current market value of that stock. And, Revlon was arguing, Pantry Pride's loans taken together—for $2.1 billion—far exceeded the maximum loan value of Revlon stock, with its current market value of $1.95 billion. The only other time in the junk-bond wars that a target had raised this margin-violation argument was in the Unocal battle against T. Boone Pickens, where it was raised not in the courts but with the Federal Reserve; Unocal and Pickens settled, however, before the Fed considered Unocal's petition.

The rest of the Revlon lawsuit centered on alleged disclosure violations by Pantry Pride and attempted to strike at the inner workings of Milken's machine. Revlon charged that when Pantry Pride did its $750 million "blind pool" public offering in early July, Perelman and Drexel in fact had known that the money was in substantial part to be used for the Revlon bid but had not disclosed that in the offering prospectus. However, Revlon alleged, Drexel and Pantry Pride were not wholly chary with this information—disclosing to certain prospective bond buyers pro-forma Revlon–Pantry Pride financial statements, to convince them that the debt could be repaid.

Moreover, Revlon charged that the prospectus failed to disclose that some $200 million of the $750 million that was raised was not for Pantry Pride's needs but for Drexel's, to enable it to sell off some of its junk-bond inventory.

Perelman testified that while he had been looking at Revlon, among other corporations, as a possible acquisition since as early as February or March 1985, he did not decide on it until about the second week in August. In an interview, Howard Gittis pointed to their interest in July in another acquisition, a Florida thrift, as evidence that they had not yet decided on Revlon. That thrift, however, would have cost only $50 million, hardly enough to warrant $750 million in the junk-bond offering, and hardly a substitute for the Revlon acquisition. Indeed, Fred Sullivan said that "one [acquisition] had nothing to do with the other—the S&L was a money-leverage deal, a way to get cheap capital."

One Revlon source said that he was told by "two top executives of two investment-banking firms" that the Revlon–Pantry Pride pro formas had been shown to prospective junk-bond buyers. But when the Wachtell, Lipton litigators took the depositions of more than twenty of these buyers—many of them loyal members of the inner circle, like Fred Carr, Nelson Peltz and Samuel Belzberg—they found none who testified that he had been told that the target was Revlon.

Rohatyn remains "convinced that the Wachtell lawyers just got stonewalled, and that there *was* a disclosure violation. Perelman came to Bergerac in June and said he wanted to take over Revlon. He said he was about to go out and raise about $400 million. He went out and raised the $750 million and came back for the company. It doesn't take a genius to figure out what was happening."

One whose deposition was not taken was Ralph Papitto, the tough-talking chairman of Nortek, a mini-conglomerate based in Providence, Rhode Island. Papitto, who describes himself as "one of Drexel's top-level clients," said that Milken has raised $600 million for him since 1983, and that he, in turn, has invested in Drexel's megadeals. In GAF's bid for Union Carbide, for example, Papitto said, he committed to buy $50 million of bonds—and had to make that decision in twenty-four hours. "I call this a renaissance," Papitto declared. "In the old days of J. P. Morgan, it would have taken four months, at least, to raise that kind of money, and you would have had reams of paper. But it's really not that complicated. We do it with just a term sheet. We're all pretty savvy. And it's one hundred thousand percent trust. Knowing Mike, if he tells me something's good, I tend to believe in it."

In June 1985, Drexel raised $300 million for Nortek, for acquisition or other corporate purposes. Papitto said he had only planned to raise $150 million. "But it was so *easy*. It was sold in two days. They forced us," he said with a laugh, "to two hundred million, then two hundred fifty million, then three hundred million. They wanted us to go to five hundred million, but I said no." It was a far cry from the early days, when Milken used to raise $25 million or $50 million for a company that wanted to expand and couldn't get that kind of bank financing. Now it was more a matter of Milken saying to his customers, "Here, want three hundred million?" and their replying, "Sure, why not?"

While Papitto did not know exactly what he would do with that money, Milken was not at a loss for ideas. In July, Papitto bought $10 million of preferred stock in Pantry Pride's "blind pool" public offering. "You buy people in this business—Perelman's a pretty savvy guy," says Papitto. "And Pantry Pride had that big tax-loss carryforward."

Did he know the money was for Revlon? "Orally, they tell you things," Papitto replied. "They say it's Revlon. They don't say in writing what they're going to do with the money, but orally."

Revlon's claim that Pantry Pride and Drexel failed to disclose that at least $200 million of the $750 million offering was for Drexel's needs was an attempt to highlight the Drexel daisy chain: Drexel raises money for one client, such as Nortek, which then buys the Pantry Pride offering, and Pantry Pride then buys the securities of other clients, and so forth. If the issuer understands at the time of his offering that he will pay the piper by buying other junk bonds, this ought to be disclosed in the prospectus. To Revlon's allegation, Perelman's response was simply that after getting the money he had decided to invest some of the proceeds from the offering—about $350 million, in fact—in other Drexel-underwritten junk bonds, in order to make up his carrying cost, of about 14.5 percent.

According to Gittis, they had told many investment-banking firms that they were in the market for junk bonds, but only Drexel had available the quantity that they wanted. "We started hearing that others were trying to buy them from Drexel, to sell to us." Gittis also points out that they brought in an "independent consultant" to recommend to them which bonds to buy.

That consultant was Mark Shenkman, one of Milken's first recruits into this market. Shenkman had recently left his job at First Investors and was about to start Shenkman Capital Management—in which one of Drexel's managing directors, the London-based Albert Fuss, would own 24 percent. Not surprisingly, Shenkman recommended Drexel bonds—original issues for other deals, he says, though he declines to name them. "We talked to Merrill Lynch and Salomon," Shenkman said, "but they didn't have the size. I told them we needed bonds in quantities of ten million dollars, fifteen million, twenty million. They—Salomon, for example—wanted to sell us oil paper [debt issued by oil companies], and we didn't want that."

Shenkman said Perelman and Gittis wanted new issues, as opposed to bonds in the secondary market, because the new issues would have greater liquidity. Pantry Pride bought ten to twelve different issues, with interest rates close to that on Pantry Pride's bonds, in blocks of roughly $15–20 million (bigger and therefore riskier than Shenkman recommended). These were sold when the Revlon deal went through.

Pantry Pride had filed with the SEC for only $350 million, back in June. But after Perelman and Gittis went on their road show, also in June, visiting ten cities in as many days, there was much greater demand. "Ronnie was in Paris, and Milken kept calling me and saying he could sell four hundred fifty million dollars, then five hundred fifty million, then six hundred fifty million," Gittis recalled, echoing Pappito. "Finally, at seven hundred fifty million, we decided to stop."

By 1985, it was increasingly more usual than not for Drexel clients to take down much more than what they initially filed for—and, by deduction, much more than they had thought they needed. Shenkman asserted, "Drexel, more than anybody else, always files for less than they think they're going to do. It's a trick of the trade. First, it shows the company how great they are. And, second, the buyers think the company must be in really great shape, to have so many more orders."

Shenkman added that, as a buyer, he does not like it when an issue doubles in size over its filing figure. "Then there are no new buyers afterward, if you want to get out. And the fact that it can double doesn't mean that the deal is great—it's just because there is so much money burning holes in people's pockets."

By mid-September, all of Revlon's claims in the federal litigation had failed (and the locus of significant court action in this battle would move to the Delaware state courts). Revlon's lawyers were unable to find any evidence that prospective bond buyers had been told the target was Revlon. Despite the fact that Pantry Pride in discovery produced documents that showed they were analyzing the Revlon acquisition—code-named Nicole, for Donald Drapkin's eighteen-month-old—from at least April, and that in late June there was a memo on the Nicole deal that stated, "Purchase price, $47.50 per share," the district court judge found credible Pantry Pride's position that no decision had been made on Revlon until early August. On the alleged margin violations, the court essentially deferred to the Federal Reserve, which would in fact take some action some months later—when the Pantry Pride–Revlon drama was history.

Another allegation which Revlon made in its complaint, that Pantry Pride and Drexel had selectively tipped certain arbitrageurs before the offer became public, so as to move large amounts of the company's stock into the hands of those arbs—who would then "warehouse" it for them—was also never proven. In the last five trading days before the Pantry Pride offer, an average of 1,258,800 shares of Revlon common stock per day traded hands, as compared to 283,760 per day in the preceding five trading days. As Wachtell's Brownstein said, "The whole shareholder base of the company had changed before anything had happened publicly."

REVLON'S ADVISERS, however, never banked on the federal litigation to defeat Perelman. Nor did they view the poison pill, an anti-takeover device instituted just before Pantry Pride first announced its hostile tender, as more than a buyer of time. It was with their major corporate maneuver that they expected to stop Pantry Pride in its tracks: an offer to exchange ten million common shares for a package of notes and preferred stock valued at $57.50, thus exchanging about one quarter of the company's equity for debt.

After the buyback was announced on August 26, Bergerac reportedly summoned a group of company executives into the large conference room opposite his office on the thirty-ninth floor of the General Motors Building and, gesturing to a sword that hung on the wall, according to a member of the Pantry Pride team, declared jubilantly, "We have just cut off Perelman's balls and nailed them to the wall."

This battle was laced with tales of such machismo. Perelman recalled that, just prior to Revlon's announcing the buyback, Rifkind had set up a meeting between him, Bergerac and Liman in Rifkind's office. "They saw the meeting as my looking for a graceful way to exit. I saw it as their looking for a graceful way to go along. I'll never forget it. Bergerac looked at me and said, 'I am not afraid of this. I am a big-game hunter. I sit there and a tiger charges me and when it gets to ten feet from me I shoot it between the eyes.'

"I said, 'Then you shouldn't be afraid of a tender offer.' "

Bergerac was, indeed, confident that he would prevail, and his confidence sprang from his advisers'. "They all were totally convinced that if we did the exchange, Perelman would be finished," Bergerac said later.

In addition to turning one quarter of the company's equity into debt, the exchange offer contained covenants which, among other things, precluded most asset sales and the incurring of other indebtedness—which any Pantry Pride deal would require. These covenants, however, could be waived by the directors.

The rest of the watching world seemed to agree with Bergerac and his optimistic advisers. Two articles appeared in the business section of *The New York Times* two days after the exchange offer was announced: "A Victory by Revlon Seen Near," in which Revlon's buyback was likened to CBS's recent successful buyback, which had thwarted Ted Turner; and "Pantry Pride Chairman Pursues Elusive Quest," in which Perelman was portrayed as tilting at windmills—an almost sure loser.

According to one source, "Depression set in at Morgan Stanley. People were going around the firm saying this hostile tender was not the firm's idea, that Gleacher had given assurances at the start that it would be friendly. Eric was being put in a pretty unpleasant position."

For nearly two weeks, Brownstein recalled, "Perelman looked like he was dead in the water. All through the period of the exchange offer, he did nothing."

Then, on September 16, four days after the conclusion of the exchange offer, Pantry Pride came back—with a $42 bid, the equivalent of its $47.50 bid with the debt that Revlon's exchange offer had incurred factored in. This bid was not conditioned, as the first offer had been, on the redemption or invalidation of the poison pill, but was conditioned on 90 percent of the stock's being tendered, so as to diminish the pill's impact. But the real point of this offer, qualifications and all, was that Perelman was still coming.

Perelman's initial offer, rather surprisingly, had stated that the $725 million from junk bonds would be raised in the public market. This set Revlon apart from most of the buyouts and the few hostiles that Drexel had backed, where the debt was raised (or commitments were made) in a private placement. These had the advantage of speed: while a private placement can be completed within twenty days, public offerings take as long as forty-five to sixty days to complete. And since public offerings have to be registered with the SEC, they can be held up even longer by regulators' objections.

But Milken's private placement distribution system was heavily stocked at this point. Some speculated, too, that Milken wanted to show the world the scope of his powers, show that even in a hostile deal the public capital markets would lend themselves to his instrumentation. "It would have been a feather in his cap, to raise the money for a hostile deal in a public offering—it would have been a first," declared Stuart Shapiro of Skadden, Arps.

A few of the Pantry Pride lawyers, however, had been unhappy about the initial plan to raise the money publicly, believing it far too slow and unwieldy a process. Now, in Perelman's revised offer, Milken had switched from public to private placement. It seemed to signal that the deal would be done expeditiously.

The Revlon advisers and directors now resigned themselves to the fact that the company would not remain independent. They began to consider either finding a white knight or liquidating the company—doing something similar to what Perelman wanted to do, but giving the premium to the shareholders instead of allowing it to fall to him.

Meanwhile, in Pantry Pride's "war room"—Perelman's office on the second floor of his MacAndrews town house, an elaborate sitting room with several large pieces of sculpture and with a Modigliani and a Léger on the walls—there was anxiety. The team frequently repaired to Perelman's haunt, the famous Le Cirque restaurant two blocks away, which one participant referred to as "our cafeteria." Don Engel tried to ease the tension, likening this contest to the color wars at Camp Winaukee, where he and Drapkin had been campers, and telling Perelman, "The blue team will win."

Perelman and Drapkin walked around the block, debating the merits of raising the bid. Perelman's new wife, Claudia Cohen, formerly a gossip columnist for *The New York Post*, was now a television entertainment reporter. Whatever else was happening, the group, led by Perelman, gathered in front of the TV set to watch her morning program. Perelman, who is about five foot five, would sometimes make Drexel investment banker Paul Abecassis take off his shoes and stand back to back with him, and then summon one of his executives and demand to be told who was the taller.

As such pastimes suggest, the Pantry Pride team was feeling stymied. True, Perelman could afford to wait it out. He was not at risk of losing more than his fees and carrying costs. He had not purchased stock, in large part because of the Delaware State Supreme Court's decision in Unocal, which had validated that company's discriminatory offer to buy back stock from everyone but Pickens. But Perelman had conditioned his new tender offer upon 90 percent of the shares being tendered. And 90 percent seemed like a lot to expect. "We spent days yelling at each other about what would happen," said one lawyer.

Revlon could, of course, have "played chicken" and simply let Perelman try to get his 90 percent—but Revlon's advisers felt that the risk of his succeeding, and thereby getting the company at $42 a share, was too great. Or Perelman might raise enough money to take over just 51 percent, in which case the shareholders in the back end would be hurt. There were any number of disastrous scenarios. The problem with Revlon's finding a white knight, on the other hand, was that no company wanted to take the polyglot Revlon whole—and no one wanted the cosmetics business, which had been in the doldrums for a few years.

Several days after Perelman made his $42 offer, a little-known private investment partnership that specializes in leveraged buy-outs, Adler and Shaykin, appeared as a buyer for the beauty business that no one other than Perelman wanted—at a price that ultimately reached a staggering $900 million.

Adler and Shaykin's entrance galvanized the situation. Now the leveraged-buyout firm of Forstmann Little emerged as a buyer for the rest of Revlon. Peter Jaquith, with whom Bergerac had explored the possibility of a management buyout of Revlon a year earlier when Jaquith was at Lazard, had moved to Forstmann Little and was eager to revive the old plan. Within the next ten days or so, a deal was hammered out in which Adler and Shaykin, in a transaction that stood independent of the rest, would buy cosmetics; Forstmann Little, joined by Bergerac and other members of management, would then acquire the rest of Revlon for about $1.4 billion (giving the shareholders $56 a share), selling off a division to American Home Products and keeping the health-care business.

While this deal was being negotiated, however, Pantry Pride was neither oblivious nor idle. The Revlon directors were kept apprised of the negotiations, and, it seemed, so was Pantry Pride. Many of the participants on the Revlon–Forstmann Little side were firmly convinced that there was at least one channel from the board of directors to the other side. Wherever the leaks to Pantry Pride came from, they were constant and handicapping for Revlon. "I have never been in a deal where there were leaks like this," asserted Loomis of Lazard. "The transmission of information was *immediate*. And it reached the point where the people we were negotiating with didn't trust some of us, so they wanted to talk to some of us and not others, and felt they had to restrict their conversations generally. For example, when Forstmann Little finally made its bid at the October third board meeting, they didn't tell any of us they were at fifty-six dollars a share until one hour before the meeting."

Pantry Pride, meanwhile, cognizant of the deal that was in the works, was desperately trying to entice Bergerac. Don Engel enlisted Harold Geneen, Bergerac's old boss at ITT, to pay Bergerac a visit. Geneen, on behalf of Pantry Pride, offered to give Bergerac his parachute, as Perelman had offered before; to give him a second one, which he would be able to cash in in two years; and then to sell him a division, one of the health divisions of his choice, at a favorable price, and finance it for him. "He didn't spell out favorable price, but these things are understood," said Bergerac. "So the package they were offering came to close to a hundred million dollars."

Bergerac's account of Geneen's offer was confirmed by a Perelman adviser—though flatly denied by both Perelman and his lawyer, Drapkin. Bergerac's continued rejection of all financial enticement, however, was mystifying to Perelman and his advisers. One went so far as to call it "irrational."

"Some people think that for one hundred million dollars you have to be crazy not to accept," Bergerac acknowledged. "But I chose to fight these characters because I found them to be undesirable."

After Geneen's failed visit, Robert Greenhill of Morgan Stanley, the firm that was playing handmaiden to Drexel in this deal, tried the emissary role. "I remember Greenhill saying he could swing it, he'd go see Michel," scoffed one Perelman team member. "If anything, he made it worse."

So in order to combat Forstmann Little, Pantry Pride had no choice but to give more money to the shareholders. On September 27 it raised its bid from $42 to $50, and then, on October 1, to $53. Stuart Shapiro of the Pantry Pride legal team remembered, "We were all standing around that afternoon, we knew they were going to have the board meeting at six P.M. And we'd heard all these rumors. We'd heard Forstmann Little was coming in at fifty-two. So in an hour and a half we convinced each other we should go up another three dollars to fifty-three.

"We drafted this letter, and since it was already six P.M. we needed somebody to bring it over. We decided that it should be Dennis Levine—it's hard to get into the Revlon building at night, and Dennis is so ingenious we figured he'd find a way. So we told him he was the messenger. He was mortified. We put him in a Rolls Royce, to make him feel better. And he got it to them."

Shapiro said that in August they had not believed that the company had these values. But since then they had learned that the divestitures could bring prices several hundred million dollars in excess of what they had estimated. And they had seen Philip Morris Companies Inc. buy General Foods Corporation for nearly $5.8 billion, and Procter and Gamble pay $1.55 billion for Richardson-Vicks, Inc., showing that established, big-name consumer-products companies were worth much more than Wall Street analysts had thought just a few weeks earlier.

"From the start, some of Perelman's advisers thought he was overpaying at forty-seven fifty," Shapiro said. "But Perelman's view was always that everyone else was being too conservative in their valuations, and that the assets were going to be worth much more."

Told by Bergerac that a management buyout at a superior price was in the works, the board made no decision on Pantry Pride's $53 offer. Two days later it met again and voted for the management buyout with Forstmann Little at $56 a share. Bergerac's parachute would be triggered, and he would invest it in the deal; management would have 25 percent of the equity. There was no lock-up (an agreement which so favors one bidder that it makes the acquisition of the target by any other bidder uneconomic) given to guard against any other bidder, but there was a provision promising Forstmann Little a bust-up fee of $25 million if it was topped by another bidder.

That was on Thursday, October 3. Finally, after close to two months of running the emotional gamut, Revlon's advisers breathed a sigh of relief. The Forstmann Little–Adler and Shaykin deal had been extremely complex, and those involved had doubted that they would succeed in putting it together with the speed that was required, but, in just ten days, they had done it. And while the company would be broken up, they had—this time for sure, they believed—escaped the unsavory Perelman.

The following Monday, Pantry Pride was back, with a $56.25 offer.

And within forty-eight hours, by Wednesday, Drexel had obtained commitments for $350 million of the next $700 million and announced it was "highly confident" of obtaining the remaining $350 million. Perelman paid a little more than $5 million in commitment fees.

On Wednesday, Arthur Liman—who had always been more open to the idea of negotiating with Perelman than his two co-defenders, Lipton and Rohatyn, and who had, after all, attempted to broker the deal at its inception in June—instigated a meeting between Bergerac, Theodore Forstmann, and Perelman, in an attempt to work out a three-way solution.

At around midnight on October 9, Perelman and his entourage arrived, for the first time, in Revlon's gilded, rococo foyer on the thirty-ninth floor of the General Motors Building. "I'll never forget those twenty or thirty guys coming off the elevators," recalled Bergerac. "All short, bald, with big cigars! It was incredible! If central casting had had to produce thirty guys like that, they couldn't do it. They looked like they were in a grade-D movie that took place in Mississippi or Louisiana, about guys fixing elections in a back room."

"What a scene," Liman concurred. "All the Drexels were in one room—these guys with their feet up on Michel's tables, spilling their cigar ashes onto his rugs."

For their part, Perelman's group thought little of Bergerac's décor: the animal heads from his safaris mounted on the walls, the elephant-leg stools, the Abercrombie and Fitch–type murals of lions and tigers, the antique commode, thronelike, in Bergerac's private bathroom. As Drapkin commented, "It was the tackiest."

The three parties met, in various groupings, until 4 A.M. At the end, there was a deal on the table in which Perelman would take over the company and then sell one of the health-care companies to Forstmann Little at a price that Forstmann now set (which Perelman would later claim was far too low). But Theodore Forstmann made clear that he would do it only if it was what Bergerac—who would run this one company—wanted; and by the next morning Bergerac said it was not.

What did emerge from the meeting, and what made the biggest impression on Perelman's adversaries, was this: Perelman declared that, since Forstmann had had access to the Revlon numbers and he had not, he would simply use Forstmann Little as a stalking horse. Whatever they bid he would raise by twenty-five cents; he had done so already when he went to $56.25.

"By that time," Lazard's Loomis asserted, "Perelman had clearly changed his thesis—from seeing this as the deal of the century at forty-seven fifty, where he would sell the rest and keep cosmetics for free, to saying, 'Anything Forstmann Little can do, I can better by a quarter.'

"It may no longer have been a phenomenal deal—but there

were his fees to pay, the interest on the money he'd raised, his reputation for efficacy as an acquirer. I'm convinced that if Forstmann Little had been at fifty-nine, he'd have gone to sixty. He *had* to do this deal."

Indeed, Perelman's debt service and dividend obligations on the $750 million of securities he had issued came to roughly $110 million annually. The Pantry Pride offering prospectus had made the disclaimer, which Drexel subsequently made boilerplate, that "funds generated by the existing operations will not be sufficient to enable the Company to meet" those obligations. Perelman had invested about half of the approximately $730 million he had received from that offering (after paying Drexel its fees) in other high-interest-paying junk bonds, but those were, of course, risky themselves. He could take a loss on the principal.

The interest on the majority of the securities Pantry Pride had issued was slightly more than 14 percent. So, assuming for the moment the bank rate, which was 8 percent, Perelman had a negative carrying charge of about $40 million a year. And it was, of course, not a case of just losing that $40 million. How was Perelman to pay back the $750 million, which even in the never-never land that Drexel had created must come due someday? If Perelman did not get Revlon, he had to get something else. Fast. And it had to be a good and reasonably priced acquisition—something that was increasingly hard to find. And if such an acquisition was hostile, then—after more months of fees and carrying costs—it too might not work. And Perelman would be no longer just a tilter at windmills, but a loser.

There was also the time and money already invested in the Revlon deal. Perelman owed roughly $20 million in lawyers' and investment bankers' fees. And he had just incurred the commitment fees of over $5 million for the $350 million he had taken down in the private placement.

Beyond these practical considerations that impelled Perelman, his advisers say, was his urgent desire to do the deal. Echoing other Perelman associates, Fred Sullivan referred to Perelman's "incredible tenacity. He was like a dog with a bone. He would not stop. I think if he'd had to bid ninety dollars he would have done it."

Drexel's Abecassis added, "I don't know *when* Ronnie would have stopped. We were getting nervous. It was getting very thin."

On the Revlon–Forstmann Little side, Loomis was not alone in his assessment of Perelman's position. In just a week, Loomis and others had gone from believing that they had buried Perelman to seeing him as someone whom no bid would stop. Bergerac said, "We really were tempted to go to sixty or sixty-five, just to watch him do himself in—but then what would we have done if by some chance he let us have it?"

Swept along in the maelstrom, the Revlon advisers and directors had gone from their initial and justifiable position of fighting Perelman's lowball bid of $47.50 to seeking a way to thwart his making an ever higher bid. The dynamics of the deal had changed, but their animus for Perelman stayed constant and blinded them.

One other element had been added to the scenario in this last week. When the board approved the buyout with Forstmann, Revlon had had to undo all the defensive measures it had instituted to ward off Pantry Pride. It had redeemed the poison pill and waived the debt covenants (imposed in the exchange offer) to allow Forstmann to leverage the transaction by borrowing on Revlon's assets.

Now the price of the exchange offer notes, which had been issued August 26 and were intended to trade at par (face value), plummeted in reaction to the announced leveraged buyout. (The notes would no longer be as secure, since Revlon's capital structure would be laden with debt.) According to an affidavit filed by Rifkind, "Since our meeting of October 3, the notes had dropped to as low as $87—a decline of about $60 million below par. I was deluged with telephone calls from irate holders who had exchanged shares for 11.75 percent notes which they believed would be worth par, and who now saw a 13 percent erosion in the value of their notes."

And on October 10 an article in *The Wall Street Journal*, entitled "Some Revlon Investors Say Company's Moves Could Cost Them Millions of Dollars in Losses," stated that some angry bondholders were considering legal action.

What Pantry Pride offered to do about the noteholders is not clear. Gittis wrote Revlon a letter on October 11 stating that Pantry Pride would pay the interest and the principal on the notes—in other words, nothing extra. But Drapkin filed an affidavit in which he stated that he had told Lipton, in a phone conversation on October 10, that they "were willing to satisfy Revlon's concern for the noteholders and that the issue should not block the deal."

What was clear was what Forstmann Little was willing to do for the noteholders: it promised to exchange the old notes for new ones that would trade at par. It also agreed to raise its bid to $57.25

—one dollar higher than Perelman's. In exchange, it demanded a lock-up option, something that would in essence preclude a bid for Revlon by anyone else. If another acquirer obtained 40 percent of the stock, that would automatically trigger the right of Forstmann Little to buy two divisions, Vision Care and National Health Laboratories, for $525 million. That price, according to Lazard, was below fair market value. And in this new version of the Forstmann buyout, management would drop out as equity partners. Lipton and Liman both advised Bergerac that, with the lock-up option given to Forstmann, he was placed in a position of intolerable conflict.

On October 12, after Drapkin had made repeated unsuccessful attempts to reach Revlon advisers by telephone the previous day in order to reopen negotiations, the Revlon board approved the new, revised Forstmann Little deal, with the essential lock-ups. These were essential not just to Forstmann Little, which wanted to halt the dance with the inexhaustible Perelman, but to the Revlon board and its advisers, who wanted the same thing. As the board minutes —which, in line with Lipton's regular policy, were taken in elaborate detail—say, "The effect of the lock-up option, Mr. Lipton stated, was to deter a bid at a higher price than $57.25 . . ."

At the decisive meeting, Forstmann addressed the board. He made it plain that he and the Revlon directors had united to defeat a common enemy, the worst sort of parvenu.

> . . . Mr. Forstmann noted that before this transaction had begun he had never heard of Ronald Perelman [say the minutes]. He stated that . . . Mr. Perelman had proposed to Mr. Forstmann that they chop up the company between them. Mr. Forstmann stated that in Mr. Perelman's proposals the word "employees" was never in his mouth. . . . A director inquired of Mr. Forstmann what his ultimate point of dispute with Pantry Pride preventing an agreement was. Mr. Forstmann stated that basically the chemistry just wasn't right. He stated that he had not entered into this transaction in order to make a deal with Mr. Perelman. Mr. Forstmann stated that he was interested in the transaction not only for the profit he could make but for other reasons as well and that the other reasons would be violated if he had entered into a deal with Pantry Pride.

WITHIN TWO WEEKS of Revlon's having granted Forstmann Little the lock-ups, they were undone by Justice Joseph Walsh of the Delaware Chancery Court. (The disclosure and margin requirements, whose alleged violation was the subject of the earlier litigation, were federal laws; but the issue that the battle now hinged upon, whether the Revlon board had failed in its fiduciary duty to shareholders by granting the lock-ups, was a question of state law.)

The court found that the Revlon board had indeed "failed in its fiduciary duty to shareholders," having breached the "duty of loyalty." While it found the Revlon board's early defensive measures—the poison pill and the exchange offer—appropriate, it opined that once it became clear that there would be a breakup of the company, the directors' role changed from one trying to thwart a hostile acquirer to "an auctioneer attempting to secure the highest price for the pieces of the Revlon enterprise."

At that point, the court was saying, the board should have been essentially blind, or indifferent, to the identity of the bidders. Instead, it acted out of favoritism, seeming to "want Forstmann Little in the picture at all costs." The reason for this, the court decided, appeared to be the directors' concern over their personal liability to the noteholders; but their sole responsibility as directors was not to the noteholders but to the shareholders. And it was their "self-interest," the court found, that led them to make the concessions to Forstmann Little that excluded Pantry Pride.

The directors had not contented themselves with giving Forstmann Little the lock-ups, but had further maneuvered to, in effect, lock up the lock-ups. The court mentioned that Revlon, after the final board meeting, had transferred into escrow the assets of the two divisions which were part of the lock-up agreement, and that the court—in response to a protest from Pantry Pride—had issued an order prohibiting any further transfer of assets until the pending motion had been decided. In Joe Flom's view, that transfer of assets was "their biggest mistake. It colored the whole proceeding."

On Thursday, two days before the final Revlon board meeting which Forstmann had addressed, Justice Walsh had seen lawyers for Revlon and Pantry Pride in his chambers. The Pantry Pride lawyers were pressing for an expedited hearing on their motion for a preliminary injunction to stop the Revlon-Forstmann leveraged buyout (which the Revlon board had voted to accept) and the Revlon lawyers said there was no reason the hearing could not be held after the weekend, during the following week, since no action was planned. The Revlon board held its meeting on Saturday and granted the lock-ups. The following Monday, a bank holiday, Revlon and Forstmann Little managed to get the assets and the $25 million breakup fee transferred from Manufacturers Hanover to Morgan Guaranty. When the outraged Pantry Pride lawyers appeared before the judge the next day, the judge, clearly angered, issued an order preventing any further transfer of assets.

On November 1 the Delaware Supreme Court affirmed the lower-court ruling, and the battle that had begun in August was finally over. The court commented:

> . . . Forstmann was given every negotiating advantage that Pantry Pride had been denied: cooperation from management, access to financial data, and the exclusive opportunity to present merger proposals directly to the board of directors. Favoritism for a white knight to the total exclusion of a hostile bidder might be justifiable when the latter's offer adversely affects shareholder interests, but when bidders make relatively similar offers, or dissolution of the company becomes inevitable, the directors cannot fulfill their enhanced Unocal duties [a reference to the court decision in Unocal, where directors were given wide discretionary scope] by playing favorites with contending factions.

The court also commented that after that initial June meeting between Perelman and Bergerac "all subsequent Pantry Pride overtures were rebuffed, perhaps in part based on Mr. Bergerac's strong personal antipathy to Mr. Perelman."

That, of course, was the key—the overriding animus that Bergerac and the rest felt for Perelman and "Panty Pride" and "the Drexels." It was not simply that the Revlon directors and advisers feared that Pantry Pride would not take care of the noteholders and so had turned to Forstmann Little; it was that they feared, more than anything, that Perelman *would* come back, offering more and more, with his limitless piles of lucre, and there would be no escape.

THE CONQUEST of Revlon signaled the end of an era. Those who defended it were struggling to perpetuate a way of corporate life—plush, congenial and secure, unmenaced by anyone but perhaps another corporate giant—that had lost its capacity to prevail in the economic world. The junk-bond marauders had won here, and if they had won here they could win anywhere. It had all happened so quickly that Revlon's advisers, when they spoke later about the company, sounded faintly archaic, unmistakably out of step with the times. Milken had not singlehandedly created a new age, but he had done more to shape it than any other individual.

Months later Rifkind returned to the MacAndrews and Forbes board, but he did not rejoin Revlon's newly constituted board. "I'd been a Revlon director since the fifties," Rifkind mused. "I had watched Revson build the company. The board was like a family. We'd known each other for years. It was collegial."

Rifkind gazed out his office window toward the dome of St. Bartholomew's Church on Park Avenue. "If somebody could prove to you that the bricks of that cathedral [sic] could fetch a higher price in the market, would you dismantle it? I know, I know, today it is put 'em together, break 'em up—no cement anywhere."

In the final days and the aftermath of the battle, Bergerac was pilloried in the press and ridiculed by Perelman and his followers, who painted him as the kind of corporate executive from whom shareholders need deliverance. When Perelman was asked by a New York Times reporter about Bergerac's claim that he had offered to improve Bergerac's lifestyle, he responded, "I don't think that could ever be improved upon."

With his enormous parachute and his elegant, European lifestyle—much of it supported by company perks—Bergerac had made an easy target. From the time the Forstmann Little–management buyout was announced, he had received a working-over in the press. At the outset of the battle he had announced that Revlon was worth $65 a share, and he had derided Perelman as a "bust-up artist." Then he helped to engineer—with his roughly $35 million severance package—his own bust-up of the company, at a price that was $9 below what he had first said the company was worth.

For this, Bergerac was portrayed as a self-interested hypocrite. But what this attack ignores is that $56 was a good price for the company, and that Bergerac had fought hard to bring it up from Perelman's $47.50 (and then $42, when he factored in the cost of Revlon's exchange offer). He had done well for his shareholders. It is true that he was attempting to do the very thing he had accused Perelman of—busting up the company. But there was no white knight to take the company whole. Was Bergerac to do nothing and let Perelman bust it up for $53? In his own bust-up, he would have been able to take care of his people, something his advisers concur was a foremost concern throughout this battle. Had Bergerac been solely self-interested, he could have accepted Perelman's lavish inducements.

Of his defeat Bergerac said, "It was a terrible experience. I would hope to never go through something like that again. At the final board meeting, people were bawling, I cried. . . . You must understand, people had a love for this company. It was like a woman's being raped."

Revlon was a public company. It did not belong to Bergerac or to the others on the board who wept for it. But shareholder ownership is an abstraction, compared to the tangible reality of a company, its directors, its employees who come to work every day, its customers and its community. It is the dislocation or destruction of that tangible reality that makes hostile takeovers so fraught with emotion.

Felix Rohatyn contrasted Revlon—which he calls his "virginal experience" in defending against a bust-up, junk-bond raid—with other hostile raids in which he has been a defender. "People on the other side are usually a company interested in a product, in business strategy, and the emphasis is on how do you put two companies together and make them grow, where do we go from here to make them bigger and better.

"Here the overriding issue was, what can we sell for how much, to be left with a small piece for nothing, or virtually nothing. On the other side was a group of people tearing at a carcass—a group of people interested in numbers on pieces of paper, and nothing having to do with people, customers, quality, is this good, bad, or indifferent."

This world *had* changed. And it had not changed for the better. It was not simply a matter of the old members of the club not liking the style of these shrewd, dollars-and-cents-driven parvenus, who had started their own club and were now running things—though that, certainly, was a part of it. It was also that these newcomers, in their desperation to break in, seemed to flout not only social values, but the law. Revlon's defenders had alleged and then failed to prove violations of the law, but they remained convinced that it was true.

As one participant declared, "In the seventies, among the people I dealt with . . . there were some I liked and some I detested but they were all bright, decent people. The arbs were Bob Rubin [of Goldman, Sachs] and Bunny Lasker [of Lasker, Stone and Stern], and they were honest, and if they thought they had inside information they'd call and ask, and if we said yes, then they'd freeze their position. And the clients were people like Larry Tisch going after CNA—or big companies going after other big companies, because they believed they could run them better.

"Now it's the Icahns and the Jacobses and the Pickenses and the Peltzes and the Perelmans.

"And," this participant continued, displaying the paranoid-sounding mind-set that the junk-bond wars had induced, "we have to have detectives in to make sure our rooms aren't bugged and our phone lines aren't tapped, and that they aren't sending electronic beams into our offices, and we have to look for hidden cameras when we go into and out of meetings. They have ruined my life. You feel like you're in the gutter, like they're piling shit on you and you have to keep struggling to get up from it. And it's all been made possible by Drexel. Without Drexel, none of it could have happened."

WHILE REVLON'S defenders mourned, the "blue team" celebrated. When the deal closed in early November, Perelman hosted a dinner for thirty aides, lawyers and investment bankers at Le Club, an exclusive Manhattan nightspot. Perelman's favorite champagne, Cristal, flowed freely, and some of the key players put on a skit which—in the continuing color-war motif—was referred to as the "songfest."

It opened with the first Perelman–Bergerac encounter, in June '85. Dennis Levine played Bergerac, dressed as a big-game hunter, mimicking his French accent, calling Perelman an "upstart" and a "Jew from Philadelphia." Engel played Perelman. Wearing Gucci loafers and one of his $3,000 Fiorentino custom-tailored suits, he fondled and puffed a fat Macanudo cigar and dropped its ashes on Bergerac's rugs. When Bergerac (Levine) offered Perelman (Engel) some Château Lafite, Perelman asked for vodka. "Peasant!" snorted Bergerac.

There was plenty to celebrate for those on hand that night. Perelman had gotten the company of his dreams—though not for free, as he had originally planned. Its real cost would not become clear for some time, until the divestitures were completed. But for

most of these merrymakers, particularly the lawyers and the investment bankers, the bust-up of Revlon had already spouted geysers of
gold. Fees paid to lawyers and investment bankers in this deal came
to over $100 million—making it the most lucrative takeover yet.
Even the $13.4 billion acquisition of Gulf Oil Corporation by Stan-
dard Oil (instigated by Pickens) threw off only $60 million in fees.

Revlon's legal bill, from Wachtell, Lipton and Paul, Weiss, is
estimated at about $10 million, while Pantry Pride's from Skadden,
Arps is estimated at $7–8 million. Fried, Frank, Harris and Shriver,
representing Forstmann Little, was paid at least $1 million.

But as is always the case, the investment bankers' take makes
the lawyers' seem modest by comparison, though the bankers typically have far fewer people working on any deal than the lawyers
do. Goldman, Sachs and Company received about $3 million from
Forstmann Little. Lazard Frères received about $11 million from
Revlon. Morgan Stanley, once all the divestitures were done, received under $25 million—far less than the $30 million that had
been established as their ceiling. In fact, Drexel had tried to persuade Perelman to ditch Morgan Stanley when they refused to put
their name on the tender offer, and Drexel continued to argue that
all Morgan Stanley deserved was its fee for having brought Perelman
the idea.

Not surprisingly, Drexel claimed the lion's share—over $65 mil-
lion. In its July public offering of $750 million of Pantry Pride notes,
Drexel received an underwriting discount, or fee, of about 3.5 percent, which equaled $25 million. It received another $11 million as
an advisory fee. And then it received on its private placement of
$770 million about $30 million.

Moreover, when MacAndrews and Forbes made its purchase of
37.6 percent of Pantry Pride stock for $60 million in the spring of '85,
Drexel-related entities known as Prime Capital Associates had
bought $10 million worth of that stock on the same terms as
MacAndrews. This stock was distributed, as such extras always are,
to those whom Milken favored—himself, his people, some of the
key individuals in corporate finance. Engel was one of those in
Prime Capital Associates.

Revlon's most senior executives lost their jobs, though they did
not walk away empty-handed. Golden parachutes totaling $42.2
million were paid out to thirteen executives. Fifteen million of this
went to Bergerac's own parachute—the largest ever given. In addi-

tion, he received five years of salary and bonus, valued at about $7 million; and stock options and accelerated payment of restricted stock worth $13 million. In all, his severance package came to $35 million.

Revlon's shareholders also did well. The stock was trading in the low thirties before the Pantry Pride rumors drove it up, and Pantry Pride paid $58 per share in the end. (Immediately after the argument in Chancery Court but before Justice Walsh wrote his opinion, Pantry Pride had raised its bid from $56.25 to $58.)

Pantry Pride shareholders were not left out. That stock was trading at about three and three quarters before Perelman took control of the company in the spring of 1985. Less than a year later it had tripled.

And those who signed up for the bonds and bought them but wanted to trade out quickly also profited. One of the buyers said that over a period of several months—starting before Perelman announced his offer, but when the company was known to be "in play"—he had accumulated about $16 million of Revlon stock. When Drexel called to sell him the bonds, therefore, he had a powerful interest in seeing the deal go through. He sold his stock for about $18 million, he says, and then put that money up for the bonds at an interest rate of 13.75 percent, plus his commitment fee of .75 percent.

The deal closed in mid-November, and within two weeks there were reports that Revlon was going to sell its Norcliff Thayer health products and Reheis special chemical businesses to the Beecham Group of Britain for about $400 million, and its ethical-drug division to Rorer for over $600 million. Both deals were announced by the first week of December. Some onlookers were puzzled by the speed with which the Rorer deal, particularly, was done, and by the absence of an auction. Howard Gittis, however, explained, "They had an exclusive. Well, almost an exclusive. We said, 'If we get the company, and you commit to us now, then we won't shop the deal.' " This agreement should arguably have been disclosed in SEC filings if it was indeed made during the course of the deal. When later asked to comment, Gittis denied that anyone had been given an exclusive.

"At that point [in December], the money was just sitting there in the bank, but they couldn't call [buy back] the bonds for six months," this buyer said. "So it was completely safe now, good for the S&Ls, and Milken wanted the bonds back." That suited him, he added, because he wanted to get his money out. And he was eager to be a team player so that Milken would come back to him in the next deal.

This is the same kind of movement of the bonds—out of the hands of a high-rolling buyer into those of the more reticent thrifts, insurance companies and pension funds—that took place in Triangle–National Can. Here the high-risk, private buyers were freed to go on to the next megadeal, which in December was GAF–Union Carbide; while the more risk-averse but still hungry players could be fed.

The only dissonant note in this chorus of happy profiteers came, as is usual in these transactions, from the bondholders of the acquired company who found their paper suddenly downgraded now that the company was so debt-laden. (Their prices, however, have since rebounded.) This illustrated the gospel according to Milken, which proselytized that while low-grade bonds might be upgraded, high-grade could go only one way—down. Of course, when he first started spreading that gospel he had been speaking as an observer; now, many years later—as Milken's raiders menaced companies which did defensive restructurings and then had their bonds downgraded, or acquired companies whose bonds were subsequently downgraded—he was often the propulsive force. According to Drexel, in 1985 $4.6 billion of junk bonds moved up into the investment-grade category, while $9.1 billion of investment grade moved down into the netherworld of junk.

ONE YEAR AFTER the "blue team" had had its high-spirited bash at Le Club, Perelman was still on the move. In October 1986 he had made a run at CPC International, the food-processing company, and had then sold his stake to Salomon Brothers for a profit of $41 million (in a trade which a *Wall Street Journal* "Heard on the Street" column suggested was prearranged, artificially inflated, and, if so, Perelman's first—albeit disguised—greenmailing).

By early November, Perelman had accumulated 15 percent of the stock of Transworld Corporation, a restaurant, hotels and food-service conglomerate. Transworld then decided to liquidate, but Perelman got the option of buying its prize, Hilton International Company, for $1 billion. That option aside, in one month he had achieved on his $223 million Transworld investment a paper profit of $55 million. On November 14, he offered $4.1 billion in cash—with Drexel's "highly confident" endorsement—for the Gillette Company, the razor-blade manufacturer.

Perelman was thriving as a predator. But whether the Revlon acquisition, which had raised him from an obscure, small-time entrepreneur to a corporate mogul, would in fact turn out to be the world-class company that he envisioned was less clear. He had purchased Revlon shares for about $1.8 billion, assumed debt of roughly $1 billion, and had expenses and carrying costs that brought his total acquisition cost to about $3 billion. He had sold several of the health-care businesses for a total of roughly $1.4 billion. He had kept National Health Labs and Vision Care, whose value at the time of the acquisition (though it has since gone up) was probably about $1.2 billion. Therefore, Perelman had not acquired the cosmetics business for free, as he had initially planned—but for roughly $400 million. And Revlon's contract to sell the cosmetics business to Adler and Shaykin—for a price that Perelman puts at $780 million, not $900 million—ended in litigation that cost Perelman $23.7 million to settle. (By year-end 1987, Perelman would augment the cosmetics business—making it the world's largest—by buying Max Factor, Charles of the Ritz and Germaine Monteil for more than $500 million. According to Revlon, operating profits for 1987 would double what they had been in 1985.)

Drapkin, who announced in October '86 that he was leaving Skadden, Arps, where he had been earning well over $1 million a year, to join Perelman as a vice-chairman of Revlon Group (Revlon was merged into Pantry Pride, which then changed its name to Revlon Group, Inc.), predicted at that time that "Ronnie is going to turn cosmetics around. I doubt very much that he'll ever sell Revlon. I think he sees it as the cornerstone of an empire."

Others are less rhapsodic. "It will be a tough struggle, very tough," says one established figure in the industry. "Too much damage has been done. I don't know any cosmetics image that has ever been resurrected." Many questioned the wisdom of Perelman's having brought Sol Levine, a protégé of Charles Revson and former consultant, whom Bergerac had let go, back into the company as its president. Bergerac had let Levine go because he considered him wanting.

Bergerac, as was to be expected, is foremost among the doomsayers. He is convinced that Perelman was seduced by the glamour of the beauty business, and that it will be his undoing. "Cosmetics was worth five hundred million at best," he declared. "But instead of taking the nine hundred million for it from Adler and Shaykin, he got good to average prices for selling the health-care businesses, which were running like a clock, generating enormous profits. So he got rid of the good and kept the bad."

That would be at odds with what Perelman had managed to do in most of his earlier, smaller acquisitions—but the cosmetics business was in itself a break with Perelman's past targets. Drexel's Abecassis admitted, "Revlon does have a fickle aspect to it that Ronnie's other acquisitions didn't have. They didn't have to depend on sophisticated selling. In Revlon, you're selling dreams—so it's a different story.

"He's done some things at Revlon—cutting expenses, consolidating. But it's certainly not done yet—not by any means. And the measures he's taken aren't going to improve the business in the long run."

Abecassis believes that Revlon could benefit from Perelman's full attention, but the peripatetic Perelman does not see it that way. "His attitude is, he came in, he cleaned it up, he's ready to go on to the next," Abecassis added. "It worked with flavors [MacAndrews], it worked with Technicolor, but here it's different. I told him this, just the other day. He said, 'What am I supposed to do, sit here and look at the business every day?'

"Ronnie is a deal person," Abecassis concluded. "He wants to *do deals*."

Given that, it is not surprising that Perelman changed the plan he and Milken had agreed upon—that he would sell off the pieces of Revlon and pay down most, if not all, of the junk acquisition debt. Instead, Perelman refinanced those notes. According to one member of the UAC (Underwriting Assistance Committee), some of its members thought that Perelman should pay down the debt, but they were overruled by others.

As for Milken's view on Perelman's keeping the cash, Abecassis said, "Mike is a trader. He has the view, you go in and out. And he's a hungry guy. So he doesn't say, 'Stop.' Also, he trusts Ronnie."

According to Abecassis, if the Transworld deal had gone through, Perelman would have had to give up (to Drexel, which would probably have distributed some to bond buyers) 30 percent of the equity. "Ronnie doesn't want to give any equity—but if he doesn't, there's no deal. In Revlon, he gave Drexel warrants in Pantry Pride, and it was not that much equity. That was really a way of paying our fee. We fought. We told Ronnie next time he would *have* to give equity."

By fall '86, Perelman was still dependent on Drexel for the multibillion-dollar deals he craved. In Transworld, which would have been a $2.5 billion deal, Perelman had no other recourse, Abecassis insisted. "You may not be able to sell assets, you need long-term money. And the banks won't do it. I went to a meeting yesterday. They [the bank] are nervous about $400 million—when we have $1.9 billion *below* them [subordinated to the bank's senior, secured debt]."

While it was not yet clear whether Perelman would succeed in resurrecting Revlon, its acquisition had certainly done wonders for his social climbing. Almost everyone who knows Perelman has a story to tell about his eagerness for that ascent (which dates back to his Philadelphia days, when he was rebuffed by that city's social elite) and for the company of the famous. He had on the payroll of Technicolor a "consultant" named Dennis Stein—known for his brief engagement to Elizabeth Taylor—who, as one associate says, is "a high-class gofer." Stein's apparent function, this associate says, was to introduce Perelman to celebrities (though with Taylor's departure it became less viable).

A few months after taking over Revlon, Perelman hired a well-connected editor from *Town & Country* magazine, Nancy Gardiner, to be his social secretary. And he brought Ann Getty onto the Revlon board ("Ronnie is *determined* to have a glitzy board," commented another of his associates). As reported by *Spy* magazine, Jacqueline Onassis, Halston, Caroline Herrara and Calvin Klein have been to the Perelmans' East Sixty-third Street town house for parties. And Perelman would become the honorary chairman at one of the most socially acceptable and literati-filled benefits of the year, for the New York Public Library.

Referring to all the gossip about Perelman's eagerness to gain entree to the rarefied social realm, Bergerac says, with an acid chuckle, "Teddy Forstmann had the best line of all: 'This has got to be the highest price ever paid in the history of this country to get a good table at a New York restaurant."

●　●

IN SEPTEMBER '86, in the opulent Revlon offices where he and "the Drexels" had arrived as hated interlopers and dropped ashes on Bergerac's Persian rugs, Perelman now seemed at home. He and Drapkin had liked calling attention to Bergerac's excesses, particularly the Boeing 727 outfitted with a gun rack for his safaris, and the Revlon offices in Paris which Perelman described as a "castle." Now the company leased its corporate jet from a Perelman aircraft-leasing company. And now that the "castle" was *his* Paris headquarters, Perelman had decided not to sell it, after all. He was having the New York offices redecorated. And James, Bergerac's butler, was now serving Perelman.

Moreover, while Bergerac's $35 million parachute had elicited from Perelman and Drapkin a mutual outrage befitting two sign-bearers of the corporate revolution, the terms of Drapkin's employment would be far richer than any that Bergerac ever enjoyed. (It is true that Perelman would take the company private in the spring of 1987, so Drapkin would not take his king's-ransom out of public shareholders' money; but his employment agreement went into effect when Revlon Group was still a public company, and after taking the company private in the spring of '87 Perelman would owe public bondholders roughly $3.7 billion. The debt-to-equity ratio of MacAndrews and Forbes, at the top of the Perelman pyramid, would be 18:1.)

In his six year employment agreement with MacAndrews and Forbes Holdings (which comes just under Perelman in the corporate chart of the Perelman empire, with all the other companies under it), Drapkin would receive $2 million as an inducement to enter into this employment agreement, which guaranteed him a salary that would escalate from $2,500,000 in 1987 to $4,192,650 by 1992. In addition, he would receive a bonus of $1 million each year. He would further be entitled to 20 percent of net trading profits in investment partnerships that would be formed. A separate five-year employment agreement with Revlon would guarantee Drapkin $1,150,000 each year. Thus Drapkin was to start his employment at Revlon—this paradigm of the new cost-cutting corporate age—with a guaranteed take by March 1988 of $6.7 million, which with Perelman-type trading profits factored in could easily range into the tens of millions. Nor would Drapkin be the sole beneficiary of such profligacy. Bruce Slovin and Howard Gittis would also be guaranteed many millions.

When this reporter came to interview him, Perelman assumed his interview posture. He was wearing his uniform navy cardigan sweater. He sank low into his chair, removed his tasseled Gucci loafers, put his navy-stockinged feet up on the coffee table, and worked his cigar. The posture was casual but the man was not. He continually ground his molars. He seemed to be straining to project a pleasant image—but what kept appearing from underneath, pentimento-like, was a mix of impatience, vulgarity and boiling temper that was anything but pleasant.

He raged at his secretary for taking six steps toward him to hand him a piece of paper after he had ordered her to summon Drapkin—something which required her to walk in the opposite direction. Associates say that he yells constantly at everyone who works with him—Gittis, Slovin, Drapkin, Drexel investment bankers. No one except for Milken, they say, is exempt. One associate remarked, "It really is pretty bad. The excuse is he can't control it."

When Drapkin arrived, Perelman addressed his erstwhile Revlon opponents' perception that by the end he was unstoppable, that if they had raised the bid to $59 he would have gone to $60. "There was no point where we were committed emotionally beyond financial reason," he declared. "Look at our record—in Richardson, for example: we have stopped where it made no sense to go forward."

What about the fact that he had by that time raised $750 million—with high carrying charges? "It was reinvested," Perelman said shortly. "Right now I'm sitting on a cash hoard of $1.5 billion. I have a negative carry of about one point. I am willing to do that because tomorrow morning, without making a phone call, I could do eighty percent of the transactions that are available."

Asked when he conceived of the megaleap he made with Revlon, Perelman replied that it was "a process of bites." No, he did not have this trajectory in mind when he started out in 1978 to buy the jewelry company, Cohen-Hatfield. "Go back to 1978: even if we'd defined it, we couldn't have funded it," said Perelman, who refers to himself in the first person plural. "This could not have been done without Drexel."

As to the changes he has made thus far, Perelman said he had hired Richard Avedon to photograph high-fashion models for a new ad campaign and had cut through the excessive bureaucracy that plagued the company, eliminating numerous levels of review. All the bureaucracy, he added, stemmed from Bergerac. "He did not *run* this company."

"It's easier to shoot little birds than to run a company," interpolated Drapkin, referring to Bergerac's yearly shooting holidays in Scotland.

"He put in layers of form rather than substance," Perelman went on. "Books this high"—gesturing above his head—"from each division. Four times a year, he'd budget and rebudget. He brought that practice from ITT. Geneen used that effectively. But Bergerac pulled out the form without the substance."

Several times during the interview, Perelman denied that he had offered Bergerac extra inducements—either at the first meeting or later through Geneen (the $100 million package, which was confirmed by one of Perelman's associates). Returning to this sore point, he put his shoes back on and paced the room, raising his voice. He demanded to know how Bergerac's charges, and his rebuttal, would be presented. "How can you believe what he says?" he demanded. "This guy was stuffing his pockets at every possible moment through the process. He had his finger in this pie from the very beginning. He was a guy totally motivated by greed. Do you think if I had said to him, 'Michel, what would it take?', he would have said, 'No, nothing'?

"Believe me, for a hundred million, he would have taken it so fast your head would spin. He was stuffing his pockets at every opportunity. . . . How can you believe this was not a guy who was stuffing his pockets?

"And what about that château bill in Scotland, prepaid for two years? [Perelman claims that before Bergerac left Revlon he wrote a company check to cover his shooting trips to Scotland; Perelman says he stopped payment on the check.] And what about the 727 with the shower and the gun rack? Maybe you can say he didn't care about money because he was never spending his own!

"And what about when he took the china and silverware? He said he'd bought it—and then I came in here," Perelman argued, "and they were rolling up the rug in his office and taking the *wallpaper* off the walls—yes, the *wallpaper*. There was this twenty-five-thousand-dollar mural, African wildlife, and they were taking it off the wall. I said, 'Wait a minute—if this stuff is his and he wants to take anything else out of here, I want to see *invoices*.'

"That mural," Perelman said in disgust, "was the ugliest thing I've ever seen. It's rolled up in the basement."

He fixed his visitor with a baleful look. "Does that sound like a guy who is bashful about *taking?*"

THE REVLON SAGA has no heroes. Bergerac, though far from being the inept villain that Perelman caricatures, indulged himself with the perks of corporate life. Perelman, cursed with his crude persona that offends so many, apparently attempted to entice Bergerac with lavish inducements and then furiously denied it. And Revlon's defenders, the cream of the legal and investment-banking establishment, allowed their professional judgment to be clouded by their passion, and their prejudice.

On Milken's chessboard, however, all that mattered was that his pawns keep moving deeper into corporate America, decimating its ranks further—making bids and acquisitions and issuing junk bonds and doing streams of divestitures and making new acquisitions—until one day the game would be won.

PART THREE

The Zenith – and the Fall

10

"Drexel is like a god..."

BY NOVEMBER 1986, Milken was scouting new frontiers. "We want to finance the world with our goodies," proclaimed Drexel chairman Robert Linton. Indeed, Milken hoped to replicate in other parts of the world the hostile contest for control that his chosen had waged so successfully in this country. Japan, where the hostile takeover was still nascent, was his first target. On November 10, Drexel held a mini–Predators' Ball in Tokyo.

Milken presided over this lavish affair. It featured two days of presentations (with simultaneous translation) by a familiar cast—a dozen of Drexel's star junk issuers, including Revlon Group, Wickes Companies, Occidental Petroleum Corporation, MCI Communications, Texas Air Corporation and Triangle Industries. The U.S. ambassador to Japan, Mike Mansfield, was a luncheon speaker. The event was organized by Harry Horowitz, Milken's Washington lobbyist and the chief organizer of the Beverly Hills bond conference in 1985. Even Don Engel, of Bungalow 8 fame, was on hand to play his accustomed part, ushering some of the Drexel clients to "baths" (Japanese massage parlors) outside Tokyo each night after dinner.

Drexel executives deemed the conference a huge success. They believed that the Japanese, while still cautious (they traditionally were buyers of triple-A credits with household names), were now ready to wade into the junk market. The Japanese seemed receptive to the gospel Milken preached: that the rating agencies were wrong and that they, the Japanese investors, should reap the benefit of those prevailing misconceptions, as so many thousands of their

American counterparts had done over the past decade, by investing in the high-yield companies of the future.

While Milken did not make it explicit to this audience, they were participating in the first phase of the process he had authored in the United States. First he would build a client base of buyers. Then he would raise capital for small-time entrepreneurs. And finally he would transform those entrepreneurs into mighty challengers, financing their raids on the giants of Japanese industry. The process would be replicated, but the time would be compressed: what had taken seven or eight years to evolve in the U.S. would probably occur within two. And even if the Japanese culture proved too inimical to the hostile takeover in Japan, Milken still wanted to tap the reservoir of Japanese capital to mount raids in this country that were far larger than any he had ever backed—ten- and fifteen- and twenty-billion-dollar bids.

It seemed only natural by the fall of 1986 that Milken should be expanding his scope to cover the world. The home territory, where he was using junk bonds to revolutionize and restructure the American corporate landscape, was in some sense already appropriated. While there were certainly many more battles to be fought, many more giant corporations to be won, Milken's gospel had gained such currency that it was no longer the heresy of an outcast but the liturgy of Wall Street. If everyone had decided to come to his first party, mustn't it be time to start another?

Milken may have been restless, but many of his colleagues would have been content to pause and savor the moment. That Milken, and Drexel with him, could have scaled the heights they had made some of them lightheaded. Who would have imagined that such a rarefied atmosphere would ever be theirs to enjoy? The payout from Milken's singular idea had been so bountiful—in terms of money, and power, and even a growing social acceptance—that the prevailing mood at Drexel in the fall of 1986 was close to euphoria.

It was captured in a framed quote, in large, bold print, which Drexel investment banker Stephen Weinroth had displayed in his office. Referring to the junk-bond market and takeovers, it read: "Drexel is like a god in that end of the business and a god can do anything it wants. . . . They are awesome. You hate to do business against them."

The quote was from Michael Boylan, the president of Macfadden Holdings, excerpted from an article in the June 1986 issue of *Barron's*. It had been sent to Weinroth and other colleagues by Arthur Bilger, of Drexel's Beverly Hills corporate-finance department.

Many of Drexel's wish lists drawn up in early Cavas Gobhai sessions—wish lists which had been wistful, grandiose, almost delusional at the time—had become reality. Among them was the goal articulated by Leon Black in 1979 when he recorded the corporate-finance team's resolution to find and help create "the robber barons of the future." Now, in 1986, Black expounded happily on his fully realized goal.

"What I like about Drexel is that our clients are the growth companies of this country, and the heads of these companies are often real principals. They are the modern version of robber barons," Black declared expansively. "These are the guys shaking up management, these are the guys who are building empires."

He ticked off his favorites: his friend and client Carl Icahn; Henry Kravis of Kohlberg Kravis, with whom he had worked on that firm's $6.2 billion buyout of the Beatrice Companies; Samuel Heyman, the chairman of GAF whose $6 billion bid for Union Carbide had been financed by Drexel; Rupert Murdoch, whose purchase of television stations from Metromedia had been financed by Drexel; and Ronald Perelman.

"I look at them as the Rockefellers of one hundred years ago," Black continued eagerly. "They're very, very bright. They keep you awake. They've got lots of guts."

But Black reserved his most exuberant praise for the man who made all this possible. "I'm not much given to hero worship, but I have to tell you I never thought there would be a Michael Milken. He's someone who sees the big picture all the time—and also the small picture, down to the details. He knows so many industries in such depth. He knows the balance sheets of companies better than many of our clients do. And he is so aggressive. He has an absolutely voracious appetite. He wants one hundred percent market share."

To be creating empire-builders—choosing them, molding them, sitting on their boards, owning pieces of their growing companies—was heady business, especially for investment bankers who, before 1985, had been the lesser-knowns of Wall Street. Black was not alone in his breathlessness. One of his colleagues in corporate finance, G. Christian Andersen, who had lived through what he refers to as the "Bataan death march" on Wall Street in the early seventies, when he bounced from one failing firm to another, declared that he once had thought of getting his doctorate and teaching history; but now, in 1986, he said he felt he was *making* history.

"We are the gentlemen who finance and create change," Andersen declared. "When I read [Alvin] Toffler's *Future Shock*, and he described this vortex of change that whirls around us, and it happens very fast in New York City, and slower in Des Moines, and even slower in the outback of Australia, the thing that was amazing to me was, when I looked at the funnel of that maelstrom, the vortex of that sits right in the middle of my desk. I am the fella who determines what the change will be. If I don't finance it, it ain't gonna happen. I get to decide who's going to get capital, to make the future. Now, I ask you—what's more romantic than that?"

As overblown as Andersen's image of himself had become, there was a germ of truth in what he said. For the most highly leveraged mega-acquisitions—the nouveaux entrepreneurs who were changing the face of corporate America—Drexel was indeed the only conduit.

What Drexel had done was to securitize the low-grade corporate loan, much as Salomon Brothers had securitized mortgages in its creation of the mortgage-backed security. In its securitizing of the corporate loan, Drexel had to some degree displaced the banks and the insurance companies, which had formerly had the acquisition-financing role to themselves—just as their clients, America's major corporations, had had the acquisitor role to *them*selves. Now those banks' clients were as likely to be prey as predator. And those clients were being felled, one after another, in acquisitions more highly leveraged than the banks would ever have financed.

The banks were lenders in many of Drexel's deals, but their loans were generally short-term and secured. Without Drexel to place the unsecured, subordinated debt, these deals would never have happened. And while other investment banking firms now were eager to play Drexel's part, the megadeals spawned securities —junk bonds—in amounts that no investment-banking firm but Drexel could sell.

Drexel's monopoly of this market, following the earlier years of monopoly of the nontakeover junk market, had resulted in a trajectory of growth that was unprecedented on Wall Street. At the end of 1977, Drexel's revenues were about $150 million; the firm had about $75 million in capital, of which less than $40 million was equity. The book value of its stock (as of August 1977) was $4.47 per share. By the end of 1985, the firm's revenues were $2.5 billion; it had about $1 billion of capital, of which over 75 percent was equity. The book value of its stock was $58.66 per share. Its profits were thought to be about $600 million pretax and $304.2 million after taxes—which would place it not far behind the mammoth Salomon Brothers, which had nearly double Drexel's capital.

And by the end of 1986, Drexel's revenues would soar to a record $4 billion and its after-tax earnings to an estimated $545.5 million—making it the most profitable investment-banking firm in America. Salomon was second in earnings, with $516 million. Goldman, Sachs is a closely held partnership which, like Drexel, does not publicly report earnings, but its earnings were estimated by Perrin Long, an analyst at Lipper Analytical Services, Inc., to have been between $475 million and $500 million.

The engine of this growth, of course, was Milken's group. In 1978 it had been contributing 100 percent of the firm's profits. With the growth of corporate finance, which Milken fueled—first with the original issuance of junk bonds and then with the LBOs and the takeovers—the share of Milken's group in the firm's profits declined to roughly 43 percent by the end of 1985. But corporate finance, his adjunct, had been increasing its profits at a rate of roughly 50 percent a year. In 1977 the corporate-finance department had $4.2 million in revenues; in 1985, it had made about $700 million.

In this entrepreneurial firm, where salaries were moderate and all the heavy compensation came in bonuses, those payouts were staggering. In 1985 Drexel is said to have devoted roughly $400–500 million of its $2.5 billion in revenues to bonuses. Milken—Drexel's highest-paid member—is said to have received about $40 million as his bonus (this did not include, of course, profits from all his trading partnerships and other investments, which associates estimated brought him closer to $100 million for the year). And even the top bankers in corporate finance—who had always felt like the poor cousins compared to Milken and his group—had little to complain about. Leon Black, for example, is said by one friend to have received about $8 million (in a bonus payment that included warrants). And in 1986 Drexel would pay out as much as $600 million in bonuses, with Milken and his high-yield department reportedly receiving over $250 million and corporate finance receiving $140 million. One corporate-finance executive, who estimated by the fall of 1986 that his bonus for that year would be roughly $9 million, commented, "This is Disneyland for adults."

As spectacular as Drexel's profits were, they were no anomaly on Wall Street in the early and middle eighties. The M&A frenzy had thrown off enormous fees to the other major investment-banking firms even before Drexel had a toehold in the business. Also, the period from 1981 to 1986 had seen one of the most powerful, sustained surges in stock and bond history. Firms were awash in trading profits. A number of Wall Street investment houses had taken advantage of this prosperity, too, to sell shares to the public and transform themselves from private partnerships into giant worldwide corporations. Salomon Brothers, which merged with the publicly owned Phibro Corporation in 1981, had increased its capital from only $200 million in 1980 to about $3 billion by mid-1986.

But no other investment-banking firm had vaulted into the financial stratosphere at Drexel's velocity. And no other firm had redefined the M&A business on its own unique terms (with the ability to raise billions of dollars almost overnight, from Milken's junk-bond network), terms which could not be matched by anyone else on the Street. Other firms sought to imitate Drexel. They attempted to break into the junk-bond market. They embarked on merchant banking. They initiated bridge financing, at great risk to themselves, in a desperate attempt to compete with the "highly confident" weapon. What had happened by the fall of 1986, quite simply, was that Milken had cast not only Drexel but to a large degree the Street in his image.

The most powerful firms, with the most cachet, had made their entrances into the heretofore disdained junk market in 1983 and 1984. By the end of 1985, Salomon; Morgan Stanley; Goldman, Sachs; and First Boston (in that order) were each making small incursions into Milken's preserve. Trailing close behind them came many other notable investment banks. Drexel's market share slipped to about 56 percent from the sovereign 60–70 percent it had held in earlier years. But even now, with its market share lowered, there was no close second, just a crowd of would-be competitors at the lower end of the chart. In 1985 Drexel had done seventy-three deals, for a total of $6.7 billion, and Salomon, its closest competitor, had done nine deals for $1.4 billion.

Some of Milken's colleagues at Drexel took undisguised pleasure in their rivals' flounderings. Morgan Stanley, for example, having first suffered the Oxoco debacle, where the company had defaulted within six months of the underwriting, had embarrassed itself further in its underwriting of $540 million of People Express bonds, some of which had plunged to as little as 35 percent of their issue price by July 1986. As Chris Andersen commented to *The Wall Street Journal*, "They [Morgan Stanley] announced with great fanfare that they were coming in to 'gentrify' the high-yield market." (Andersen was referring to a trade-publication headline that had trumpeted Morgan's entrance.) "I wonder how they feel about it today. Maybe it's a tough business. Maybe it isn't any more genteel than the steel business or the auto business or the banking business."

Milken struck a different note. He told this reporter in an interview in 1987, "I welcome competition. Other people might see things we don't see. We might see things they don't see. The negatives are—and I'm trying to state this in a positive way—that some deals may get done that shouldn't get done, and then that may hurt the perception of the high-yield market. People have a tendency to remember only the ones that didn't work out.

"Financing is an art form," Milken added. "One of the challenges is how to correctly finance a company. In certain periods of time, more covenants need to be put into deals. You have to be sure the company has the right covenant—to allow it the freedom to grow, but also to insure the integrity of the credit. Sometimes a company should issue convertible bonds instead of straight bonds. Sometimes it should issue preferred stock. Each company and each financing is different, and the process can't be imitative."

By 1986, Milken's rivals had also followed in his footsteps by venturing into "merchant banking"—a term borrowed from the British, whose investment banks in the nineteenth century had pooled capital to buy businesses and thus had built empires. In this country it meant that the firms were putting up their own capital in deals, mainly takeovers and buyouts. They were no longer acting solely as agent, but also as principal. This was something, of course, that Drexel, through Milken (as well as a few others, such as Allen and Company), had been doing for years.

But Drexel's rivals had also come up with a new variation on merchant banking: the bridge loan. There, the investment bank puts up its own capital as a loan in order to facilitate a client's deal.

That loan in effect "bridges" the time from the closing of the deal to the time when the junk bonds are sold; the proceeds of the sale then pay off the loan or (if the investment bank is leaving some of its capital in the deal) part of it. In their enthusiasm, Salomon and a group of institutional lenders who were participating in thus funding deals together dubbed themselves "the Bridge Club."

It was inevitable, once these firms—tantalized by those 3–4 percent spreads—had followed Milken into the original issuance of junk bonds, that they would then attempt to follow him the next step: to the junk-bond-financed takeover and buyout. How could they not try, after watching Drexel garner a financing fee of $86 million in the Beatrice buyout? Milken had no patent on greed. (Although he did, arguably, give the word new meaning. Drexel's financing fee in Beatrice was dwarfed by the amount Drexel partners were said to have earned by 1987 from their equity stakes in the deal—close to $800 million, several hundred million of which was said to have gone to Milken personally.)

But none of these investment banks had Milken's ability to tap into his network and raise billions overnight. None of them could enlist his buyers to give them a bridge loan—which is in essence what these buyers did for Milken. His first-tier buyers—who committed to buy the bonds and earned the commitment fees, but were often replaced by second-tier buyers by the time the deal was funded, or shortly thereafter—provided him a bridge.

Milken's rivals had two problems. First, they didn't have Milken's distribution system, and so they were unable to place $4–5 billion in junk. Second, they needed more time to place what they could. The bridge loan cured the time problem and made deals with less than $2 billion in junk financing viable for them. From the client's standpoint, the bridge went the "highly confident" letter one better. While that letter had been largely accepted in the business world as transmutable into cold cash, it was not cold cash. But now First Boston, Morgan Stanley, Shearson Lehman, Merrill Lynch, Salomon Brothers and others were offering to put cash into their clients' hands—and take the risk of the refinancing themselves. That risk was considerable, for time here was a two-edged sword: crucial for them to be able to place the bonds, but dangerous in that the market could change.

That, of course, had been the beauty of Milken's system—that there was such bountiful reward for so little risk to him or the firm.

When Icahn suggested that Drexel in essence give him a bridge loan in Phillips, his proposal had been dismissed and the "highly confident" letter conceived instead. But in their desperation to reap Drexel-like rewards, other firms were seduced into greater risk than Drexel had ever taken.

These firms' deepest obeisance to Drexel, however, came not when they tried to imitate and compete, but when they simply gave up and encouraged their clients to bring this much-hated rival into their deals—so that the dreadnought would be on their side. According to two executives at Donaldson, Lufkin and Jenrette, which along with Drexel represented management in the buyout of Viacom, they had urged their clients to hire Drexel, for just that reason. And it was the same thinking, according to a well-placed source, that led Goodyear Tire and Rubber Company, in planning a defensive restructuring after a month of frenzied trading in its stock during October 1986, to hire Drexel along with its traditional investment-banking firm, Goldman, Sachs.

While the rest of Wall Street was trying occasionally to disarm but more often to compete with the renegade firm, Drexel was not only fighting to keep its lion's share, but also gearing for posterity. Fred Joseph had become the firm's chief executive officer in May 1985. And Joseph was intent on building a towering, enduring financial institution from the foundation that Milken's machine had laid.

Over the past several years, Drexel had been plowing some of its enormous profits into new areas. Dr. Richard Sandor, generally considered the principal architect of the interest-rate futures markets, joined Drexel in 1982 to develop a financial-futures division. Joseph's brother, Stephen Joseph, joined Drexel from Salomon Brothers in 1984 to start a mortgage-backed securities department. By 1986, his department had 280 employees and ranked in the top five of the industry. In municipal finance, where it also expanded enormously through lateral hiring, Drexel in '86 underwrote some $15 billion in offerings, up from $1 billion two years earlier; it went from being ranked as the fortieth-largest participant to number eleven or number twelve. And in '86 Drexel also moved from fifteenth to eighth place in U.S.-government-securities trading. And Drexel—albeit far more measuredly than some of its compatriots, such as Salomon—followed the Wall Street trend toward globalization, expanding its offices abroad, particularly London and Tokyo.

Symbolic of this drive to make itself into a well-rounded Wall Street titan was Drexel's decision, in July 1986, to move from its scattered quarters at 55 and 60 Broad Street into the brand-new two-million-square-foot, forty-seven-story tower, Seven World Trade Center. Drexel, which acquired a minority interest in the skyscraper, committed to lease the entire building for $100 million a year. In 1986 the firm had 4,300 employees in New York, but the new tower, it was planned, would eventually house 10,000 employees.

This institution-building was Joseph's vision more than Milken's. It always had been. What motivated Milken was a consuming passion for dollars, and for an empire—ever widening—to control. But Joseph was bent on fulfilling the ambition he had expressed to Mark Kaplan, Drexel's then president, six months after arriving at the firm in 1974—when he said that, given fifteen years, he could create something as important as Goldman, Sachs. The iconoclastic Milken would have derided such an aspiration. Joseph, however, did not wish to remain the outsider forever. He would join the club. And now, twelve years after his declaration to Kaplan, he was on track.

As Stephen Weinroth remarked, "Don't take me literally, but Fred [Joseph] would like to travel around the country and say, 'Drexel is the largest underwriter of corporate securities, and of this, and of that'—he'd like to say, 'the largest in all things.' And if he had to say that we were second-largest in trading of government securities of Somaliland, he'd say, 'But we're gaining on the leader.' And if we were the largest in everything, and we made only $10 million, he'd still be happy. He's a market-share guy."

A central tenet at Drexel, frequently articulated by both Milken and Joseph, was that it was not capital but people that were the scarce resource. Both of them, therefore, were willing to pay more than anybody on the Street in order to hire and keep those they considered the best. In Milken's group, where the pay had been astronomical since the seventies, there were few defections. It was a historic event when, in the fall of 1986, one of Milken's traders of more recent vintage, Eugene Wong, was hired away by Prudential Bache; the headhunter had made a host of calls, seeking "one of Milken's disciples."

People did burn out, or worse, under Milken's ceaseless lash (one trader was rumored to have been found under his desk chewing his phone cord one day), but then they were generally shifted to less stressful positions off the trading desk, or placed outside Drexel to operate as adjuncts. A few simply retired, at an early age. Charles Causey, who had been with Milken since the Drexel Firestone days, gave it all up in 1981 and moved to Islamorada in the Florida Keys, to devote himself to bone-fishing.

In 1985 and '86, Joseph had gone on a firmwide hiring binge, as part of his goal of diversifying the firm's strength and expertise. By early 1986, one big drawing card he was playing as a recruiter was that Goldman, Sachs was the only other highly profitable private firm on the Street. If Drexel ever went public, its shareholders (and the stock was widely held throughout the firm, with about eighteen hundred stockholders in all) would be likely to reap a bonanza.

Now, in the fall of 1986, Joseph pointed with pride to some of his star recruits: Martin Siegel, whom he had finally succeeded in wooing from Kidder; Sam Hunter and Michael (Jack) Kugler from Merrill Lynch; Jeffrey Beck from Oppenheimer and Company; and Robert Pangia from Kidder. He had had some rejections, among them Bruce Wasserstein, the M&A star at First Boston, who would later leave to start his own firm, and Michael Zimmerman, a fast-rising M&A banker at Salomon Brothers who would soon become co-head of M&A there. But Joseph was still ardently recruiting. "The day Drexel gets the last of the best people [for each position] is the day the battle's over," he promised.

And the buckets of money that Drexel was offering were not only for the superstars. Offers to the lower-tiered people also made the pay at other firms seem, as Martin Siegel had once commented, like the margarine spread. The case of one analyst at Donaldson, Lufkin and Jenrette is typical. DLJ had hired him out of Harvard Business School at $80,000 a year. After he had been with them for one year he was doing good though not exceptional work in the health-care field, and his salary and bonuses had risen to about $110,000. Drexel, meanwhile, had hired a corporate-finance team specializing in health-care businesses from Kidder, but it lacked an analyst. So Drexel targeted the DLJ analyst. They offered him $350,000. According to a DLJ executive, the analyst had been happy at the firm, content with his salary, never even imagining that he could be making more than three times as much. But when that tripled offer came, it was too much to resist.

● ●

IT WAS CLEAR by the fall of 1986, however, that in Drexel's sweep of the Street, in its self-touting as the hottest firm, one with a derring-do, entrepreneurial culture where there was virtually no limit to the dollars that someone with talent and drive could make, it had attracted some so greedy that even Drexel was unable to sate their hunger.

Dennis Levine was a warm, jovial investment banker whose personality outshone his intellectual attributes. Nonetheless, he had made himself into enough of an M&A presence that when he was passed over for a managing directorship at Shearson Lehman in 1984 and decided to leave, he received job offers from three other top investment-banking firms. But it was Drexel—which guaranteed the thirty-three-year-old an income of $1 million a year—that won the auction.

On May 12, 1986, Levine was arrested, handcuffed and taken off to spend the night at the Metropolitan Correction Center. He was accused by the SEC of having made $12.6 million in illegal profits through insider trading in fifty-four stocks. And in June he pleaded guilty to four felony counts and agreed to cooperate with the government in its continuing investigation.

Drexel reeled from the scandal. "It's more than embarrassing," Linton, the firm's chairman, told Business Week. "It's like someone breaking into your home. You almost feel dirty about it." In private at the firm, it quickly became material for gallows humor. "Did you hear why Mike fired Dennis?" quipped one Drexel investment banker. "Because anybody who had to do fifty-four trades to make twelve million dollars couldn't be any good."

Levine's case quickly mushroomed into the scandal of Wall Street as his cooperation with the government led to charges against members of his ring—investment bankers from Shearson Lehman, Lazard Frères and Goldman, Sachs and a lawyer from Wachtell, Lipton. Moreover, within the next several months there were two other indictments, unrelated to the Levine case, brought against Drexel employees. One was arbitrageur Robert Salsbury, who was alleged to be a member of yet another insider trading ring. The other was senior vice-president in the firm's expanding international-finance department, Antonio Gebauer, who was charged with having misappropriated funds from client accounts while he was a banker at Morgan Guaranty Trust Company. Milken had hired Gebauer to work on his Third World debt project, attempting to find some original approach to the crisis (which, if found, would probably rival the original issuance of junk bonds in its payout). Both these individuals ultimately pleaded guilty.

Drexel officials pointed out that all three—Levine, Salsbury and Gebauer—had been at Drexel for less than a year, and that their criminal conduct had started (and, in Gebauer's case, occurred wholly) before they arrived at Drexel. Furthermore, Drexel was by no means alone in this spreading scandal. With Goldman, Sachs; Lazard Frères; Morgan Guaranty; and Wachtell, Lipton, Drexel was arguably in better company than it had ever been.

By the fall of '86, the shock of Levine, who had been by far the most high-profile of Drexel's miscreants, had faded at Drexel. Soon, Drexel officials hoped, he would be forgotten, erased from public memory, as cleanly as he had been wiped from Drexel's annals. Copies of Drexel's glossy 1985 annual report had just been distributed in the firm when the news of Levine's arrest hit; they were quickly recalled. New copies were issued, and in place of Dennis Levine's smiling image Martin Siegel's appeared.

Siegel moved from Kidder to Drexel in February 1986. In so doing, he was betting more on Joseph than on Milken. After about a half-dozen meetings with Joseph through the summer of 1985, he had gone out to the West Coast in October to meet Milken. Siegel had found Milken almost frightening—like a speed junkie, he thought, incapable of sitting still, shooting off ideas, here, here and there, like a sparkler. Milken told him, "When you start to add up how much you have, I don't want you working for me. Then you're not hungry anymore." Siegel thought Milken wanted to be the richest man in the world.

That kind of rawness was not something Siegel wished to see in himself. He felt more comfortable with Joseph—a bright, smooth-talking and attractive salesman, like himself—and with Joseph's projection of their building a world-class financial institution together. He and Joseph were both builders, Siegel decided—he had built Kidder's M&A department from nothing, and Joseph, powered by Milken's engine, might indeed create an institution comparable to a Morgan Stanley, a First Boston, a Goldman, Sachs. Siegel thought it was a historic opportunity, to be in the vanguard of such an enterprise. And he and Joseph agreed that his presence would accelerate that process. Siegel had a franchise in tender-offer defense, a whole roster of blue-chip and loyal clients, who, he guessed, would follow him anywhere—even into Drexel's lion's den.

He made sure, too, that his relationship with Martin Lipton, with whom he had worked on so many deals and who was also a kind of father figure to him, would remain intact. That relationship had been soldered in 1983 when together they had inaugurated the poison pill (Lipton's creation) defending Lenox, Inc., against an attempted takeover by Brown-Forman Distillers Corporation.

Other investment bankers on whom Lipton had tried to foist his poison pill had been reluctant to use it. It was sure to be open to legal challenge, they argued, and if successful it might kill the golden goose, the takeover business. But Lipton had urged Siegel that they should implement it, that if they did they would *own* the defense market. And that is not far from what had happened. Lipton had proceeded to carve out his defense franchise, refusing to represent aggressors in hostile junk-bond-financed deals and, of course, becoming one of the fiercest, most outspoken critics of what he derisively called Drexel's "hostile, junk-bond, two-tiered, bust-up takeover."

Now Lipton promised Siegel that despite Siegel's joining the Huns, he would continue to work with him—but only on defense. So Drexel got not only Martin Siegel, but the promise of a sometime alliance with the dean of the defense bar in M&A, and the erstwhile leader of the establishment onslaught against Drexel into the bargain. Lipton negotiated Siegel's employment contract with Drexel.

That contract assured that at the same time that Siegel would be satisfying his image of himself as a builder, he would be getting richer. He had obtained from Drexel a guarantee of $3 million a year for three years. With possible further bonuses and his investments in Milken's trading partnerships, he was sure to make much more. Drexel had also promised to make him whole on the profit he would have reaped on his Kidder stock (he was that firm's fourth-largest shareholder) if Kidder went public or was sold within two years of his coming to Drexel. Kidder was bought by General Electric about six months after Siegel left.

If Siegel needed further confirmation of the financial opportunism of his move, he got it when the results of the first two months of 1986 came in at Drexel. In each of those months, Drexel made more money than Kidder had in the entire preceding year.

However leery of Milken Siegel had been at their initial meeting, once he joined Drexel he too came under Milken's spell. He went out to Beverly Hills for three-day periods, spending from 4 A.M. to 8 P.M. with the indefatigable Milken, and was awed by the fecundity of ideas that had first seemed to him wild and uncontrolled. At Kidder, he had had to generate the new ideas, and they had never come to him from the trading side. Now Milken was the generator.

Siegel's primary mission, however—as conceptualized by him and Joseph—was to build a defense business at Drexel, with the kinds of blue-chip clients the firm had never had. If Drexel was to become a major financial institution, it could no longer be merely a haven for renegades. Siegel's goal was to have twenty-five or thirty clients on a tender defense retainer, much as the law firm of Skadden, Arps did. And he got off to a good start. In his first month at Drexel, he contacted about twenty of his old clients. He began to represent several, either on defense or on financing.

One was Lear Siegler, the aerospace concern and manufacturer of auto parts, which needed help because its stock was being accumulated by the greenmailing Belzberg brothers. Siegel was, of course, well situated to mediate with the Belzbergs (they had been part of Milken's coterie ever since Mesa-Gulf), and ultimately the Belzbergs were bought out by Lear Siegler. According to Dan Dorfman in *New York* magazine, the Belzbergs made a profit of almost $7.5 million.

But the potential conflicts that could arise in Drexel's attempting to go both ways were vividly illustrated at this time. Contemporaneous with Drexel's representing Lear Siegler *against* the dreaded Belzbergs, it was also representing the Belzbergs as they greenmailed Ashland Oil. Here the Belzbergs reaped a profit of $15.4 million, according to Dorfman. If there was not an ethical dilemma (conflicts of interest are rarely recognized in the investment banking world), such dual purpose might give pause to the sort of client Siegel was trying to bring aboard. Potential clients might wonder, as they disclosed their financials to their investment banker, where his loyalty, or that of his partners, really resided.

Siegel decided that the best way for his Kidder clients to overcome their fear of Drexel would be for them to become acquainted with his partners, to meet Milken, to understand that true security lay in their being in the Drexel camp, not outside it. So he invited more than a dozen of them to the 1986 Predators' Ball.

In one year so much had changed that even the old name, Predators' Ball, sounded faintly archaic. Among the two thousand guests were many CEOs of major corporations. T. Boone Pickens, the raider who had started it all with Mesa-Gulf, and had been a keynote speaker at Drexel conferences in 1984 and 1985, attended but was not invited to speak (and was clearly miffed). Ronald Perelman, now chairman of Revlon, opened the conference, and Dr. Armand Hammer, chairman of Occidental, closed it. There were also presentations by Beatrice, Gulf + Western, Burroughs, Warner Communications and Lear Siegler. As one of the conference organizers exclaimed excitedly, "It's the Academy Awards of business!"

The old ethos was still there, though not as strident and all-encompassing as in years past. In one of the videos that are produced each year at Milken's direction, *Dallas'* J. R. Ewing (Larry Hagman) appeared, flashing a "Drexel Express titanium card," which, he declared, had a $10 billion line of credit. J. R. urged, "Don't go hunting without it!"

But the best line of the conference, most participants agreed, was delivered by Nelson Peltz, who was asked to give a presentation for the first time. A year earlier, Peltz had been a nervous hopeful, with nothing to his name but a controlling interest in a meager wire and cable company. Now he was magically transformed into one of the nation's industrialists, with a controlling interest in a $4 billion empire. In a play on Winston Churchill's famous declaration, Peltz gazed out at the crowd, many of them holders of his bonds, and declared, "Never have so few owed so much to so many."

Martin Siegel played a prominent role, appearing on a panel and at one point, in reference to his move from the bluenose Kidder to the dread Drexel, donned first a white cowboy hat and then a black. His old Kidder clients, among them the chairmen of Lear Siegler and Pan American, seemed rather dazzled by it all. One guest wondered, "Wow, Marty, does Kidder throw these kinds of things?" But probably no one was more dazzled than Siegel himself. The personal wealth there, he calculated, was three times the GNP. And it was not only the sheer dollars but the power and influence that he found so awe-inspiring.

One manifestation of that growing power and influence was a political presence far larger than at any previous conference. Senators Bill Bradley and Frank Lautenberg of New Jersey, Howard Metzenbaum of Ohio and Alan Cranston of California all spoke at the conference. Senate Majority Leader Robert Dole was supposed to appear as a surprise speaker at a corporate-finance breakfast, but he canceled at the last moment. Representative Timothy Wirth of Col-

orado and Massachusetts Senator Edward M. Kennedy came, but they were not speakers. "Kennedy told me," recalled Tubby Burnham, " 'I'm here to listen and to learn.' "

Drexel had spared no effort—and no expense—in educating Congress over the past year and a half.

Representative Wirth was one of the early recipients of Drexel's lavish attentions—not surprisingly, since he chaired the hearings of the House Subcommittee on Telecommunications, Consumer Protection and Finance on takeovers, in 1984 and again in the first half of 1985. At first, Wirth spearheaded the congressional assault; but by April 1985, when he attended the Predators' Ball, he was straddling the fence, and by the end of that year he had become a staunch supporter of Drexel and its junk bonds. In fact, one of his top aides, David Aylward, left his job with Wirth to help organize Alliance for Capital Access, a lobby formed to oppose federal limits on junk-bond financings, formed by Drexel clients at Drexel's prompting. The leader of Alliance was Larry Mizel of M.D.C. Holdings, a longtime issuer of junk bonds and also a major subscriber to the bonds in the takeover deals.

Under the Federal Election Campaign Act, the limits on contributions to candidates per election are $1,000 for a contribution by an individual and $5,000 by a multicandidate committee (the category in which Drexel's Political Action Committee falls). In 1985, Drexel's PAC donated $2,000 to Wirth, falling short of its limit by $3,000. But contributions by individuals at the firm (including $1,000 from both Michael and Lowell Milken, and $1,000 from Gary Winnick, who left the firm in the fall of '85) totaled about $17,000. Roughly $9,000 of this was comprised of donations of $250 from members of the Milken group. There were also some contributions from Milken's extended family. Donations from Tom Spiegel, Abraham Spiegel, Helene Spiegel, Edita Spiegel, Lee Eckel (a Columbia Savings director) and a Columbia PAC totaled $7,150.

While Drexel executives knew that Wirth was their supporter by the latter half of 1985, Wachtell, Lipton—with Martin Lipton spearheading the anti-junk crusade—apparently did not. In late 1985, twenty members of the Wachtell firm each donated $500 to Wirth—for a total of $10,000.

By mid-1985, the center of activity for anti-takeover legislation had shifted from the House to the Senate, and Senator Alfonse M. D'Amato of New York, chairman of the Senate Banking Commit-

tee's subcommittee on securities, had primacy. Drexel was by far the biggest donor among financial firms to D'Amato from 1981 to 1986; its contributions totaled $70,750. (The next-highest D'Amato contribution from an investment-banking firm was Morgan Stanley's at $40,600.)

As reported by Bruce Ingersoll and Brooks Jackson in *The Wall Street Journal*, Drexel's courting of D'Amato moved into high gear at the end of May 1985, when D'Amato was preparing to hold hearings on proposed legislation. One bill would have curbed the use of junk bonds in takeovers and buyouts, and another would have limited junk-bond purchases by thrifts. Harry Horowitz, Milken's boyhood chum who joined Milken's group in 1979 to perform administrative functions and by the mideighties was his Washington lobbyist and Predators' Ball organizer, set up a fund-raising dinner for D'Amato at Chasen's in Beverly Hills. The guest list at that dinner included twenty-three executives from Drexel and a half dozen from Columbia Savings and Loan, including Thomas Spiegel. D'Amato's take from this dinner was more than $33,000.

During the late spring of 1985, the wave of anti-takeover sentiment in Congress was cresting, and many legislators were eager to take some action. According to the *Journal* account, D'Amato assured his fellow senators that he would have legislation ready to be considered before the summer recess. That, however, did not happen. It was December 1985 when D'Amato finally had his draft bill readied, and by that time the issue had lost its heat. In any event, D'Amato's proposed legislation carried no provisions onerous to Drexel. On the subject of junk bonds, he suggested a federal study. Five days after D'Amato introduced his innocuous bill, Fred Joseph and thirty-five other Drexel executives each donated $500 to the Senator's campaign.

In the end, of the thirty bills that dealt with regulating takeovers in 1984 and 1985, not one passed. While Drexel's (and other investment-banking firms' too) lobbying efforts were herculean, at least as much credit for their nonpassage must go to the Reagan Administration, which had said that it would veto any such legislation.

And the SEC, which was of course the agency most involved, did not support any of the proposed bills. This was hardly surprising, considering that it was the pro-takeover attitude of the SEC and the Justice Department (in its antitrust policies) under Reagan that had

fueled the M&A activity of the early eighties. The SEC did do a study of junk bonds in takeover financing, which reached the predictable conclusion: Released in June 1986, it stated that there was no "justification for new regulatory initiatives aimed at curbing the use of this kind of debt issuance in takeover bids or indeed as it relates to any other aspects of corporate financing activity."

In their 1985 annual report, the President's Council of Economic Advisers had weighed in with its conclusions, surprising only in their ambitiousness. They purported to settle once and for all the decades-long debate over whether takeovers are beneficial or harmful. This august council concluded that mergers and acquisitions "improve efficiency, transfer scarce resources to higher valued uses, and stimulate effective corporate management." The conclusion was remarkably definitive but, apparently, more polemical than proven. In some of the more interesting testimony that emerged from the congressional hearings on takeovers, F. M. Scherer, a Swarthmore College economics professor, had rebutted the Council's findings. In his testimony in March 1985 he pointed out that the report's conclusion that takeovers improve efficiency relied on stock market event studies, which are short-run in orientation (examining stock prices during periods ten to thirty days before and after the announcement or consummation of the merger). If one looks at a period of ten years or so, Professor Scherer testified, the results are very different.

Scherer has developed the premier data base in this country for looking at the financial consequences of merger. This data base draws upon twenty-seven years of merger history and seven years of sell-off history for nearly four thousand individual businesses.

These are some of Scherer's findings, from his case studies and statistical research:

• Contrary to the Council's view that merger-makers sought companies where management had failed, most in fact targeted well-managed entities (such as National Can). What they were generally attracted by was not sick companies or slipshod management but undervalued assets.

• Takeovers by firms with no managerial expertise in the acquired company's line of business tended to impair, not improve, efficiency.

• Takeovers frequently led to short-run profit-maximizing strategies, such as the "cash cow" strategy under which "a business is starved of R&D, equipment modernization, and advertising funds, and/or prices are set at high levels inviting competitor inroads, leaving in the end a depleted, non-competitive shell."

• On average, acquisitions were less profitable for the acquiring firms than the maintenance of existing businesses and the internal development of new business lines.

• Many takeovers led to selloffs, which did improve the efficiency of the simpler, self-standing entity.

• While Scherer had relatively few hostile takeovers in his sampling, in those he did study he found that the takeover aggravated performance deficiencies that existed earlier.

In response to questions from panel members, Scherer also made an interesting point about the high-leverage, or debt-intensive, capital structures of many U.S. companies, which are coming to resemble Japanese companies' financial structures. Indeed, in the gospel according to Milken which is spread by so many of his acolytes, it is often noted that Japanese companies have for years carried much higher debt-to-equity ratios than American companies. True enough, Scherer commented, but the Japanese are able to carry such high levels of debt because when they get into financial difficulties the government bails them out.

Scherer's testimony was followed by that of Warren Law, a professor at Harvard Business School. Law too had come to rebut the "glittering generalities" of the Council's report. The Council's reliance upon short-run stock market behavior as evidence that takeovers are beneficial, he said, could be accepted only if the stock market were a good judge of intrinsic values. (As Milken and his entire coterie of raiders—who had made billions by identifying assets undervalued by the market—could have told this group, it is not.)

Law added that he did not believe that it could be strictly proven that takeovers deter or promote growth and productivity. Inasmuch as "we cannot run history twice with and without them, we can only speculate." With this caveat, however, his speculation is that takeovers decrease productivity. He bases this view on a number of factors. Through takeovers, bigger firms are created, and he believes that large firms "make fewer but bigger errors, tend to continue wrong policies too long, and have the resources to delay until crisis is unmistakable."

Furthermore, he pointed out that in the late 1970s approxi-

mately half of all corporate acquisitions were also corporate divestitures, many of them businesses which were acquired during the
last merger heyday of the 1960s. That wave, he said, was accompanied by "an increasing tendency of executive suites to be dominated by people with financial and legal skills, executives who
believed a manager with no special expertise in any particular industry could nevertheless step into an unfamiliar company and run
it successfully through strict application of financial controls. The
present dismantling of many conglomerates is the result of this
folly. There is no reason to believe the result will differ this time."

The takeover debate would be laid to rest neither by the 1985
annual report of the President's Council of Economic Advisers nor
by Professor Scherer's research. While Scherer's conclusions appeared to be much more soundly based, one reason the debate has
been so long-lived is that there is some truth on both sides. Some
takeovers do result in more efficient and profitable companies, even
when the new manager-owner has no expertise in the industry and
has been, as Frank Considine put it, a *financial* operator, but not an
operator—as in the case, thus far, of Carl Icahn and TWA. Some,
on the other hand, do result in companies so debt-laden that their
R&D budgets are starved and they become noncompetitive—as
could conceivably become the case with Uniroyal Chemical, which
was the profitable, healthy core of the old Uniroyal and in its brief
tenure under Nelson Peltz's aegis earned barely enough to cover the
interest charges on its mountain of $1.06 billion debt. The questions
that remain, of course—which of these scenarios occurs more often,
and whether there is indeed a preponderance sufficiently quantifia-
ble and large that one can conclude that most takeovers are beneficial or harmful—will not be able to be meaningfully addressed for
the most recent wave of buyouts and takeovers for years.

Despite the reservations that both Scherer and Law voiced
about takeovers during their testimony before Congress, neither professor was wholeheartedly endorsing anti-takeover legislation, since
both were wary of efforts of the federal government to tinker with
the tender-offer process. Law, however, did favor legislation to abolish greenmail. And Scherer was in favor of changing the tax law
that favors the issuing of debt over equity by making interest payments (on debt) deductible but dividends (on stock) not.

No law to abolish greenmail was passed. While sweeping
changes were made in the Tax Reform Act of 1986, that debt-favor-

ing provision was not one of them. And the only regulatory measure affecting takeovers that *was* put into effect gave credence to the view that the government might as well stay out of the takeover arena, since its rules are no sooner passed than they become obsolete.

In December 1985, the Federal Reserve Board had proposed a measure that would apply its margin regulations to junk bonds issued by shell companies to finance acquisitions. Margin rules restrict the use of borrowed money in buying stock, generally allowing no more than 50 percent to be borrowed.

As the Fed's proposal was interpreted at the time, this would mean that buyers intent on financing a takeover would be allowed to borrow only 50 percent of the purchase price against stockholder equity of the target, rather than what had become the vogue in 1985 —80 percent or more. In other words, they could no longer buy a company by using the company's own equity as collateral for loans. It was just such an enforcement of the margin rules which first Unocal (in its petition to the Fed) and later Revlon (in court) had argued for when they were under attack.

The Fed's proposed ruling elicited an extraordinarily vehement response from the Reagan Administration. The Justice Department was joined in its opposition by the Treasury Department, the Office of Management and Budget and others. Even within the Fed there was dissension. Chairman Paul Volcker, who had been an outspoken critic of high leverage and debt-financed acquisitions, was the measure's driving force, but the two Reagan appointees to the Fed's board of governors, vice-chairman Preston Martin and Martha Seger, both dissented from the board's recommendation.

Wall Street was divided on the measure. Salomon Brothers, for example, was in favor of it, while Drexel of course mounted a blitzkrieg of lobbying against it. Even Milken, who typically did not make the politicking treks to Washington that Fred Joseph, Chris Andersen and others in the firm did, tried to lend a hand. "Milken wanted to come and see the chairman and talk about capital markets," recalled Michael Bradfield, the Fed's general counsel. "We wouldn't let him come.

"Everybody considered that bad form, trying to initiate exparte contact, trying to get in the back door. It was supposed to be all public comment," Bradfield continued. In February, after the proposal had been approved, Joseph paid a visit to Volcker.

The rule was finally adopted, but considerably watered down. The original proposal might have let the government review proposed takeovers based on the respective sizes of the acquirer and the target. But the rule as passed applied only to hostile takeovers by shell companies—and shell companies narrowly defined as having *no* assets or operations.

After all the furor, the rule was irrelevant. One way to get around it was to use as acquiring vehicle a company that had some business, however slight. Another way was to use preferred stock instead of bonds. Preferred stock generally acts like debt (it pays an interest-like dividend, and it gives the holder certain rights a common equity holder does not have), but it counts as equity.

In the Drexel-financed $487 million takeover of Warnaco in late April 1986 by a group that included Andrew Galef, the chairman of four small, diverse companies, and Linda Wachner, a former president of Max Factor and Company, Drexel almost seemed to be thumbing its nose at the regulators.

W Acquisition Corporation (WAC) represented the ultimate in the shell acquirer. Not only was WAC a shell corporation with no publicly available financial statements, but the individual bidders —who were providing only slightly more than one percent of the needed financing—were disclosing no financial statements with respect to *anybody* on the bidders' side. Indeed, it was not clear who would be in control of Warnaco, should the WAC tender offer succeed. All that was really known was that Drexel was expected to raise the financing.

At least Icahn and Perelman and Peltz had been identified bidders, with some investment in the offer through their respective vehicles; it was clear they would control, if their tenders succeeded, and they each had to disclose their business histories. But by the early spring of 1986 Drexel was telling the world (including its lawmakers and regulators, all abject) that it had ceased to matter *who* the bidders were; it was a tender offer and it was money-good, because Drexel was behind it, and that was all that mattered.

Drexel got around the Fed rule by raising half the financing as common and preferred stock and the other half as debt. Following the announcement of the merger agreement, most of the equity financing was converted into debt. So much for the Fed.

11

Proven Prophet — So Far

IT WAS NO WONDER that by the fall of 1986 the Drexel juggernaut seemed unstoppable. Congress had been quieted. The takeover debate would continue—but in academia, not in the halls of Congress. And the Fed's action had been rendered impotent.

"The force in this country buying high-yield securities has overpowered all regulation," Milken had announced to a group of pension-fund managers and others in April 1986, as reported in *The Washington Post*. "The investors have recognized increased value, and those financial institutions who dare to move into this area have been well rewarded." Indeed. Free of any constraints, Milken's machine was working like a dream. And his critics, many of whom had been prophesying a debt-triggered doomsday for the last two years or so, were twisting in the wind.

One of the most thoughtful was James Grant, editor of *Grant's Interest Rate Observer*, who had carved out his anti-junk position back in September 1984. Grant explained that he had reached this point of view, first, because the world even at that time was long on debt and short on equity, and he followed the old investment adage that one should own the thing in short supply and shun the thing in surplus. What an illiquid world needs is cash, he reasoned, and so the debt security to own (if one chooses to own debt at all) is the one with the highest ratio of cash flow to interest expense—not, in other words, the junk securities of companies which typically have little financial leeway.

Second, Grant reasoned that the holdings of junk bonds were so concentrated in a handful of institutions (Milken's inner circle)—which issued bonds and bought each other's paper—as to invalidate the argument of safety through diversification in one's portfolio. And, third, he declared that the junk idea had been carried too far, and that a faddishness had grown around its progenitor and prose-lytizer, Milken. Thus, Grant declared in September 1984, ". . . our hunch is . . . that, in some basic way, junk has had its day."

Two months later, in November 1984, when Drexel refinanced John Kluge's leveraged buyout of the Metromedia Broadcasting Corporation and issued $1.3 billion of junk bonds—then the largest junk issue ever—Grant had sounded the alarums. He quoted extensively from the prospectus, which said, in the plain, daunting language that would thenceforth become junk boilerplate, that the company might not be able to pay its investors their interest or, for that matter, their principal. Grant's concern, however, was apparently not shared by the buyers, who grabbed up the Metromedia bonds, some of which promised (if all went well) interest of 15⅝ percent.

Six months later, Grant was eating crow. In May 1985 Rupert Murdoch, the publishing magnate, bid $2 billion for the Metromedia television stations (not the radio stations). And he agreed to assume the whole Kluge debt—and pay some $650 million besides—for the television assets. In a mere six months, the value of the stations had appreciated by $650 million. This, Grant noted rightly, had added vitality to the already prevalent investment outlook that assumed not a recession but prosperity, that counted on something good just around the corner to make the balance sheet balance.

Hot on the heels of Murdoch-Metromedia came Storer Communications, at $1.93 billion further testament to this kind of investment faith. Like Metromedia, Storer did not have enough money to meet its fixed charges out of cash flow, and like Metromedia it contained a healthy quantity of zero-coupon bonds (one third of the total) in its mix of securities.

The zero-coupon bond was vital to these deals. Sold at a discount from its face value, it requires no interest payments (hence, "zero-coupon") until maturity, when the annual accrued interest and the principal are paid out. Drexel had pioneered the heavy use of zero-coupon bonds in junk deals (especially in the communications industry) where the company in the foreseeable future could not make its interest payments. The day of reckoning for many of these deals, with securities issued in 1985 and 1986, would be years away.

Now, in early fall 1986, Grant was still in print, and unswerving. He articulated a theory of a credit cycle in debt expansions, in which a gradual shift from vigilance to recklessness in lending and borrowing takes place, and he postulated that the current cycle had reached the reckless, or manic, phase. In this phase, the public competes frenziedly for securities of higher and higher yield—and poorer quality.

Using the junk mutual funds as a benchmark, Grant pointed out that as recently as 1982, only 45 percent of the funds' holdings had comprised bonds rated single B— or lower (or not rated at all); and as of mid-1986 such securities made up 68 percent of those funds' portfolios. Edward Altman, a finance professor at New York University who wrote a book entitled *Investing in Junk Bonds*, also asserts that credit quality of new issues—after improving over the 1978-to-1984 period—began to deteriorate in 1985. And Gail Hessol of Standard and Poor's asserted in *Business Week* in November 1986 that within the junk universe the new issues were at the lower end of credit quality.

It was noteworthy that at the same time that junk was becoming junkier, it had been comprising a growing percentage of the entire corporate-debt market. A total of $50 billion of junk was issued in 1985–86. Junk rose from 11 percent of the total corporate debt issued in 1982 to 24 percent in 1985. (This does not include all the debt that was downgraded into the junk nether regions—$20 billion over the 1985–86 period—much of it as a result of takeovers and buyouts.) By year-end 1986, the junk market had grown from $15 billion a decade earlier to about $125 billion.

If the quality of junk was deteriorating, one would expect there to be an increasing number of defaults—although the junkiest of issues, being the most recent, would not yet have had time to go into the can. For the period 1978 to 1985, the average default rate as a percentage of the junk debt outstanding was 1.222 percent. The year with the highest default rate was 1982, with 3.12 percent. Nineteen eighty-five, by comparison, had only 1.68 percent. But then in July 1986 came the fall of LTV Corporation, the largest bankruptcy ever, which helped to produce a 1986 default rate of 3.394 percent —marginally higher than the 1982 rate and the highest ever since 1970, when Milken was a newly hired researcher and trader of arcane bonds at Drexel Firestone. While 1985 had seen a par (face) value of defaulting debt of $992 million, in 1986 it was $3.2 billion.

LTV—whose defaulted debt had been underwritten by Lehman,

not Drexel—caused some nervousness among junk-bond investors. But there was no rush to sell from institutional investors, no large withdrawals from the fifty or so high-yield funds investing about $20 billion—in other words, none of the panic that leads to distress selling, that triggers further panic, that causes a market to collapse. And within about two weeks, the junk market rallied to its pre-LTV state.

Thus LTV was perceived as, and quickly became, an isolated event. It was one that caught even Milken off guard, since he had not believed that a major steel company would go into bankruptcy. When one of Drexel's senior investment bankers told a client that Milken had taken an $11 million loss on LTV, the client—in perfect synch with the Drexel mood in summer '86—quipped, "Lunch money."

It is true that by the fall of 1986 there was a growing chorus of business analysts worrying about the amount of debt in this country and the signs of strain it was causing—in the increasing numbers of loan defaults, bankruptcies, bank failures and savings-and-loan closings. By the end of 1986, total debt—federal plus other borrowing—would top $7 trillion, up nearly $1 trillion in one year. Debt would total 1.7 times gross national product, the highest such ratio since the worst years of the Depression. The market-value debt-to-equity percentage—a key measure of the corporate-debt burden—was 71.4 percent for 1985; that compared with 35.3 percent in 1961, 46.7 percent in 1971, 91.1 percent in 1974, and 70 percent in 1981. But the concern of these business analysts tended to be global—running the gamut from federal debt to corporate to consumer—and was not focused particularly on Milken and his enclave in Beverly Hills.

It could not reasonably be, because there debt was not a problem, leverage was not a problem, the thrifts that were failing were not Milken's protégés, and the deals that were going into default in the main were not his, either. Many of the most highly leveraged acquisitions that he had backed were now refinancing their debt at lower rates. Taking advantage of the surging bull market, many were replacing straight bonds with either convertible bonds or equity; "Equitize," in fact, was the new slogan at Drexel. By the end of 1987, Drexel would say that almost $22 billion in public high-yield debt had been retired in 1985–87, during which time about $99 billion of such debt was issued.

Despite these signs of growing stability in Milken's empire, the Isaiahs of the financial world were still proclaiming that the Milken experiment had worked so far only because interest rates had gone down and the stock market had continued to soar, but when the next recession came, they declared darkly, that empire would be shown to be made of mirrors. Some of Milken's rival investment bankers too suggested that he—with the help of his and his group's capital, and Drexel's, and that of his ever-ready inner circle—had been able to create the *illusion* of a thriving supply-and-demand market, by fixing the trouble spots and providing liquidity when and where it was needed. When the recession came, they predicted, even Milken at the controls, with all his machinations and his billions of dollars of capital, would not be able to forestall a tidal wave of defaults.

In the fall of 1986, however, that recession—which was indeed the necessary test for Milken's grand design—was nowhere in sight. And the critics, who in the face of Milken's success had begun to sound niggling, were all but drowned out. A spate of magazine articles about Milken appeared, rivaling each other in the lavishness of their praise. *Forbes*, which in 1984 had featured a cover showing Milken and his favored (Fred Carr, Tom Spiegel, Saul Steinberg and others) riding a merry-go-round, with an accompanying article by reporters Allen Sloan and Howard Rudnitsky that detailed the interlockings of his network, now published a piece (by the same reporters) laced with admiration and entitled "A One-Man Revolution." *Business Week*, with Milken on its cover, quoted Harvard Business School professor Samuel Hayes comparing Milken to J. P. Morgan and ran an editorial headed "Junk Bonds Deserve a Little Respect." For *Institutional Investor*, the headline said it all: "Milken the Magnificent."

Even *The Economist*, that sober periodical, gave its imprimatur to Milken's accomplishments in November 1986. In an editorial, "In Defence of Raiders," its editors essentially sided with the President's Council of Economic Advisers. The editorial declared that the raiders in their junk-bond-financed acquisitions were helping to make American business leaner and more competitive, instituting operating efficiencies through better management. The assumption of debt, it noted, is not necessarily profligate but can, in fact (as Milken had been repeating in his tireless litany year after year), impose a most wondrous discipline.

All these plaudits did nothing to mellow Milken or soften his iconoclastic edge. Overriding confidence, the utter conviction of his rightness, had been his insignia even when he was a twenty-two-year-old summer intern at Drexel Firestone in Philadelphia and wanted to bring salvation to that firm's beleaguered back office. Now, after more than a decade of having preached his unorthodox gospel about low-rated bonds, after having pioneered their issuance, eliciting first the disdain and later the antipathy of the corporate establishment, Milken had the certitude of the proven prophet. That he had been so right about so much (while others were so wrong) was a point that no one who listened to the few speeches he had given in early 1986 was allowed to ignore.

His recurrent theme was "perception versus reality," or, put more bluntly, how he could see what most of the world could not. Self-serving as it was, he had in fact built his legendary career and fortune upon this ability: first, in seeing the creditworthiness of companies that the rating agencies deemed junk, and later in seeing the undervalued assets of companies that were candidates for buy-outs or takeovers.

His was the clairvoyance of the outsider. He held himself apart from the mainstream. He had become both prophet and engineer of change. And that was why, he believed, resistance to his endeavors had lately been so violent.

"We're faced with change," Milken told a group of money managers in Boston in February 1986. "And all of us have resisted this change. Our regulators have resisted change, our politicians have resisted change, portfolio managers have resisted change, traders have resisted change, salesmen have resisted change.

". . . We're not willing to recognize that James Dean, in the movie *The Giant [sic]*, was really the person who was financially strong, not Rock Hudson. . . . That many of our money-center banks today are financially weak, even though we might perceive them to be strong. That many of the insurance companies in the United States that are considered to be mavericks are the strong insurance companies today, not the weak. That many of the savings and loans, who have used different investment techniques, and different ways to build their capital structures, will be the survivors and the strong savings and loans of the future, not the weak. Why [are they not accurately perceived]? Because their customs, their methods, their personalities, their people, are not the way they were . . . in the past, and are not immediately accepted. . . . Often, what's old is weak and what's new is strong."

The common perception is that capital is scarce, Milken declared in his timeworn message, but in fact capital is abundant; it is vision that is scarce. In a favorite exercise, Milken offered example after example of disastrous investments of excess cash made by those blue-chip companies rated triple A, the companies he had always disdained.

The major international oil companies have had from $2 billion to $7 billion in excess cash for a ten- to twenty-year period, he said. Exxon squandered perhaps as much as $3 billion in its foray into information systems. Standard of California made an $8 billion bid for a company named American Metal Climax which, had it been accepted, would have caused Standard to lose $12 billion. Atlantic Richfield lost in excess of $2 billion in the metals business. "So we see here," Milken drew the moral, "excess capital is not strength. It leads to the opportunity of weakness."

But if one has vision, the results are very different. While Milken had not mentioned them by name, his star protégés, Columbia Savings and First Executive, were clearly in mind when he spoke of those savings and loans and insurance companies that are today's mavericks and would be the strong institutions of the future. Now he tallied his triumphs:

"Even though *Forbes* magazine would have us believe otherwise, Mr. Perelman, who runs Pantry Pride today, seems to have had the ability of knowing what to do with his money. . . . In the last six to seven years, not only has he taken a few million dollars and purchased MacAndrews and Forbes, and then bought Wilbur Chocolates, and then took the company private, and then bought Consolidated Cigar, and then bought Technicolor, but [he] has subsequently invested money in Pantry Pride. . . . Pantry Pride was only selling at three and three quarters before Mr. Perelman took it over, and is now selling somewhere between eleven and twelve—in a matter of less than one year. Why? Because a management team has been brought to bear, which was willing to take the risk, who had the vision of value, and to find the backing of you in this room and other institutional investors around the country, willing to loan them money with the understanding that they had to commit to repay your interest and principal, and have the vision or foresight, which was the scarce resource, to identify those assets that are undervalued in the marketplace, the difference between a perception and the reality, and to use your money wisely. . . .

"*Forbes* magazine (I don't mean to dwell on their articles) recently wrote about two people who run a company called Triangle, who took advantage of the poor unsuspecting public, I don't know how, and bought National Can. Anyone in this room, anyone at Drexel Burnham, anyone could have bought National Can. . . . It required a downpayment of one hundred million dollars in equity, four hundred ninety million dollars in debt. Today the company will make in 1986 probably one hundred forty to one hundred fifty million dollars from operations, and the stock of the public company that bought it has increased fourfold.

"So," Milken summed up, "the opportunities are there. The question is—who sees the value?" A rhetorical question if ever there was one.

Milken heralded the return of the owner-manager, back in American corporate life after an absence of thirty or forty years. This had been Milken and Joseph's tenet, from the time they started raising debt for their junk issuers back in 1977. They had wanted those clients to have significant stakes in their companies. In 1980–81, three key Drexel clients, Meshulam Riklis, Carl Lindner and Saul Steinberg, had each taken their companies private, in the ultimate extension of the owner-manager philosophy. And then the mammoth LBOs of the mideighties—largely financed by Drexel—had further amplified the trend.

On another occasion, in 1986, Milken pointed to the Beatrice buyout as an example of the efficiencies that can be wrought by owner-management. "Why is this company worth fifty dollars a share three months after the company decided to sell stock at thirty-two? This company spent hundreds of millions of dollars on things an owner-manager might not spend money on. The company spent as much as seventy million dollars a year sponsoring races. Elimination of seventy million dollars a year in cash outflow increases your value by half a billion dollars a year.

"The company spent thirty to fifty million dollars on corporate-image advertising, so that people would know what a Beatrice was. Maybe as an owner you feel it is not important to know what a Beatrice is. You think knowing what Tropicana orange juice and Samsonite luggage [Beatrice products] is is good enough. And so there you can add another three to four hundred million a year.

Corporate-home-office overhead was two hundred twenty million–plus a year to run a twelve-billion-dollar business. Esmark [purchaser of Beatrice] ran a six-billion-dollar business on a twenty-three-million-dollar corporate-overhead level."

Milken speaks extemporaneously. He usually scribbles a few notes on his way to his speeches, but he only glances at them. He never gropes for a number; the facts and figures pour forth, as effortlessly as though on a computer printout. The set of his jaw is as taut as his delivery. While he strives occasionally for some humorous one-liner, he is most himself when he is serious, hammering home one purposeful point after another. But at his February 1986 speech in Boston, to a group of high-yield-fund money managers whom he first had courted back in the late seventies, he did make one remark, lighter than the rest, that seemed to engage his fancy.

"There are at least five hundred people in this country worth one billion dollars," Milken said intently. Skip a beat. "That gives us all something to shoot for," he added, with a smile of pleasure that told his listeners he was already over the mark.

12

Milken's Money Machine

In the fall of 1986, the Street was filled with Milken imitators. They underwrote junk bonds, cutting the once-secure 3–4 percent fees, and sometimes to Milken's fury they beat him out on a deal. Now they were offering bridge loans in an attempt to cut into his buyout and takeover business. But try as they might, what they could not do was *be* Michael Milken.

They did not have the storehouse of knowledge about this market that he had built since his earliest infatuation with it in the sixties. Much of that knowledge he had fed into his computer system which, as he liked to say, "shows who owns securities, when they bought them, where every security might be in the Western world." They did not have Drexel's portfolio of about $5 billion in junk, more than ten times larger than any of theirs. And, most important, they could not sit out in Beverly Hills at Milken's NASA-like console of direct phone lines to buyers whom he had cultivated, enriched, in many instances created—buyers whose commonality was that they owed him—and parcel out billions of dollars of bonds among them in pieces of $25 million, $50 million, $100 million, more. In that, he was inimitable.

In December 1985, Drexel had backed the bid of GAF, a chemical and building-materials company controlled by its chairman, Samuel Heyman, for Union Carbide, a chemical giant more than ten times the size of GAF. Drexel had said it was "highly confident" that it could raise $3.5 billion—the largest "highly confident" claim up to that time.

Ultimately, GAF chairman Samuel Heyman decided to stop

raising his bid and to sell into Union Carbide's defensive counteroffer (made to all shareholders), thereby reaping a profit of $250 mil-
lion for GAF. He stopped, he would later say, because he thought
the price had simply gotten too high to make good business sense.
Milken and Drexel had wanted him to go higher, and had assured
him that the firm would raise the additional financing required to
top the Union Carbide recapitalization offer.

Heyman recalled going out to see Milken in early December
1985, a few days before GAF announced its offer. "I wanted to look
him in the eye in order to take the measure of his confidence level
in getting the job done. He gave me his personal assurance that he
would be able to raise the financing, and he reviewed with me a list
of individual and institutional investors who had customarily participated in similar Drexel transactions, and indicated which ones
he thought would be likely purchasers of the Carbide issue. Within
three weeks of that meeting, Mike had delivered to me on New
Year's Eve signed commitments for three and a half billion dollars
from substantially the same list of buyers he had earlier predicted
would be interested in the deal.

"Considering the mammoth size of the financing, that it was a
complicated hostile transaction, and that it was accomplished in
three weeks over Christmas vacation, it was a herculean effort,"
Heyman concluded.

CAPITAL, AS MILKEN LOVED to say and to prove to the world,
time and time again, is not a scarce resource, indeed. But there had
never been quite so much at his fingertips as there was by the fall of
'86. This was a tribute to his money machine, which had of course
flowed most copiously at its fount but had also spread its abundance, increasingly, through all its parts.

First Executive and Columbia Savings, both of which Milken
had an equity stake in, as well as pride of authorship, had flourished
and continued to gorge on the junk bonds that had transfigured
them. By the fall of 1986, Thomas Spiegel was investing at least $3
billion of Columbia's $10.2 billion in assets in junk. And that was
conservative compared to Fred Carr, who was investing in junk
about $7 billion, roughly 60 percent of First Executive's assets. In a
sense—considering the enormity of their investments and their
closeness to Milken—these institutions functioned as his merchant-
banking arms. (Some who understood this relationship found it

amusing that a branch office of Columbia Savings should be on the second floor of Milken's building—which was locked, and could not be entered except with clearance.)

On a smaller scale, others in this game had also prospered. Money managers who had started in the late seventies with $50 million or $200 million to invest in Milken's junk bonds were now managing portfolios of $1–2 billion. James Caywood, for example, who had been managing money for American General when Milken visited him in Houston in 1978, was now running his own fund, Caywood-Christian, which had about $1.5 billion of mainly S&L money. Howard Marks, who had been managing money at Citibank in New York when he came out to visit Milken in Century City and concluded that Milken's shop should be a Harvard Business School case study, was now managing about $1 billion (some of it First Executive's) at Trust Company of the West. And David Solomon, who had started out at First Investors when it was a fledgling in junk and then had become by 1978 the giant of the high-yield-fund buyers, with about $500 million to invest, was, by 1986, running his own fund, Solomon Asset Management, and investing about $2 billion.

Then there was the Milken placement service. "Michael is known for placing people who lose jobs, or who want to change jobs," commented one rival. "That way, he gets the reputation for loyalty, and he also has all these different pots to draw upon. It's a double whammy."

Mark Shenkman, who had first met Milken in 1977 when he was an equity-portfolio manager at the Fidelity Fund in Boston, became the portfolio manager at First Investors after David Solomon's abrupt departure in 1983. Shenkman left First Investors in the spring of 1985. For a brief interim period of a couple of months he advised Ronald Perelman on how to invest (mainly with Drexel) the money Drexel had raised for him in its blind pool. Then, in the early fall of 1985, he opened up Shenkman Capital Management—with Albert Fuss, of Drexel in London, as his 24 percent partner. By the fall of 1986, Shenkman Capital Management had about $500 million to invest.

Shenkman also was now investment adviser for two Drexel offshore funds for foreign investors—Finsbury and Winchester Recovery. Finsbury was a general high-yield fund; Winchester Recovery invested only in bankrupt securities (Milken's specialty, from the early seventies). Shenkman and David Solomon each were managing 50 percent of Finsbury. By having ostensibly independent managers, Drexel avoided the conflict-of-interest problem it would have had if it had put its own new issues into these funds.

And for Drexelites who wanted to leave the firm (and were doing so on friendly terms) Milken often found or created new situations. Thomas Sydorick, whose brother, David Sydorick, was one of Milken's troops in Beverly Hills, worked briefly at Drexel in New York and then decided he wanted something different. He became the manager of a $300 million junk portfolio at Coastal, a thrift in L.A. "No one ever really has to leave Drexel, that's what is so great about it," Thomas Sydorick declared. "If you say you're tired, you want a change of pace, they say, 'Fine—we can put you over here.' "

Joan Conan had moved out from New York to join the Milken group but never made the adjustment to California and wanted to return home. Milken is said to have helped her find a job at the Equitable, where she was now, in '86, running a $2 billion fund, investing mainly in buyouts.

Another of the old-timers, Dort Cameron III, who had been with Milken from the Drexel Firestone days, left Drexel in 1984 to join the Bass Investment Limited Partnership, subsequently renamed Investment Limited Partnership, in Greenwich, Connecticut. He did it with Milken's blessing and some of his money. Cameron's partners there were Drexel, the Bass family and Richard Rainwater, who was the Basses' chief deal-maker until he went independent in 1985. By 1986, Cameron had at least $2 billion to invest, mainly for LBOs.

Gary Winnick, who had joined Milken's group in 1978 and had become one of his key salesmen, followed in Cameron's footsteps. In 1985 Winnick moved across the street from Milken's Beverly Hills office to open Pacific Asset Holdings. Winnick invested about $30 million, a Drexel Burnham group put in $40 million, and the Bass family and related entities put in $45 million. With that equity base, slightly less than $500 million of junk debt raised by Drexel, and bank borrowings, Pacific Asset had over $1 billion.

Both Pacific Asset and ILP are structured in ways that ostensibly limit Milken's and Drexel's role in decision-making. At Pacific Asset, for example, the two general partners are Winnick and Richard Sandler, Milken's ubiquitous lawyer and his brother's boyhood friend, who appears in so many Milken partnerships. Winnick needs the approval of Sandler, his general partner, for certain transactions. The strived-for illusion here, of course, is that Sandler is something other than Milken's proxy.

It is no different from Belvedere, the firm in which Milken owned the majority interest but was only a limited partner—and thus when asked about it in an SEC deposition could profess general ignorance about its operations, pointing to his limited-partner status. This was, in fact, the position he took in a 1985 SEC deposition with regard to all the limited partnerships in which he was an investor. "I don't have, you know, investment authority for any of these accounts," Milken testified. Questioned again on this point, Milken testified, "I would not make the investment decisions, correct." The idea of Milken allowing his control over his investments to be so usurped, however, is simply not believable. Indeed, Otter Creek, that early investment partnership for his group, had a revolving investment committee of three Milken group members who theoretically made all investment decisions. Said one former member of Milken's group who served on that investment committee, "I never made one decision. It was all Mike."

Cameron and Winnick had done their hard time with Milken, accumulated many millions, and then moved out to augment their fortunes as Drexel adjuncts. But probably no one else joined Drexel, was relocated in a satellite group, and made his fortune, in as short order as did Guy Dove III.

Dove had worked at Drexel Firestone in the early seventies. He had left Drexel and bounced through four other firms. When, in 1982, he was rehired at Drexel in Washington, D.C.—where he did some selling for Milken—Dove had just signed a consent agreement with the SEC. The SEC alleged that he had sold stock short on inside information for a profit of $22,906.25, which he was made to disgorge.

Dove had been an institutional salesman at Schroder Capital Management when he did the trades that were the subject of the consent decree. After signing it, he realized—according to Schroder's then senior vice-president Howard Cuozzi—that he would neither move ahead nor make more money at Schroder. So he went to Drexel. Cuozzi recalled, "Guy was always really aggressive in his own account—not like the rest of us money managers. We might have tried to enhance our personal wealth now and then, but he was *really* aggressive."

In 1984 Dove moved to California and went across the street

from Drexel to be chief investment officer at Atlantic Capital. This was the Atlantic Capital that committed to buy bonds in Icahn's bid for Phillips, in Peltz's and May's for National Can, in Perelman's for Revlon. In the $725 million that Milken raised for Revlon, Atlantic Capital (through its various subsidiaries) committed to buy $130 million of the bonds. In the $3.5 billion of commitments that Milken had collected for Heyman in his Union Carbide bid, Atlantic Capital had come in for $155 million. This was the ubiquitous Atlantic Capital. In the Drexel megadeals of 1985, it was among the biggest buyers, if not *the* biggest.

Of all Milken's ready pools, Atlantic Capital was the one about which other investors, even those close to Drexel, knew the least. While other buyers sometimes used Street names, probably no other buyer went by as many names or used as many subsidiaries in these deals as Atlantic Capital. (In Revlon, there were commitments to buy bonds not only from Atlantic Capital Corporation, but also from these related entities: Worldwide Trading, SSC III Corporation, Garrison Capital Corporation and First Oak Financial Corporation.)

In its 1984–85 heyday, Atlantic Capital had at least $3–4 billion to invest. While First Executive's investment pool was somewhat larger, First Executive, like all insurance companies, had to submit a list of all securities in its investment portfolio to the state insurance commissioner at the end of each year. By the fall of '86, in fact, the New York State Insurance Commissioner (who had jurisdiction over Carr's Executive Life in New York, a smaller subsidiary of the California company) had indicated that he was considering imposing a limit on the amount of junk bonds an insurer could buy.

Similarly, Tom Spiegel's $3 billion pool at Columbia Savings was overseen by increasingly critical regulators at the Federal Home Loan Bank Board. And by the fall of '86 those regulators indicated that they expected to propose regulations that would limit thrifts' junk-bond investments in some way—perhaps by limiting the amount that could be invested in a single company, or by requiring that investments be spread among various companies and industries. Tom Spiegel and Fred Carr had enjoyed great license for years, but theirs were not wholly unmonitored investments. Atlantic Capital's were.

Atlantic Capital's game was the brainchild of a former investment banker in municipal finance at Shearson named Peer Wedvick. In the early eighties, when interest rates went sky-high, single-family mortgage revenue bond issues began to proliferate, since financing a home in the private sector had become extremely expensive. Typically, in these housing deals, a municipality would sell its bond issue and invest in an investment contract with the proceeds (which would remain in that investment contract until they were needed to purchase mortgages). That contract, which had to be provided by an institution with a high investment-grade rating, promised to pay a certain rate of interest on the funds, and to repay the principal in an allotted period of time. In most of these housing deals, the bulk of the funds were moved out of the investment contracts and used either to purchase mortgages or to repay the bonds, generally within three years. However, some of the funds (approximately 10 percent) were invested in a debt-service reserve fund for the full term of the bond issues (usually thirty-plus years).

Wedvick's idea was to sell these investment contracts to the municipalities and—somehow—make a big spread between the rate he had to pay and what he made on his investments. An arbitrage. All he needed was an institution with a high investment-grade rating, and a crackerjack investment strategy.

An AA rating was provided through a Mexican named Rodrigo Rocha, who in 1981 had taken over a Bermuda-based reinsurance company, Clarendon. Rocha's cohort at Clarendon was Eerki Pesonen, then chairman of Kansa General Insurance Company in Helsinki, Finland. Kansa owned about 35 percent of Clarendon. Kansa was also a member of a pool of reinsurers for First Stratford, the reinsurance company formed in 1982 and owned primarily by a Milken group and First Executive. Most important, Kansa had an AA rating from Standard and Poor's. So Atlantic Capital was created, as a subsidiary of Clarendon. Atlantic Capital issued the investment contract, which was backed by Clarendon, which was covered by a "cut-through" agreement (assuming liability) from Kansa.

That, however, was only half the farrago. The other was an investment strategy. And that, as Wedvick and Rocha soon discovered, they did not have. When they started selling these investment contracts in 1982, they invested the money in Treasuries, which they attempted to hedge. "They lost their asses on that," recalled one former Drexel executive. "I remember going to a cocktail party in '84, and Rodrigo was introducing his hedge guy from Stanford, who had all these computer models. About four or five months later, I heard they took a really big hit."

By mid-'84, they had moved to Milken's junk (bonds and preferred stock). Now they were making a spread of at least 400–500 basis points (there are 100 basis points in one percentage point), sometimes as much as 1,000. They would promise a return of 8 percent or so and then invest the money in junk that was paying 13–18 percent. Guy Dove came to be their trader—and Milken's man in the shop. It was rumored at Drexel that Milken had an equity stake in Clarendon through his investment partnerships. But those partnerships were essentially run as blind pools, so even those at Drexel who had money in them generally did not know what their investments were.

It was great while it lasted. Wedvick, who had reportedly been making no more than $70,000 a year at Shearson in his pre–Atlantic Capital days, now was said to be making about $10 million a month. His lifestyle lent credence to the talk. "I saw Peer not long ago," one friend remarked, "and he was driving a Rolls Royce. But it was only one of them [that he owns]." When Wedvick married in early 1985, Drexel threw a bachelor party for him in Las Vegas and flew in friends and key clients. It was an extravaganza worthy of someone who was said at the time to be Milken's biggest client.

In these bond deals, it was typically the underwriter who decided which bidder would be awarded the investment contract. Major commercial banks and insurance companies flooded this market in the early eighties. But in California, where Atlantic Capital was most active, no institution could compete with it. There was no disclosure required as to how the funds would be invested, and most underwriters who accepted Atlantic Capital bids apparently looked to the AA rating and not beyond. Of a half dozen interviewed by this reporter, all said they did not know the money was being invested in junk bonds.

One asserted, "For about two years, they [Atlantic Capital] were tearing up and down the state, getting any deal they wanted —it was almost impossible *not* to do business with them. And for a long time they managed to keep it very quiet, the rates they were getting. I remember I was with Peer in a restaurant in early 1985, and I said, 'Peer, how *are* you doing this?' And he said, 'We've got the best options guy in the country.'

"I can't say what they were doing was illegal," this underwriter concluded. "But it certainly failed the good-faith test."

If the underwriters were ignorant of how the money was being invested, FGIC (Financial Guarantee Insurance Company), the bond insurer which insured some of Atlantic's investment contracts, was not. One analyst at FGIC says, however, that it was their knowledge of Atlantic's investment strategy that caused them to limit the coverage to $300 million. What was worrying, this analyst adds, was not only that Atlantic was putting the money into junk, but that it was also committing a cardinal investment sin. Like the S&Ls which had borrowed short-term money and lent long, and so got caught when interest rates skyrocketed and had to pay more for their money than they were receiving on their long-term loans, Atlantic Capital had borrowed short (most of these funds had to be repaid in three years) and lent long (the securities they bought typically had maturities of ten years or more).

"It was a game of musical chairs," this analyst said. "They were using the new money that came in to make payouts on the old contracts. They weren't liquidating the securities. So there was certainly the risk that if interest rates had risen, in the end there would not have been enough money in the securities [whose price would have fallen] to make the payouts. Or if there had been any big defaults [in the junk issues]. But there weren't."

By the fall of 1985, it was essentially over. Standard and Poor's finally exerted sufficient pressure on Kansa that that company refused to extend its "cut-through" agreements to any new investment contracts. Atlantic Capital stopped selling these contracts (it had sold about one hundred) by the late fall of '85. Within the next year, Pesonen, who had led Kansa into the foray with Rocha and Clarendon, left Kansa to join Clarendon full time in its London office. He was replaced by a new chairman and management from outside the company who vowed to refocus Kansa on its domestic, rather than international, activities. And in December 1986 Standard and Poor's downgraded Kansa from AA to A− (a substantial downgrade) in large part because of its relationship with Atlantic Capital and its concern about Atlantic Capital's investment portfolio. Standard and Poor's noted, however, that Kansa had already taken steps to allay its concerns. "In particular, Kansa General's intention to no longer reinsure new exposures of its one-third-owned Clarendon Group will reduce over time the overall role in the company's portfolio as those exposures run off." Many of the bonds which had been backed by these contracts would also be downgraded by early 1987, so the bondholders were left with devalued bonds.

Dove too by 1986 had shifted his base of operations to Clarendon's London office. In December 1986, U.S. District Judge Owen Panner granted a preliminary injunction to the Princeville Development Corporation, allowing it to block the attempts to acquire control of it by Dove (through Garrison Capital Corporation, affiliated with Clarendon), Charles Knapp (through Trafalgar Holdings) and others.

Among his other findings, Panner cited numerous disclosure violations by Garrison, including its having failed to disclose that it was acting as part of a group, in an attempt to seize control of Princeville. Panner also found that, while Dove and Knapp were posing as only sources of financing for the tender offer for Princeville, in fact that financing—through the issuing of warrants—would place between 40 and 90 percent of the equity in Dove's and Knapp's hands. The offer to purchase was fraudulent, Panner found, inasmuch as Princeville shareholders "were prevented from discovering that managerial control of Princeville . . . could pass to persons with, at best, dubious pasts: Dove and Knapp."

For Dove, Atlantic Capital was surely a once-in-a-lifetime kind of opportunity. Like other members of the Milken network, Atlantic Capital benefited enormously from the halcyon financial times in which it operated. Because Atlantic Capital's gamble on interest rates was so great, the superb economic climate probably meant the difference between striking it rich and suffering a disaster. For others—companies which had issued mountains of debt, for example —the climate may have meant the difference between scraping by and prospering. But for everyone in this magnificently orchestrated, highly interdependent production—and for Milken, its maestro, most of all—timing was key.

13

The Enforcer

IN THE VERY BEGINNING, from 1973 to 1977, when Milken's universe extended no farther than to the next trading area, he had controlled the members of his small, clannish group with the investment partnerships. As the junk market began to take shape, he controlled some of the buyers, some of the issuers. The larger that market grew, the more important it became to him to control the whole, the more he conceived it in fact his responsibility to do so—because there was more opportunity for error, more that needed constant fine-tuning, so much more to protect; one tremor could be costly. And as Milken's power grew, commensurate with his creation, the opportunities for abuse in the name of control, of expansionism, of disciplining the intransigent, of uprooting the indolent entrenched, also increased. It was for the greater good. He remarked to someone once that there was no corporate democracy in this country and there never would be unless it was forced. Milken was, self-appointed, the enforcer.

It is axiomatic that the more powerful one is, the easier control becomes. As Milken became exponentially more powerful than the vast majority of his clients, many would not challenge him. And so he could gouge them, freely. As one Drexel employee said, "Mike is always saying, 'If we can't make money from (that means overcharge) our friends, who can we make money from?' "

Norman Alexander, the chairman of Sun Chemical Corporation, met Milken in the midseventies when Milken sold him some of Riklis' Rapid-American bonds. "I remember meeting Mike in Schrafft's, and him showing me all the companies [whose bonds he was trading] on one sheet," recalled Alexander. "He had made a market in these bonds. He had organized himself among the players so that he could take you out when you wanted to be taken out—either because he had the capital or because he had the place to put it."

Alexander added that through the last fifteen years, that liquidity has remained constant. "So far, he's always been there, and he's been able to provide whatever oil was needed."

Once the original-issue market started, Sun Chemical became one of Milken's early issuers, doing a $50 million offering of junk bonds in 1978. Alexander remained a satisfied customer of Milken's through the years, investing personally in some of the superleveraged acquisitions when they came along. On these deals, he said that he, like many others, tends not to read "the fine print." Alexander explained, "The investment is made largely on your confidence in Mike's ability to appraise the value of a deal."

Alexander is a longtime admirer of Milken, but he did register one muted complaint. In 1986 Drexel was selling a small company for him. It was charging him a commission fee that he estimated was double what other investment bankers would have charged him. But he did the deal with Drexel anyway. "Because if I didn't," Alexander recalled, "the next time I would say, 'Mike, you have to get me out of Revlon,' or 'You have to get me out of Boesky,' he would say, 'Oh, and for twenty-five thousand you went somewhere else?' So, you see, you tend *not* to go somewhere else."

One of his clients going somewhere else—not just on a deal, but even on a trade—Milken took as a personal affront. And he was so vigilant that he missed little that occurred in his market. One client recounted getting a call from Milken in 1986, when Milken was steeped in multibillion-dollar transactions. " 'You people just bought five million dollars' worth of bonds through Oppenheimer,' Mike said. 'I could have gotten you those bonds for half a point better.' I said, 'How do you know, and more important, why do you care?' And he said, 'We want every piece of business.' "

One rival trader said Milken's omnivorousness goes even further. "Mike wants not one hundred percent but one hundred and one percent—because not only does he want to do *all* your business, but he also is not happy unless you actively trade, churn the account."

When Milken had 60–70 percent of the market, no one who

intended to stay in it could afford to alienate him. Knowing they were being gouged by Milken but thriving on his merchandise, many of his clients had what one Drexel employee described as a "love-hate relationship" with Milken. Even some of those clients closest to him—Fred Carr, for example—actively (though privately) encouraged competitor investment-banking firms to enter the junk market. But while those firms did enter, they were not committed to that market the way Milken was. And how could they be? He had created it, he viewed himself as not only its progenitor but its guardian. They had come along, late in the day, for the ride.

Morgan Stanley, which by 1985 was emphatic about its determination to be a serious participant in this market, underwrote $540 million of junk bonds for People Express from December 1983 to April 1986. But in the summer of 1986, when People was on the verge of bankruptcy and some of its bonds plunged to as low as 35 percent of their issue price, Morgan Stanley made itself scarce. No bids were forthcoming. James Caywood, who first started buying bonds from Milken as a money manager in the late seventies, said, "Where was Morgan? Nowhere! Who's the only one who can tell you what's going on? Mike. So you go crawling on your knees. I was only in it for five million, but still. He took me out of it. I thanked him. He said, 'You don't have to thank me, Jim—it's my obligation.' "

As Milken was approaching the zenith of his power, in 1985, there were some clients who so suited his larger purpose that he was willing to grant them more autonomy than most, or even take a beating from them in a negotiation. Carl Icahn was one, and Samuel Heyman was another. Heyman is a Harvard-educated lawyer and successful real-estate developer, who had taken over GAF in 1983. By the spring of 1985 he had substantially improved GAF's earnings. Heyman was smart, studious, polished (a different breed from Peltz and Perelman), and he was gearing up for a major acquisition. That spring, he was talking to a premier investment bank about its underwriting $150 million of junk for GAF.

Heyman had been a close friend of Eli Black, the former United Brands chairman, and had known Leon Black, Eli's son, as he was growing up, so Leon Black became Drexel's emissary, along with Fred Joseph. Heyman ultimately agreed to give the deal to Drexel, but he drove a hard bargain. Underwriters generally will not commit to exact terms until the night before the offering, when the deal

is priced—and then issuers are at their mercy because they already
have too much invested in the deal's consummation to walk away.

So Heyman insisted that Drexel agree to a fixed formula, with
no leeway for negotiating at the end. He argued that the rating
agencies were wrong in their assessment of GAF as a below-investment-grade credit, because they were so biased in favor of "companies with little debt, whose managers buy Treasuries and have no
ideas." This, of course, was an argument close to Milken's heart. He
told Heyman that in his next life he was going to set up his own
rating agency. And he agreed that the issue should be priced as
though GAF were an investment-grade credit.

The formula Heyman bargained for was 115 basis points over
Treasuries. The other firm which had been talking to Heyman about
the issue was not willing to commit to a fixed formula. Milken,
however, accepted Heyman's terms. "Then Treasuries went down
two hundred basis points, and the spread between the Treasury rate
and the junk-bond rate widened dramatically," Heyman recalled.
This meant that Milken was committed to sell these bonds at a rate
that was well below the lowest end (strongest credits) of the junk
market. The GAF bonds were issued at eleven and three-eighths. "In
the end, most firms would have said, 'We just can't do it,' " said
Heyman. "But Drexel gave some customers a big discount, they did
swaps, they put their commission money into it. Mike told me later,
his blood was spilling."

From Milken's standpoint, however, it was all for the usual
good cause. Less than six months later, he was raising $3.5 billion
for GAF's bid for Union Carbide, and by that time Milken had
achieved his accustomed bargaining position: on top. For this
amount of money, in a hostile bid, Heyman had nowhere else to
turn. And though Heyman fought hard with Milken's assistant,
Peter Ackerman (Milken remained characteristically above the
fray), in the end Heyman had to agree that in the event GAF did
acquire Union Carbide, not only would the refinancings and some
of the divestitures have flowed in a golden flux through Drexel, but
Drexel would also receive (ostensibly to distribute to the bond buyers, but maybe to keep for Drexel) 15 percent of the equity in the
newly constituted company.

By 1986, when "merchant banking" arrived as the new craze
on Wall Street, Drexel had already amassed equity stakes in more
than 150 companies. Milken had had the principal mentality from

his earliest days as a trader, and the firm had followed his lead. It had become partners with many of its clients. This approach suited Milken especially, because not only did it mean sharing in the upside of the companies he was backing, but it augmented his control. With Milken and his group owning a sizable chunk of a company's stock—and being just a few phone calls away from amassing a much larger block—the chairman of that company would tend to be pliant.

Drexel had started demanding its pound of flesh in equity back in the late seventies, when the firm sought warrants as well as fees in its junk-bond underwritings. But its amassing of equity took a quantum leap as Drexel moved into financing leveraged buyouts in 1983–84, and then the hostile LBOs, or takeovers. The equity in these deals is, of course, where the massive upside potential lies. And Drexel typically demanded warrants (to purchase the stock cheap) as equity kickers to help sell the bonds. It seems, however, that much of that equity never reached the bond buyers.

Richard Cashin, of Citicorp Ventures, who has worked with Drexel on a number of LBOs, said, "Drexel was developing a clientele in these deals that was rate-oriented, like mutual funds. So Drexel would sell them the bond, maybe at a discount—and Drexel would keep the equity. They would say, 'The buyers *need* the equity.' Well, *Drexel* needs the equity.

"A lot of the bonds are done on swaps—Drexel will give someone a Levitz bond for a Safeway. It's so Byzantine, you never know how much the trade was, where the equity has really gone. They register the equity in Street names out in L.A.

"In Levitz," Cashin continued, "they said, 'The bond buyers *need* the equity.' Then we find out, who has the equity? It's Drexel. It's a movie, you've seen it a hundred times before, you could cut it short but you don't. Look, we're Citibank—it's crazy for us to go on bended knee to L.A. But we do. Because we find they're very smart and they benefit fifteen ways to Sunday, but they do what they say they're going to do and they get the deal to close."

One former Drexel employee confirmed Cashin's view. "In a buyout, Mike's guys might say, 'OK, we need twenty-five percent of the equity in order to sell the debt.' But then it never goes to the bond buyers. Mike's salesmen know their accounts, they can say, 'Buy this,' and they will. And the buyers don't even know that the warrants are available."

As the competition with rival firms intensified and the options of clients grew—especially prospective clients, not already wedded to Milken—he encountered some resistance. In one instance in early 1985, Merrill Lynch offered to do an offering of about $200 million of preferred stock at 14.5–14.75 percent (depending on the market at the time of pricing) for Home Insurance. Hearing about the deal, Drexel quickly offered to do $250 million at 14 percent. "We had the order and were writing the prospectus, but George Schaffenberger [then chairman of Home Insurance] said, 'I have to give Drexel a chance,' " recalled a Merrill investment banker. "They came back with American Financial [owned by Carl Lindner] as the buyer for the whole thing—and they were demanding warrants for twenty to twenty-five percent of the company. George told them to stick it." Merrill did the offering, raising $285 million, at 14.75 percent.

"It was their old bait-and-switch, what they do all the time," this banker continued. "Do you know what 'highly confident' means? It means that Mike is highly confident that he's *got* you, one way or the other, and he's going to change it fourteen different ways at the last minute, and the deal's fine but you're not."

Some prospective clients too just wanted to do a debt issue, and did not want to become dues-paying members of Milken's club. Not everyone for whom Milken raised money also bought others' junk bonds—but those who did not were the exception rather than the rule. One of the driving forces of Milken's machine, after all, was overfunding: he would raise more than a company needed (or had filed for), and then the company would invest the surplus (or, in some cases, the entirety) in junk. Fred Joseph once told *Business Week* that 70 percent of their deals were overfunded (by which he meant they raised more than their initial filing). One chairman of a company recalled that he wanted to raise about $100 million of junk bonds, with which he planned to refinance his bank debt. "Drexel said, 'We'll raise a hundred twenty-five million for you. You'll have twenty-five million extra. You'll be paying fifteen percent [interest], so you'll want to invest in an issue we have coming up, which will pay fifteen percent.' " This prospective client went to a rival of Drexel's for the underwriting.

Lawrence Coss, chairman of Green Tree Acceptance, a Minneapolis company that services sales contracts for mobile homes and recreational vehicles, is one Drexel client who did not want to play the game—and believes he paid the price. In early 1985, Green Tree hired Drexel to underwrite a unit offering of bonds and stock. Midwest Federal Savings and Loan Association, its then 71 percent shareholder, wanted to sell most of its stock, so the offering would include over 50 percent of Green Tree's shares. Since it was such a sizable block, Green Tree officials expressed their concern that it be widely distributed, and Drexel, they said, assured them that it would be.

Shortly after the offering, however, Coss said, James Dahl, who was Milken's most aggressive salesman by early 1985, called Coss and gave him a list of purchasers of his stock who would be filing 13Ds: Columbia Savings, Strong Capital Management, Martin Sosnoff and Reliance Insurance Company. It was Saul Steinberg at Reliance who, with his block of 9.3 percent, set Coss most on edge, since Coss thought immediately of Steinberg's greenmail of Disney, in 1984. However, Coss received assurances from his investment banker at Drexel, Gerald Koerner, that the stock was just "parked" with these longtime Drexel customers to prevent there being a surplus in the market, and that when the stock price went up, the shares would be distributed out.

According to one source, Coss then began receiving calls from Milken or one of his salesmen, offering him junk bonds to buy or acquisitions to consider. Coss didn't want to buy the bonds, this source added, and none of the suggested acquisitions was just right. So he declined everything. Over the course of the next five months, Steinberg raised his stake to 10.3 percent, then 11.8 percent, then 14.9 percent, and then indicated he was going to raise his stake to 20 percent and eventually 25 percent. Coss, said this source, was convinced that because he had refused to play the game he was paying the penalty—by being the target of either a real takeover threat or at least tactics of terror.

In October 1985, Green Tree sued Drexel and Reliance, charging violations of trust and fiduciary duty, breaches of contract, and fraud, among other things. In March 1986—while he was at the Predators' Ball—Steinberg sold his Green Tree stock back to Green Tree, reaping a profit of about $26 million. The suit against Reliance was dropped, but in the fall of 1986 the Green Tree litigation against Drexel was still pending—one of the few clouds in that fair-weather season.

•   •

COSS'S ANXIETY would have been shared by most chief executives if they were not members of Milken's inner circle. Some did business with Drexel but still tried to protect themselves. One deal that Milken is particularly proud of is the financing he did for the toy-makers Mattel, Inc., when that company was on the verge of bank-ruptcy in 1984. After a $231 million cash infusion, the company went through a dramatic turnaround. Milken and many in his group, through their investment partnerships, were among the investors. Drexel, however, was not the lone money-raiser. It was accompanied by E. M. Warburg Pincus and Company and Reardon and Joseph.

As Mattel's then chairman, Arthur Spear, explained, "Drexel wanted to do it alone—but we said they couldn't. It was going to be more than bonds [also stock], and, knowing their stable, we were concerned about who the shareholders would be. I told Michael [Milken] that."

Milken accepted the compromise in Mattel. And despite his craving for every last piece of business, after Green Tree filed suit he may have realized that there were some clients who—either because they didn't want to play the game or because they were unnerved by having their bonds and, especially, their stock held by his coterie of high-rollers—were better off elsewhere. But there were some clients who were potentially so integral to Milken's vision that he would not tolerate either losing or sharing them.

Wickes was one. Sanford Sigoloff, Wickes's chairman and chief executive, sees himself as the doyen of troubled companies. In the seventies, Republic Corporation and then the Daylin Company, both of which had gone into Chapter 11, were successfully reorga-nized under his aegis. And by early 1985, after Sigoloff had steered Wickes, a lumber and building-materials retailer, out of its bank-ruptcy, he was intent on raising about $300 million in junk bonds in order to make an acquisition.

Troubled companies, of course, were the specialty not only of Sigoloff but of Milken, who had seeded his fortune in the seventies by analyzing the assets of troubled or bankrupt companies and buy-ing the bonds of those with value at rock-bottom prices. Thus, he had accumulated a sizable portion of Daylin's debt, which then led to his futile attempt to exert control over Sigoloff at that abbrevi-ated lunch where Sigoloff told Milken that the last time he had checked he was still chairman and CEO of the company. Later, Milken had acquired Wickes's debt.

Now Wickes, having emerged from Chapter 11 in January 1985, had one enormous asset: a $500 million tax-loss carryforward. Sigoloff believed that the best way to capture the value of that enormous tax benefit was to raise debt capital and make a major acquisition. Drexel was by no means his only option as an underwriter. Nearly everyone was eager to break into Milken's market by early 1985, and Salomon Brothers courted Wickes vigorously. According to one associate of Sigoloff, Sigoloff favored doing the deal with Drexel but members of his board of directors, worried about Drexel's reputation, preferred the prestige of a Salomon underwriting. So Salomon got the deal.

Milken had apparently not been paying much attention to the Wickes deal—perhaps because he doubted that Sigoloff, who had made a presentation at the 1984 bond conference about taking Wickes through bankruptcy, and who was Drexel's Santa Monica neighbor, would dare to go anywhere else. But in early March a Drexel employee told Milken that he had just seen Sigoloff socially and learned that he was preparing for his road show—with Salomon.

On Friday, March 22, after Salomon had already drafted and printed its red herring (the preliminary prospectus that must be filed with the SEC prior to the underwriting) for the Wickes offering, Saul Steinberg's Reliance Financial Services Corporation filed with the SEC a 13D (required whenever one acquires more than 5 percent of a company's stock) stating that he owned 10.4 percent of Wickes's stock. Sigoloff received a call from Milken, and the two arranged to meet on Saturday, March 23.

On Saturday, "Mike told Sandy [Sigoloff] what Saul held, what Drexel held, and how, when you combined that with whatever other pockets Mike might have placed the stock in, it meant they would have control of the company," said a Wickes director close to Sigoloff. "So Mike told him the facts of life." If they were indeed in collusion, Steinberg and Milken at least—and the other "pockets" if they were aware of this anticipated action—were violating the securities laws by not filing 13Ds as a group.

According to Steinberg's 13D filing, he had started his accumulation of Wickes stock on March 12—by which time Milken had been apprised by the Drexel employee that Salomon had won the Wickes deal. He crossed the 5 percent line on March 14 and continued to add to his position aggressively. However, according to a Drexel spokesman, this 13D—reflecting the purchases of approximately 8 million shares during the period March 12–21, 1985—reflects the settlement date of the purchase of "when-issued" Wickes shares by Reliance back in November 1984 (5 million shares) and in January 1985 (5 million shares). (Approximately 2 million shares had not yet settled.)

It seems noteworthy, however, that this 13D gives no hint that these transactions occurred as Drexel claims. It states that these purchases of securities were made "during the past sixty days, all . . . by brokerage transactions." It does not mention that these are settlement dates rather than trading dates—though 13Ds generally reflect trading dates. And (suggesting that this is not simply a carelessly drawn 13D) it takes the trouble to state that a Reliance official's 1,200 shares (less than .1 percent of Wickes's outstanding stock) were acquired under Wickes's "Plan of Reorganization"—which would seem to refer to the kind of "when-issued" transaction that Drexel claims accounted for the entire 10 million shares.

During the March 23–24 weekend, Sigoloff suggested to Salomon that Drexel co-manage the deal. Sources say Salomon replied that the quid pro quo for Drexel's joining the deal should be that Steinberg sell his stock. John Gutfreund, the chairman of Salomon, is said to have been so enraged that he attempted to intervene. He phoned Sigoloff during the weekend.

According to one Drexel source, Drexel was assured of being co-manager from the time of the Saturday Milken-Sigoloff meeting, and an investment banker from the Beverly Hills office, Joseph Hartch, met with Sigoloff and started working on the deal the following Monday morning. "But it is obvious that two giants can't walk the earth," this source declared. And by the next Thursday, Salomon was out, and Drexel was in as sole manager.

Sigoloff reached Milken by phone on Thursday in the Beverly Hilton auditorium, where he was holding court at the 1985 Predators' Ball. Sigoloff told Milken he was giving him the keys to the washroom and Milken had better not let him down. The next day's conference schedule was revised to insert a Wickes presentation. And there, attentive in the front row, was the company's 10 percent holder, Saul Steinberg. Sigoloff and he had a friendly conversation, and Sigoloff felt threatened no longer; they were in the same camp. Within the next couple of months, Steinberg reduced his position to 3–4 percent.

At the conference, Sigoloff also met Martin Davis, chairman of

Gulf + Western. Some four months later, Wickes bought Gulf + Western's consumer- and industrial-products group for about $1 billion. Drexel raised the debt for that acquisition, and one year later, in June 1986, it raised another $1.2 billion for Wickes in a "blind pool"—the largest ever. Its coffers brimming with that cash, in early November 1986 Wickes announced that it was buying Collins and Aikman Corporation, a manufacturer of fabrics and wall coverings. And only days later, Wickes announced it had completed negotiations to take over Lear Siegler, the aerospace concern and maker of automotive parts. Together, these acquisitions would cost nearly $3 billion.

Wickes, like Heyman's GAF, had been the kind of client Milken simply refused to lose. Each became one of the handful of quintessential players, Milken's giant acquisitors with appetites large enough to be Milken's "monsters," as Riklis had put it. To win GAF, Milken had done a deal that probably cost him money, one that no other firm would have done. To win Wickes, he had used a different kind of persuasion—in this writer's view, extortion. Milken, of course, would not have used that word. He was recruiting his players, aligning them, disciplining when necessary, forcing when he had to force, and reforming the corporate world.

MESSIANIC VISIONS aside, there was also the visceral satisfaction of having taken on a competitor, Salomon, a Wall Street titan. In 1985 Salomon was perceived as the most powerful investment-banking firm on the Street, with a viselike grip on underwriting and trading. Milken had beaten it to a pulp. The fact that they had been able to expunge Salomon from a done deal was a source of great glee and self-congratulation at Drexel. Referring to Steinberg's sudden appearance and Salomon's disappearance, Leon Black said, laughing, "That's power investment banking. Things like that have always happened on the Street—although," he added with a grin, "they're not usually so blatant."

In fact, in this never-never land at Drexel where Gobhai wish lists kept being granted one after another, the Wickes deal marked the fulfillment of one more. In the notes of a Gobhai meeting back in 1983, this goal was recorded in block letters: "TO BE AS BIG AS SALOMON SO WE CAN BE AS ARROGANT AS THEY ARE AND TELL THEM TO GO STUFF IT." And at the Wickes deal's closing dinner, held in the Garden Room at the plush Hotel Bel Air, one Drexel employee presented to Milken, Joseph and others framed copies of three prospectus covers, mounted side by side—a Wall Street triptych. The first was Salomon's red herring; the second was the prospectus with Drexel and Salomon listed as co-managers; the third was Drexel's. The inscription that ran across the bottom of the mounting read, "As Yogi Berra said, 'It isn't over 'til it's over.'"

14

Sovereign Privileges

IN FEBRUARY 1986, when Milken appeared before the money managers in Boston, speaking about the difference between perception and reality and ticking off his triumphs, he had begun by noting that he had seen pickets as he entered the building. That had reminded him of the time he offered to finance Frank Lorenzo's bid for TWA. "We had pickets circling our building night and day in Los Angeles, until we explained to them that we were just a small branch office and what they really wanted was 60 Broad Street [the executive offices of Drexel, in New York]."

It was an "in" joke that could only be relished by those who understood Milken's relationship to Drexel. But in this group, comprised of many old-timers in the junk market who had known Milken since he first came pushing his oddball product in the late seventies, it brought the house down. This audience realized that however much of a Wall Street powerhouse Drexel had become, it was first and foremost a facade for Milken.

Moreover, while Milken had fastidiously shunned the trappings of power at Drexel—refusing to be elevated from a mere senior vice-president, refusing to be mentioned in the annual report—he was not averse to the thing itself. He did not exercise power in the administration of the firm, because it did not interest him. But in his operation, which was all he cared about, he enjoyed untrammeled power. The trading floor in Beverly Hills, notwithstanding the fact that he expected no one there to work any harder than he did, notwithstanding his unwillingness to refer to his people as "subordinates," notwithstanding his having no office, was his throne room. And every other office—including Drexel headquarters in New York—was the hinterlands.

In L.A., Milken had gradually created his separate firm—much as earlier, after the Drexel Burnham merger, he had created his separate group. By this fall, 1986, his traders in Beverly Hills were trading not only junk bonds (straight and convertible debt) but common stocks, preferred stocks, the securities of bankrupt companies, and mortgage-backed securities. Drexel's mortgage-backed-securities and common-stocks departments were back in New York, but Milken traded whatever interested him in Beverly Hills. And in an adjacent building, connected to Milken's trading floor by a walkway, was the corporate-finance department. John Kissick, Drexel's investment banker in Beverly Hills (who had worked with Milken on that first Golden Nugget transaction for Steve Wynn), had built this department from three professionals in 1982 to about ten in early '85 and to sixty in '86. According to Kissick, 30 percent of the firm's investment-banking revenues then came from his group. Being in this corporate-finance department was still not the same as being in Milken's enclave. Milken insisted that not only these corporate finance people but *his* salesmen cover the accounts he cared most about, so that he ceded no control. But it was the next closest group to "the Department."

Kissick idolized Milken. ("Mike," said Kissick, "is what we would all like our sons to be.") And since he and his colleagues were so close to the fount, they tended to incorporate the Milken ethos. Arthur Bilger had moved from the corporate-finance department in New York to L.A. in 1982, in order to be close to Milken. Being close to Milken, Bilger had found, meant living (more or less) on his schedule. "Mike gets in at four-thirty, and it's sort of a competition among guys out here, who gets in the earliest," Bilger remarked. "Although Mike always wins.

"I'll be with him at the end of a day," Bilger continued, "and I'll say, 'I have to see you.'

"Mike will say, 'How about in the morning?'

" 'What time?'

" 'How about four-fifteen?' "

Bilger sighed. "And I smile and say, 'What am I going to do with myself between two-thirty and four-fifteen?' "

It was Bilger who in the summer of 1986 sent the framed quotation "Drexel is like a god . . . and a god can do anything it wants" to several of his colleagues. But Bilger's excitement was mild compared to that of some of the younger associates in Beverly Hills. They had received their primer in corporate finance from Milken as he wrested control from the corporate elite and passed it to his chosen, the have-nots of American business life. Many of these investment bankers—and, even more, Milken's troops in "the Department"—felt that they were in the vanguard of a force that would change the world.

"There was no legacy out in Beverly Hills. They started out fresh. It was a real Wild West thing," said one former Drexel investment banker from New York. "I remember [in 1986] one of the young corporate-finance associates in Beverly Hills said to me, 'Maybe we'll take a run at IBM'—and he was only half kidding.

"Don't take me literally," this investment banker added, "but I used to think about what was happening in Beverly Hills as the 'five-o'clock what-if sessions.' In a sense, the most dramatic events in corporate takeovers in the last few years have come about because some guys out in Beverly Hills, tired at five o'clock after a day of trading, sat around saying, 'What if . . . ?' " He gestured, one hand seizing the other. "And then, instead of going out and getting a beer, they'd get on the phone and make it happen."

BACK IN '79, key members of the New York corporate-finance team had resolved in their Cavas Gobhai session to "merge with Mike." That goal had been only partially realized. The investment bankers in New York had "merged" with Milken in that they had helped him build the junk business, prospered mightily from it, and invested as principals in some deals along with him. But as Milken's L.A. firm grew, the schism widened between East and West coasts. The Beverly Hills contingent tended to look upon at least some of their East Coast partners as ciphers who lived off the fruits of the West's labors, and the New Yorkers, for their part, looked askance at Beverly Hills as too wild, too reckless—and too greedy. The jealousy over the amount of money being made out in L.A.—which had spurred the resolve to "merge with Mike" in the first place—had not abated.

Much of the wealth that was being amassed in Beverly Hills, of course, came through Milken's investment partnerships, and while he had allowed some members of the corporate-finance department to participate in several of them, the overwhelming majority of these partnerships were for him, his brother and his group (and at least a few of them included individuals wholly unrelated to Drexel). Corporate finance, for example, had not been allowed into probably one of the more lucrative of them, Belvedere Securities—which was by its very existence testament to Milken's sovereignty. For Milken to be the majority owner of another brokerage firm, which according to an SEC lawyer traded some securities that Drexel underwrote and took orders from members of Milken's group for clients of "the Department," was a situation so rife with conflict of interest, and so ripe for abuse, that it is difficult to imagine how it could have been allowed, even at Drexel, even for Milken.

Nor was Belvedere an isolated instance. A related entity, controlled by two of the same general partners, operating out of the same space in Chicago (although its official address was c/o the American Stock Exchange in New York), with 75–100 percent of its capital at the outset contributed by Milken, was EGM Partners, a broker-dealer in options. Among EGM's limited partners were Milken; many of his favored from his group; and James Regan and Ed Thorp (general partners of both Belvedere and Dorchester Government Securities). EGM Partners was formed in late 1982 and stopped doing business less than two years later, within a month after signing a letter of consent with the Chicago Board of Options Exchange for violating Exchange rules concerning size of positions.

Even when the New York corporate-finance members did participate in the partnerships, they still felt underprivileged. Particularly once the buyout boom was under way, much of Drexel's and Milken's profits came in the form of warrants in the newly formed companies. The bulk of these were in the investment partnerships —including at least one in which corporate finance participated. But even here, where there was joint participation between New York and Beverly Hills, the warrants were distributed in unequal proportions between the two coasts, with Milken's group taking the lion's share.

Another portion of warrants, many of them received as part of fees in underwritings, did not go into the investment partnerships but was available for more general distribution. This distribution, however, differed on the two coasts, according to a former Drexel investment banker. In New York, they went into a pool, known as the warrant strip fund; each year a certain percentage of those warrant strips were sold, and the proceeds distributed on a pro-rata basis to the partners in corporate finance, according to their allotted percentages (senior partners had the largest slices of the pie). But in L.A., this banker said, Milken distributed the warrants not on a pro-rata basis but directly to those in his group he deemed deserving. The largest portion, to the most deserving, he is said to have allotted to himself.

"There were two separate firms, and Milken's was more of a meritocracy," declared this former Drexel investment banker. "He was giving direct incentives. Bringing in one deal could make you a millionaire. It worked on a microlevel—you had guys who were really incentivized, which is what Mike wanted. They were animals, threatening companies and making a million dollars on a single piece of business they brought in. But Fred Joseph's problem was that it wouldn't work on an institutional level—you couldn't run a firm with ten thousand animals. So he had to institute a different system, where you did well if the firm did well."

The schism was reflected, too, in the battle fought between the two groups on behalf of their respective constituencies—a battle that L.A. almost always won. As one corporate client recounted, "The way it works is that the New York office sort of represents you, and L.A. represents the bond buyers. Part of Mike's success, I think, is attributable to the fact that he negotiates a very, very favorable deal for the bond buyers. It was a great source of friction between Drexel and us—we thought L.A. was exacting much too much. But L.A. had the power."

A former Drexel investment banker from New York added, "It is more true at Drexel than anywhere else that their real clients are not corporate; they are the buyers of the bonds. They feel they have a patrimony to protect. So if you're a corporate client, and you're not part of the inner circle, you are ripe for a raping.

"Usually, when it comes to a pricing for a deal, you [as the investment banker] have to fight with the client to get him to pay a sufficient amount [in interest]. Here the fights were with the guys from Beverly Hills, to get them to a point that was reasonable enough that you could even go to the client with it. At Drexel, the most difficult, contentious, acrimonious discussions were with your own people—in Beverly Hills."

While Milken's reign showered gold upon his associates, his was not a pleasant dominion. Some at Drexel perceived him as an insatiable, abusive tyrant, who by 1986 was operating—and demanding that others operate—at a whirlwind speed that no one else could, or should, emulate.

Shortly after the April 1986 Predators' Ball, one Drexel investment banker commented that it had struck him as a "feeding frenzy, everyone doing deals, deals, deals, so thrilled at being part of the new power elite." That spectacle had caused him to think about what had drawn him to this business, back in the seventies. "To me, the appeal was essentially academic. You learned about the companies. You tailored the transaction. Lastly, I noticed, it paid well. But that was like a bonus.

"The trading mentality is supposed to be quick—traders are supposed to know prices. We [in corporate finance] are supposed to understand things. But when you start making these deals look like trades, you begin to question whether it's worthwhile. And what I came away from California with was [the realization] that we are essentially a processing arm for Michael and his trades—and he doesn't pay attention to nuance, and he wants them as fast as possible.

"Michael is interested in power, dominance, one hundred percent market share. Nothing is good enough for Michael. He is the most unhappy person I know. He never has enough. He drives people by insult. He drives everything—more, more, more deals. Michael doesn't care if it's a bad deal—he sees bad deals as an opportunity. You can refinance, restructure, do an exchange offer. Everything is an opportunity."

The firm's founder, Tubby Burnham, also struck one of the few dissonant notes amid the euphoria at Drexel in 1986. For Burnham, who had built the firm by carefully husbanding its capital, the abundance of easy money that spilled from Milken's machine was discomfiting. He disagreed with the overfunding that was fundamental to that machine's operation. "Companies have been piggish," he complained. "It's wrong for an underwriter to say to a company that needs fifty million dollars, 'We can get you a hundred million.' I am always telling my guys, it's wrong!

"It's like a kid saying, 'I want five dollars,' and you say, 'Take ten dollars, have fun!' It's not right, it's too loose."

Burnham was also skeptical of the way fortunes were being made by the nouveaux entrepreneurs, by what sometimes seemed little more than sleight-of-hand. "It took me fifteen–twenty years to become a millionaire—not like today, when it happens overnight. When this is over, some of these people are going to find out they're not millionaires anymore—they're going to be looking for their next meal."

Whatever reservations brewed quietly in the more conservative corners of Drexel in New York, however, were irrelevant. People might carp now and then, but who could afford to challenge? Milken's hegemony was nearly complete. In 1978 he had announced to Edwin Kantor, head of all trading, that he wanted to move to California; Burnham had had a fight with Milken about it; but as Kantor later said, "What could we do?" All that had changed was that Milken had made the firm's executives wealthy beyond their dreams, and had made Drexel into the most fearsome investment-banking firm on the Street. Drexel chairman Robert Linton, when asked in early 1986 who was the person to whom Milken answered, looked bemused for a moment and then replied, "Kantor, Fred [Joseph]—but that's a question that never gets asked."

There apparently were occasions on which Milken did yield to Joseph. They had, after all, been partners from the beginning, when they started the original issuance of junk bonds. It was Joseph who had brought in many of the early corporate clients, and who was the superb salesman, and the genuine leader of the corporate-finance team. It was Joseph who attempted to make amends with clients or competitors whom Milken's crew had roughed up. When Linton had ceded the position of chief executive officer to Joseph in the spring of 1985, the strongest opposition to Joseph's appointment came from Milken, who did not want to lose him as head of corporate finance. In 1985, as the firm moved into the eye of the political storm, it was Joseph who was the consummate front man, and Milken who was able to remain cloistered.

Some of their associates suggested that Milken gave Joseph latitude because the two supersalesmen were simpatico, Joseph with his drive to be number one, Milken with his drive to have it all; Milken with his penchant for thirty-second phone conversations, Joseph agile and fast on the comeback. But, for Milken, who had so distilled his life that his smallest action was calculated and purposeful, compatibility would have meant nothing unless it enhanced efficacy. He must have deemed Joseph extraordinarily useful.

One occasion on which Milken paid attention to Joseph was in Drexel's financing of Ted Turner's $1.25 billion acquisition of the

MGM/UA Entertainment Company. Drexel had issued its "highly confident" letter in August 1985. But after the letter was issued, there was deterioration at MGM. And the "highly confident" letter, which drew its almost mystical powers (it was after all merely a letter stating intent, and not legally binding) from its record of irrevocability, was altered twice to reflect a restructured deal. It changed first in October 1985 and again in January 1986. Arthur Bilger worked on that deal and said that "forcing its restructuring is the greatest value-added thing I've done at Drexel.

"Mike did not want to do it. He still could have sold the paper, and he had this relationship with Kirk Kerkorian [MGM/UA's majority shareholder], and everybody was watching, saying, 'Mike can't do the deal.' And he *could*. But it would have been wrong. So we had to bring Fred [Joseph] in to persuade him. And he did." Milken did not discount Joseph, as he did most people. But in the main, he did as he pleased. And by 1986 he was doing it with ever greater frequency.

In theory, the Underwriting Assistance Committee (UAC), formed in 1982, had to approve every underwriting the firm did. On the committee were about eight or ten (it varied slightly over the years) corporate-finance professionals. The investment banker for every proposed underwriting wrote a memo to the UAC, outlining its substance and the pluses and minuses of Drexel's doing the deal. Also, in 1984 or so, Leon Black introduced into his memos (which then became the form) a first-page paragraph stating what Drexel's compensation would be. "That marked a subtle shift here," claimed one investment banker. "The fees don't belong there. The deal should be judged on its merits, not the fee. It was going public with our venality."

UAC meetings were held weekly in New York (with a phone hookup for members in corporate finance in Beverly Hills), and they lasted from several hours to more than a day. Everyone was expected to have read the memos beforehand, and the meetings were by no means a rubber-stamp process in which every deal was approved. But after all the memo-writing, the homework and the hours-long debates, Milken simply went ahead and did some deals that the committee had rejected.

By the fall of 1986, some of the committee members thought that Milken's increasingly frequent flouting of this fundamental process was a serious problem. They compiled a list entitled "Difficult Deals." On it were about twenty to thirty deals that had been bones of contention between Milken and the UAC—about half of which Milken had then proceeded to underwrite. A couple—for Sea-Containers and Bright Star, for example—had gotten into trouble within their first six months.

Others were not in trouble—yet. Milken had done an $80 million underwriting for Compact Video, owned by Perelman's MacAndrews and Forbes—a deal whose sole claim to viability was that the successful Perelman would make it work.

Milken had done a $135 million blind pool for Banner Industries, controlled by Jeffrey Steiner. Here the committee had argued that they ought not to be doing a blind pool for an individual like Steiner—a former oil trader and arbitrageur who had zero record as either a raider or an operator of companies—but should instead wait until he had chosen his target and then finance its acquisition.

Milken had also done a $50 million deal for Great American Management and Investment (GAMI), a holding company controlled by Chicago entrepreneurs Sam Zell and Robert Lurie. Zell had made his fortune as a savvy bottom-fisher in real estate, picking up valuable properties at distress-sale prices. Now, however, he was trying to apply that strategy to companies and had purchased a diverse mix of troubled companies over the previous five years or so. But thus far these acquisitions were still dismal, and it looked like Zell's bottom-fishing knack was restricted to real estate. The UAC had vetoed the underwriting.

And then Milken had done a $640 million deal for Ivan Boesky's arbitrage partnership. This had been one of the most hotly disputed deals within the firm. The arguments against doing it were compelling. It was a very large private placement with no registration rights, because Boesky's business changed too rapidly to be able to comply with the disclosure demands of a public offering. Therefore, if Boesky got into financial trouble, there would be no public market for the debt and only the thinly traded (though not so thinly as it was supposed to be) private market to rely on. Holders who wanted to unload their securities would look to Drexel. It would be placing hundreds of millions more in the hands of an arbitrageur who many thought was already overcapitalized. Drowning in dollars, he might chase the bad deals as well as the good and therefore not obtain the return he had in the past.

Over the years, there had been SEC investigations of Boesky.

Though none had borne fruit, rumors of insider trading persisted about Boesky, far more than about any other arbitrageur. He was simply too prescient. And if he were ever caught, Drexel might be tarred.

Even without such a tarring, executives worried, the firm could be criticized for its conflict of interest. Drexel would be raising capital—and, as usual, taking an equity stake—in an arbitrage partnership where Boesky would be betting on the outcome of deals, many of which would be Drexel's. If he bet correctly, Drexel, which would have inside information on those deals, would share in his profits.

According to one Drexel executive, it was not only the more conservative New York contingent but those closest to Milken on the West Coast who had argued against doing it. Peter Ackerman, Milken's right-hand man for buyouts, had reportedly subscribed to the overcapitalized argument. Lowell Milken, the one individual whom his brother was most likely to heed, had reportedly been against it because he neither liked nor trusted Boesky. "But Michael," said this executive, "thought Ivan was a winner."

What Milken was doing violated the social contract of the firm. While Drexel prided itself on being nonbureaucratic and free-spirited—an institutional mirror of its entrepreneurial clients—it still had rules which were essential to its functioning as a coherent whole, rules which were meant to safeguard it against financial disasters and/or lawbreaking.

The UAC, formed after the debacles of the American Communications and Flight Transportation underwritings, was designed to carry out corporate-finance and executive functions—analyzing a company and a deal, determining whether Drexel should be its underwriter. All proposed deals came before the UAC: plain vanilla underwritings for general corporate purposes as well as those more adventuresome ones for acquisitions and blind pools.

No one from the trading side sat on the UAC. For Drexel, like other investment-banking firms, had built into its structure a "Chinese Wall," meant to restrict the flow of information between its deal-making and its trading or arbitrage bodies. Such walls had been erected in investment-banking firms after the Texas Gulf Sulphur Company case in 1964, which expanded the definition of insider trading from company insiders to include anyone possessing material inside information.

Because of Milken, however, such separation was antithetical to Drexel's very nature. Fusion had been the order of the day, ever since the members of the floundering corporate-finance department collaborated with Milken on the restructuring of the troubled REITs, back in the midseventies. From that time on through the original issuance of junk, Milken and corporate finance had been frequently intertwined. And while Milken had at first functioned as researcher, trader, salesman and business-getter and left the investment-banking, or deal-structuring, side of the transactions to his corporate-finance colleagues, he limited himself no longer after he moved to California. As Kissick, the Beverly Hills corporate-finance head, told *Institutional Investor* in 1986, "Prior to 1977, Michael had never done any traditional corporate-finance work. By 1978 he knew as much as virtually anybody on Wall Street."

In that same article, an unnamed investment banker commented, "Mike is the only person in the securities business today who can do it all. He is a master trader, salesman, deal structurer, credit analyst, merger tactician, securities venturer. And he does these things at the level of the best guy in each of these categories. You look at the difficulty *firms* have in putting all these together— and here you have *one man* embodying all these attributes."

In effect, Milken had appropriated all these diverse functions for himself. Just as he had no use for organizational demarcations in his group, because he believed that they subverted productivity by boxing people in, so he certainly would not allow himself to be constrained. For him, there was only one test: who had the best skills to get the job done? It was hardly surprising that Milken, who must have considered himself the best investment banker and credit analyst at Drexel, would simply subsume the function of the UAC and do the underwritings they had rejected. In earlier years he did not override the firm's veto so flagrantly, but by 1986 he seems to have considered it his sovereign prerogative. Just as there were few clients who would challenge him as his power increased, there was only one partner, Joseph, and he did so rarely.

Milken's subversion of the firm's authority in the underwritings was one problem. But another, potentially more explosive, was engendered by his being a kind of Renaissance man of finance. While it was indeed marvelous for Drexel to have one man who embodied all those attributes, whose talents ran from trading and sales to corporate finance and M&A, Milken was a walking contradiction of the Chinese Wall principle.

Most firms tried to erect Chinese Walls between their deal-making group and their arbitrage department, which traded securities for the firm's account. In the gold rush of the eighties on Wall Street, however, even this relatively simple separation was not always maintained. At Kidder, for example, Martin Siegel had both headed its M&A division and helped create its arbitrage department.

But at Drexel, which had been practicing merchant banking before much of Wall Street knew the words; where Milken had invested for himself and the firm and his group and his customers in the REITs, many of which were Drexel restructurings; where he had then gone on to invest in both the debt and the equity of Drexel deals for his investment partnerships; and where he was often not only the source of the business but, increasingly, the structurer of the transaction, there could be no Chinese Wall. The only check upon Milken, who, as he had shown the UAC, did just as he pleased, was that Kantor theoretically had to approve all his trades.

One Drexel employee, asked about Kantor's supervision of Milken's trades, answered that that was indeed the rule. "Mechanics," he added, "can mask substance." For Milken, he said, opportunities for profiting on his inside knowledge were plentiful and the possibility of penalty slim. "If Mike sees bonds busting, lets them go to forty, thirty, twenty, all the while knowing that a deal is coming that's going to make them worth sixty-five, and if he buys up a bundle when they're at twenty, well, that's insider trading if there ever was. But who's ever going to be able to prove it?"

That may have been the problem that the SEC confronted in a 1984–85 investigation of Milken. That investigation—like at least two others since 1980—ended without the government's taking any action, and the SEC does not comment on investigations that are thus closed. But much can be gleaned from Milken's deposition testimony, given in January 1985, a copy of which was obtained by this reporter through a Freedom of Information Act request.

A major focus of the investigation was Milken's trading in the securities of Caesars World, the gambling casino. Milken, Kissick and John Taylor (one of the original salesmen who had joined Milken's caravan to the West) had attended a meeting at Caesars World corporate headquarters in Century City, Los Angeles, with the company's new chairman, Henry Gluck, and several other employees, on June 29, 1983. At that meeting, one of the topics discussed was the possibility of Drexel's doing an exchange offer—the popular 3(a)9—for some of Caesars' outstanding debt.

Either on that day or the next, Milken had purchased slightly more than $3 million (face amount) of Caesars World bonds which went into the firm's account. According to a trading ticket, they were moved into Milken's personal profit-sharing account at Drexel on July 1. Those bonds, within about two weeks, became the subject of an announced exchange offer on which Drexel was the adviser. Milken bought them at 81.5 and sold them at 101.67—making a profit of approximately $635,500.

From the deposition, it was not clear just when Milken had bought the bonds. The trading ticket for the purchase was stamped 11:05 A.M., June 30—the day after the meeting. But on the ticket was also written, in one corner, "as of June 29." Milken, who professed ignorance of the hieroglyphia of trading tickets, declaring repeatedly that he had not written a ticket in fourteen years, nonetheless went on to insist that the "as of June 29" must have meant that that was when the trade was executed, and the stamping must have been done the following day because the order had gotten temporarily lost. He also was adamant that they had been intended for his account at the time of their purchase, and that it was not an after-the-fact decision made on July 1 (as the trading ticket that showed them moving from the firm's account into his might suggest).

Milken is famous for his memory. Members of the Milken cult love to tell stories about how, in random conversation about a company on which he has not recently been focused, he will remember not only how many bond issues that company has outstanding, but the maturities and coupons of each one, and, more, the call provisions on a given issue. Joseph recounts Milken's recalling the trading pattern of a bond as much as ten years earlier—the bid, the selling price, how much was left in the portfolios of the buyers and the sellers.

At his deposition, however, Milken was positively forgetful on certain points. He could not, for example, recall the names of any limited partnerships in which he was an investor. He did not remember why the meeting with Caesars had come about; who had arranged it; when he had known about it; or much of anything specific that transpired at it. Asked repeatedly whether Caesars World doing an exchange offer had been discussed, or whether, indeed, there had not been an agreement at the meeting's end that Drexel would look into Caesars' doing an exchange offer, Milken asserted that they had "talked about fifty things at the meeting."

And when pressed as to the agreement reached at its conclusion, Milken testified—after extensive maneuvers by his lawyer that seemed aimed at keeping him from having to answer—that he did not recall.

According to Caesars chairman Gluck, however, in an interview with this reporter, the meeting had come about because a Drexel gaming analyst whom Gluck had recently met at a business conference had been "pitching our doing an exchange offer." Given Caesars' 3:1 debt-to-equity ratio, Gluck said, the idea of giving bondholders equity in place of some of that debt was very attractive. The meeting, Gluck added, was held to discuss the exchange offer, which was then carried out. "I thought it was not all that likely that the exchange offer would be widely accepted," Gluck recalled. "If we had gotten a fifty percent acceptance rate, I would have thought we'd done extraordinarily well. But we got over eighty percent!"

While Milken was vacant on most of the above matters, he was crystal clear on others. He was adamant, for example, that he had purchased the bonds before the meeting. He was also vivid in his recollection of having spoken to Edwin Kantor and gotten his approval to buy these securities for his profit-sharing account. He invoked Kantor's name many times. He testified that when he decided to sell the bonds about a month later, he had again sought Kantor's approval. Asked whether in that conversation he and Kantor had had any discussion about the fact that Drexel had recently worked on the exchange offer, Milken replied, "I think as a senior member of the firm and on the firm's Executive Committee, Mr. Kantor should have more knowledge than I did related to any of the firm's activities on Caesars."

Asked a second time whether they had discussed it, Milken said he did not recall.

It is, of course, possible that Milken has an astonishing memory for the bonds he loves and little memory capacity left over for ordinary human events, or for the trivia of life, like the names—any name—of his limited partnerships. Even so, the picture that emerges from this deposition is of someone who was full of certitude about details that would help him but aphasic on those which would not, and who was shockingly eager to pass the buck to Kantor (who had been his loyal partisan through the years).

Milken bought these bonds from Mark Shenkman, at Shenkman

Capital. Shenkman supports Milken's recollection that Milken bought the bonds from him on the morning of June 29, before the meeting at Caesars World (though Milken would have known the meeting was scheduled for later that day, and would probably have known its purpose). Shenkman added, however, that when the SEC questioned him in connection with this investigation, he was shocked to learn from the government lawyer that Milken had bought these bonds from him, an institutional client, and put them into his personal account. Recalling his days at Lehman Brothers, Shenkman said, "At most Wall Street firms—certainly at Lehman —you could never have mixed professional and personal that way, buying securities for your account that you were trading for the firm. There's too much opportunity for self-dealing." Somewhat rueful about having made that losing trade, Shenkman calculated Milken's profit (as $635,500) and remarked, "People work a lifetime and never make that kind of money, and Mike made it in a three-minute phone conversation."

Finally, from the line of questioning at this deposition, it appears that Columbia Savings, First Executive, and the Princeton-Newport Limited Partnership (controlled by James Regan and Edward Thorp, Milken's partners in Belvedere Securities, the Chicago brokerage firm in which he had the majority interest) may have done well, along with Milken, on the Caesars World exchange. Milken was asked whether he had had any conversation about the Caesars World bonds with Tom Spiegel, Fred Carr, James Regan or Edward Thorp between the time of his Caesars meeting and the announcement of the exchange offer about two weeks later. Milken testified that he had not. He was also asked if he was familiar with a sale of Caesars World bonds from the Drexel account of Prudential's high-yield fund (decidedly not an inner-circle member) to the Columbia Savings account, about a week before the exchange offer was announced. Both accounts were covered by James Dahl, Milken's favored, superaggressive salesman. Milken said he knew nothing about it.

This was the kind of rumor that had swirled around Milken and his inner circle for years: that first he had created these players such as Spiegel and Carr, made them his captives with their pools of capital at his disposal, and then rewarded them further (sometimes personally, other bond buyers speculated) with this kind of inside information. Regan and Thorp were slightly different, insofar as they were not running financial institutions dependent on Milken's junk bonds but were money managers and Milken's partners in some of his lucrative investment partnerships. He could conceivably have profited directly from rewarding them. At the close of this deposition, when Milken was asked whether he had any knowledge of certain individuals or any interest in certain limited partnerships (which presumably had been buyers of the securities that were the subject of this investigation), one entity about which he was asked was One First National Plaza, Suite 2785, Chicago—the address of at least two Milken-Regan-Thorp partnerships, Belvedere Securities and Dorchester Government Securities. "Don't recognize the name," Milken replied.

One former Drexel employee, who was not aware of the Caesars World investigation, commented, "What I think may happen is this: An exchange offer is coming up, and Mike wants it to go well [have a high acceptance rate]. So he gets his clients to buy the securities with advance knowledge that there will be an exchange offer in three weeks. That way, they all make out—plus the exchange offer goes through."

Even if all this were true, the government could pursue it as they did in Caesars World; but without an informant they would be hard pressed to make a winning case. For Milken—as for Boesky, in the government's numerous investigations of him, prior to Dennis Levine's turning state's evidence—there was always a credible explanation for his having bought a security.

What was telling in interviews with scores who knew Milken, however, was that so many thought he was not above reproach, simply beyond the reach of the law. Some thought that he would violate the securities laws because he had the archetypal outsider's disdain for convention and the established rule, because he believed he was responsive to some higher law. Some thought he would do it because he was increasingly possessed by the machine he had created and would do anything to fuel it. Some thought he would do it because he had the trader's compulsion always to beat his record, and, after ten years of beating the previous year in a blinding winning streak, there was no way to go on beating it without having an edge.

Almost no one, however, thought he would do it out of something as simple, and base, as avarice. In fact, many who know Milken marvel at how a man of such wealth can remain so indifferent to its usual pleasures. By 1986 a few close to Milken estimated his net worth at $1 billion or more. Moreover, it was said at Drexel that with the help of his brother, Lowell, he had been able to shelter much of it.

But Milken was clearly not seduced by the material things his money could buy. For Milken, there was no equivalent of Ivan Boesky's statue garden, or Peltz's Palm Beach palace, or even Icahn's Foxfield. Milken's house in Encino is charming but unprepossessing, no twenty-two-room manor house. It has no surrounding acreage for isolation but sits on a fully developed cul-de-sac where neighborhood children (and probably Milken's own) ride their bicycles up and down.

He was said, by one client who visited his home, to have an old nineteen-inch color TV that was always on the blink, and to have only recently purchased a VCR. His home was decorated with inexpensive wicker furniture, no antiques, no art. Until lately, too, he had driven a dated Oldsmobile. The firm had finally prevailed upon him to get a driver—an insistence that may have been triggered by an auto accident Milken had in 1984, resulting in a lawsuit that he finally settled in the fall of '86 by paying $30,000. Now he owned a Mercedes Turbo Diesel and had a driver—but the driver was a concession to personal safety, and the antithesis of Milken's style. In another such concession, Milken had recently hired four bodyguards.

His wife, Lori—who was Milken's high-school sweetheart and, according to Steve Wynn, the only girl Milken ever dated—apparently had no greater desire for conspicuous consumption than her husband did. She was said to appear at black-tie gatherings, such as those for the Simon Wiesenthal Foundation (the Nazi-hunting organization) wearing a cloth coat and inconspicuous jewelry, while other women were swathed in furs and bore rock-size gems. What Lori Milken did care about, apparently, was writing; it was said to be her consuming interest, and she had been enrolled in various writing workshops over the years. She wrote fiction, mainly short stories, apparently none of which had been published. Milken reportedly offered to buy her a publishing company, something she declined.

There seemed to be, then, literally no personal use for the fortune Milken had built. He did contribute in a low-profile way to certain causes, like the Simon Wiesenthal Foundation and (through the Milken Family Foundation) many programs in the field of education, both in California and nationally; but if he was a major philanthropist, that was a well-kept secret.

While Milken apparently chose to not spend his money, however, he certainly had been driven to accumulate it from the very start. And, after all these years, he was still trying to shave every trade, still trying to milk his best clients ("If we don't make money from our friends, who will we make money from?"), still demanding everything but the firstborn son in deals where he could get it. And still, in the view of one Drexel employee, shortchanging his partners.

"Michael has a deal with the firm on every LBO," said this employee. "Michael [with his group] gets a piece, the firm gets a piece, a fund that corporate finance has gets a piece. Michael, of course, gets the lion's share.

"Then Michael goes and tells the client that ten percent of the equity has to go to Drexel and thirty percent has to go to the investors, because they [the investors] need that much to get the proper risk–reward ratio for taking all this subordinated debt. Then he doesn't give the thirty percent to the investors. He gives maybe ten percent. And the other twenty percent he squirrels away.

"That," this employee added, "has caused tremendous ill-will within the firm. Fred [Joseph] knew about it, did nothing. It's like, a lot of people will cheat on their income tax, they figure it doesn't hurt anybody but the impersonal government, but not many people will cheat on their friends.

"In addition to being a talented, creative genius," he concluded, "Michael is among the most avaricious, ruthless, venal people on the face of the earth."

By 1986, it seemed to some who had known Milken for years that he, always wired, was now like a whirling dervish, spinning out to the very edge of control. One longtime buyer commented that there seemed to be less and less joy in Milken—something that had been part of him in the early years—and more compulsion. Others agreed that he was far more "driven" than when they had met him in the seventies, though even then he had been one of the most intense and kinetic people they had ever encountered. In a deposition taken during a 1980 SEC investigation, Milken testified that in 1979 he had had about two hundred phone conversations on a routine day. Moreover, he added, while he was speaking to someone he could be carrying on "ten other conversations" at the same time. "I would say that I listen to no more than twenty-five percent of the conversations I have with anyone during the trading day. . . . I would come in and out, buy and sell securities during any conversation."

In an SEC deposition in 1982, during another investigation, Milken testified that he had about five hundred phone conversations a day. And in a deposition in September 1986 he said he participated in "potentially one thousand transactions every day." But this superhuman acceleration was not without its cost. "If you talk to Michael for three or four minutes," said one associate, "he can grasp what it may take other people hours or even a week to learn. But when you take three or four minutes down to two minutes, his reliability starts being worse. But he still wants to be in the decision process. Then he gives you forty seconds, and his decisions are bad, made on too little input. Add to all that his imperialness and sense of his own infallibility."

Out of about thirty or forty conversations that this associate had with Milken on a given bond issue, he said they did not have "more than two or three half-meaningful discussions. Most of those conversations lasted about thirty seconds, conversations where you're on the phone with him and you don't know if he's listening to you or talking to someone else, covering the mouthpiece. You're talking, you finish making your point, and then he says (one of his most often-used expressions), 'I'm back.' "

By 1986, he concluded, Milken "never had enough information. His retentive powers were amazing—but then that phenomenal repository got filled up, wasn't retaining any more."

Some thought that Milken was increasingly out of touch, not only because he was operating at such velocity, but also because in his somewhat calmer moments off the trading floor he had succumbed to hubris. He had always cultivated a personal style that was modest, deferential. He liked to think that he appeared even humble. But years of rarely being challenged, of seeing his influence skyrocket, of having his acolytes and clients hang on his words, had taken their toll. So many treated him as though he were the oracle —and Milken began to act as though he were.

Throughout 1985 and 1986, the chairmen of American companies—not the Fortune 500, but sizable, $300 million companies— had been making the trek to Beverly Hills to pay homage. Milken would see almost no one during the trading day, so he scheduled these appointments before the market opened (starting at 4:30 A.M.) and after its close. And there, in his throne room, he would finally forsake the thirty-second bursts and segue into monologues on macroeconomics, on the state of the world, on whatever came into his imperial mind.

On the final morning of the Tokyo bond conference in November 1986—the inaugural of Milken's effort to target Japan, having already captured so much of the domestic territory—Mike Mansfield, the crusty eighty-seven-year-old U.S. ambassador to Japan who had been a luncheon speaker at the Drexel conference, invited Milken to a private breakfast meeting at the embassy. It was without specific purpose, a formal, courtesy visit. Such meetings have their own protocol: polite conversation, filled with give-and-take, not overextended. Milken, however, reportedly held forth for close to an hour in a monologue that barely allowed Mansfield to get a word in edgewise. Off and running, he is said to have pontificated until the visit's end on the economy, bonds, world politics, currency rates, macroeconomics. The gospel according to Milken. He had long been the fiscal evangelist, but now there was a self-importance which was blinding him, certainly to social conventions—and probably to much more.

15

Boesky Day

DREXEL EXECUTIVES had just returned from the Tokyo bond conference in November '86, flushed with the success of that international inaugural, when—at the market's close on Friday, November 14, 1986, the day that they would thereafter refer to darkly as "Boesky Day"—the announcement came across the tape that Ivan Boesky had pleaded guilty to insider trading and had agreed to pay the largest fine ever, $100 million. He would, moreover, be cooperating with the government in its ongoing investigation of insider trading on Wall Street. At Drexel in New York, the leatherbound volumes of the $640 million much-disputed Boesky underwriting done in the spring of 1986 had been delivered that day to the office of Stephen Weinroth, the main investment banker on the deal, who would typically add these volumes to those of his other deals on his office shelves. Weinroth was not in the office. Hearing the news, his secretary put them in the closet.

Over the next four months, Weinroth, who like several others is said to have argued against doing the Boesky underwriting, was responsible for its unwinding. In the end, the bondholders were made whole on their investment; it was Boesky's equity partners in his arbitrage fund who suffered losses, and who sued Boesky, Drexel, and Fried, Frank, Harris, Shriver and Jacobson, the law firm that was counsel to Boesky in this and most other matters. When the unwinding was completed, in mid-March 1987, Drexel commemorated it not with the traditional deal paperweight, a Lucite-encased miniature prospectus cover, but with a giant pink eraser, bearing the amount of the ill-fated offering in parentheses ($640,000,000).

The Boesky-Milken relationship, however, was not so erasable. Within minutes of the announcement of Boesky's plea, the SEC issued subpoenas seeking information about trading in a dozen securities and the role in those transactions of Michael Milken, Carl Icahn, Victor Posner, Boyd Jefferies of the Los Angeles–based brokerage firm of Jefferies and Company, and others. Drexel executives knew then that their worst fears at the time of Dennis Levine's arrest in May, which had receded amidst the euphoria of the summer and fall of '86, had been realized.

When Levine was arrested, the quick consensus at Drexel was that he would do anything, say anything, to save himself. He had been at Drexel for only a little over a year, however, and his colleagues in corporate finance in New York didn't think he had been close enough to Milken and his group to know much about what really went on in the Wild West. But what if he knew just a little? Or what if he made it up? Or what if he squealed on someone who did know?

Through the summer, those whom Levine had earlier convinced to trade information with him, and whom he now was trading to the government, emerged to take their pleas: investment bankers Ira Sokolow from Shearson Lehman Brothers; David Brown from Goldman, Sachs; Robert Wilkis from Lazard Frères; and lawyer Ilan Reich—Martin Lipton's protégé—from Wachtell, Lipton. With each successive revelation, however, the scandal seemed to move farther away from Drexel, becoming more and more the Wall Street scandal; and the Levine ring, moreover, appeared to have been comprised of second-tier M&A players. There was no hint of its touching the figure at the apex of that world.

Then came Boesky. For years, other arbs, investment bankers and traders had talked among themselves and, occasionally, on a background basis with this reporter and others about Boesky's trading on inside information. The shock that seized the Street on November 14 was not at what Boesky had done—who had not surmised it?—but at his having been caught. His prescient trading patterns had sparked SEC investigation after investigation, but until there was a cooperating witness in the person of Levine the fortress had been impregnable. Now it was falling like a house of cards.

Suddenly, most of Wall Street seemed vulnerable. Boesky, the biggest arb on the Street by far, with hundreds of millions to bet, who lived and breathed the M&A game through all his frenetic, obsessive twenty-one-hour days, had been at that game's nerve center. He had monitored it from his command post, where he stood for hours at a time, surrounded by computer screens flashing stock prices, manning a switchboard with 160 direct phone lines to stockbrokers, arbs and others. There was not a significant M&A player on Wall Street who had not gotten the hyperkinetic Boesky's calls. And at least one star player, Martin Siegel when he was at Kidder, had long been rumored to have provided Boesky the inside information he continually sought.

Now, like Levine, Boesky would doubtless offer up his Wilkises and Browns and Sokolows and Reiches. But just as Boesky had dwarfed them in Levine's trade, so would Boesky's ultimate target dwarf his middling ones. Because his ultimate target was the King.

Boesky had been doing business with Milken since at least mid-1983, when Drexel raised $100 million for the Boesky-controlled Vagabond Hotels, a subsidiary of the Beverly Hills Hotel Corporation. In 1981 Boesky had gained control of the lush Beverly Hills Hotel from his in-laws after their patriarch, Ben Silberstein, died. In that Vagabond offering—the proceeds of which were in part devoted to Boesky's risk arbitrage—Drexel in its time-honored tradition took as part of its fee a slug of warrants that gave it an equity stake in Vagabond (later renamed Northview Corporation).

Then, in April 1984, Drexel had done a $109 million private placement of junk bonds for Boesky's arbitrage partnership. While $109 million seems paltry compared to the $640 million that Boesky would raise just two years later, at that time it probably comprised roughly 50 percent of his capital. So Boesky was relying heavily on Drexel for his funds.

Interviewed in early 1984, Boesky's lawyer and close friend Stephen Fraidin of Fried, Frank had listed Milken as one of a handful of people, important to Boesky, who knew him well. This friendship —or, more likely, this relationship based on mutual exploitation, since few more purposeful people than Boesky and Milken exist in this world—had begun even before Milken became the full-fledged maestro of the takeover world. But the relationship—and its potential for abuse—must have intensified once Milken possessed so much of the information the omnivorous Boesky craved. According to one associate of the two men, Boesky (who made it a point of pride that he slept only three or four hours a night) would call Milken (who did the same) most mornings as soon as Milken arrived at his desk, between 4 and 4:30 A.M.

The relationship was fraught with a conflict-of-interest potential that was extreme even for Milken. He, of course, would not have seen it as a conflict. It had, rather, the synchronicity of interest that he had long cultivated in his interdependent universe, where he underwrote debt securities, and owned them, and owned those issuers' equity as well, and placed others' debt with those companies. Here Milken (and Drexel) not only underwrote Boesky's debt and probably owned some of it but had profit participation in Boesky's arbitrage activities as equity holders. In those activities, Boesky was betting—in the kind of volume that could influence their outcomes—on the contests that Milken was strategizing and backing. They might be, if they so chose, perfectly complementary.

And they had been, as Boesky began telling the government, or at least it appeared so from stories in the press, mainly those written by James Stewart and Daniel Hertzberg in *The Wall Street Journal*, during the six months after Boesky Day.

Within the first two weeks Drexel was identified as the subject of an investigation by the SEC and also a federal grand jury. By early February 1987, the outlines of what was reportedly the government's case were being sketched in the *Journal*.

The centerpiece of that case against Milken and others at Drexel appeared to be a $5.3 million payment made by a Boesky entity to Drexel in March 1986. As reported by Stewart and Hertzberg, that payment was questioned by Boesky's auditors at the accounting firm of Oppenheim, Appel, Dixon and Company. Boesky had told his auditors that it was for "consulting." Unable to produce documentation explaining the payment, Boesky had then called Drexel's Beverly Hills office and obtained a letter—signed by Lowell Milken and Donald Balser, a member of "the Department"—stating that the payment was for "consulting and advisory services."

Stewart and Hertzberg, however, quoted sources "familiar with the government's case" who said that the payment appeared to be the settling of differences in a series of profits and losses incurred by Boesky and Drexel, respectively. These profits and losses apparently had resulted, sources said, from Boesky's having bought and "parked" stock at Milken's behest, and Milken's having done a similar favor for him. "Parking" refers to one investor's holding stock for another, in order to conceal the true ownership of the stock—and it typically involves the holder's being guaranteed against losses. In some instances, these sources said, it appeared that Milken had not only agreed to protect Boesky from loss on the stock purchase Boesky made for him, but had promised him a percentage of the profits on the eventual sale of the stock. Thus, to arrive at the $5.3 million, Boesky totaled the losses and profits from the stock positions he had been parking for Drexel, and subtracted the percentage he was allowed to keep.

If this were true, prosecutors would have a multitude of potential violations of the law to draw upon for indictments: failure to disclose these arrangements in SEC filings; net capital violations; violation of prohibitions against market manipulation, of tender-offer regulations, of record-keeping requirements, of prohibitions against falsifying documents, and of antifraud provisions of the securities laws; and conspiracy to commit any or all of these offenses. Beyond all this, if Boesky had parked stock for Drexel in the context of a coming takeover about which Drexel officials had inside information, then Drexel might be subject to triple damages under the insider-trading act for all or part of its profits.

There are numerous ways that such a reciprocal parking arrangement could have worked to Boesky's and Milken's mutual advantage. Boesky, who was always straining his net-capital requirements with his gargantuan appetite, could have disguised the true magnitude of his holdings by parking them with Milken. Or he might not have wanted to make the required public 13D filing stating that he had acquired over 5 percent of a company's stock, if he were contemplating an acquisition. (Boesky had said, in early 1984, that he intended to expand from arbitrage into "merchant banking.") Or he might have been buying stock on the basis of inside information about a coming deal, and he would have wanted to disguise his purchases so as to avoid SEC investigation.

For his part, Milken might have wanted to park stock with Boesky if it were stock that Drexel was restricted from buying because of its knowledge of a coming deal. Or Milken might have wanted to seem not to own stock but have it on call to pressure a targeted hostile takeover subject as in, for example, the Wickes situation. Or he might have wanted, as was allegedly the case in Victor Posner's acquiring control of Fischbach, to have freed Posner to act via a stock purchase—one he was unable to make himself. For Milken—deftly moving his players across the board, strategizing many moves ahead—the potential uses for disguised stock purchases were myriad.

Fischbach was among the eight stocks that Stewart and Hertz-

berg listed, in articles in the *Journal*, as allegedly having been involved in the $5.3 million payment. (The others were Gulf + West-
ern, Unocal, Transworld, Phillips Petroleum, Diamond Shamrock,
Lorimar-Telepictures, Harris Graphics.) According to Drexel executives, it was Fischbach that the government in depositions appeared to be focusing on the most.

Indeed, in April 1987 when Boesky would take his criminal plea
(having agreed to a consent decree regarding the SEC charges earlier), he would plead guilty to a criminal information that charged
him with conspiring to make false statements to the SEC in the
context of a conspiracy to gain control of Fischbach, an engineering
company. The document charged that a conspirator had instructed
Boesky to acquire Fischbach stock, and that Boesky was later reim-
bursed for losses as "part of an attempt to reconcile other outstanding money differences." According to sources quoted by Stewart and
Hertzberg, that conspirator was Milken, and that settling of differences was part of the $5.3 million payment.

The Fischbach saga, which had been partially told (minus the
alleged Milken-Boesky parking arrangement) by reporter Allan
Sloan in the December 1985 *Forbes*, certainly looked like a classic
Milken orchestration. It had begun back in 1983, when Victor Posner—then still a client in good standing at Drexel, and one of Milk-
en's circle of high-rollers—was being thwarted in his desire to gain
control of Fischbach. Posner had entered into a standstill agreement
with Fischbach in 1980 which prohibited his buying more than 24.9
percent of the company unless someone else acquired more than 10
percent. In December '83, Fred Carr of First Executive converted his
Fischbach convertible bonds to stock, which gave him a 13.1 percent
holding in the company. In January '84, Fischbach bought Carr out
at the market price.

In April '84, Posner sued Fischbach, claiming that Carr's holding had voided the standstill. Also in April, Boesky began acquiring
Fischbach stock. By the summer, Boesky had acquired 13.4 percent.
Posner—who now could argue that the standstill had been doubly
voided—increased his stake in Fischbach to 28 percent and sought
antitrust clearance to acquire more than 50 percent. Fischbach gave
up the fight and agreed to give Posner control, once he had bought
51 percent of the company's shares.

In February 1985, Drexel raised $48 million for Posner's Penn-
sylvania Engineering. Also in February, Boesky sold all his Fisch-

bach stock for $45 a share in London, when Fischbach was trading in the high thirties in New York. Boesky also sold Fischbach convertible debentures in the over-the-counter market at a premium over their face value. The same day, Pennsylvania Engineering purchased the identical number of shares, for $45 each, in the over-the-counter market, and the same amount of convertible debentures that Boesky had sold. The bulk of the $48 million Drexel raised for Pennsylvania Engineering was used to purchase these securities. Ultimately, Posner bought more than 50 percent of Fischbach's stock. He became chairman of the company in October 1985.

The Pennsylvania Engineering underwriting occurred while Posner was struggling to raise money to take over National Can— and several months after Drexel executives said they had decided to raise no more money for Posner. One Drexel executive said, "It's true, we *had* made that decision. But the Pennsylvania Engineering underwriting was for the Fischbach stock, and that whole thing had started before we made that decision, although it happened afterwards."

It is true that Posner's Fischbach machinations predated the firm's decision to raise no more funds for him—but that would in itself have been no reason for Milken and his investment-banking colleagues to rescind their decision, unless they were already involved. If the government is right in what it is alleging in the criminal information, of course (and assuming the conspirator *is* Milken), then they were.

According to the criminal information, and as agreed by Boesky in his guilty plea, Boesky was assured by the conspirators that he would be made whole on any losses resulting from his Fischbach stock purchases at the outset. Boesky also confirmed that the conspirators arranged for the purchase of the Boesky holdings at the above-market price. Boesky took a loss on Fischbach—but it would have been much greater if he had not been able to sell to Posner at about 20 percent above market. With the Pennsylvania Engineering underwriting, Posner got the money to acquire the company, and Milken got a way of cutting Boesky's losses, which he had allegedly guaranteed.

Remember Milken's maneuverings (scouring the country for a buyer, finally settling on Peltz when no one else was willing, raising all the money for the acquisition) to rescue Posner from the trap he found himself in at National Can, and the government's Fischbach scenario becomes utterly credible. It is, in fact, vintage Milken: at the controls, fine-tuning here, adjusting there, advancing his players, using them to pressure some reluctant party, moving one to help another—fiercely intent, always, on expanding his scope, and maintaining the delicate equilibrium of the interconnected whole.

Ironically, all the machinations were for no profitable end. The Pennsylvania Engineering debt, raised at rates of 17 percent to 22 percent, coincided with a slump in that company's main business, making the interest payments crippling. Fischbach's construction business suffered at the same time, so that it was unable to help with those interest payments. Profitable when Posner first targeted it—Fischbach's earnings were $26.7 million in 1983, its peak year— Fischbach lost $29 million in 1986. And by mid-1987 the downward spiral of Posner's empire had accelerated, accentuating the wisdom of Drexel's decision in the fall of '84 to do no more financings for him—a decision that Drexel executives must fervently wish they had adhered to.

Sometimes, as seems to have been true in Fischbach, the actions performed by Milken's machine, in its diverse parts, were complex; sometimes they were brutally simple. Milken's apparent use of Steinberg as a club to gain Wickes's business was an example of the latter. As was the attempted extortion that Staley Continental alleges took place in November 1987—just days before Boesky Day, when Milken's troops had no idea the end was near and so appear to have been carrying on business as usual in "the Department."

In February '87 Staley filed suit against Drexel, alleging that Drexel had made an "extortionate attempt to force Staley to use it as an investment banker so that Staley could be taken over by a Drexel-Staley Management leveraged buyout group." The suit was proceeding along its private, civil track, but Drexel executives said that it had obviously aroused government interest, as the SEC in its depositions was focusing intensively on Staley also.

According to one former Drexel executive, Drexel had attempted to court the blue-chip food company Staley as a client in the early eighties, through a contact at Bruxelles Lambert, but had been rebuffed. The Drexel of the mideighties, however, was not so easily discouraged. The Staley suit alleges that Drexel and some of its customers began making purchases of Staley stock in late October '86. On November 3, it says, a representative of Drexel contacted Staley's chief financial officer, Robert Hoffman, and expressed an interest in establishing an investment-banking relationship. Three days later, the person in charge of accumulating Staley stock at Drexel, Milken's favored salesman-trader James Dahl—also a central figure in the Beverly Hills Savings and Loan suit against Drexel —allegedly told Hoffman that Drexel had acquired approximately 1.5 million shares (more than 5 percent of the company's stock) and might buy more. Dahl is said to have advised Hoffman against Staley's doing a planned common-stock offering.

On November 11, the complaint continues, Dahl suggested a management-led leveraged buyout to Hoffman. He also warned against Staley's proceeding with its planned stock issue with any investment banker but Drexel. On November 13, Staley registered a four-million-share offering with the SEC, with Merrill Lynch and First Boston as lead managers. Dahl allegedly threatened to disrupt the offering, and over the next several days heavy selling forced Staley's stock price down $5. Drexel "sold into our offering," Staley's general counsel, Robert Scott, told *The Wall Street Journal*.

On November 21, Staley withdrew the offering and filed with the SEC for a new issue of preferred stock. Additional costs associated with this revised deal were $70 million—for which Staley was suing Drexel, as compensatory damages. It was also suing for twice that in punitive damages.

At least as provocative as what Drexel did, as alleged in the Staley complaint, is what Dahl said. He allegedly acknowledged that Drexel had not yet filed a 13D, despite the fact that he said the firm owned more than 5 percent of Staley's stock; 13Ds, he explained, were "bad for business." In assuring Hoffman that Drexel was genuinely interested in pursuing a leveraged buyout of Staley with its management, Dahl allegedly explained that "Drexel drew no distinction between debt and equity because companies' life cycles were so short," and that Drexel could "take Staley private in forty-eight hours."

In warning Hoffman against Staley's doing the common-stock offering, Dahl allegedly said, "It is very important for us to sit down and talk before you do something that hurts me and before I do something that hurts you." The equity offering, Dahl allegedly made plain, would hurt Drexel (by diluting the value of its holdings), and if that happened, "the next thing that happens is someone files a 13D at $40 a share and management is thrown out." Later, after Staley had decided to go ahead with the offering, Dahl allegedly asked how its pricing would be handled and commented that he would "hate to see Drexel have to sell into the offering."

This was the Drexel—the brass-knuckles, threatening, market-manipulating Cosa Nostra of the securities world—that its rival investment bankers and corporate targets loved to hate. Drexel was already down, three months into the government investigation, when the Staley suit was filed, but a round of cheers went up in the investment-banking community. Just as rivals had circulated copies of the Green Tree complaint when it had been filed, so now—Drexel executives alleged—Salomon sent its clients copies of the Staley complaint.

To many who knew Dahl, his alleged comments rang with authenticity. Seeming not only literally but symbolically true, they captured the zeitgeist of the Beverly Hills operation. While these acquaintances of Dahl speculated that he might have been off on an entrepreneurial spree, unauthorized by Milken, they agreed that it was the kind of action that the culture of "the Department" encouraged. One former Drexel employee claimed, "What Jim Dahl is alleged to have said was not the exception [in Beverly Hills] but the norm."

Moreover, it seems unlikely that Milken, who was obsessed with controlling his people and everything that he touched, who in an SEC deposition several years earlier had spoken about his gradually developed ability to hear everything that went on on his trading floor, would have utterly missed Dahl's machinations in Staley. As one former member of this group declared, "Mike controlled everything. He was like Patton, up on the hill. He saw everything that went on, heard everything."

Drexel took the position publicly that the suit was "totally without merit." According to one Drexel employee, the firm's officials to whom Staley complained in November decided that Dahl had said some things that were "inappropriate," and they hastened to reassure Staley that Drexel would do nothing to destabilize the company. Drexel and Staley were in the midst of executing a standstill agreement, this executive says, when Staley suddenly filed suit. This executive also adds that Drexel was a net buyer, not seller, during the Staley aborted offering; therefore, he states, Dahl was all talk and no action, Drexel did not ruin the stock offering, and there were no grounds for a suit.

Even if Drexel did not carry out Dahl's alleged threats, the

Staley situation exemplified, in this writer's view, conduct that was probably central to the Milken machine and that could be a 13D violation: assembling control of more than 5 percent of the stock but not disclosing it publicly while using it as a threat privately. Milken was the great choreographer. He knew where convertible bonds were and where lots of stocks were, or he could advise clients to buy them and then he could bring their cumulative weight to bear—all without filing a 13D and disclosing that these shares were being used in concert to achieve his end.

From his earliest days as a bond trader, when his fellow bond-holders typically were a passive lot, Milken had understood that controlling a position of size in a company's securities, even its debt securities, meant a chance to exert control over that company. He had tried this with Riklis (in Rapid-American) and been well received. He had tried this with Sigoloff (in Daylin) and not been. The Milken who years later reportedly told Sigoloff, in Wickes, that (with the stock that others held but he controlled) he effectively had control of the company, was simply a Milken who had grown far more powerful, who could direct the movement of stocks owned by others—but it was the same Milken.

In addition to looking for evidence of Drexel's having assembled blocks of stock without complying with disclosure requirements, and of its having parked stocks to disguise their true ownership, the government also appeared, during the first few months of '87, to be looking for evidence of the more garden-variety misuse of inside information. Passing inside information about coming deals to favored customers was something for which the SEC had investigated Milken in earlier years, always fruitlessly. According to press reports, the government had subpoenaed both Rodrigo Rocha and Guy Dove, attempting to ascertain whether Atlantic Capital—on tips from Drexel—had invested in common stocks before announced tender offers. If true, this would have given Atlantic Capital added motivations (beyond the high yield of the bonds) for being probably the single largest subscriber to the junk bonds in the 1985 takeovers; it would have had a powerful interest in the deals' going through, since it was a shareholder in the target company, and it would also be repaying the favors of Drexel's tips.

As the investigation continued, the government would become interested in another satellite group with which Milken had done business, the Regan-Thorp entities. James Regan and Edward Thorp and their associates had been Milken's partners at least since the Treasuries-stripping days of Dorchester Government Securities and Belvedere Securities, and they had been a focus of SEC interest in the 1985 investigation into the trading of Caesars World securities. In December 1987, federal agents would raid and confiscate more than sixty boxes of documents and business records going back to January 1984 from three firms which operated from the same address in Princeton, New Jersey—Princeton-Newport Arbitrage Partners, Englewood Partners and the Oakley-Sutton Management Corporation. According to search-warrant filings, the government was hoping to establish that a network of traders had been involved in a scheme of stock parking. It also sought evidence of improper tax deductions taken on losses that were generated from hedging on trades involving convertible bonds and warrants, according to the court documents. Among those named in the warrant was Bruce Newberg, who had been a trader in convertibles for Milken and was still a member of Milken's group though no longer on the trading desk.

In the early months of the investigation, however, it had not seemed plausible that it would continue for over a year without producing indictments. Nearly every Friday in March and April of 1986, Wall Street gossip had predicted that the Milken and Drexel indictments would be announced at the market's close—gossip fueled, of course, by press reports which purported to spell out the government's impending case against Drexel in great detail.

While those reports were not borne out within the six months following Boesky Day, other events had occurred. Boesky, to the surprise of few on the Street, had offered up Martin Siegel. On February 13, Siegel had pleaded guilty to two felony counts of tax evasion and conspiracy to violate securities laws, and also agreed to pay $9 million in civil fines. The insider trading with Boesky to which he pleaded, however, had occurred while he was at Kidder, before he went to Drexel.

Siegel, in turn, had offered up Robert Freeman, head of the arbitrage department at the impeccable Goldman, Sachs; Richard Wigton, head of arbitrage at Kidder, Peabody; and Timothy Tabor, former head of arbitrage at Merrill Lynch. These three men were arrested the day before Siegel took his plea, and they were charged with being part of an information-swapping conspiracy. But by May their indictments had been dropped.

On March 20, Boyd Jefferies, chairman of Jefferies Group, the Los Angeles–based brokerage firm that had become a major force in takeovers, pleaded to two felony counts of securities-law violations, and settled related charges with the SEC relating to market manipulation and to parking stock in a scheme with Boesky.

By April 1, the opening day of the 1987 Predators' Ball, it seemed to many Drexel employees and their clients that the government's drumbeat was almost deafening. Freeman, Wigton and Tabor had been arrested without warning, Wigton led from his Kidder office in handcuffs, and the nightmare of some at Drexel was of Milken being arrested onstage at the Predators' Ball. The conference drew a record crowd, some probably out of curiosity but many out of loyalty.

Fred Joseph appeared ill and suddenly aged. Other Drexel executives were depressed and fatigued. Cary Maultasch looked especially haggard. Maultasch was the Drexel official, formerly in Beverly Hills but now based in New York, who according to sources quoted by Stewart and Hertzberg handled all Milken's personal trading and, at the end of each day, destroyed computer printouts of his trades in a shredder. The mood at the Polo Lounge, where for the first time Engel's "girls" were absent, was wakelike. ("It's because of the First Amendment," one Drexel executive explained sourly, referring to press reports.)

Milken alone looked well. He did not introduce as many of the client presentations as he had done in years past, having accepted the view of Joseph and others that for the good of the firm he should recede somewhat at this conference lest he soon have to recede forever. But when he mounted the stage at the Beverly Hilton during the closing gala, his loyalists, over two thousand strong, gave him an ovation that seemed as if it would never end.

16

The Center Cannot Hold

IN THE SIX MONTHS that followed Boesky Day, Drexel was a reminder of the old adage that the higher they rise, the harder they fall. The heights that Drexel's executives had scaled had been so dizzying, and their descent was now so sudden, that some felt themselves on a roller coaster.

Many at Drexel looked for the root of their downfall, outside. The press—mainly *The Wall Street Journal*, which, shortly after Boesky Day, had begun to describe in increasingly greater detail Milken, Drexel, and Milken's takeover machine as targets of the investigation—was one scapegoat. The government, as personified chiefly in the SEC and the U.S. Attorney's Office, one or both of which was presumed to be leaking to the press, and secondarily in a newly aroused Congress, was another. America's corporate elite, those Business Roundtable types who had fought the hated Drexel and their arriviste clients on every possible front (in Congress, in court, at the Fed) and lost, but who now saw a chance to reverse that rout, was a third. And Drexel's investment-banking rivals on the Street, who had marshaled much of corporate America's attack on the upstart firm but in the end had decided to play its game, were yet a fourth. The more conspiracy-minded at Drexel saw combinations of the four, in unholy league.

"The distortions and even falsehoods being uttered about our firm and some of its personnel are so rampant and willful that one wonders if it isn't a plot to destroy us," wrote Tubby Burnham, the then seventy-seven-year-old honorary chairman of the board, in an anguished letter to Drexel Burnham employees ten days after Boesky Day.

Arthur Bilger, corporate-finance partner in Beverly Hills, spoke for many of his colleagues when he pointed out that "between twenty and twenty-five percent of Fortune 500 companies disappeared in 1986. I am convinced that it is that, generally—plus our having gone after the major oil companies, Gulf, Phillips and Unocal—that has caused our troubles."

Others at Drexel saw the backlash springing from a resentment more deep-rooted and age-old. Now they harked back to the fears expressed by many Jewish members of the business establishment ever since Drexel had first conjured up its armies of takeover entrepreneurs. Paul Levy, one of Drexel's 3(a)9 (unregistered exchange offer) specialists, put it bluntly. "There is a lot of anti-Semitism at work," Levy declared. "People see Drexel as a bunch of Jewish guys who have been making too much money."

Amidst all the talk of persecution, however, there was a certain amount of self-examination and recrimination. What the aftermath of Boesky Day made crystal clear was that Drexel had no friend on the Street. In the early eighties, as its junk business flourished, the firm had been disdained by Wall Street's titans. Not hated, but disdained. Once Drexel had become a titan itself, it had seemed to take pleasure in remaining the outsider, in flouting the rules of the fraternity, in crushing that fraternity's members when it could. Other firms syndicated deals (in common stock and investment-grade-bond issues) not only to share the risk but to spread the goods about the Street in a collegial fashion. Milken hated syndicated deals. He hated having a co-manager. He would not spread the goods, and they could *keep* their fraternity.

Now was the comeuppance. Howard Brenner, a member of Drexel's Executive Committee who had been at the firm since it was Burnham and Company, admitted, "Some of our colleagues [at Drexel]—especially the younger ones—were very arrogant, and it's come home to bite us."

"To me, the investigation is a parable," declared another Drexel executive. "It has brought us down for our hubris—in our not paying sufficient attention to our transactions, in our dealings with other people. Things like sending people to another city for a road show. Not giving any bonds to a co-manager. Taking a piece of business from another firm which had already filed a prospectus. Other people have occasionally done this kind of thing to us, but I have a hunch that we started it. So far, the government doesn't seem to have evidence of anything illegal. But we are already so weakened [by the press reports of the investigation], it is as though we are paying the penalty for our other sins."

In the months after Boesky Day, it seemed plain that even if Drexel and Milken were to survive, their idyll—in which Milken could raise billions in a matter of days for a hostile bid, in which no company in America was safe from him—would be ended. It was a time for epitaphs.

"I think the systematic realigning of corporate America, and putting parts of companies in the hands of guys who have major equity stakes in those companies, is the best thing we have done for our society," commented corporate-finance partner Stephen Weinroth. "The cat's out of the bag—and if the old-guard establishment puts us out of business, they're not going to put the concept out of business, be it the LBO or the hostile takeover or valuing a company and breaking it up because the assets are worth more broken up than whole."

Weinroth lapsed into the familiar refrain (articulated by Milken, Icahn and others of their persuasion) about the decline of corporate America in the hands of its managers, and its rescue by the new breed of manager-owners. "Old companies were started by true entrepreneurs, who had children some of whom were affected by the ills of the rich," he continued. "They brought in professional managers, who ran the companies in a conservative fashion . . . but those professional managers didn't have an ownership stake. Their risk–reward ratio was skewed to being a conservator, not an initiator. Then the second-generation [managers] grew to the top. And even if they were high quality as managers, they were certainly not entrepreneurial. And then that group promoted people who couldn't threaten them, and they in turn hired people inferior to them, who lived for their perks and compensation and ran their companies conservatively because they had no upside interest. And by the time you go through several generations of these managers, you have a company run by dull-normals!

"It started to change in the fifties," he said. "As new businesses sprang up largely out of a new spurt of technological innovation, there were some entrepreneurial guys. More recently all the LBO guys have said, 'We want the managers to have a stake in this business, because we want them to get rich if they do well' (typically, five to twenty percent of a deal would be owned by management).

"I think the principles are right," Weinroth concluded, "and the fact that some of our players are venal or self-interested or unpleasant is almost beside the point. There is a greater machine going, and if these guys don't make a go of it, then somebody else will buy the stock, and the ownership will reside very close to the helm. And Drexel had more to do with it than anyone else."

The months after the November Boesky Day were rife with signs of Drexel's ebbing power. The first and most symbolic was Drexel's decision, announced in early December, to abandon its much-heralded move to the forty-seven-story tower, Seven World Trade Center, which it had agreed to lease in its entirety in June '86. Just as the announcement of the impending move to that imposing building had been a dramatic statement that Drexel was assuming its place among the established giants of Wall Street, so its cancellation suggested that that ascension was no more.

The most mammoth publicly announced deals that Drexel had been backing when the Boesky news hit, Icahn's bid for USX, Perelman's for Gillette and Sigoloff's (Wickes's) just-announced acquisition of Lear Siegler, came to a total of roughly $14 billion. For Icahn, Perelman and Sigoloff, these deals would have represented an enormous expansion of their respective empires. In addition to collecting a king's ransom in financing fees in these deals (in USX, for example, Drexel's fee would have been roughly $250 million), Drexel would have reaped a golden harvest of divestiture business. But after Boesky Day, despite Drexel's assertions that it could still place the debt for these deals, those financings were deemed sufficiently questionable that the bidders' hands were weakened. Ultimately, all three deals foundered: Wickes abandoned its acquisition of Lear Siegler, and Perelman and Icahn were beaten back from their targets. In the next six months, the whole of the first half of 1987, Drexel did not back a single hostile bid.

Other hallmarks of the Milken regime also disappeared, casualties of this new epoch in which Milken and Drexel would be forced to live under the government's microscope. Privately placed, unregistered bonds, for example, no longer changed hands en masse, moving from Milken's high-rollers to the second-tier buyers in that flow that was so integral to the Milken machine. Mark Shenkman of Shenkman Capital commented about two months after Boesky Day, "Privates still trade—but now precise logs are kept, and they [Milken's salesmen and traders] can only talk to twenty-five people about it. It can't be a public distribution. They are reining Mike in."

And at least some of the gold-mine investment partnerships, through which Milken had built wealth first for his own people and then for a wider group in corporate finance, were closed down. The major partnership with corporate finance, which invested in buy-outs, was named Concordia. In 1985, Concordia's return had been close to 100 percent. By the end of 1986, when it was closed out, it was flat for the year. This was strange, since 1986 had been a soar-ingly profitable year at Drexel. "That had to have been done on purpose," insisted one former Drexel employee, "so that they could say, 'See? We always knew that with the kind of risk we take we'd hit a bad year sooner or later.' "

Within days of the Boesky plea, rival investment bankers had begun going down the list of Drexel clients, soliciting their business. While Drexel's traditional stable appeared still loyal, the blue-chip clients that Drexel had been struggling to win (whether by court-ship or by coercion, whether by Martin Siegel or by Jim Dahl) quickly fell away. Theirs had been an uneasy alliance with Milken. In the months just prior to Boesky Day, Goodyear had brought Drexel in along with Goldman, Sachs to advise it on a defensive restructuring. Viacom had hired Drexel along with Donaldson, Luf-kin and Jenrette to assist in its management buyout. Ralston Purina had added Drexel as a third co-manager, along with Goldman, Sachs and Salomon, for an investment-grade-bond issue. According to well-placed sources in each of these deals, Drexel was brought in for only one reason: so that it would not bring in a competing bidder or finance a raid on the company.

The uneasiness, moreover, had existed not only on the part of these corporate clients, but within Drexel. Such client representa-tions were integral to Joseph's and Siegel's shared vision of institu-tion-building, were in fact the mission with which Siegel had come to Drexel. But they were at odds with the gospel according to Milken—a gospel which taught that these corporate behemoths de-served to be taken over because they were being run inefficiently, so it was not only profitable to do so, but right. In the above in-stances, however, Milken had apparently acceded to Joseph and agreed to allow his peace to be bought.

Now Milken's hands had been involuntarily tied. And the cor-porate establishment, no longer afraid, was no longer interested.

Lear Siegler, for example, had followed Siegel from Kidder to Drexel. In its sale to Wickes, Drexel had been its investment banker. But about a week after Boesky Day, when that sale fell through, Lear Siegler brought in Goldman, Sachs to study the alternatives of a leveraged buyout or a corporate recapitalization.

"With the Fortune 500 companies, it was all fear," remarked one former Drexel employee. "[In the summer and fall of '86] I would make a call to a CEO and the call would be returned in a half hour. Once Drexel started to fall, they never returned my calls."

Now Drexel, which had used fear to wedge its way into corporate suites, was riddled with fear itself: Fear of what the government might find. Fear of losing business. Fear of seeing the value of the firm's stock (widely held among about 2,050 employees) and its capital decimated, in the event the firm had to pay crippling damages as a result of the investigation. Fear of the damage to recruitment. And, because of all this, fear of a mass exodus of employees (draining the firm not only of talent but of capital as they demanded payout on their stock).

In the first few months, about a half-dozen associates in corporate finance and M&A did leave Drexel. This was followed by a major defection in April, when an entire group of seven professionals, including one senior-level executive—all of whom had been hired from Kidder within the past year—departed for Paine Webber.

So fearful was Fred Joseph of an exodus, according to one Drexel employee, that in December '86 he broached the idea of soliciting signed loyalty pledges from all senior employees, promising that they would not leave the firm for at least one year. Executives reportedly tried to dissuade him, arguing that it was distasteful, a sign of weakness on the firm's part, and in any case unenforceable. Finally, Joseph abandoned the idea.

For Joseph, who had had false starts in the business, who had dreamed back in the seventies of building an institution "as important as Goldman, Sachs," and who had felt he was tantalizingly close to that goal, it must have been an agony to see it slip through his fingers. While Milken remained protectively cloistered as always, Joseph, the front man, had to step into the glare of the public spotlight. Looking gray and puffy-eyed, photogenic no longer, he was shown (incredibly enough) sitting on the floor in his office on the cover of a December '86 issue of *Fortune* magazine, where the subtitle described him as "Floored by the crisis." The ready and confident, albeit superficial, answers he had always produced were now replaced by ones so tentative and unsure that they invited parody among some of his partners—such as his quote in *Business Week*, dated December 22: "What I think I'm confident of is that we don't know of anyone here who's done anything wrong."

It was Joseph's personal crucible. He had assumed the post of CEO—from Robert Linton (who retained the title of chairman, but had clearly yielded the leadership of the firm to Joseph)—only about eighteen months before Boesky Day. Back in the early seventies, Joseph had become chief operating officer of Shearson, Hamill —which, six months later, had had to merge into Shearson Hayden Stone (through no fault of his). One Drexel executive recalled ruefully that at a meeting immediately after Joseph had assumed the top post at Drexel, John Sorte, who had been with Joseph at Shearson, quipped, "Fred, how many months do you give us before we fail, with you as chief executive?"

Joseph, more than anyone else, had been the architect of the institutional expansion of Drexel. For Milken the firm was a vehicle, but for Joseph it was an end in itself. And Joseph possessed certain traits which had, in his lexicon, added value to the firm. First, he was a supersalesman, a great complement to Milken on the corporate-finance side, especially in the early days before Milken started doing everything himself. Second, he had a front-man personality that was so good it made you forget that that was what it was: down-to-earth, good-humored, redolent with boyish charm, but all bright surface, with a veneer that never cracked. And, third, he had that overriding desire to win, which was probably the key to his and Milken's compatibility.

His paramount contribution, however, was in a role that was much like that of a manager of a great Hollywood star. Joseph had managed Milken. "Fred grabbed onto those [Milken's] coattails, directed them some, orchestrated them a lot to the public and to us," commented one Drexel executive.

Now the firm's shining star had become its greatest liability, and it was not so clear that Joseph's dominant traits were what this crisis required. In a time of terrible uncertainty, when the firm was being publicly tarred with the suggestion that its key employees had committed crimes, its ideal leader would be decisive, strong and principled, the personification of integrity.

There were at least two views of Joseph within the firm. One was that while he came closer to monitoring Milken than anyone else, he still was kept in the dark about some things that transpired on the West Coast. Somewhat short of information, therefore, he was nonetheless seen as an honest, restraining force. Former corporate-finance partner Julian Schroeder claimed, "Mike would do *anything*. I would have felt naked there without Fred."

Schroeder added that on a visit to Drexel in the spring of '86 he had found Joseph in the midst of one of his many daily phone conversations with Milken, in which Joseph was saying, "Michael, you are the only one who can put yourself in jail—now, *don't do it*." To Schroeder, this remark indicated that things had not changed since he left the firm in 1984: Joseph was still struggling to control Milken.

Another view, however, was that Joseph and Milken, consumed by a similar, religious fire to win, were more in league than in counterpoint. And that Joseph, therefore, was more pragmatic than principled. As one Drexel employee maintained, "Fred is great in an up-market. In an up-market, the leadership, the salesmanship, the upbeatness are the important things. But all the quick moves that in good times looked like a great salesman, in bad times looked dishonest. And when things are bad, he can't make a decision."

Joseph, this employee said, "is the consummate rationalizer about why somebody doesn't have to get fired." There was a case to be made that the firm should have either fired or suspended Martin Siegel in December, after he had been subpoenaed in the grand-jury investigation and it seemed all of Wall Street was convinced that the Boesky-Siegel game was finally exposed. Siegel remained at the firm until his plea was announced in February. (Indeed, even the hiring of Siegel in early '86 arguably attests to Joseph's being long on pragmatism and short on principle, since Siegel was so widely rumored on the Street to be involved in insider trading with Boesky.)

A stronger case could be made for the firing of Jim Dahl, if Joseph believed that Dahl had in fact said what Staley alleged. And this was not the first complaint about Dahl. Beverly Hills Savings and Loan, in its lawsuit against Drexel and Dahl, had accused him of fraudulent misrepresentation. The same employee declared, "Dahl was a loose cannon. He has put securities in people's accounts without calling them. We knew what he was—but Mike liked him, because he was productive. The Staley threats might not be illegal, but there should be a standard of conduct. But Fred's attitude when it came to firing Siegel or Dahl was, If we get rid of them, they will hurt us."

Joseph, of course, would not have been the first chief executive to keep employees on so as not to create witnesses friendly to the government, with an investigation in progress; his lawyers might well have advised him not to fire the two. But a less defensible example of Joseph's elevation of pragmatism over principle was his decision, also urged by Milken, to bring Donald Engel back into the firm.

Engel had been a fixture at the firm since the days of Burnham and Company. As Victor Posner became a more important Drexel client in the late seventies and early eighties, Engel had handled his account on the corporate-finance side and become a director on several of the Posner-controlled companies' boards. According to many of his colleagues, Engel knew little about corporate finance, particularly in the sophisticated way that Drexel practiced it by the eighties, but he did have a way with clients. And, since the earliest days of the Predators' Ball, he had been extremely useful to Milken on the social side—a perpetual gladhander, a happy panderer. "Mike always respected Don's usefulness," declared one former member of the Milken group. "Don could make sure the clients got laid—and Mike didn't have to dirty himself."

But in 1984 Engel was forced to resign. According to one Drexel executive, Engel had taken money from a Drexel client that should have been paid to the firm. (Engel denies this charge.) Some executives wanted to sever all ties with Engel, but Milken reportedly argued in his behalf, and in the end Engel became a "consultant," negotiating a lucrative fee arrangement for any business he originated.

Ironically enough, it was as a "consultant" that Engel saw his wealth accumulate. The clients with whom he had relationships—among them Peltz and Perelman—were Drexel kingpins by 1985. One Drexel employee said that Engel's compensation for 1986 (probably including warrants) was about $9 million. And while Engel had had to relinquish his office at Drexel when he was forced to resign (his new business habitat was the third floor of his friend Perelman's town house), he still presented himself as a member of the firm. To reach Engel's office one called the Drexel switchboard.

It was, then, the cushiest of exiles. But in January '87, when Drexel's push for new clients had ground to a halt, and the firm seemed to be in danger of losing much if not all of the territory it had appropriated over the past decade, Engel was deemed too valuable to not be a full-fledged member of the team.

Soliciting new clients was the business of the Investment Banking Group (IBG), formed in early 1986 and headed by corporate-finance partner Chris Andersen. Even before the trauma triggered by Boesky Day, however, the IBG had been a failure (and by late 1987 the group would be disbanded). Andersen, who has a rambling, free-associating habit of mind, was considered by his colleagues to be a creative investment banker but a poor administrator and ill-suited for this management post. Moreover, Andersen's attention to the IBG was sporadic, inasmuch as he and Stephen Weinroth in May of '86 had bought a 13 percent stake in Centronics Data Computer Corporation, a Drexel investment-banking client. Though he and Weinroth had done this with Joseph's permission, their move had caused bad blood among many of their colleagues, particularly when Weinroth, Centronics' new chairman, discussed its becoming a deal-making vehicle whose deals might be in competition with some Drexel clients'.

Some at Drexel maintained that the real problem of the IBG lay in the firm's generally freewheeling, unstructured approach—exemplified in part by the Centronics situation. The Drexel culture encouraged entrepreneurism at every turn. Compliance, capital allocation, exposure and accounting were centralized, but all other decisions were left to the head of each group, so that the firm was run as a loosely connected association of free enterprises.

"Drexel was made up of little fiefdoms, with no rules," recalled one former IBG member. "Joseph wanted it to be that way. It was supposed to be more entrepreneurial, and I guess it had worked for a while, especially when the place was smaller, but it didn't anymore. You'd [as a member of the IBG] call on a company and find out that, four weeks before, someone from corporate finance had been there; three weeks before, someone from M&A; and two weeks before, one of Mike's guys. No one had any idea what anyone else was doing. It was chaos."

Now, in January '87, Engel was brought back to the firm to be co-head (with Andersen) of the IBG. Engel invited one of the IBG members, a recent recruit from a premier Wall Street firm, to breakfast. He reportedly told this associate that he, Engel, was his new boss (not Andersen) and that he would be dealing directly with Milken. Symbolic of his stewardship, Engel had rechristened the IBG the "Relationship Group." He is said to have explained that it was emphasizing relationships that would win the new clients, that that was the style of business at which he excelled and that the way to establish relationships was by "getting in the minds" of prospective clients, and providing them what they wanted.

This associate had heard Engel's analysis before. At the Tokyo bond conference, when he had first met Engel, Engel had allegedly remarked to him, "I understand CEOs, CEOs don't care about money, power or fame. They have all that. What they want is *pussy*. And I'm going to make sure they get it."

Then, however, Engel had been only a consultant to the firm. Now he was this young investment banker's boss, ready to school the IBG in his kind of business-getting. One Drexel executive recalled, "He [the associate] said, 'Omigod, everything they told me about Drexel over at . . . , it was all true, the place is a total slime-bucket!' " He immediately resigned from Drexel and returned to his former firm.

At Drexel, the melodrama continued. Word had circulated about what had precipitated the associate's resignation. Younger employees at the firm did not know why Engel had been forced to resign in 1984; many, knowing Engel as a notorious, compulsive womanizer, believed it had been for the kind of incident that had just occurred. But whatever the reason had been, it was clear to these fresh-faced Harvard M.B.A.'s, who had had their pick of the firms on Wall Street and had chosen Drexel, that Engel (like his longtime client Victor Posner) was an unsavory reminder of the *old* Drexel, which would be better forgotten. If there was ever a time for the firm to cultivate a straight-arrow image, they thought, surely this was it.

Andersen and Weinroth, who both had opposed Engel's reinstatement, now threatened to resign unless he was forced to resign again. And within two weeks, by early February, there was such a popular groundswell against Engel that people were calling it a "revolution." When Engel tried to enter an IBG meeting on February 6, Andersen ordered him out. Engel left the room and called John Kissick in Beverly Hills, who was participating in the meeting via a hookup. Engel's strongest support had always come from the

Coast. Kissick said he thought it was OK for Engel to attend. As soon as the meeting broke, Andersen walked across the street to Drexel's executive offices to deliver his resignation to Joseph. Weinroth said he would resign, too. Another corporate-finance partner, Alan Brumberger, calling in from out of town, said he would join them.

Joseph—who in earlier, more upbeat times had described himself as the "Dr. Feelgood" of Drexel—reportedly asked for one week to try to resolve the problem in a way that would "make everyone happy." That, however, was not possible, and Engel was forced to resign. He resumed his "consultant" status.

Engel's reinstatement had lasted less than a month. It is true that in the larger scheme of Drexel's troubles it was only a sideshow. But at a time when Drexel employees were already shell-shocked, depressed, embarrassed, defensive and fearful for their futures, it managed to make morale even worse, holding up a mirror to the firm and reflecting an unsightly image.

That image had nothing to do with what the government was investigating, and yet it had everything to do with it. Engel's procurement of women for clients was not conduct the government would likely seek to prosecute, but its significance lay in the larger truth that it revealed about Drexel. For whether it meant procuring women, or threatening would-be clients, the resounding credo at Drexel was to do whatever it took to win.

Everything bowed before that credo. Morality and legality became mere conventions, accepted modes of conduct for the foot soldiers of the world—the less creative, less aggressive, less visionary. The iconoclastic Milken, in whose image the firm had been formed, had always disdained conventional ways of seeing, conventional ways of doing business. And, thanks to his flouting of convention, Drexel had apotheosized out of nothingness.

It was that credo that had led to Engel's reinstatement. Joseph is said to have personally abhorred Engel. He may have also personally abhorred Engel's function, though he must have known and accepted it for years. He had made a show of enormous though disingenuous indignation to *Institutional Investor* in an interview for its August 1986 Milken profile, when the subject of hookers at the Chasen's dinner and Bungalow 8 was raised. Telling *Institutional Investor* that he "went bananas" when he heard the stories, Joseph added, "I discussed it with Michael and I said, 'If there ever is a hooker there, I'll fire everybody in sight, I'll kill everybody . . .' And everyone said, 'Fred, it's not true, you're overreacting, you're nuts.' I said, 'All right, but not one woman who would embarrass us if someone knew exactly what she did for a living.' And I think I can guarantee you that there isn't a single woman there who doesn't have a legitimate reason to be there and that none of them are hookers."

It may well be that had history allowed Joseph to pursue his longtime vision of building an institution comparable to Goldman, Sachs, he ultimately would have done away with Engel and his cast of (in case anyone asked) aspiring actresses and would-be models. But when the firm began to disintegrate around him, Joseph applied Drexel's one abiding test to the question of whether to bring Engel back. "He thought," said one employee, with a shrug, "that Donnie would be good for business."

That quintessentially pragmatic credo—whatever it takes to win—may have shaped Drexel's response to the investigation, as well. In the first month or two after Boesky Day, the firm was in turmoil, apparently without a fixed defensive strategy, taking the crisis day by day. There was a considerable amount of anxiety about who might be cooperating with the government. Some days, corporate-finance executives in New York considered casting the West Coast adrift, telling the government that they had known things were not right out there (but never been sure of the specifics, so had not gone to the authorities) and that they wanted now to make their separate peace.

But ultimately this notion had been vetoed as too ignoble, too disloyal to the regent who had made them all richer than they would ever have been without him—and also impractical, since it would have been difficult for the firm to escape liability. Instead, Drexel would present a united front and—unless the government came up with a "smoking gun"—fight back.

Apparently, the closest thing to a smoking gun that the government had was that $5.3 million payment made from Boesky to Drexel in Beverly Hills. And after Boesky's auditors had demanded some documentation, Lowell Milken and Donald Balser had signed the invoice stating the payment was a fee for "consulting and advisory services." In an article in *The New York Times* in February by James Sterngold, several Drexel executives were quoted, elaborating on this, saying that the payment was for several takeover bids—for the Financial Corporation of Santa Barbara, Scott and Fetzer, and *U.S. News & World Report* magazine, among others—that Boesky had asked them to work on but had never consummated. One Drexel official added that in some instances Boesky had backed out at the last minute, and that part of the $5.3 million was meant as compensation to Drexel for its work on these deals.

After-the-fact explanations, however, accompanied by no corroborating documentation tend to fall rather flat—particularly when set alongside the "paper trail" of records kept by Boesky which corroborated his version and which the government was said to have collected, according to sources quoted by Stewart and Hertzberg in *The Wall Street Journal*.

One Drexel employee claimed that this problem—the lack of a paper trail for their side—had been solved by Drexel's fabricating one. Interviewed in early April '87, this employee claimed that "the books were cooked" in the previous month or so, to show at least one specific charge to Boesky that had never existed, as part of that $5.3 million: about $1 million for research, related to Boesky's abortive takeover bids. If true, this was not only a desperate but an ill-considered gambit, since it appeared somewhat implausible on its face. While Drexel's research has become well regarded in the last couple of years, it was considerably less strong back in 1984, when the work on these bids would have occurred. It is especially unlikely that Boesky, who prided himself on his research capabilities in his own shop, would have paid for Drexel's. Moreover, when Boesky did utilize research from Wall Street firms, he was often given it gratis, in exchange for the commission dollars that the firms earned from his trading.

A Drexel spokesman has stated that contemporaneously with the billing of the $5.3 million fee in March 1986, an internal memorandum directed that the fee be allocated among the corporate-finance, research and high-yield-bond departments, and there have been no subsequent changes.

17

The Humbling

ONE YEAR AFTER Boesky Day, Drexel was still in limbo—its likely indictment spelled out in great detail in the press many months before but not yet issued by any grand jury. In the world at large, however, events had not stood still. On October 19, 1987, the stock market's horrific crash was thought at the time to signal the end of an era—an era in which a five-year surging bull market whipped Wall Street into a frenzy of deal-making, an era in which financial fantasy routinely came true. In the wake of the crash, "debt" and "leverage"—which had seemed to possess magical properties for the conjuring of enormous wealth in the corporate arena—were demystified, seen as tools of excess which might now, in the harsh light of day and a possible recession, exact their toll. The spell—for the moment at least—was broken.

Milken had not created the M&A binge of the eighties. Indeed, he had been an outsider, relegated to the sidelines until he and his colleagues provided their chosen with war chests and refined the concept of the Air Fund (conceived of in a Gobhai seminar but never implemented) into the "highly confident" letter. But once Milken won entry to the game, he did more to shape it than any other individual. It seemed only appropriate, in a sense, that this era might draw to a close now that its impresario was so hamstrung (though by early 1988 M&A would again be thriving and Milken would not yet be enjoined from the scene).

For the past several years, while Drexel and its rivals were underwriting billions of dollars of junk bonds to finance scores of superleveraged acquisitions, critics had predicted that this mountainous debt's test—and failure—would come in the next recession. They pointed out that in the early eighties' recession the megadeals' junk bonds had not yet existed, and that credit quality of junk had been deteriorating in the last couple of years. Therefore, they maintained, there had been no test of the junk market in its current, $150 billion form.

In the October 1987 crash, junk bonds did fall in price, with the average junk portfolio losing at worst about 10 percent of its value. This was not surprising, since they are really part debt, part equity, and their value tends to fluctuate with the equity markets as much as or more than with the bond markets, their key variable being less the direction of interest rates than the perceived ability of the issuer to service its debt. While investors fled to Treasury bonds, which staged a huge rally as the stock market plunged, junk bonds yielded a near-record 5.5 percentage points over Treasury bonds with comparable maturities. In the weeks after the crash, the market for new junk issues was scarce, even at interest rates of 17–18 percent. And a scattering of obituaries for junk began to appear in the press.

But they were wrong. For by mid-November, one month after the crash, the prices of the stronger junk issues had rebounded dramatically, while the weaker issues—among them credits which were dependent on asset sales to meet their debt obligations, for example—did not. At this point, it was a winnowing out of the junk market, not its demise.

Moreover, the issues and deals that got so badly pounded by the crash that they overnight became symbols of the changed world in junk were by and large not Drexel's. Fruehauf bonds, for example —underwritten by Merrill Lynch—were at 82–84 just before the crash, and two weeks later were at 60–70. Also, in the wake of the crash the Thompson family's management buyout of Southland Corporation was temporarily stalled, mid-deal, when its $1.5 billion of junk bonds could not be sold, even at rates of 18 percent. The investment banks at risk in Southland—at risk because they had been the lead lenders in a $600 million bridge loan extended to Southland the previous August, and now it was not at all clear that the bridge loan could be paid down—were Salomon and Goldman, Sachs. About two months later, however, the Southland deal was restructured to offer investors an added sweetener of warrants, and it proceeded. After the crash, too, bridge loans suddenly lost their panache. They were now seen for what they had always been—

serious risks to the investment banks which had extended them. Drexel had extended some, but had been far charier than most of the other major firms.

Milken rejected the critics' premise that the market had not been tested. Critics, he said in a late-November interview with this reporter, were using the wrong benchmark, because they lacked historical perspective. While it was true that broad public issuance of non-investment-grade securities had started in 1977, he repeatedly emphasized that there had been a large high-yielding market (comprised mainly of fallen angels and paper issued in exchange offers) by 1960. And this market, he asserted, had been tested in 1970–71, and even more severely in both 1974–75 and 1980–81. The success of high-yield investments during these three periods was testimony to the diversity and underlying strength of high-yield companies themselves, Milken added. "We were there to help provide advice and liquidity to both companies and investors during those periods, and we will be again," he declared. "In reflecting upon it, the greatest opportunity to help, strengthen and build is during difficult economic times."

By late '87, those difficult times had not yet impacted the rest of the country, but they had hit Wall Street. The retrenchment had started earlier in the year, after several major firms suffered severe trading losses because of interest-rate volatility, but after the crash it proceeded with a vengeance. E. F. Hutton was purchased by Shearson Lehman Brothers. Some specialist firms were bought by Drexel; Merrill Lynch; Bear, Stearns; and others. Layoffs, bonus-cutting, and reduction of overhead expenses were pandemic. Drexel was no exception, though its cuts were less dramatic than some firms'; one hundred of its eleven thousand employees were laid off, and its bonuses were reduced (less so for star performers).

Corporate America, witnessing Wall Street's distress, might have felt a certain mean-spirited gratification. For while hundreds of public companies had undergone paroxysms of restructuring, overhead-cutting, layoffs and elimination of research and development in order to escape an acquirer's clutches, Wall Street, inciter of and handmaiden to all this frantic activity, had only grown fatter. But it could not last; most of the Wall Street firms, after all, had relinquished their private-partnership status over the last decade and become public companies themselves.

Now the scythe had turned in their direction. Salomon, its

earnings down and management poor, had become quarry for Ronald Perelman in August 1987. Salomon had managed to fend him off by selling a substantial stake to Warren Buffett's Berkshire Hathaway. The event served not only as an indicator of Wall Street's vulnerability but also as a reminder of how quickly this world had changed. Exactly two years earlier, the bid for Revlon by the unknown Perelman had seemed, almost, amusing. Now Perelman was a corporate titan to be reckoned with.

Barring an apocalypse—the chain-reaction collapse of dozens of junk-bond-financed, highly leveraged companies, which would then impact the junk portfolios of insurance companies, thrifts, pension funds, mutual funds and others—it will be ten years before Milken's legacy becomes clear. Takeovers, buyouts and restructurings would have occurred if there had been no Michael Milken, but it is hard to imagine that they would have occurred in the size and volume that they did.

And it will take time to discern whether, on balance, those financial maneuvers created leaner, stronger companies, by imposing the discipline of debt, by dismantling inefficient giants and putting their parts into the hands of managers who owned a piece and so did a better job; or whether they created undernourished, nonproductive, noncompetitive companies, crippled by the debt which in many instances had served only to enrich the short-term investors —and, of course, their investment bankers. In all likelihood, both scenarios had occurred, and the question would be which was demonstrably more prevalent.

This, of course, was the debate that had raged through the mideighties. In the speeches Milken gave in 1986, when he was at the zenith of his power, he had risen to it eagerly. Peltz and Perelman, Beatrice and Metromedia, had been his glowing success stories. But by late 1987 the companies that Milken and others at Drexel were pointing to with pride were Comdisco, the computer company; Hovnanian, the successful home-builder; Kinder-Care, the provider of day care (although by late 1987, contrary to Drexel's depiction, the firm was moving into the financial-services area and becoming a buyer of junk bonds). These were all companies which over the last decade had issued junk bonds and used the capital to grow, but not through acquisition, not by doing buyouts. It was as though Milken had entered a time warp; as though he were back in the late seventies and early eighties, raising junk bonds for small and medium-sized companies that needed capital and couldn't get it anywhere else; as though the last several years of his raising hundreds of millions for the high-rolling entrepreneurs who barely knew what to do with such sums (until he told them), of raising billions of dollars for the biggest, most leveraged acquisitions ever done in the history of this country, had not happened.

The ultimate goal of the massive public-relations campaign Drexel would mount in ads in newspapers and magazines throughout 1987 was to obliterate Drexel's M&A spectacular of 1985–86, to purge the public memory of Drexel's leading role.

In the first few months of 1987, the campaign was more defensive and less focused. Drexel ran one centerfold in *The Wall Street Journal* listing, all in identical tiny print, with no titles, the names of its ten thousand employees, as though to emphasize that there were thousands of other people at Drexel in addition to the ones whose names were appearing regularly in the *Journal*'s articles on the government investigation. And in an effort to counter persistent rumors on the Street that it was losing business, Drexel ran ads that listed hundreds of its faithful clients.

But by the spring of 1987, the campaign developed a stronger message—that junk bonds (after years of hating and resisting the nomenclature, Drexel officials had decided there were more important battles to fight) were good for America. Inside the firm there was a two-week-long "celebration," open to all employees, of seminars, sports events and films, all devoted to this proposition. Thousands of square green pins were distributed, reading: "Junk Bonds Keep America Fit." (One music video, along more general morale-boosting lines, showed Drexel employees mouthing the words to a hit song by Billy Ocean. "When the going gets tough," chanted Bob Linton and Fred Joseph along with brokers and mail clerks, "Drexel gets going.")

The message Drexel was attempting to convey in its in-house and public campaigns was that junk bonds provided the only access to the public debt market for mainstream America—95 percent of American businesses. That the companies that issued them were the vital, growing sector of American industry that had provided new jobs in the last decade, while the employee ranks at investment-grade giants were declining.

There was a sort of truth to this. The 95 percent figure is somewhat obfuscating. Drexel's reasoning went this way: There are about 23,000 companies in the United States with sales over $25 million. Only 800 of them, however, qualify for investment-grade ratings. Therefore, that leaves some 22,000—or 95 percent—that are in the junk bailiwick. The problem with this arithmetic is that the vast majority of those 22,000 companies have not applied for ratings and have not issued junk bonds. From 1977 to 1986, about 1,200 companies, not 22,000, became issuers, of over $114 billion of junk bonds.

The job-formation claim suffered from a similar vulnerability. In the last three years, Drexel stated in 1987, America's largest companies have been cutting their work force; they have decreased employment by 4 percent. Junk issuers, however, have expanded employment by over 24 percent. What was left unsaid was the fact that the employment rolls at some of those large companies had been cut after defensive restructurings—undertaken to fend off Drexel-backed bidders.

Sometimes Drexel attacked the problem head on, as in ads stating that a prevalent "misconception" is that junk bonds are "responsible for the recent proliferation of hostile takeover activity." On the contrary, Drexel asserted, less than 10 percent of successful tender offers (1981–86) were funded by junk bonds. True enough, except that the junk-bond-financed hostile takeover had only two preliminary runs (Mesa-Gulf and Reliance-Disney) prior to 1985. And this statistic also omits, of course, all those raids which threw off hundreds of millions in profits to the bidder, the shareholders and Drexel, which intensified the fever of restructuring through corporate America—but which did not take their targets.

In the last few months of 1987, however, Drexel forsook such didacticism in favor of a softer, more impressionistic approach. One full-page ad in The Wall Street Journal featured a photograph of a group of workers at an Arkansas steel plant, where Drexel claimed to have saved jobs through its financing for the plant's parent company, Quanex; another showed a picture of a couple (the wife pregnant) and their toddler in front of a house under construction, being built by Hovnanian—a company which, without its access to junk bonds, would not have been able to "provide 50,000 people with a living room and 20,000 people with a living."

Drexel also took its campaign to television, spending some $4 million. In late '87 two 60-second commercials, in the same soft, sentimental vein as the recent print ads, appeared. One of them

featured an energy plant in Vidalia, Louisiana, whose construction
was financed by Drexel's junk bonds—with a resultant reduction in
unemployment in Vidalia by over 20 percent. Before the plant was
built, the commercial stated, over 16 percent of the residents of
Vidalia had been unemployed. Among the problems here, as pointed
out in an article by *Wall Street Journal* reporter Laurie Cohen, was
that the commercial was not shot in Vidalia; that unemployment
statistics for Vidalia, as distinguished from the surrounding parish,
do not exist; that a Louisiana Department of Labor official stated
he disagreed with the claim that the plant had helped to reduce
unemployment by 20 percent; and that moreover most of the people
who worked at the plant didn't live in Vidalia.

In its eagerness to alter its image radically—from the host of
decadence at the Predators' Ball, the raiders' money machine, the
firm that in 1985–86 gave new meaning to greed on Wall Street, to
a wholesome, civic-minded provider of capital (and thereby jobs)
to this nation's little people—Drexel was fudging facts. The problem, however, was not so much these specific obfuscations as the
overall image.

Drexel *had* provided financing for growth to small and medium-
sized companies which would have had trouble finding capital elsewhere. It *had* built a thriving market of this original-issue debt
where none had existed before. It could reasonably sustain the
claim made in its '87 ad campaign that it had furthered the "democ-
ratization of capital."

But if Drexel had limited itself to that initial source of supply
—never financing the buyouts, or the leveraged acquisitions of
1985–86—it would have remained one of the second-class citizens
of Wall Street, highly profitable, because of those 3–4 percent
spreads, but barely noticed by the premier firms and their clients. It
would have been an outsider in the M&A world, instead of its hot
center. Without that new supply source, the junk market—the best
barometer of Drexel's influence—would never have increased in
size so quickly. In 1981, before Drexel had started issuing junk for
LBOs, the new-issue market was $1.3 billion. In 1986—a year when
the new-issue market increased by 52 percent—it was $32.4 billion
(not including private placements). And all junk debt outstanding
was approximately $125 billion.

While Drexel was striving to expunge from history its period of
triumph and sovereignty, it was not disowning the King. It is true

that in the early months of the investigation, when Drexel employees feared that indictments and perhaps the firm's collapse were imminent, there had been some sentiment in New York that Milken and his troops should be cut adrift. But as time passed without indictments, hope grew that the government was having difficulty making its case, and solidarity took hold.

As one Drexel employee claimed in the summer of 1987, when hope was probably at its high point, "The government is right in principle, and maybe in fact, but they won't be able to prove it. No one is going to tell on Mike—who didn't take bags of money like Marty [Siegel, who took satchels filled with money from Boesky in return for inside information], but broke the securities laws. And who made them very rich."

Issues that had been sore points within Drexel prior to Boesky Day—such as Milken's flouting the decisions of the UAC—now were put aside in favor of a united front. The "Troubled Deals" list seemed to have evaporated. In a *New York Times* article by James Sterngold in November 1987, Joseph insisted that Milken had lost arguments before the UAC. Joseph was supported in this claim by other, unnamed Drexel executives, who said that Milken had pushed hard to do an underwriting for Rooney, Pace, for example, and that that deal nonetheless had been rejected. True enough— except that that was the deal, listing Rooney, Pace itself as the underwriter, which was then placed by Milken. (The judgment of the UAC was vindicated, moreover, inasmuch as within one year of that offering Rooney, Pace was all but broke and it had defaulted on the second interest payment on the bonds.)

In its now fully engaged struggle for survival, an attitude had evolved at Drexel which might win the day—or at least mitigate defeat—if successfully imparted by its defense lawyers to a jury. It could be summed up with this statement: a 13D violation isn't murder. Translated into strategy, it meant attempting to fragment any pattern of conduct, isolating its particulars—an alleged 13D violation here, a claimed parking violation there—and then minimizing their significance.

Indeed, if seen separately, Milken's actions could be effectively trivialized. Assume, for the moment, that the following were true: the "mass distribution" of privately placed bonds; Milken's buying bonds and alerting favored customers (such as Tom Spiegel, Fred Carr and Jay Regan) to do so before an announcement of an exchange offer, such as in the Caesars World issue; the failure to disclose (except to some favored investors, who may then have bought the stock) that the Pantry Pride "blind pool" was actually intended for the acquisition of Revlon; an undisclosed arrangement with Boesky in Fischbach; and an undisclosed arrangement with Saul Steinberg in Wickes.

Any one of the above, by itself, might seem an offense which, if proven, could be plea-bargained away without severe sanction. But seen in concert—and in concert is how they must be seen if any true sense of Milken's machine is to be grasped—these individual acts take on different dimensions. Their gravity becomes inescapable. Indeed, it seems plain to this writer that if the above or some similar assortment of Milken's and, by extension, Drexel's actions are not worth prosecuting, then the securities laws were not worth passing. Assuming these actions occurred, it is difficult for this writer to imagine a manipulation of the securities markets that is more broad, more powerful or more frightening.

What Drexel could be banking on, of course, was that the fully integrated, multidimensional picture would remain forever shrouded in Milken's legendary secrecy, and that those bits and pieces that did emerge could be kept separate and trivialized. As 1987 drew to a close, however, despite the firm's united, defiant front, the hope of the summer that indictments might not come had ebbed away. Morale, again, was sagging. Reserves of at least $500 million had been set aside in expectation of a civil fine that the firm would have to pay, according to several sources close to Drexel. And the future of Drexel as envisioned by some had begun to bear a grim resemblance to its distant past. "Drexel is dead," commented one banker in the firm. "Not in the short term, and I don't mean literally dead—but Drexel as we have known it is gone. Even if we win at trial, our reputation, already so tarnished, will be so much more tarnished that it will hardly matter. We won't be doing the big deals anymore. We won't be making the same money. And the good people, little by little, will leave—because if you're not going to make that kind of money anymore, why not at least be at a firm with a good reputation, where you can be involved in big deals?"

Asked whether Joseph shared this view—that Drexel would now fall back to the point from which its meteoric rise had started a decade ago—this banker shook his head. "Fred is still fighting," he said.

And Milken was in the vanguard of that fight. By the summer of '87, officials at Drexel had apparently decided that as a countervailing weight to Milken's violations on the scales of justice there should be Milken himself. He had long been the firm's single greatest asset. He had briefly been perceived as its single greatest liability. But wasn't he still the best thing Drexel had? Shouldn't they play from their strength, however flawed? Lawyers for Drexel started referring to him as a "national treasure."

Before the start of the government investigation, some of Milken's admirers had spoken wistfully of harnessing his energy to the federal government. They pictured him, for example, as the Secretary of the Treasury—his obsession with increasing his fortune and his influence over corporate destinies in this country replaced by an obsession with the budget deficit, the trade deficit, Latin-American debt. The idea of Milken in the Cabinet would remain sheer fantasy, but Milken's lawyers needed to convince the government that he was a human being so visionary, and so willing to serve in a private capacity, that he was simply not expendable.

At about the same time that his lawyers began referring to Milken as a "national treasure," Milken had let it be known that he would be devoting up to 25 percent of his time to the Latin-American debt crisis. He made trips to Mexico to discuss international debt with President Miguel de la Madrid. This was not a new project at Drexel—a Latin-American debt team from Citibank, headed by Gerald Finneran, had been hired in 1985—but it was certainly being given new emphasis.

In October '87, Drexel announced that the DBL Americas Development Association had been capitalized with $170 million of equity, raised from forty U.S. corporations. Its aim was to invest principally in equity and convertible debt securities of Latin-American businesses; it might also purchase debt securities and use them in debt-for-debt or debt-for-equity swaps. If Drexel possessed any original solution to the crisis, however, it was being kept under wraps; and $170 million would hardly make a substantial dent in a $600 billion problem. Skeptics referred to this as Milken's missionary work.

Milken also made his press debut. Under carefully controlled conditions (he would not discuss the investigation, and he would have the right to approve the use of any quotes, in context), he met with a handful of journalists. That he did so at all served to underscore his plight. He had always distrusted the press—it was inimical to his penchant for secrecy, and outside of his control. Happily for him, considering that distrust, he had not needed it for his business. As he used to say to Steve Wynn, "You can't make a dime off publicity."

In the early days, his investors had been glad that Milken and his arcane bonds kept a low profile—the better for the spread. Once Drexel entered the spotlight as the backer of the junk-bond takeover and needed a spokesman, Fred Joseph had assumed the role. But now the mystique that had long surrounded the cloistered Milken was suggestive of secret, illicit dealings. He had to come into the light. Moreover, it was hoped that as a "national treasure" personally revealed for the first time, Milken might be Drexel's hidden ace.

That was unlikely. Years of reclusiveness coupled with Milken's extraordinary feats had engendered a legend that was larger than the man. He had been widely portrayed as a profoundly enigmatic and mesmerizing figure who caused even nonbelievers to fall under his spell. In a long interview and subsequent conversations with this reporter in late '87, however, Milken was deeply knowledgeable about his twenty-year obsession but not spellbinding, and more transparent than enigmatic. If Drexel officials were hoping for magic as Milken went public, he would disappoint them.

Milken speaks often about the importance of remembering one's roots. He certainly has done so. He married his high-school sweetheart. He left New York for California when it was unthinkable that someone who aspired to success on Wall Street should do so. He moved back to his old neighborhood in the unfashionable San Fernando Valley, where he remained after accumulating his hundreds of millions of dollars. He brought his brother and high-school friends into his group. Unlike some powerful individuals who assiduously remold themselves in the course of their ascent, Milken made no such effort.

Perhaps as a consequence of that, one can still see vestiges today of the oddness that always set him apart, making him slightly misfitted for any group but the one he eventually created. He was, after all, the teenager who slept only three or four hours a night, who was not the football player but the cheerleader, who in L.A. and Berkeley in the sixties not only never smoked or drank or experimented with drugs but did not even drink carbonated beverages.

He was the new Wharton student, made fun of by his pipe-smoking Ivy League classmates, but vowing he would be number one in his class. He was the Jew at the blueblood Drexel Firestone, segregated off in a corner of the trading floor. He was the bond trader at Drexel Burnham who, even as he began making millions trading his strange bonds, still looked so strange, with his shirt-and-tie combinations that made him the brunt of others' jokes, with his dreadful "rug" that Saul Steinberg once, in a bit of office horseplay, pulled off his head. He was the Drexel junk-bond trader from *California*, no less, who, when he asserted to a roomful of investment bankers and lawyers in '83 that he could raise $4–5 billion for Boone Pickens' Mesa-Gulf bid, which Pickens was having trouble financing, was greeted by snickers from the men from Cravath, Swaine and Moore, and Lehman Brothers, the aristocrats of the Street.

Milken must have been determined from his youth to show the world just how smart he was, and to make wealth his measure. One of his favorite anecdotes concerns a recent Wharton graduate who returned to the school to speak while Milken was a student. The graduate had blueblood credentials. He had attended a prestigious prep school and an Ivy League college. He was twenty-nine years old, and he told the assembled group of students he was worth $30 million. Milken was impressed. But what emerged a little later— the punch line that so delighted Milken—was that the young multimillionaire had inherited $50 million when he was twenty-five. (This was the individual-squandering-wealth analogue to those corporate-disaster stories Milken also loved, about the blue-chip, triple-A companies that lost hundreds of millions, even billions, of dollars of capital in foolish business decisions.) The moral, of course, was that however impressive appearances might be, it was not birth, not a prestige education, and not inherited wealth that counted at the continuing, year-after-year bottom line, but performance. Nothing else. Milken resolved to outperform them all.

And for him, high-yielding bonds were a custom-made vehicle. They were the outcasts and misfits of the securities world, disdained by the rating agencies and the establishment, many of them victims of misconceptions. In that gap between perception and reality, as Milken liked to say, there was money to be made. Later, when he began to underwrite them, and when they were eventually used by his chosen—the outsiders of American business life—to challenge the corporate giants, his operation of course metamorphosed into something far larger and more powerful than even the farsighted Milken could have dreamed when he first started trading these contemned bonds at Drexel Firestone in 1970. But the whole long journey, starting with the bus ride from Cherry Hill and culminating at the pinnacle of power in American finance, was an unbroken continuum.

Milken's group, the first one ever which fit him like a glove, had been cloaked in mystery for years. As bits and pieces of information emerged, they added descriptive detail to the image of the peculiar, cultlike whole, but did not explain it. Milken, however, did that. It became clear, in listening to him, that his group was the physical embodiment of his theory of productivity, fused with his need for absolute control.

Milken believed that people were at their most productive when they felt they were part of a collective enterprise. There could, therefore, be no stars, and that included him. That was why he refused to have his picture in Drexel's annual report—it would detract from the team spirit. He had no office, only his desk on the trading floor, for the same reason. He had no meaningful title in the firm, and there were no meaningful titles in his group; no one was to be ranked over someone else. (As Milken had mentioned, his group's Christmas card, in the form of a bond, was an undifferentiated printing of the names of all its members—a graphic illustration of this principle.) He would not, of course, have allowed the members of his group to speak to the press, because of his insistence upon secrecy and control; but he also mentioned that he did not want his people to start thinking of themselves as stars. It would be harder to motivate them, come four-thirty Monday morning.

Keeping his people pure—consumed and fixated on the work at hand—was his perpetual effort. Milken believed that two of life's major distractions, romance and wealth, were counterproductive, diminishing the kind of intensity he required of his people. He therefore advocated long-term, stable relationships; he took pride in what he claimed was the group's low divorce rate. Wealth, of course, was a double-edged sword for Milken. Its achievement (largely through the equity stakes in the investment partnerships) was what gave his people incentive. But once he had made his people wealthy beyond their imaginings in order to both motivate them and bind them to him, that very wealth tended to divert them with life's pleasures.

Milken attempted to cure this dilemma through control. Much of his people's wealth, of course, was in the investment partnerships, kept out of their reach, although as the years went on and the accumulated wealth of the group grew mountainous, a substantial portion did reach its owners. Still, when Milken was displeased, he manipulated the levers of the partnerships, reducing someone's existing percentage, freezing him out of the next.

There were other, more subtle but probably more powerful means of control, understood by any charismatic, messianic leader. Milken sought to inspire by example. He expected no one to work any harder than he did, and as his power increased he worked the same punishing hours he always had, or longer. He climbed no social (and time-consuming) ladder. He had been married to the same woman, with whom he had three children, since 1968. He lived simply, rejecting the symbols of materialism that he wanted his people to reject, in emulation. He lived in the Valley, not in decadent, splashy Beverly Hills, and he urged his people, also, to buy homes outside of Beverly Hills (many, indeed, lived in the Valley). For a man who was driven by limitless greed (one could hear the pleasure that money gave, sometimes, when he spoke), he espoused—in terms of lifestyle—anti-materialism. Everything, but everything, in Milken's life—and, if he had his way, in his people's lives—was subsumed to productivity.

Milken meant to inspire so that his people would feel like cathedral-builders, not bricklayers, and he did so. "If he was walking over a cliff," declared one former disciple, "everyone in that group would have followed him."

As Milken himself suggested with his allusion to Gandhi, he had not built this holy army for the sole purpose of buying and selling securities. It had begun that way. But by the late seventies, when Milken was providing capital to an underclass of corporate America that had not been able to obtain it before, he had started to envision his larger purpose. That was also when he moved back to California and began building his cadre in earnest.

One of its former members recounted that in 1979 he had read a thriller, *The Matarese Circle*, by Robert Ludlum, whose plot revolves around a worldwide terrorist conspiracy orchestrated and financed through the largest multinational corporations. The goal of the Matarese fanatics, who are so imbued with their cause that they willingly sacrifice themselves, is to plunge the established world powers into chaos and then impose their own new order, in which all power will be held by the Matarese through the corporations they control. The conspiracy's mastermind is a brilliant, megalomaniac naif. Once a Corsican shepherd boy, he has built an inestimable fortune and is so consumed by his vision of world control that he bends everything in life to its shape.

"My nickname for Michael was 'the Shep,' " commented this former disciple. "A few other people in the group read it, and they saw it, too. The incredible thing was, that was 1979—and then, over the next five or six years, we watched it happen."

The comparison to the murderous "Shepherd Boy," of course, is not meant to be taken literally. But the parallel that struck this former member of Milken's group lay in the force of the obsession, the megalomania, the conviction of a cause so just that the end justified the means, and, finally, the conceptualization of the corporate vehicle as a means of extending control nationwide—and then worldwide.

The Michael Milken interviewed by this reporter displayed no hint of such rapacity. Though naturally intense, he seemed to strive for a casual manner. He was painstakingly modest, praising the achievements of others at Drexel, repeatedly attempting to shift the focus from himself. He refused to criticize rivals at other investment-banking firms, though he was well aware that many of them show no such restraint about him and Drexel. He spoke repeatedly of his pride in having financed companies which had been small, or in dire financial straits, when he first underwrote their bonds, and which had grown and prospered (not via acquisition). He described Drexel's paradigmatic trait as an eagerness to help. He pointedly mentioned his being around to help in the hard times that would come in the future, as he has been in earlier hard times.

The problem with all this was its utter transparency. Milken, the world's greatest bond salesman, was now attempting to sell himself—as a low-key, humble, beneficent public-servant type, who makes more money than other public servants because he does his version in the private sector. "I *welcome* competition," insisted the individual whose hallmark since the seventies had been his relentless craving for 100 percent market share, who for years when competition arose would try to either crush it or buy it. What this sales pitch showed, more than anything else, was Milken's shockingly poor judgment about himself in relation to others, to the wider world—a world that is not confined, as his has been for so long, to his beloved bonds.

Nearly two years earlier, when he was approached by this re- porter after the speech he gave to the money managers in Boston, and was asked for his cooperation with this book, Milken replied that he had heard about the book from Fred Joseph. He asked a few questions about its genesis and its aims and then declared, "I do not want it to be done." When he was told that it was already in prog- ress, he reiterated that he did not want it done. He seemed surprised, almost, by the assurance that it would be done. Then he said, "I was saying to Fred, why don't *we* pay you the commitment fee that your publisher would have paid you—except we'll pay it to you to *not* write the book?

"Or," he went on, as though he had not heard the response, "why don't we pay you for all the copies you would have sold if you had written it?"

That was in February 1986. That was Milken in his prime, at the very apex of his power: assuming that in the wider world, as in trading, a price exists at which any transaction can be done; com- fortable that the end justifies the means; determined that nothing which he did not control should come close to him. So cloistered, and so accustomed to people's hanging on his words and bending to his will, Milken had not had any idea how to relate to the world outside his own.

He never had. But it seemed hardly to matter while the param- eters of *his* world—in which he was not a misfit but sovereign— were so wide, and growing by the day. He was feared by his enemies, idolized by his followers. He was soon to be universally lauded by the business press and slavishly imitated by the rest of Wall Street. Many billions of dollars were at his command; capital, as Milken had been saying and proving for a long time, was not a scarce re- source. The only limits to his power, it seemed, would be the limits of his febrile imagination.

After the speech to the money managers—many of whom he had first met nearly a decade earlier when he came knocking on their doors, peddling his oddball product—Milken was surrounded by well-wishers paying tribute. One longtime client, unable to see him through the press of the crowd, asked Milken's assistant, Susan Cochran, where he was.

"The King," she said, with a nod in his direction, "is over there."

Afterword

IN SEPTEMBER 1988, nearly two years after "Boesky Day," the SEC finally filed its charges against Drexel, Milken, his brother Lowell, and four other individuals. While the SEC's action had long been anticipated, there had been some press speculation, instigated by Drexel's public relations team, that the government's case was wanting, and its complaint would be narrowly drawn. Instead, this 184-page document depicted a veritable panoply of violations of the securities laws, and constituted the most sweeping enforcement action that had been taken since those laws were passed in the 1930s. It charged that the defendants had traded on inside information, manipulated stock prices, filed false disclosure forms with the SEC in order to disguise stock ownership, filed fraudulent offering materials, kept false books and records, and defrauded their own clients.

In that long litany of alleged abuses, the last—the defrauding of clients—stands out in bold relief. While it shocks because it is such an egregious violation not only of the law but of the most fundamental ethical precepts, it was not exactly news. One of Milken's long-time favorite sayings to others at Drexel had been, after all, "If we can't make money off our friends, who can we make money off of?" Many Drexel clients knew that Milken had been gouging them for years. Some knew, too, that it was his habit to demand warrants from an issuer, claiming that they were necessary as a sweetener in order to place the bonds—and then to keep them for himself or for his favored at Drexel. While in this writer's opinion this was clearly unethical and most likely illegal, in the universe that Milken had created and ruled, it was a fact of life. In a contemporary, financial version of droit du seigneur, whatever Milken fancied was his to take.

But now other means that he had used to defraud clients were coming to light. The SEC was charging that when financier Charles Hurwitz, the chairman of MCO Holdings Inc.'s Maxxam Group, balked at the high fees Drexel was demanding for its proposed acquisition of Pacific Lumber, Milken, uncharacteristically, relented. Milken then allegedly instructed Boesky to buy Pacific Lumber shares at prices higher than Maxxam's tender offer price. Ultimately, this caused Maxxam to raise its offer from $36 to $40 a share. Because the acquisition became more expensive, Drexel's fees, too, were raised— probably higher than when Hurwitz had had the temerity to argue about them.

And Wickes, it would now appear, was victimized more than once. In the spring of 1985, of course, Milken had applied his form of persuasion by telling Sigoloff that, with the stock that Saul Steinberg owned and that which Milken owned or controlled, they had effective control of the company (and so Drexel, not Salomon, should do the underwriting). Now the SEC alleged that in 1986 Milken had instructed Boesky to buy for Milken and Drexel shares of National Gypsum before Wickes's, whom Drexel was advising, tender offer for that company's shares was announced—and, after the announcement, at prices higher than Wickes's tender offer price. In the bidding war that ensued as National Gypsum's share prices were driven even higher, Wickes lost.

The ledger on Drexel's defrauding of clients was being amplified, too, with information gathered by Rep. John Dingell's Oversight and Investigations subcommittee of the House Energy and Commerce Committee. At a hearing in April 1988—where Milken took the Fifth Amendment—it was demonstrated that Milken and Drexel had engaged in self-dealing, putting its interests ahead of its clients'. Having offered for sale to the public a new debt issue and received a request from clients for a portion of the offering, Drexel either rejected those requests or gave the clients less than they wanted. Drexel then placed a portion of the issue in the gold-mine investment partnerships owned by Milken, his brother, and senior members of his group. A few days later—the scarcity in the market having driven up the price, the committee alleged—Milken and the others sold the bonds back to Drexel for a profit of $2-4 for each $100 of face value. Drexel then sold the bonds to outside buyers for an additional mark-up of $2-4. According to the subcommittee, Milken's partnerships made $936,000 on such transactions in one bond issue, and $2.2 million on another.

What the trading records subpoenaed by the subcommittee really reveal is the Milken machine at work. Trade by trade, one sees Milken doling out his patronage. One sees his investment partnerships getting the choice issues, the best prices; the most favored clients, such as First Executive and Columbia Savings & Loan, getting the next best; and the host of regular clients coming in after that.

While some obviously enjoy the benefits of this favoritism more than others, the real losers are the issuers. They are not only getting gouged on fees and having to surrender warrants, but they are also suffering from the extra points Drexel gains on its trading, which indicates that the bonds could probably have been issued at lower rates. One is reminded of the battles that used to rage regularly between Drexel's corporate finance department in New York (representing the issuers) and the high-yield department in Beverly Hills (representing the buyers), when issues were being priced. It appears that Milken did indeed view his network of buyers as his patrimony, as one Drexel investment banker had explained to this writer. It was, after all, his placement power that made Milken inimitable, and invincible. So while he did exploit the buyers (as the self-dealing illustrations make plain), he apparently abused the issuers more.

One of Drexel's co-venturers in a buyout recalls an instance in 1987 when discussion arose at a board meeting, attended by a director from Drexel, about taking the company public again. At that time, Drexel owned less than 10% of the equity in the company. Shortly after the board meeting, Drexel bought a large amount of the company's bonds, which were issued with warrants. Drexel then sold the bonds, but kept the warrants—giving them a 17 percent stake in the company. "When you've got a Drexel representative on the board, they think they can do whatever is in the bondholders' interest, or whatever is in Drexel's interest," says this investment banker. "They don't seem to have any grasp of the meaning of a fiduciary obligation."

Milken's trading practices, increasingly revealed by the government's investigations, seemed almost a parable on the evils of monopoly. For years driven to control all that he touched, Milken needed most of all to control this junk bond market, a market that he had virtually created and that remained the wellspring of his ever-expanding wealth and power.

He was able to exert that control because he established his dominance early; because it is a byzantine market, its trades conducted privately, trader to trader, with no electronic tape flashing the last price; because he had more knowledge and more trading capital by far than any of his competitors; and because he would stop at nothing to kill a competitor's deal. No newcomer was able to make any meaningful encroachments on Milken's preserve; and without competition, Milken ruled, unchecked. Even as this market mushroomed to $180 billion, its command center remained a locked room, off-limits to outsiders, on the third floor of a building at the corner of Wilshire and Rodeo. "Michael *is* the market," his followers used to echo rhapsodically, as though they were repeating a mantra, in the days when it seemed that Milken's reach would soon be global. But that monopoly would eventually be his undoing. If he is forced to leave the securities business forever, "Michael *is* the market" will be a fitting epitaph for him.

Even with these successive revelations of Milken's client abuse, however, there were by the end of 1988 no large-scale Drexel client defections. Drexel's relationship with its clients has always been unique among Wall Street firms, of course, inasmuch as Drexel created so many of its clients from whole cloth. (Nelson Peltz should go down in history as Milken's single most magical transfiguration. Shortly after taking Triangle Industries private in mid-1988, Peltz and his partner, Peter May, sold the company to Pechiney S.A., a French state-owned aluminum company—reaping a profit of about $740 million.) It is possible that some of these clients continued to feel sufficiently indebted to their progenitor, that they would not abandon Milken in his hour of need. More likely, though, what bound them to him was roughly the same thing that had bound them before. For, toward the close of 1988, even with the SEC charges filed and the criminal charges expected, Milken *still* controlled this market.

Drexel, after all, won the vicious battle against Salomon and Shearson to become sole manager of the junk offering in the mammoth RJR Nabisco deal. And Kohlberg Kravis & Roberts insisted that the deal go to Drexel—despite the fact that, as had emerged in the Dingell hearings, KKR had been one of the clients defrauded by Drexel. In 1986, Milken had demanded warrants in the $6.2 billion Beatrice deal, saying they were needed to sell the debt—and then put about 70 percent of them into his and his group's investment partnerships. According to the subcommittee, Milken and Drexel made a profit of roughly $750 million on those warrants. "Henry [Kravis] was very angry about that," commented one KKR adviser in the RJR deal.

"But he and Mike talked about it, and they resolved their differences. Henry feels very loyal to Mike."

How Milken was able to forge such extreme client loyalty—loyalty that survives the most fundamental breach of fiduciary responsibility on Milken's part, and that overlooks his alleged gain of $750 million from that breach—is not yet clear. One factor (though this is insufficient to explain the phenomenon) may be that by November 1988, when the RJR deal was in progress, Milken's exodus from the market was far from guaranteed. However unlikely, it was then still conceivable that—if he and Drexel fought the criminal charges expected to be filed by then–U.S. Attorney Rudolph Giuliani of New York's Southern District, went to trial, and won an acquittal—he would remain in control forever. And in that event, few, if any, of Milken's clients could afford to be on his enemies list.

When the SEC charges had been filed in September, they had seemed only to fan the flames of Drexel's and Milken's fighting spirit. Drexel spokesmen had argued that the overwhelming majority of the charges appeared to rest on the testimony of Boesky, a convicted felon. The Drexel ranks had held fast; except for Charles Thurnher, a Milken employee who had been granted immunity early in the course of the government's investigation (and who, Drexel employees said at the time, was telling the government nothing), no Drexel employee was cooperating with the government. If the eventual trial was, essentially, a swearing match between Boesky and Milken, Milken might well win.

In the week after the filing of the SEC charges, Milken—expertly groomed by the public relations firm of Robinson, Lake, Lerer & Montgomery—hit the campaign trail. Gone was the reclusive financier who had always shunned the press, telling his friend Steve Wynn that "you can't make a dime off publicity," forbidding the use of his picture in Drexel's annual report, buying the rights to all photographs of himself. And gone was the intense, imperious individual who had said, when told of this writer's projected book, "I don't want it to be done."

In his place was an eager, affable Milken, seeking out not only speaking engagements but tête-à-têtes with select members of the press. At a breakfast seminar with Gov. Rudy Perpich of Minnesota and New York City schools chancellor Richard Green, Milken spoke about problems in education. Later that day, he made a trip to a New York Mets game, accompanied by 1,700 underprivileged youngsters. (This trip was part of Drexel's alliance with Variety Clubs International, begun in 1987. Milken had made his Variety debut months earlier in a telethon presided over by Monty Hall, of "Let's Make A Deal.")

Over the next several days, Milken gave two speeches in Philadelphia, one in Hartford, and one at Princeton, on subjects ranging from Third World debt to education to drugs. At Princeton, he was introduced by Ralph Ingersoll, the publisher of the newspaper chain that bears his name, a long-time Drexel client, and probably—of all Drexel clients—the most impassioned and most fatuous defender of Milken. "Michael Milken is a social scientist, in my view, who happens to make his living as a banker," Ingersoll was quoted as saying in a *Wall Street Journal* article by Bryan Burrough. Ingersoll added that Milken is the target of a "Salem-style witch hunt."

While Milken kept trying to perfect his new public persona—that of a mild, deferential, civic-minded individual—behind the scenes he and Drexel continued to resort to tougher tactics. In the spring and summer of 1988, they had mounted a campaign of innuendo against this book. Milken's lawyers from Paul, Weiss, Rifkind, Wharton & Garrison, and others had contacted book reviewers and insisted that the book was filled with "hundreds" of (non-specified) errors. Moreover, a Drexel client at a major financial institution recounts having received a call he considered "extraordinary" from one of Milken's employees. "This guy told me, 'We figure we can keep [*The Predators' Ball*] off the bestseller list by buying books directly from the distributors, since it is bookstore sales that the list is drawn from. So we'll ship you [give you] however many you need—just don't buy them,'" recalled this Drexel client. (The book made the *New York Times* list—briefly—in September.)

And in their legal strategy, Drexel and Milken were still embracing the credo "whatever it takes to win" that for years had guided their juggernaut. With the help of their lawyers, they seem to have attempted to manipulate the judicial system as deftly as Milken, for years, had manipulated the market.

Although the SEC did not file its charges until September, Drexel had been on notice since June that charges would be forthcoming. In June, in an unusual maneuver, the SEC had voted to file charges against Drexel (an action duly leaked to the press) but had delayed their filing. This, according to one SEC lawyer, was done in order to strike a compromise between the conflicting demands of Congress, particularly Dingell's committee (which wanted the SEC to act) on the one hand, and the office of U.S. Attorney Rudolph Giuliani, which was conducting the criminal investigation of Drexel (and which wanted the SEC to wait until the criminal charges were ready), on the other.

Meanwhile, in New York's Southern District, civil cases brought by various plaintiffs claiming to have been harmed by insider trading, against Ivan Boesky and, in some cases, Drexel Burnham (as the former employer of insider traders Dennis Levine and Martin Siegel, and as the underwriter of Boesky's arbitrage fund) had all been consolidated and placed before one judge: U.S. District Judge Milton Pollack. According to a piece by Steven Brill in the *American Lawyer*, Drexel's and Milken's lawyers were concerned that, when the SEC did file its case against Drexel and Milken, the Commission might assert that Milken and Drexel's case was related to the above cases, and that it must therefore join the group before Judge Pollack.

They had reason for concern. Judge Pollack, a crusty, opinionated, intellectually daunting jurist, has been reputed for years to favor the government in his rulings. Worse, a vicious enmity has existed between the judge and Milken's lawyer, Arthur Liman of Paul, Weiss, Rifkind, Wharton & Garrison, for more than a decade—ever since Liman tried a complex securities case, Chris-Craft Industries v. Piper Aircraft, before Judge Pollack. There would arguably be no worse judge for Milken and Drexel in the Southern District than Judge Pollack.

In September, with Congress due to decide on appropriations to the SEC shortly, the SEC could withstand the pressure from Dingell's committee no longer, according to an SEC lawyer. So, Giuliani's displeasure notwithstanding, the SEC filed its case. And, as the Drexel contingent had long feared, the SEC lawyers filed it as a related case under Judge Pollack.

The case was filed on September 7. Two days later, according to subsequently filed Drexel affidavits, Fred Joseph returned a call from W. Mitt Romney, managing general partner of an investment group called Bain Venture Capital in Boston. Drexel was to do the junk-bond portion of the financing for Bain's buyout of two Southwest apparel chains, Palais Royal and Bealls. And Romney—having read that Judge Milton Pollack was to preside over Drexel's case, and knowing that the judge was married to Moselle Pollack, the chairman and major shareholder of Palais Royal—wanted to make sure there would be no problem with the deal.

According to Drexel's and Milken's lawyers—Peter Fleming from Curtis, Mallet, Prevost, Thomas Curnin from Cahill, Gordon & Rheindel, and Liman—this was the first that Drexel or they knew of the connection between the judge and Palais Royal. What ensued over the next couple of months was a circuslike extravaganza (replete with courtroom vitriol that radically diverted attention from the charges that had been filed against Drexel) in which Drexel sought to recuse the judge.

Drexel argued that because Moselle Pollack, whose family had owned Palais Royal for over fifty years, was to receive about $30 million from the buyout, Judge Pollack had a conflict of interest—or, at least (and this would be sufficient for recusal), the appearance of one. The SEC, on the other hand, argued that the buyout was being done by Bain, not Drexel; that Drexel was merely providing the subordinated debt portion of the financing (approximately $50 million in a $250 million deal), one that could have been raised by another investment banking firm, and therefore they were not indispensable to the deal; and that, moreover, Drexel might have purposely created the very alleged conflict of which they were complaining.

This last allegation elicited screams of outraged denial from Drexel's lawyers. There was, however, a series of suggestive circumstances. According to sources at Bain, the people who had worked on the deal there had known since at least early 1988 that Moselle Pollack was the wife of Judge Pollack. They mentioned this relationship to Bain's lawyer, Karl Lutz of the Kirkland & Ellis firm in Chicago (which has done substantial work for Drexel). Lutz and his associates were negotiating with Cahill, Gordon, which was representing Drexel in the Palais Royal buyout (as well as being the firm's lead counsel in its fight against the government). Cahill, Gordon lawyers, therefore, were working on copies of the merger agreements, in which Moselle Pollack's name appeared prominently as the chairman and major shareholder. Cahill's Thomas Curnin has known both Milton and Moselle Pollack for years. Palais Royal (primarily, Moselle Pollack and her family) was being represented in this deal by lawyers from Skadden, Arps, Slate, Meagher & Flom—the firm which, after Cahill, has done most of Drexel's legal work. Finally, it emerged that Paul, Weiss (Arthur Liman's firm) recently had done work for Palais Royal as well.

Nevertheless, no matter how numerous the possible nexuses, they do not in themselves prove the transfer of the information. And the lawyers who were working on Palais Royal at Cahill, Gordon and at Paul, Weiss were not the same lawyers who were obsessed with the Drexel defense, and with the looming shadow of Judge Pollack. So what the circumstantial evidence suggests may not be what occurred.

But it seems almost certain that, notwithstanding courtroom histrionics and affidavits to the contrary, Drexel employees—at the least, those who were working on the Palais Royal deal—knew by mid-summer 1988 of the relationship of Judge Pollack to the company. Palais Royal for years has been run by a manager, Bernard Fuchs. After the buyout, it was planned that Fuchs would run the combined entities of Palais Royal and Bealls. When potential lenders visited the company during the spring and summer—as Drexel did—Fuchs gave the presentation. According to a banker and a lawyer who have participated in this deal from the outset, Fuchs is a voluble individual who had a set, long-winded spiel that he delivered at each and every presentation, which they heard many times. "Bernie is a meticulous person," said this lawyer, "and in these presentations he would explain that the chairman of the company does not live in Houston but in New York—because she is married to a federal judge, Judge Milton Pollack. And he would always say that with a lot of pride."

In a carefully crafted affidavit, Drexel's Frederick Moselev, one of the senior members of the Palais Royal team, stated, "I have no recollection of ever being so informed [of the relationship of Moselle Pollack to Milton Pollack] . . . and I have spoken to each person who has worked on this transaction and have received confirmation that they have no memory of being so informed."

More credible than this collective aphasia would have been an admission that the relationship had been spelled out emphatically by Fuchs—but, they might have contended, its significance was lost upon them because they had not realized the role that Judge Pollack was likely to play. Instead, they are all devoid of memory. What is also telling is the fact that the senior Drexel partner on the deal, who also swore to having had no knowledge of the Pollack relationship, was Fred McCarthy. McCarthy, one of the "Shearson Mafia" who has been with Fred Joseph for many years, heads Drexel's Boston office, where this deal was done, but he is also the person who, from "Boesky Day" onward, was Joseph's lieutenant in the fight against the government, operating much of the time from a desk just outside the door of Joseph's office. Even if one assumes that there was only a handful of people at Drexel for whom the name "Milton Pollack" would have sounded alarms back in the summer of 1988, McCarthy was unquestionably one of them.

Judge Pollack—clearly infuriated by the Drexel motion, calling its claim "ludicrous" and "bizarre"—ruled that he had neither a conflict of interest nor the appearance of one, and refused to recuse himself. The Second Circuit Court of Appeals supported Judge Pollack's position. Drexel then appealed that decision, asking that argument be heard en banc. But by late December—with the announcement that Drexel and the government had agreed in principle to a settlement of the criminal case brought by Giuliani, contingent upon its reaching a settlement agreement with the SEC—the whole tawdry charade (for Drexel, if not for Milken) had become moot.

Drexel agreed to plead guilty to six felony counts of mail, wire, and securities fraud—charges that largely paralleled those in the SEC complaint—and to pay a record $650 million in fines and restitution. The firm, stunningly enough, also agreed to cooperate in the government's ongoing investigation of some of its clients and its own executives. Including Milken.

No sooner had the settlement been announced than opinion pieces by Drexel sympathizers began to appear. They argued that the firm, which had protested its innocence so vigorously for two years, had been deprived of its right to a trial by the government's use of the Racketeer-Influenced Corrupt Organizations law, or RICO. RICO, which has mainly been utilized against organized crime but is increasingly being employed in the area of white-collar crime, is a powerful weapon because of the severe penalties it carries. In addition to offering prison sentences of many years, RICO allows for the forfeiture of ill-gotten gains, and, moreover, for the pre-trial freezing of assets.

U.S. Attorney Rudolph Giuliani had brought the power of RICO to bear in a related case several months earlier against Milken's old friend and partner, Jay Regan, and others at the brokerage firm of Princeton/Newport, as well as a former Drexel trader who worked for Milken, Bruce Newberg. In these indictments, the defendants—charged with racketeering, conspiracy, and mail and wire fraud—were alleged to have participated in a scheme to create illegal tax losses through bogus stock deals.

Princeton/Newport, the first securities firm ever to be labeled a "racketeering enterprise," closed its doors for good in early December

1988. Lawyers for the Princeton/Newport defendants maintained that it was largely the threat of the government's freezing of the firm's assets—at that time, still uncapped—that caused its demise. They also argued that U.S. Attorney Rudolph Giuliani had abused his prosecutorial discretion by transforming a tax fraud case into a RICO case, in order to attempt to pressure the defendants to cooperate against Michael Milken and Drexel, among others.

In the case of Princeton/Newport, the use of RICO may well have been unwarranted. But if ever there were a case outside the organized crime area that seemed appropriate for RICO prosecution, it is the case against Milken and Drexel. If the SEC allegations are true, Drexel under Milken was a major, ongoing enterprise where continuing violations of securities and mail fraud statutes were perpetrated over a period of years, accumulating hundreds of millions of dollars. Indeed, if one puts aside violence, there are parallels between traditional organized crime and the organization that the patriarchal Milken built—as described here earlier, "the brass-knuckles, threatening, market-manipulating Cosa Nostra of the securities world."

Moreover, if Drexel and its lawyers had believed that the government had no case, they would surely have elected to fight, even against the formidable might of RICO. (With over $2 billion in capital, the firm could easily have posted a bond to satisfy the government's pre-trial forfeiture claims.) What really had happened by the end of 1988 was not that Giuliani's threat of a RICO indictment deprived Drexel of its right to a fair trial, but that the government's case had grown immeasurably stronger.

No longer was it a contest of Boesky's word against Milken's. For by mid-fall, Drexel's ranks, which had held fast for nearly two years of ever-increasing pressure, had finally broken. James Dahl, Milken's favorite trader-salesman, was given immunity in return for his cooperation with the government. His testimony is said to have led the government to issue about a dozen subpoenas to Drexel employees. Then Cary Maultasch, who was said to have handled all Milken's personal trading, and who had for months been threatened with RICO indictments, followed in Dahl's footsteps. So did Terren Peizer, a 29-year-old trader who sat beside Milken in his Beverly Hills office, and is said to have participated in many of the trades for which the government is intent on prosecuting Milken. As reported in *Business Week*, by late January 1989, Giuliani was said to be trying to recruit six more witnesses from the Milken group.

It was not surprising, therefore, that by then Milken's lawyers had had some discussions with the government about a settlement. Milken had long prided himself on his ability to perceive value where others do not, to find the positive in what others might see as negative, to discern the undiscovered upside. But this situation must have sapped even his formidable powers. There were two courses from which to choose; both were terrible.

If he pleaded guilty, he would have to drop the banner of the holy war that he had carried for the past two years. He would have to admit that the price he was paying was not for having challenged the establishment, as he had been insisting it was, but for having broken the law. (Back in November, Milken had told *Washington Post* reporter David Wise that one of his sons had compared him with Socrates, who also was persecuted for his unconventional views, even though his life had been dedicated to the pursuit of truth and goodness.) And, finally, he would have to turn in his friends and clients— forsaking any code of honor, as so many of his erstwhile confreres had.

If, on the other hand, he went to trial, he would have to confront not only Boesky but those like Dahl whom he had created and, to some limited degree, trusted. Each of them knew only a small part of the whole. But the cumulative weight of their knowlege was almost surely enough to convict him and—under RICO provisions—seize a considerable amount of his fortune and send him to prison for as much as twenty years.

Milken was cornered; the government had won. It was the right outcome, for in this writer's view Milken had had to be stopped. But this was no straightforward morality play of good and evil. Milken had been dangerous, but he had also been one of the most imaginative, visionary financiers of our time. He could probably have had nearly as much impact as he had had upon the corporate restructuring of this country (the merits of which will long be debated) without ever violating the law. With Milken, creation had come first and his alleged lawbreaking, later. In that lies an element of tragedy.

The government's efforts to bring him down, moreover, were no model of restrained, evenhanded justice. Throughout the two-year investigation, there had been frequent leaks of non-public information to the press, much of it apparently emanating from the SEC. Congressman Dingell's investigators leaked non-public information to the press on a regular basis. (By way of disclosure, this reporter— whose job is to ask—was denied information by Dingell's committee.) These leaks served the purposes of achieving publicity for Dingell and recognition for the investigators' work and, on at least one occasion, embarrassing the SEC and attempting to force its hand in its negotiations with Drexel. (As SEC enforcement chief Gary Lynch told the *Wall Street Journal*, "I think you ought to put it high up in your story that you were provided non-public documents by a committee of Congress. Because that's how Washington works. . . . I think it stinks. The whole thing stinks.") And Giuliani, who was preparing to launch his political career as he pursued this case, in this writer's view shares some notable traits—an overriding ambition, an instinct for the end justifying the means—with his quarry, Milken.

In the end, what made Milken's defeat most poignant was that he was so betrayed. He had constructed a universe in which he made people wealthy beyond their dreams, in which he could rely on their loyalty because they owed everything to him. But he had not counted on a force more powerful than he, that could deprive his once-faithful of both their wealth and their freedom.

Now, Dahl, who had worshiped Milken and tried to mold himself in Milken's image, was divulging their secrets to the government. Fred Joseph, the personable salesman who had ridden Milken's coattails, was leading the firm in its decision to abandon him—to fire him and to withhold his 1988 compensation of about $200 million, and to cooperate with the government against him. There were those who were expressing rage at Joseph for his treachery. But skeptics countered that some of these Milken loyalists probably had much to fear from the government and had been put at risk themselves by the firm's decision to cooperate.

It was a sorry, bitter comeuppance for the man they had in brighter days revered, whom they had referred to as "the King."

ACKNOWLEDGMENTS

THIS BOOK is the result of interviews I conducted with 250–300 people, during a two-and-a-half-year period. Many of these people I interviewed many times, often for interviews of several hours' duration. Some of their names appear; others said that they could speak candidly to me only on a "background" basis, meaning that their comments would not be attributed to them. While I interviewed dozens of people who had been antagonists of Drexel and its players, the overwhelming majority of my interviews were with the subjects of my book themselves—employees of Drexel, and its network of clients. The hosts, and the guests, of the Predators' Ball.

Fred Joseph's agreement to cooperate with this book spoke for all of the firm with the exception of the West Coast—Milken and his group—a bifurcation that, as I would learn over the next two years, was a way of life within Drexel. Joseph agreed to grant me access in February 1986, nine months before Boesky Day; I therefore had the opportunity to learn about Drexel and its players at a time when their idyll was at its height. Awash in triumph, people spoke quite freely. Had I started to do the reporting on this book after Boesky Day, when the Drexel saga went from being publicly perceived as the success story of Wall Street to, perhaps, its greatest embarrassment and scandal, I would never have been granted such a frank and full view, by the participants themselves.

My meetings with Milken were the bookends of this project, coming at the beginning, when I asked for his cooperation, and very close to the end, when I received it. I feel confident that he never would have decided to go public if he were not in effect fighting for his life, in this battle that must be his worst nightmare—the government's strobe lights playing mercilessly over what was once his perfectly controlled universe, full of secret pools and pockets known to him alone.

Milken almost surely believes, as some close to him have indicated, that he is paying the price not so much—or not at all—for having violated the law, but for having led the revolt of an underclass to scale the walls of corporate America and depose the rich, credentialed and powerful. This he did indeed do, and for this I (while not endorsing his selection of players to replace the captains and the kings) applaud him. Although I suspected when I set out to write this book that this stunning success story might well have some unholy if not illegal underpinnings, my sympathies were more toward Milken and his band of renegades than toward the corporate establishment they were attacking. To the extent that Milken, particularly, feels he is judged harshly here, he should know that these are judgments that were neither predetermined nor fueled by prejudice but that simply became—after more than two years of reporting—unavoidable.

Realizing the irony involved, I would nonetheless like to thank the many people at Drexel who spent countless hours explaining to me the workings of their world. The firm is of course filled with honest, very bright, hard-working people. I hope they will enjoy at least those parts of the book that describe the glory days of Drexel.

Drexel has been a much-covered story over the past couple of years, and articles by other reporters helped me in writing this book. Among them were pieces by James Stewart and Daniel Hertzberg in *The Wall Street Journal*, Chris Welles and Tony Bianco in *Business Week*, Allan Sloan and Howard Rudnitsky in *Forbes*, James Sterngold in *The New York Times*, and Cary Reich in *Institutional Investor*.

One researcher, Natalie Byfield, assisted me in the early days of this project, and she was followed by Todd Woody, who assisted me over the longer haul; I am grateful to both of them. My fact-checker, Karen Dillon, was superb, with a spirit and determination that kept going when mine started to flag. Her services were lent to me by *The American Lawyer*, whose editor and publisher, Steven Brill, has provided me with unstinting and vital support from the first moment of this undertaking to its last. His 1985 piece in *The American Lawyer* about Icahn's raid on Phillips Petroleum, entitled "The Roaring Eighties," provided the initial inspiration for this book. I owe him a considerable debt of gratitude.

I want to thank my editor at Simon and Schuster, Alice Mayhew, whose legendary abilities I can now attest are real; I am fortunate indeed to have had the benefit of them. I also want to express my gratitude to her assistant, David Shipley, and to Elizabeth McNamara, associate counsel at Simon and Schuster, whose sound judgment was a great asset in the closing days of this book.

Finally, I want to thank my friend Deirdre Fanning, who provided a tireless and excellent sounding board; my mother and father, both of whom have never doubted for a moment that I could do anything, and always have tried to make it possible for me to do everything; my brother, David, for his continual generosity; and my son, who, through years of enduring either uncooked or burned dinners, fits of temper and general abstractedness, has displayed the patience, cheer and relentless humor that have made my life bright.

CONNIE BRUCK
February 1988

INDEX

FOR THE BEST IN PAPERBACKS, LOOK FOR THE 🐧

In every corner of the world, on every subject under the sun, Penguin represents quality and variety—the very best in publishing today.

For complete information about books available from Penguin—including Pelicans, Puffins, Peregrines, and Penguin Classics—and how to order them, write to us at the appropriate address below. Please note that for copyright reasons the selection of books varies from country to country.

In the United Kingdom: For a complete list of books available from Penguin in the U.K., please write to *Dept E.P., Penguin Books Ltd, Harmondsworth, Middlesex, UB7 0DA.*

In the United States: For a complete list of books available from Penguin in the U.S., please write to *Dept BA, Penguin*, Box 120, Bergenfield, New Jersey 07621-0120.

In Canada: For a complete list of books available from Penguin in Canada, please write to *Penguin Books Ltd, 2801 John Street, Markham, Ontario L3R 1B4.*

In Australia: For a complete list of books available from Penguin in Australia, please write to the *Marketing Department, Penguin Books Ltd, P.O. Box 257, Ringwood, Victoria 3134.*

In New Zealand: For a complete list of books available from Penguin in New Zealand, please write to the *Marketing Department, Penguin Books (NZ) Ltd, Private Bag, Takapuna, Auckland 9.*

In India: For a complete list of books available from Penguin, please write to *Penguin Overseas Ltd, 706 Eros Apartments, 56 Nehru Place, New Delhi, 110019.*

In Holland: For a complete list of books available from Penguin in Holland, please write to *Penguin Books Nederland B.V., Postbus 195, NL-1380AD Weesp, Netherlands.*

In Germany: For a complete list of books available from Penguin, please write to *Penguin Books Ltd, Friedrichstrasse 10-12, D-6000 Frankfurt Main 1, Federal Republic of Germany.*

In Spain: For a complete list of books available from Penguin in Spain, please write to *Longman, Penguin España, Calle San Nicolas 15, E-28013 Madrid, Spain.*

In Japan: For a complete list of books available from Penguin in Japan, please write to *Longman Penguin Japan Co Ltd, Yamaguchi Building, 2-12-9 Kanda Jimbocho, Chiyoda-Ku, Tokyo 101, Japan.*

FOR THE BEST IN PAPERBACKS, LOOK FOR THE 🐧

Other business books available from Penguin:

FOR THE BEST IN PAPERBACKS, LOOK FOR THE 🐧